RESISTING INDEPENDENCE

RESISTING INDEPENDENCE

POPULAR LOYALISM IN THE REVOLUTIONARY BRITISH ATLANTIC

BRAD A. JONES

CORNELL UNIVERSITY PRESS

Ithaca and London

First published 2021 by Cornell University Press

Library of Congress Cataloging-in-Publication Data

Names: Jones, Brad A., author.
Title: Resisting Independence : Popular Loyalism in the
    Revolutionary British Atlantic / Brad A. Jones.
Description: Ithaca, [New York] : Cornell University Press,
    2021. | Includes bibliographical references and index.
Identifiers: LCCN 2020035173 (print) | LCCN 2020035174
    (ebook) | ISBN 9781501754012 (hardcover) |
    ISBN 9781501754029 (pdf) | ISBN 9781501754036 (epub)
Subjects: LCSH: United States—History —Revolution,
    1775–1783. | Great Britain—Colonies—History. |
    Great Britain—Colonies—America.
Classification: LCC E277 .J75 2021 (print) |
    LCC E277 (ebook) | DDC 973.3 / 41—dc23
LC record available at https://lccn.loc.gov/2020035173
LC ebook record available at https://lccn.loc.gov
    /2020035174

For my mom and dad

Contents

RESISTING INDEPENDENCE

Introduction
A Revolution in British Loyalism

"But what do we mean by the American Revolution?" John Adams asked the Baltimore printer Hezekiah Niles in 1818. "Do we mean the American War? The Revolution was effected before the war commenced. The Revolution was in the minds and hearts of the people." Adams maintained that there had been a "radical change in the principles, opinions, sentiments, and affections of the people," who had renounced their king and government and broken from their "habitual affection for England, as their mother country."[1]

Many historians have agreed with Adams that in the aftermath of the Seven Years' War, parliamentary taxes aimed at raising revenue led to "an awakening and a revival of American principles and feelings." Looking back across almost half a century, Adams recalled that the political crises of the 1760s had excited "an enthusiasm [among Americans] which went on increasing till, in 1775, it burst out in open violence, hostility, and fury." The American colonists had together moved toward rebellion, Adams believed, despite the fact that "their customs, manners, and habits had so little resemblance, and their intercourse had been so rare." Now, on the eve of war, "thirteen clocks were made to strike together—a perfection of mechanism which no artist had ever before effected."[2]

Adams's explanation of the revolution remains a powerful, persuasive story of the nation's founding, one that has resonated with many Americans for two centuries.[3] Yet his interpretation was inaccurate, if not deliberately mislead-ing. Adams completely disregarded the fact that the American Revolution was a civil war, which deeply divided Britons on both sides of the North Atlantic.[4] Between five and eight hundred thousand of those Americans Adams described as radically changed in their republican sentiments actually remained loyal to Britain and their king.[5] And in the summer of 1776, thirteen of Britain's twenty-six colonies, and many inhabitants of the British Isles, chose loyalty over re-bellion. In fact, the American War for Independence helped trigger a new understanding of and enthusiasm for loyalty to the Crown and Parliament, which united colonists and mainland Britons alike.[6] The American Revolution, it turns out, was as much a story of loyalty as it was rebellion.

The causes of the American Revolution were also less clear, and the out-come more contingent, than the eighty-year-old Adams would have us believe. Both loyal *and* rebellious subjects were committed to the Protestant Whig ide-als of political liberty, economic prosperity, and religious toleration that were first secured in the 1689 Glorious Revolution against alleged Catholic tyranny and then extended to Scotland in the 1707 Act of Union. In a festive culture and in print, Britons throughout the empire expressed this shared ideology through common language, symbols, and rituals, which came to define popu-lar understandings of Britishness. By the middle of the eighteenth century, in fact, Britons everywhere self-consciously identified themselves as sharing the heritage and rights of all British subjects in the empire. Many proved more than willing to defend those rights in wars against Catholic France and Spain, and in instances when they believed their own government acted oppressively.[7]

Perhaps the greatest irony of the American Revolution is that it was pred-icated on a commitment to the very ideals that shaped eighteenth-century British attitudes toward liberty and political authority. During the decade leading to the Declaration of Independence, many American colonists had come to believe that rather than protecting the rights and liberties of their subjects, Parliament and the king had become a threat to them.[8] Once the war began, loyal Britons on both sides of the Atlantic faced the Herculean task of defeating a rebellion rooted in a defense of an inherently Protestant British conception of liberty: ideologically as well as literally, Britain was fight-ing itself. While we know a great deal about the making of American inde-pendence, we know far less about how and why Britons on either side of the Atlantic rejected revolution and, instead, embraced a renewed attachment to the Crown and empire. This book will tell their story. It will show that the challenge posed by American revolutionaries inadvertently forged a new, shared Loyalist ideology and identity with implications for Britons at home and across the empire.

Adams's questions about the American Revolution, in other words, would have been just as revealing had they been addressed to loyal Britons. What was the American Revolution to them? What did it mean to those living throughout the nation's Atlantic empire who remained loyal? Was there also a "radical change in the principles, opinions, sentiments, and affections" among those who did not rebel? And how did the crisis and war force them to reconceptualize *their* sense of belonging and *their* understanding of what it meant to be British? This book seeks to answer these questions through a close examination of four port cities spanning the North Atlantic: New York City; Kingston, Jamaica; Halifax, Nova Scotia; and Glasgow, Scotland.

As we will see, these communities provide an especially useful way to think about the ways in which the American Revolution shaped a popular transatlantic understanding of British Loyalism. By the 1760s, Glasgow, Kingston, Halifax, and New York City flourished as burgeoning North Atlantic commercial centers within the "first British Empire."[9] Each had experienced significant demographic and economic growth over the first decades of the eighteenth century, and residents (for different reasons) found meaning in an imperial identity rooted in their nation's commercial and military dominance. But these communities were also located in places distant from the nation's political and cultural capital and in areas populated by often hostile non-Britons (Europeans, Indians, and Africans). Over time this situation led to the emergence of distinctive local political cultures that distinguished inhabitants of these four port cities from one another and from places elsewhere in the empire. Broader questions of loyalty were often filtered through these local political cultures, revealing an Atlantic empire that was at once united and divided. It is along these points spread across all corners of the North Atlantic that we can best view the challenges of what it meant to belong in and to the British Empire.

During the early stages of the revolution, a shared transatlantic understanding of what it meant to be British in these four communities initially crumbled in the face of the Patriots' assertion that their cause was rooted in a defense of Protestant British liberty. Patriot arguments led loyal Britons in these places to question what defined their attachment to the empire. Out of these crises there emerged a new understanding of Loyalism rooted in a strengthened defense of monarchy and duly constituted government. After the Franco-American alliance of 1778, loyal Britons were also able to reclaim their belief in the supremacy of Protestant British liberty, which they contrasted with the alleged tyranny of American Patriots and their French Catholic allies.

Scholars have long insisted that British Loyalism as it developed in the wake of the American war was more conservative and authoritarian, reaching its apogee in the reaction against the radicalism of the French Revolution and the despotism of Napoleon. Crucially, such work has also tended to restrict this understanding of Loyalism to the inhabitants of the British mainland. According to these historians, imperial officials and Britons at home had a monopoly over popular understanding of Britishness. Beginning in the 1780s, they began to draw clearer distinctions between the metropole and their colonies in an effort to maintain supremacy over an expanding and ever more diverse empire. Additionally, as the empire expanded into areas of India and Southeast Asia, many residents of Great Britain came to view these new colonial subjects as outsiders, incapable of enjoying the same rights and liberties as the nation's Protestant, white subjects.[10]

This book challenges that assertion. White British subjects who lived and worked beyond mainland Britain were just as involved in this popular reimagining of loyalty and Loyalism. The inhabitants of these four communities, this book contends, emerged from the American war even more committed to a balanced, representative British monarchy, an institution that they believed was uniquely capable of protecting their cherished rights and liberties as British subjects. Like their fellow subjects in Great Britain, those who lived in these communities also thought their nation remained the great bulwark of Protestant Whig liberty against the continued threat of Catholic tyranny. In the closing years of the eighteenth century, loyal residents of New York City (until 1783), Halifax, Kingston, and Glasgow did not need to be told by metropolitan authorities what it meant to be subjects of their empire, for these individuals had already helped shape a new, empire-wide definition of Loyalism.[11]

This process of redefinition, however, did not unfold uniformly. The revolution and ensuing war had occasioned a crisis in understandings of what it meant to be British, which led Britons across the empire to highlight certain rights and liberties over others. Over the course of the eighteenth century, white Kingstonians had constructed a brutal, violent society, where race was inextricably linked to ideas of freedom and national identity. Their claim to the rights of freeborn British subjects came to depend almost exclusively on their ability to dominate the island's nearly two hundred thousand African slaves. As such, Kingstonians ultimately came to see the events of the 1760s and 1770s as an American Patriot assault on their right to buy, sell, and own other humans. The slavocracy in Britain's largest remaining city in the Americas emerged from this period dedicated to an imperial British identity premised on the right to participate in slavery and the slave trade, despite an increasing uncertainty about the institution in Britain and amid calls for the abolition of the slave trade, which began to be heard in the 1780s.

Residents of Halifax (Haligonians) and loyal New Yorkers, for their part, suffered for nearly two decades under cruel, repressive governments (both British and American). This experience helped shape their unusually fervent emphasis on the principles of consent and representation as key components of their patriotic identity. Meanwhile, residents of Glasgow (Glaswegians) experienced the American War for Independence as an attack on their economic interests and Protestant loyalties. Glaswegians emerged from the war committed to a far more radical and inclusive conception of Loyalism, demanding greater representation in Parliament and a more determined defense of their Protestant faith. Thus, while Britons across the North Atlantic shared a renewed patriotic commitment to the British monarchy in the aftermath of the conflict, the ways in which these Britons defined and expressed their loyalty were not identical, shaped as these definitions were by local experiences and circumstances. From the Caribbean to Canada to Scotland, Britons were both united and divided by their understandings of loyalty to the Crown, Parliament, and Protestant Whig liberty.

Forging a shared understanding of Britishness in the first half of the eighteenth century was no easy task, for either imperial authorities or the nation's diverse colonial subjects. This was especially true of the inhabitants of Glasgow, Halifax, New York City, and Kingston, who may all have been British but who were remarkably different from one another. As Britain's leading Caribbean city, Kingston was built on sugar and slavery, and the city's white merchants, planters, and others connected to the institution believed that they alone knew best how to manage an enslaved population that outnumbered whites by more than nine to one.[12] Two thousand miles to the north, a powerful merchant and political elite had assumed power in Halifax in the years after Britain had conquered the region. Dependent on the British army and navy for protection and on financial support from Parliament, elite Haligonians struggled to control a larger population of former New Englanders, whose spirited independence and commitment to Protestant Whig values often set them at odds with their superiors.[13] New York City had been in English and then British hands longer than Halifax but was nevertheless one of the most religiously and ethnically diverse places in the Americas. Partly as a consequence, the city boasted intensely partisan politics, and residents' persistent defense of self-rule, personal liberty, and free trade shaped their interactions with outsiders, including imperial authorities.[14] And in Britain itself, the fast-growing Atlantic port city of Glasgow combined a uniquely Scottish adherence to an extreme form of Protestantism and anti-Catholicism with a reliance on Atlantic trade and British mercantilism. The city's Tobacco Lords, who dominated the trade with planters in Maryland, Virginia, and the Carolinas, ruled their city and presided over its growth as an imperial entrepôt.[15]

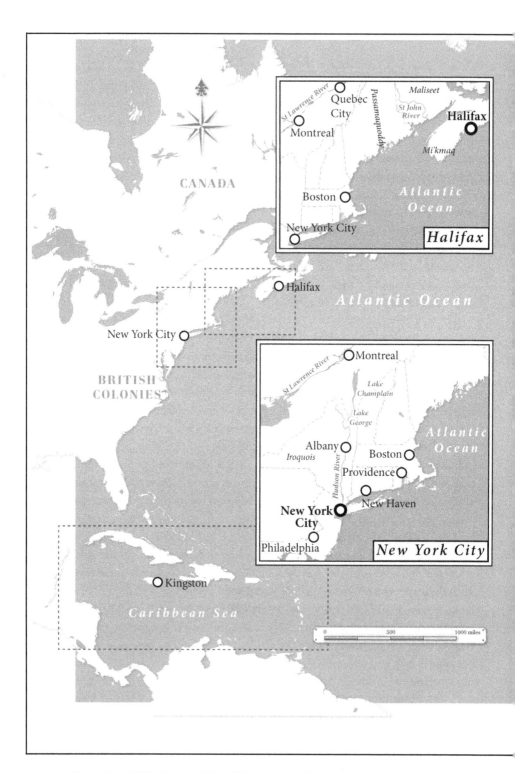

MAP 1. The British Atlantic, c. 1770, with insets. *Drawn by Gerry Krieg.*

Glasgow

Glasgow ○
Edinburgh

River Clyde

Firth of Clyde

Belfast ○

Dublin ○

Liverpool ○

SCOTLAND

Glasgow ○

IRELAND

ENGLAND

Atlantic Ocean

○ Havana

CUBA

HISPANIOLA

Atlantic Ocean

Kingston ○

Fort Omoa ○

JAMAICA

GUADELOUPE
DOMINICA
MARTINIQUE

Caribbean Sea

Kingston

In the years before the revolution and war, a loyal political culture thus emerged, tenuously, against the backdrop of a diverse and often divided British Atlantic. Britons in these four communities, and elsewhere in the empire, came to depend on an understanding of Loyalism that described a pervasive and deep-seated fear of Catholicism and authoritarian French and Spanish rule. Britons, in short, found it far easier to unite around a common enemy than to see themselves as common friends.

While these same subjects held Catholic enemies responsible for the 1715 and 1745 Jacobite rebellions, and the many wars fought across the globe in the first half of the eighteenth century, the American crisis of the 1760s and early 1770s was a different matter. This fact has been so obvious to historians that few have considered its significance. During the American Revolution, British subjects in the North American colonies, the Caribbean, and mainland Britain were forced to debate the nature of consent, representation, sovereignty, liberty, and freedom without reference to their standard lexicon of the dangers of Catholic tyranny. When deprived of the familiar principles and arguments of anti-Catholicism, Britons had to consider the challenge posed by a Patriot ideology from other and often conflicting vantage points. The crises of this period—over things like taxes, boycotts, and massacres—were debated, interpreted, and at times reimagined from the distinctly local perspectives of subjects in Glasgow, Halifax, New York, and Kingston. Loyal subjects in these and other locations around the British Atlantic contributed to the construction of new imperial understandings of British patriotism and loyalty to the Crown and Parliament. Historians are accustomed to thinking of this period as the prelude to independence, but most Britons living in these communities did not have the benefit of hindsight. They experienced this as a crisis of empire, which required a reconceptualization of the British state and their loyalty to it.

It was not only the events in North America that shaped Britons' attitudes toward their nation and empire. The last half of the 1760s produced a long list of crises across the empire: battles over liberty poles; growing fears over the establishment of an Anglican episcopacy; disputes over John Wilkes and his Liberty movement; debates over the motives behind, and enforcement of, colonial boycotts; competing views on the need for British soldiers and the purpose of standing armies; arguments over the limits of free ports in the Caribbean and free trade in the empire; celebrations in Scotland for a victory in a civil lawsuit involving the country's most famous noble family; the increasing possibility of another war with France over the Falkland Islands; and clashes in Nova Scotia over the salaried appointment of Catholic missionaries. In different ways, and at different times, these events forced Britons to consider questions of loyalty and national belonging. What did it mean to be British? To be free? And, perhaps most important, what exactly constituted tyranny, which Britons believed to be an ever-present threat to their liberties? Previously, anti-Catholic rhetoric had often provided handy, albeit simplistic, answers to such questions, but now new answers were required.

Historians of the American Revolution have invested considerable time and effort into explaining Patriots' efforts to create consensus from the early 1760s onward. Moving on from their early preoccupation with taxes and trade policies (hardly the kind of stuff they would risk their lives over), many Patriots did turn briefly to the familiar British trope of Catholic tyranny. Parliament's passage of the Quebec Act in the summer of 1774 invited American Patriots to imagine Catholic French Canadians and their Indian allies ravaging American communities. Significantly, this law also led many colonists to believe that their king had abandoned his oath to protect the Protestant faith within the empire. During the months before Lexington and Concord, these fears of Catholic atrocities filled the pages of colonial newspapers and were preached from New England pulpits as well as appearing in the addresses and proclamations of the Continental Congress and regional assemblies.[16] The fear of French Catholic tyranny was familiar, but not since the reign of James II nearly a century earlier had it appeared in the laws and actions of the British king and Parliament.

At the same time, other equally terrifying anxieties also surfaced, with rumors of British soldiers inciting slave revolts or actively courting Indian alliances. These stories offered further proof of the cruel tyranny of the British monarchy. This is the narrative that historians of the revolution use to explain the unification of a disparate colonial population, ultimately drawn together by a familiar language of patriotism common to all eighteenth-century British subjects.[17]

We know far less, however, about how loyal Britons around the North Atlantic reacted to Patriots' actions and their interpretation of British policies. How did those who remained loyal define themselves and their beliefs in the face of a Patriot ideology that challenged the very legitimacy of Britain and its core constitutional values? How did loyal Britons continue to articulate and even celebrate being British against the backdrop of a rebellion grounded in eighteenth-century understandings of British loyalty and patriotism? Indeed, the American Patriots insisted that *they* were now the true guardians of ancient English liberty. To win this war, and more important to reaffirm and protect British political beliefs and values, loyal Britons had to construct a competing narrative capable of justifying war against fellow British subjects who shared the same political and ideological creed.

This new Loyalism began to take form in the months before Lexington and Concord in colonial cities like New York City, where loyal subjects suffered at the hands of dangerous and seemingly implacable Patriot crowds. Like their opponents, these loyal subjects were just as committed to defending their liberty and were just as fearful of encroaching tyranny. Yet they held to the belief that monarchy and legitimately constituted government offered the surest protection against arbitrary rule, especially when contrasted with what they portrayed as the despotism of extralegal Patriot committees and mob violence. Stories circulating in British Atlantic newspapers described a dangerous social rebellion orchestrated by a small cabal of men—now delegates to the Continental Congress—inspired by selfish economic motives to mislead the mass of colonists into an unnatural war against their own countrymen.

Still, while loyal Britons across the empire opposed the American rebellion, few were initially inclined to wage a long, bloody, and expensive war against their own people. Following the outbreak of hostilities in April 1775, there was no Loyalist *rage militaire* to match the enthusiasm of volunteers for the Continental army. Kingston's representatives to the Jamaica Assembly, for instance, actually petitioned George III in favor of American grievances, while admitting that the island's dependence on slavery ensured the white inhabitant's loyalty to the Crown. Although a majority of Haligonians actually supported the American cause in principle, their efforts to join the rebellion were squashed by the colony's political and commercial elite, whose authority depended on the support of the government in London. The city's political leaders actively suppressed Patriot writings, arrested or exiled known conspirators, and required inhabitants to take public oaths of loyalty to the Crown. Glaswegians, though critical of the Patriot cause, were quiet at the start of the war. The interruption in the tobacco trade upon which the city depended was a cause of deep concern, and citizens refused to send a loyalty address to the king for fear that choosing sides might jeopardize their valuable Atlantic trade. Even loyal New Yorkers struggled to see the American rebellion as anything more than an unnatural war instigated by a small group of self-interested men. After all, to take seriously American Patriots' rhetoric about British betrayal of core principles would undermine the very foundations of British loyalty and patriotism.

During the early stages of the American war, loyal Britons on both sides of the Atlantic struggled to shape and articulate a transatlantic ideology of Loyalism designed to unite them in opposition to the rebel colonists. This changed in the spring of 1778, however. News of the Franco-American alliance drew together these Britons by turning to understanding of Loyalism that was dependent on age old definitions of Britishness.[18] For the remainder of the war, stories circulating the British Atlantic remade American Patriots—especially those responsible for the rebellion—into friends of their traditional Catholic foes. The Patriots' alliance with Louis XVI came to demonstrate their betrayal of the British Protestant values they had previously claimed to champion. This account of the war and criticism of the Patriot cause restrengthened ties to the empire among loyal subjects, convincing many of the divinely ordained supremacy of their nation and its commitment to liberal, Protestant values. In consequence, loyal Britons in these four communities embraced a far more enthusiastic and martial spirit of Loyalism beginning in 1778, which echoed the Patriot *rage militaire* of 1775.

But this reinterpretation of the enemy also pushed Britons toward a new understanding of Loyalism. Residents of these four communities emphasized their devotion to a representative British monarchy but they also placed greater demands on that government to protect their rights and liberties as British subjects. Loyal refugees in New York City grew increasingly frustrated with the military's unwillingness to reinstate civil rule in the city, while also pushing for their government to wage a more aggressive, vengeful war against their former countrymen. For Kingstonians, the new war led to renewed fears of foreign invasions and slave uprisings, and the city's inhabitants grew frustrated with the lack of naval and military protection on the island. Haligonians also worried that a war with France might revive latent tensions with the region's Indian and Acadian populations and thus set about actively courting the allegiance of their old enemies. Finally, for devout Presbyterians in Glasgow, their renewed defense of Protestant British liberty was undermined by their government's attempt in 1778 to relieve some of the penal laws affecting Scottish and English Catholics. The dispute over Catholic toleration while the nation was at war against France nearly drove Scots (and some others in the British Isles) to their own rebellion and ultimately resulted in the deadly Gordon Riots in London in 1780. The resurgence of British Loyalism, in other words, was both unifying and inherently fragile.

Historians of Loyalism have largely failed to grasp the importance of the British Atlantic.[19] They continue to frame the ideology in parochial terms, as defined by a North American population seemingly independent in their thinking and actions and both separate and different from loyal Britons elsewhere in the North Atlantic. These historians also tend to focus on Loyalists' personal interests to describe their political allegiances: they were motivated by economic self-interest, or political or religious obligations, rather than a commitment to a broader Loyalist ideology encompassing the entire North Atlantic. This focus has allowed some to mistakenly describe both Indians and free and enslaved African Americans as fellow Loyalists, for they too were driven to the British cause for particular personal reasons.[20] Even Maya Jasanoff's study of the Loyalist diaspora, which she shows was more a global than an Atlantic phenomenon, continues to represent the American Loyalist experience during the war as exceptional rather than as intimately linked to the experience of Britons elsewhere in the empire. Like these other historians, Jasanoff also sees Loyalists' particular understanding of the conflict, which she describes as the "Spirit of 1783," as deeply personal and local.[21]

This book instead offers a new, transatlantic understanding of Loyalists and Loyalism by featuring the people within *and* beyond the thirteen American colonies. The book conceives of the British Atlantic not as populated by isolated groups of British subjects separated by innumerable barriers but rather as a connected community of different people who were forced by the American Revolution to collaborate in a reimagining of their British identity. This study is a cis-, circum-, and transatlantic history of the American Revolution. First and foremost, it is a close study of four British Atlantic communities (*cis-*), but it is also about those points of difference that help us to see how the revolution influenced the shaping of Loyalism in certain localities across the empire (*circum-*). And finally, this study also uses those local histories and points of contrast to paint a broader picture of the impact of the revolution on the wider British Atlantic (*trans-*).[22]

Popular understandings of Loyalism were ultimately contingent on the events of this period and the ideas circulating the British Atlantic, and, crucially, these changed and developed over time. Therefore, this book follows a chronological narrative of the American Revolution and War. It begins by first explaining the growth and importance of a British Atlantic print culture and the role that newspapers in particular played in shaping popular notions of Loyalism in each of these communities. Chapters 2 and 3 consider how the political and economic crises of the 1760s and early 1770s began to divide Britons, and communities, across the North Atlantic over the meaning and importance of a shared imperial identity. Chapter 4 looks closely at the start of the American war and how a common transatlantic Loyalist ideology emerged in response to an American Patriot cause that appeared dangerous and threatening to the rights of loyal British subjects. Chapter 5 examines the disastrous first years of the war, in which loyal Britons struggled to make sense of the conflict and whom it was they were fighting. This struggle changed in 1778, however, when the Americans agreed to a formal alliance with Britain's longstanding enemy, France. The final two chapters look at the consequence of this alliance and the outcome of the war on popular expressions of loyalty across the British Atlantic.

Many histories of the American Revolution seek to tell the story of America's founding or describe Britain's defeat. This book does neither. Instead, it represents the first attempt to map the British Atlantic's reaction to the American

Revolution. The book tracks the many ideas and events of the period as they crisscrossed the ocean, entering into distant communities of subjects scattered across Britain's vast Atlantic empire. Ultimately, those ideas and events remade the British Atlantic. More so than previous or later wars against France, the American Revolution led to new understandings of loyalty and Loyalism amongst the diverse inhabitants of New York City, Glasgow, Kingston, and Halifax. These subjects had resisted independence, and a revolutionary assault on their Britishness, to embrace a renewed commitment to monarchy and empire and a more determined defense of their rights as British subjects.

CHAPTER 1

A Body Politic

Newspapers, Networks, and the Making of a Nation

In October 1756, the printer Daniel Fowle devoted almost half of the second issue of his newspaper, the *New Hampshire Gazette*, to an essay on the advantages of printing and the press.[1] Fowle described "the *Art of Printing* . . . [as] one of the most useful Inventions the World has ever seen," for it had enlightened individuals and freed them from the tyranny of governments. If absent, he warned, "the common People [are] deprived of all the Means of Knowledge, and taught nothing but what qualifies them to acquiesce under the most abject Slavery." Absolutist monarchs, Fowle continued, knew full well that a free and open press "was an admirable Instrument of promoting *Knowledge*, and . . . would prove the Bane of that *absolute Authority*, that *inhuman Tyranny* practiced by them."

Fowle contended that "Weekly Mercuries," or newspapers, offered the most immediate and accessible check to those in power. He compared newspapers to the human body's circulatory system, arguing that they "keep the Body Politic (if not alive, at least) in sound Health," through the "speedy Communication of the State of Affairs, from one part of the World to another, that easy Intercourse maintain'd between the different Parts of a Kingdom." This observation was true of Britain's far-flung empire, he believed, where this circulation of news and information allowed subjects to stay abreast of events occurring far beyond their own towns and villages.

According to Fowle, newspapers were also capable of enlightening readers of all rank in society, regardless of wealth, status, or proximity to the nation's capital. "By this Means Knowledge is spread even among the Common
People," he insisted, "a useful Curiosity is rais'd in their Minds, their attention is rous'd, their Minds are enlarged, their Views extended." Through the
regular reading of newspapers, a diverse British Atlantic public was drawn into
an imperial political culture that encouraged subjects to see themselves, "not
in that contracted View they did . . . but in a more useful Light, as Members
of a large Society . . . whose particular Welfare is in many Respects blended
with the whole."[2]

Newspapers, more than anything else, helped to integrate the vast British
Atlantic.[3] Reports and editorials appearing in the dozens of "Weekly Mercuries" carried by ships crisscrossing the ocean gave meaning to an emerging,
shared understanding of loyalty and Loyalism among the ocean's many and
varied British inhabitants. Newspapers were especially useful in generating
what one historian has called a "currency of political exchange" by giving tex-
tual existence to nonliterary events, such as riots, protests, and celebrations.
Local political occurrences could now achieve supralocal significance and
meaning, helping to shape a broader British Atlantic political culture.[4] This
point was not lost on Daniel Fowle. Later in his 1756 essay he argued that reading about events that took place beyond one's local community "brings Men
by Degrees to consider themselves as Neighbours and Fellow citizens with all
Mankind. The Transition in our thoughts from others to our selves, is natural
and easy; and we can't avoid imagining . . . that the Adversities which happen
to others, may meet us too." The movement of information along develop-
ing local, regional, and imperial communication networks fostered an imagined
community of subjects around a common national identity.[5]

Formed in the pages of the many "Weekly Mercuries" read, discussed, and
debated by subjects throughout the North Atlantic, this shared understanding of Britishness drew on Protestant subjects' deeply held fears of their nation's long-standing Catholic enemies, France and Spain. Stories, both real and
imagined, regularly described the alleged cruelty and despotism of these Catholic nations to encourage inhabitants of these four communities, and Britons elsewhere for that matter, to think of themselves as part of a progressively freer,
wealthier, Protestant nation. This language of loyalty, of Britishness, enabled a
distant population of subjects to see themselves as "Members of a large Society . . . whose particular Welfare is in many Respects blended with the whole."

Britons living in these four North Atlantic port cities were especially receptive to this narrative, not least because they lived in such close proximity to

their nation's many enemies. Haligonians were surrounded on three sides by Indian societies previously allied with France and a smaller Acadian population that still haunted many of the town's residents. New Yorkers worried, too, about the combined threat of Indian and French-Canadian enemies who might descend on the city via Lake Champlain and the North River.[6] Kingstonians also lived among and around their nation's greatest rivals, who regularly threatened invasion and were often thought to have instigated the many slave uprisings that occurred on the island.[7] Even Glaswegians, though far more secure than Britons living in the other three communities, were near the center of the twice-failed Jacobite uprisings and living among an increasing number of Highlanders who relocated to their city in the 1750s.[8] The city and towns along the Clyde River were also thought to be likely destination points for invading French armies in the first half of the eighteenth century. When they read in their local newspapers of the dangers of their Catholic foes, the inhabitants of these four communities would have certainly understood "that the Adversities which happen to others, may meet us too."

The makings of Fowle's "Body Politic," however, depended on reliable Atlantic communication networks, a circulatory system capable of carrying news quickly and regularly to all corners of Britain's vast empire. The establishment of a government-sponsored packet service during the Seven Years' War strengthened communication between the colonies and the metropole, but information traveled best within a far more robust and complex system of local and regional networks. News of national importance was thus filtered through these more immediate webs of contact, which played a significant role in shaping distinctive local political cultures and identities in places like New York City, Glasgow, Halifax, and Kingston. During the many wars fought against France and Spain in the first half of the eighteenth century, anti-Catholic rhetoric was able to overshadow divisions within the empire, providing a language of national unity that was so intentionally broad as to appeal to the nation's diverse inhabitants. But in the absence of these wars and these enemies, as was the case for much of the 1760s and 1770s, subjects in these communities struggled to understand what exactly united them as Britons.

By the 1750s, the British Atlantic was awash in a sea of print. Newspapers and other forms of print flooded cities, towns, and villages throughout mainland Britain, the Caribbean, and North America. Londoners, of course, enjoyed the largest and most accessible newspaper industry, while provincial printers on both sides of the ocean often published verbatim articles taken from metropolitan newspapers.[9] The provincial press, however, was more than a mere extension of London's printing industry. Local publishers had a wide variety of

sources to draw from, including local and regional newspapers, personal letters, and locally written essays and editorials. These publishers also had access
to newspapers and printed matter brought by ships from more distant communities across the empire.[10]

A vibrant and growing provincial and colonial printing industry helped to
level the playing field with subjects living in London.[11] By the late 1760s, provincial English newspapers numbered in the thirties, while there were nearly
thirty newspapers published in British North America and more than a half
dozen in both Scotland and the British Caribbean.[12] On the eve of the American Revolution, Britons living in the most remote corners of the empire read,
discussed, and debated ideas and events published in their local gazettes just
as readily and enthusiastically as their compatriots in the nation's capital.

Several factors contributed to the significant growth of the printing industry in the first half of the eighteenth century. A dramatic surge in the British
population led to port cities emerging as regional and national centers of importance, not just in terms of trade and commerce, but also as points of contact along a complex transatlantic information network.[13] New York City and
Glasgow, for example, were sparsely populated provincial port towns at the
turn of the eighteenth century. Fewer than 5,000 inhabitants called New York
City home, while roughly 18,000 Scots lived in Glasgow. Six decades later, however, New York's population had quadrupled to over 20,000 people, while
Glasgow's had nearly doubled to roughly 30,000.[14] Even smaller port cities like
Halifax and Kingston experienced some growth during this period, especially
in relation to their colony's population. Nearly half of Jamaica's 13,000 white
inhabitants lived in Kingston by the start of the American war, while several
thousand of Nova Scotia's roughly 20,000 inhabitants called Halifax home in
the early 1770s.[15] These port cities served as crucial information gateways both
to the surrounding communities and with other regions of Britain's ever-
expanding Atlantic empire.

Imperial wars with Britain's longtime European rivals also helped to expand
the printing industry in these communities. The War of the Spanish Succession and that of the Austrian Succession, followed by the Great War for Empire in the 1750s, threatened Britain's valuable Atlantic trade routes and often
forced Caribbean and North American colonists to take up arms in defense
of the Crown. In doing so, colonial subjects acted as agents of the state, playing a critical role in the formal expansion of their empire.

These wars forced Britons to take up their pens, too. The very act of imperial expansion required explanation. If subjects across the North Atlantic were
expected to participate in the nation-building process—to risk their lives and
livelihoods in defense of the state—they needed a narrative, a shared cause,

to rally around. Scholars have emphasized the power of print in shaping national identities. "Acts of war," argues one scholar, "generate acts of narration . . . [which] are often joined in a common purpose: defining the geographical, political, cultural, and sometimes racial and national boundaries between peoples."[16] For eighteenth-century Britons, wartime stories printed and reprinted in newspapers across the North Atlantic enabled a diverse and distant populace to find common ground, to imagine themselves as part of something greater, and to commit themselves to a vision of empire distinguished from that of their rivals in Europe.

These narratives, however, depended on reliable communication networks, which struggled to keep pace with Britain's rapidly expanding empire in the first half of the eighteenth century. Until the Postal Act of 1711, there existed no imperial postal system by which Britons on both sides of the ocean could easily and regularly send letters or exchange newspapers. And even after the passage of that act, networks within Britain, and in the North American and Caribbean colonies, continued to suffer from poorly kept postal roads (made worse during inclement weather), exorbitant postage rates (and successive stamp tax increases in Britain), and a chronically underfunded system.[17]

Reformers attempted to expand the communication infrastructure within England and lowland Scotland in the first half of the eighteenth century. Officials in London invested in improving and adding roads as provincial towns and cities grew both in size and importance. The process, though, was far from even. For instance, Glaswegians relied almost entirely on nearby Edinburgh for their news, despite their city's increasing commercial importance to the empire.[18] Scotland's capital city profited from a three-day-a-week postal service with London, and the nearby port town of Leith connected Scotland with the latest news from continental Europe. After 1749, a daily postal service connected Edinburgh newspaper printers to Glasgow, but it was not until 1788 that Glaswegians enjoyed a direct postal route to London.[19] The city's dependence on Edinburgh not only inhibited the growth of the newspaper industry in Glasgow but also delayed communication with London at a crucial moment in the city's commercial development.

Of greater concern to officials was the need to connect the metropole to the colonies, a project that required considerable resources and manpower. At the turn of the century, imperialists like Edmund Dummer and William Warner briefly established a system of packet boats to facilitate communication with political and military officials stationed in the Caribbean, in part by carrying metropolitan and provincial newspapers. The service lasted just nine years, but it offered a radical reimagining of transatlantic communication networks by establishing a fairly routine, considerably faster method of contact between the metropole and colonies. The service also represented another way in which the government in London sought greater administrative control over its fledgling empire. Like later taxes and trade regulations, the purpose of the imperial packet service was to make London the hub of several spokes on a wheel, with information spreading to all corners of the empire from the nation's capital.[20]

Officials revived the service in 1755 in response to the beginning of the Seven Years' War. This time they focused their efforts on a regular route from Falmouth to New York City, the British military headquarters in North America.[21] The first ship, the *Earl of Halifax*, arrived in New York City on February 3, 1756, after fifty-three days at sea. It carried copies of the addresses of both Houses of Parliament to the king in support of his decision to ready the navy and army for war with France.[22] The following Tuesday those addresses appeared in *The New York Mercury* and copies were then sent along an imperfect network of postal roads dotted by inns, taverns, coffeehouses, and even people's homes, which stretched north to Boston and Montreal and south toward Williamsburg.[23] For mail going to Halifax, officials agreed to send it by way of the postmaster in Boston (at least until 1775), who often added local correspondence and newspapers to the bag while he waited for the next merchant vessel destined for that port.[24] Near the end of the month, on February 26, the *Earl of Halifax* began its return journey to Falmouth (which took only twenty-six days) loaded with bags of personal letters, business correspondence, and newspapers gathered from colonists across the Eastern Seaboard.

A total of nine ships made that same journey in 1756, and during the 1760s and 1770s an average of nearly eleven ships, or almost one per month, traversed the North Atlantic.[25] The time it took to cross from Falmouth to New York City averaged between six to eight weeks, but the return voyages were often shorter. Delays were common, however, especially in the winter months when poor weather conditions might postpone departures or force ships off course.[26] Enemy navies and privateers also often targeted packet boats, knowing that they carried official civil and military correspondence.[27]

After several unsuccessful attempts in the 1750s, officials succeeded in establishing another packet service for the Caribbean and southern colonies in 1764. The service was much smaller than its northern counterpart, likely because there was more commercial traffic between the Caribbean islands and Great Britain. Under this new plan, packet ships regularly stopped in Kingston before traveling north to places like Pensacola, Savannah, and Charleston.[28] The *Suffolk* packet, for instance, departed Falmouth on April 19 and docked in Kingston on June 4 after forty-seven days at sea.[29] The letters, business correspondence, and newspapers left at the post office in Kingston were then delivered by enslaved postal couriers across a network of poorly kept roads to inhabitants living in all corners of the island.[30] Just three days later, the *Suffolk* departed Kingston harbor laden with news from that island for Britain's North American colonies, making stops at Pensacola, St. Augustine, Savannah, and Charleston before returning to Falmouth on November 10.

The lengthy return time—nearly a half year passed between the *Suffolk*'s departure from Kingston and arrival in Falmouth—suggests some of the communication problems that persisted between the capital city and the empire's most valuable colony. Kingstonians were far more likely to know what was going on elsewhere in the empire than mainland Britons were to know what was happening on that island.[31] Records are incomplete for the years 1765 to 1783, but it is safe to assume that an average of about six ships made the journey annually across the Atlantic to Kingston.

While the primary purpose of the Northern and Caribbean packet services was to share political and military intelligence, imperial officials also believed they could be useful in spreading news and shaping popular attitudes toward the nation and empire. The first ships to arrive in North America in early 1756, for example, carried advertisements for annual subscriptions to virtually every metropolitan newspaper and magazine "sent regularly by every packet-boat, so as to contain the freshest advices to the very time that each of them sail from Falmouth."[32] Though imperfect, in the context of eighteenth-century communication networks, these packet services represented the nation's best attempt at formalizing contact between the metropole and colonies, which helped to transform the Atlantic into the British Atlantic.

British commercial expansion in the middle decades of the eighteenth century also improved communication among communities throughout the empire, though in far more informal ways. By the 1740s, at least 1,000 ships were involved annually in Britain's Atlantic trade, double the number from just six decades earlier.[33] In 1762, 477 ships cleared New York City's harbor for ports across the North Atlantic. By 1772, that number jumped to 709.[34] Several decades earlier, half of those ships went to the British Caribbean, mainly to Jamaica, supplying many of the sugar planters with food, clothing, and other necessities for their slaves.[35] Another quarter to a third of ships departing New York City's port traveled to other North American port cities, from Charleston to Boston, dispelling popularly held myths that American colonists interacted very little with one another.[36]

The explosion of Glasgow's tobacco trade in the 1750s led to a substantial increase in the number of ships traveling from that city to the Chesapeake region. During the 1760s, an average of eighty-six ships each year left Port Glasgow for Maryland, Virginia, and the Carolinas. Glasgow's tobacco merchants perfected the North Atlantic shipping routes, completing the round-trip journey at a faster rate than competing merchant vessels or official packet ships.[37] With Congress's expansive boycott looming in the fall of 1775, John Glassford's ship *Cochran* made the round-trip journey to the Chesapeake in just sixty-five days.[38] While the *Cochran's* main purpose was to transport hogsheads of tobacco, it also carried British manufactured goods to the colonies and likely facilitated the exchange of mainland and colonial newspapers. During the American war, many of these ships were redirected to New York City, Halifax, and ports throughout the British Caribbean, linking Glaswegians to the remaining loyal regions of Britain's Atlantic empire.[39]

The expansion of trade led to the emergence of multiple webs of decentralized networks that threatened the official imperial modes of communication established by government-sponsored packet boats. More and more Britons were able to indulge in a local print culture that drew from a variety of presses across the British Atlantic, some distant and some very close. Absent, or even alongside, the arrival of a packet boat from England, Haligonians often read reports and editorials taken from New England newspapers (or actually perused copies of those gazettes), while New York City printers often relied on news taken from nearby Boston and Philadelphia prints. Glaswegians mostly turned to Edinburgh papers for their news, but as the city's commercial interests increasingly looked west to the Chesapeake, local printers began to publish more news from that region.[40] Perhaps only in Kingston did residents continue to rely mostly on London newspapers, though the colony's dependence on North American staple goods meant that ships regularly arrived from ports to the north.[41] London remained the information center of the empire, but these new webs of contact—small networks competing and combining with larger ones—both encouraged the greater circulation of information across the North Atlantic and established new modes of communication between the nation's diverse and distant communities.[42]

Of course, these extensive if informal networks belie easy explanation. Ships traveled to and from ports across the ocean in irregular patterns dictated by trading interests, harvest schedules, weather conditions, and wars, among many other factors. When (or if) they arrived at their final destinations, then, they constituted a complex information hub—a floating transatlantic newspaper—with reports and rumors, some written, others spoken, whose provenance was not always clearly known. In some ways, this represented one of the great strengths of Britain's transatlantic print network. News of all kind traveled relatively quickly to even the most remote corners of the empire, but the lack of organization made it difficult for officials in London to control the message, to define the narrative.

These irregular and informal communication networks also often raised questions of authenticity and accuracy in the minds of British subjects, most of whom trusted newspapers for their understanding of the world around them.[43] Printers were certainly aware of this trust and tried to convince their readers from the start that they intended to publish only the most reliable news.[44] Printers also went to great lengths to explain the often circuitous origins of the news they printed. Virtually every report, editorial, or essay included an origins story that described where it came from, who it was written by, and when the event took place.[45] Sometimes this was a simple task, as was the case with the addresses to the king that arrived by packet boat in New York City in early 1756, although those too were explained to readers in the article's opening paragraph.

More often, however, printers faced the difficult task of mapping an information network that defied easy explanation. Less than a decade later, for instance, Bostonians learned of the repeal of the unpopular Stamp Act in a "Letter from a Member of Parliament . . . to his Friend in Ireland." According to the opening paragraph—the origins story—the letter appeared first in a Dublin newspaper before being reprinted in a Cork newspaper, a copy of which found its way across the ocean to Oxford, Maryland. From there the letter moved northward, appearing in the *Pennsylvania Gazette*, news of which occasioned the "spread [of] a general Joy all over the City." The letter, now accompanied by a description of the celebration in Philadelphia, was then exchanged in both New York City and Newport newspapers, before arriving in Boston in early April. By the following month the letter, along with the news from Philadelphia, had recrossed the Atlantic, appearing in a Dublin newspaper as well as in papers across England and Scotland.[46] If Daniel Fowle was right that newspapers functioned as a sort of circulatory system that kept the body politic in sound health, printers often acted the part of the doctor, explaining to readers how that system worked.

The story of how that report traveled across the Atlantic also demonstrates how an imperial political culture interacted with, evolved, and drew new meaning and importance as it passed through different localities. The report began as a story of national importance, originating from the very pen of an imperial official in London. But as it crossed the ocean and entered into new political cultures, ones that had violently resisted the despised tax over the preceding months, it acquired new significance. Philadelphians made news by celebrating the news of the repeal with bonfires, bells, and toasts, a report of which was added to the original story and sent northward to other North American cities. From New York City to Boston, colonists read of the repeal *and* the celebrations in Philadelphia, which they replicated in their own city streets. As the news moved east across the Atlantic, mainland Britons now read excerpts of the MP's letter in the context of colonial celebrations. Thus what was originally a story of administrative action, of elite officials deciding the fate of imperial legislation, was turned into one that made clearer to readers how colonists understood the tax and their rights and liberties as British subjects. In doing so, the story not only blurred both imperial and local information networks but also demonstrated the gradual, if limited, expansion of the political sphere whereby the words and actions of the empire's diverse subjects interacted with the decisions of imperial officials.[47]

While most Britons on all sides of the ocean opposed the Stamp Act and celebrated its repeal, accounts of other, more contested events changed dramatically and divisively as they moved across the North Atlantic. That tension between an imperial and local political culture, between a broader narrative of British loyalty and patriotism and more parochial customs and attitudes shaped by local news and events, was especially evident during the 1770s when the nation found itself engaged in a civil war. The arteries that had sustained Britain's vast transatlantic networks of communication—its complex, tangled circulatory system—collapsed in some places, replaced by new networks formed in opposition to the old ones.

By the 1760s, the number of locally printed newspapers in each of these communities compared favorably with towns and cities of similar size and location within Britain's Atlantic empire. Most of these newspapers tended to be weekly or biweekly publications, with printing schedules timed to the arrival of ships and postriders bringing news from the surrounding region and across the North Atlantic. The newspapers' contents were diverse but tended to reflect the beliefs and interests of their many readers and played a crucial role in creating and defining a local political culture. Rumors and reports from near and far, essays and editorials, proclamations and addresses, and the many advertisements that filled the back pages shaped how residents understood their empire, and their place within it.

During the revolutionary era, one newspaper was published weekly in Halifax, the *Halifax Gazette*, which later became the *Nova-Scotia Gazette*.[48] Except for a brief period in the late 1760s, the printer was Anthony Henry, a German immigrant and veteran of the British army who settled in Halifax after the Seven Years' War. Henry operated the newspaper within a printing network almost entirely dependent on New England for its news, which both reflected and strengthened his readers' close cultural and political ties with that region. During the Stamp Act Crisis, Henry actually employed the editorial services of Boston native Isaiah Thomas, who "brought with him the Boston notions of liberty," which he openly expressed in the pages of the gazette.[49] The city's ruling elite feared the influence of Henry's newspaper during this period and often forbade the publication of radical texts produced by the city's southern neighbors. Yet even after Thomas's forced departure in 1766, Halifax's only newspaper continued to defend colonial rights, shared in a wider transatlantic radical political culture, and expressed support for a burgeoning Patriot cause. It was not until news of the Franco-American alliance in 1778 that Henry adopted a more loyal tone and began to draw from other British and Loyalist newspapers across the empire.[50]

Kingston had a far more robust local printing industry than Halifax, despite having only a slightly larger population. Local officials, merchants, planters, and many others depended on the sea for their livelihood and thus recognized the need to solidify the island's place within burgeoning Atlantic communication networks.[51] During the 1760s and 1770s, the island produced four newspapers, two of which were published in Kingston (the *Kingston Journal* and *Jamaica Gazette*). Few copies of either newspaper remain, but both appear to have emphasized the city's commercial ties to the empire. Whereas most provincial and colonial newspapers devoted a page to advertisements, as much as half or more of a typical issue of a Kingston newspaper listed manufactured goods for sale and ships departing for ports across the North Atlantic, evidence of the city's close ties to a broader British imperial commerce and culture.[52] Columns devoted to announcing upcoming slave auctions and offering rewards for the capture of those who had run away also spoke to a local economy defined by its dependence on enslaved labor.

Reports and essays printed in these newspapers (alongside the many runaway slave advertisements) reflected the community's commitment to defending the rights of white colonial subjects. Kingston's newspapers were largely supportive of North American colonists in their ongoing disputes with the government in London, at least until the war began in 1775.[53] By 1779, however, two Loyalist refugees, William Aikman and David Douglass, began publishing a third newspaper in Kingston, the *Jamaica Mercury, and Kingston Weekly Advertiser*, which later became the *Royal Gazette*.[54] They drew mostly from mainland and Loyalist publications to fill the columns of their gazette, reflecting a broader ideological shift that occurred in Kingston during the final years of the war. White residents, fearful of the war's effect on their slave-driven economy, denounced the rebellious Americans and their European allies and reaffirmed their support for the British monarchy.

Like Kingston's, Glasgow's newspaper industry was closely tied to the city's commercial importance within the empire.[55] Moderate in tone, and supportive of the Crown during the '45 Rebellion, early newspapers like the *Glasgow*

Courant and the *Glasgow Journal* were intended to draw residents of the city and surrounding communities into a prosperous and expanding Atlantic empire.[56] During the revolutionary era, just two newspapers (the *Glasgow Journal* and the *Glasgow Chronicle*, the latter replaced in 1778 by the *Glasgow Mercury*) served a city of nearly forty thousand inhabitants. Both covered events in the colonies in close detail. They were largely critical of the growing violence, which threatened the traditional political order of society and, worse yet, might ruin the city's prosperous tobacco trade. Glaswegians also regularly read as many as eight newspapers published in nearby Edinburgh, which reflected a diversity of political views and opinions.[57] Additionally, the *Scots Magazine*, modeled after a popular London periodical, the *Gentlemen's Magazine*, was also widely available in Glasgow and throughout all of Scotland.[58] Like the other communities in this study, both of the city's newspapers and the *Scots Magazine* turned decidedly in favor of the British cause after 1778, when the war expanded to include their longtime enemies, the French. But these same newspapers were also critical of the government's decision to repeal certain Catholic penal laws in 1778 and helped to inspire a popular and, at times, violent movement throughout Scotland to oppose the legislation.

New York City's local newspaper industry was the largest of these four communities. Since the Zenger Crisis of the mid-1730s, the city's residents had come to view their local press as indispensably tied to British ideas of liberty and freedom, which gained greater traction in a city so riven by political factions.[59] During the 1760s and early 1770s, there were at least two and sometimes as many four weekly publications, all of which were largely supportive of colonial grievances against Parliament. Printers like Hugh Gaine, James Parker, and William Weyman published widely read newspapers along with numerous pamphlets and broadsides that were instrumental in shaping how residents understood the contentious politics of the period.[60] In 1766, the radical Whig John Holt began publishing the *New-York Journal, or General Advertiser*. Holt filled his paper with content drawn from a growing network of similar-minded printers and writers in Boston and Philadelphia, which began to give shape and meaning to a nascent Patriot cause.[61]

Beginning in April 1773, New York City was also home to the most important Loyalist newspaper in the empire, James Rivington's *New York Gazetteer*.[62] Rivington's biweekly gazette became the mouthpiece for the British cause in the American colonies, providing readers with reports and essays that ultimately came to define an emerging transatlantic Loyalist political culture. Though a Patriot crowd forced him out of the colonies in 1775, he returned in 1777 as the king's printer and published his loyal gazette for the remainder of the war. Other printers also took advantage of the city's growing print market, the consequence of an ever-expanding population of Loyalist refugees and British soldiers. Hugh Gaine returned shortly after the British occupation of the city in 1776 to publish his *New-York Gazette* in support of the Crown. By 1779, there were a total of four newspapers published in New York City, with a new issue printed every day but Tuesday and Sunday.[63] The city had a composite daily newspaper; nearly every day the inhabitants could read fresh columns of print that supported the Crown.

Of course, these locally printed newspapers enjoyed an audience wider than just those living within each city. Copies of the latest gazette traveled, formally and informally, across local and regional communications networks and even boarded ships destined for communities elsewhere in the North Atlantic. After 1758, colonial printers were also able to send copies of their gazette by post for free to other printers in their region and beyond. The practice, known as franking, had existed for most of the century in mainland Britain and enabled printers to clip popular reports and essays from one another's newspapers for publication in their own gazettes.[64] This movement of newspapers beyond their own locale, and the method of printers exchanging news, helped to blur local and regional distinctions, drawing distant settlements into an ever-expanding British Atlantic information network.[65]

To some extent, it is possible to map the movement of newspapers in each of these four communities, even in the absence of subscription records. Glasgow newspapers, for instance, blanketed much of west and southwest Scotland, traveling by way of a series of postal roads first constructed in the 1720s to connect wealthy Scottish lairds invested in the burgeoning Atlantic trade to their nation's most important port city.[66] By 1780, Alexander Duncan and Robert Chapman, printers of the *Glasgow Mercury*, were asking for subscribers as far away as "Argyllshire and [the] Western Islands" to "pay their accounts."[67] Some newspapers even made the long journey across the Atlantic, likely aboard one of the city's many tobacco ships. In 1774, Alexander Thomson, a recent Scottish immigrant in Pennsylvania, reported to a friend back in Glasgow "that when I was at Philadelphia, I saw some Scotch news-papers."[68]

New York City newspapers traveled similar distances, carried by one of the many ships departing the busiest harbor in British North America or by horseback across a stretch of roads that connected the city to communities throughout New England and the mid-Atlantic. Hugh Gaine declared in 1762 that his *Mercury* could be found in "every Town and Country Village in the Provinces of New-Jersey, Connecticut, Rhode-Island and New-York; to all the Capital Places on the Continent of America, from Georgia to Halifax; to every

Island in the West-Indies, and to all the Sea Port Towns and Cities in England, Scotland, Ireland and Holland."[69] James Rivington made similar claims a decade later, telling readers that he had as many as 3,600 subscribers from across North America, the Caribbean, the British Isles, and even continental Europe.[70]

We know less about the geographical reach of the *Halifax Gazette*. Isaiah Thomas alleged "not more than seventy copies were issued weekly from" Anthony Henry's press, which, if true, would have made his printing business financially insolvent without the support of government contracts.[71] Most copies of Henry's paper were probably sold locally, while the few destined for settlements to the north would have had to travel by boat because of the colony's poorly kept roads. Henry most likely also sent issues to printers in New England and perhaps further south. During the Stamp Act Crisis, a story circulated claiming that Philadelphians "hung up in the Coffee-House . . . a stamped news-paper from Halifax," and in the evening, "the paper was set on fire, accompanied with loud huzzas."[72]

Kingston printers appear to have carried on a brisk newspaper business that stretched across the entire island. In 1779, Aikman and Douglass requested their "Country Subscribers" to pay their subscriptions for the *Jamaica Mercury*, because the "above Five Hundred Papers sent weekly to the Country, amounts every Half Year to a very large Sum of Money."[73] Their newspapers also crossed enemy lines. When news arrived in Kingston in 1779 that Spain had joined the American war, Aikman and Douglass published a letter to Comte d'Arguout, governor of the nearby Spanish colony of Hispaniola. As he was "a man of letters," they began, "we make no doubt but he will read the Jamaica Mercury; therefore, we take the liberty to remind him, that a *little, thieving, predatory war*, is a disgrace to a generous nation, and ought to be discountenanced."[74]

As their own local newspapers left the city, many others arrived in these four communities having traveled along the same local, regional, and Atlantic communication networks. For example, a recent analysis of William Bradford's 1774 and 1775 subscription books for his popular *Pennsylvania Journal* reveals a print network extending across the North Atlantic, with twenty-six subscribers in New York City, nine in Jamaica, and three in Halifax, while a single copy also found its way to a customer in Glasgow, likely a printer of one of the city's two newspapers.[75] John Dunlap's *Pennsylvania Packet* had a similar reach, with subscriptions for sale at Hugh Gaine's print shop in New York City and "by all of the Printers and Booksellers on the Continent and the West India Islands."[76] Anthony Henry certainly depended on the flow of British Atlantic newspapers into Halifax, where fresh intelligence was often hard to come by. In 1772, he complained to his readers that someone was stealing "News-Papers sent to him from *England* and from different parts of the Continent," which he relied on to fill the columns of his gazette.[77]

Similar networks also emerged in the British Isles during the first decades of the eighteenth century as printers realized that the commercial success of their press depended on gaining more and more subscribers. Though London publishers continued to dominate the industry, the provincial press expanded both in number of titles and subscriptions in the years preceding the American Revolution.[78] By tracking provincial English printers' use of newsmen and agents, one scholar discovered wide distribution networks that averaged between one thousand and three thousand subscribers and stretched to all corners of England, across to Ireland, and in some cases, north into parts of lowland Scotland. From as early as 1756, for example, Glaswegians were able to peruse the latest issues of *Williamson's Liverpool Advertiser* and the *Cumberland Pacquet and Ware's Whitehaven-Advertiser*, in addition to various London titles and the several newspapers published in nearby Edinburgh.[79] Though their account books have long since disappeared, it is likely that Robert Urie's *Glasgow Journal* and Duncan and Chapman's *Glasgow Mercury* relied on these networks, and many more, to fill the pages of their own newspapers.[80]

On the eve of American independence, there were dozens of these webs throughout the North Atlantic, creating communication networks that, as one historian notes, were "overlapping, extensive, and thick."[81] They connected Britons at multiple levels to a local, regional, and increasingly national political culture, helping to overcome the challenges of distance and time. From Kingston to Halifax, from New York City to Glasgow, and all places in between, mid-eighteenth century Britons took part in a print revolution, one that allowed more and more subjects to see themselves, as Daniel Fowle argued, "not in that contracted View they did . . . but in a more useful Light, as Members of a large Society."[82] Print facilitated this view, this idea of nation and empire.

Still, as much as this national political culture enveloped the British Atlantic, these communication networks functioned best in local and regional contexts. Imperial efforts to bridge these networks, to draw Britons into a London-centric transatlantic print culture, worked to some degree, especially in times of war when communication was especially critical. But these efforts ultimately depended on creating an efficient, fast-moving packet service, which improved steadily over the latter half of the century but never overcame the sheer distance of the empire. Broader national narratives, though persuasive and widespread, were thus filtered through more substantial local and regional print cultures that often played just as important a role in shaping popular attitudes and beliefs. Britons' imagined communities were simultaneously wider *and* closer than ever before. But their real communities—the streets, wharves, public houses, and people—still shaped how they digested news.

As countless numbers of newspapers circulated the North Atlantic, they entered into an expansive community of readers numbering far more than could be found on simple subscription lists. Britons of all rank engaged with the nation's far-reaching transatlantic print culture, creating their own smaller information networks that connected to these larger ones. In their homes, at places of work, in coffeehouses and taverns, through traveling libraries and at universities, as members of clubs and societies, and even gathered on street corners, Britons avidly and regularly devoured the latest gazettes. They read, discussed, and debated news of events at home and abroad. They argued over the meaning and importance of what was happening around them, and out of all of this, they began to make sense of their world. Fowle's "Body Politic" was a vast population of people who habitually turned to their nation's newspapers, an act that began to draw them out of their own parochial settings and into larger regional and national political cultures.

British writers on both sides of the ocean certainly understood this. When describing the importance of a free press, they almost always portrayed it in broad, expansive terms, as benefiting all Britons. A writer in a 1762 issue of William Weyman's *New York Gazette*, for instance, delighted in the ability of newspapers to spread "Knowledge of *Geography, History, Mechanicks,* and indeed the principles of every species of useful Science, through the whole mass of the nation."[83] "Quidnunc," writing late in the American war, explained to both New Yorkers and Glaswegians that without newspapers, "our coffeehouses, ale houses, and barbers shops, would undergo a change next to depopulation; and our country villagers, the curate, the excise-man, and the blacksmith, would lose the self satisfaction of being as wise as our first minister of state."[84] So ubiquitous was this idea of a widely accessible print culture, that eighteenth-century prints almost always depicted the reading of news as a public act involving both poor and wealthy Britons.[85]

Newspapers proved popular, in part, because they were substantially cheaper than other forms of printed material, such as pamphlets or magazines. If a pamphlet might cost several shillings, a single issue of a newspaper typically cost only two or three pence, while an annual subscription cost somewhere between ten and fifteen shillings, depending on location, the size of the newspaper, and the method and distance of delivery.[86] Even successive stamp taxes in mainland Britain did little to hinder the growth and spread of the industry. These rates were likely too expensive for laborers, but middling shopkeepers, storeowners, small farmers, and certainly wealthy merchants and landowners regularly subscribed to their local gazettes.[87]

For those unable to purchase subscriptions, or even single issues, there were any number of ways to gain access to the latest news. In fact, historians believe that as many as five to ten readers perused an issue of a newspaper and that number increased over the course of the century.[88] Readership was also higher in urban areas, like the four communities in this study, where residents lived closer together and frequently socialized. There were also more readers to be found in places with higher literacy rates, as among more devout Protestant communities in western lowland Scotland and in cities on both sides of the Atlantic.[89]

Reading newspapers also often and necessarily combined a growing popular print culture with long-standing oral traditions, or what one literary scholar has called the "orality of print."[90] Printers often wrote their news reports to be read aloud, adopting a narrative style that led readers through a story whose importance was not learned until the very end.[91] If the news was especially important, printers actually encouraged purchasers of their gazette to post the story in a window, or at a shop or tavern, for others in the community to read aloud. When John Holt published the Declaration of Independence on a single sheet of his paper, for example, he instructed his readers *"to separate it from the rest of the paper, and fix it up, in open view, in their Houses, as a mark of their approbation of the INDEPENDENT SPIRIT of their Representatives."*[92]

Specific spaces within a community also emerged as public gathering points in a city's local information network. Through a process known as bridging, literate members of the community would actually read the newspapers aloud to residents who were either illiterate or unable to purchase their own copy of the latest gazette.[93] This was especially common in Glasgow, where a growing population of working class residents could ill afford the purchase of a newspaper.[94] An early historian of Glasgow recalled how citizens would gather at the "'Lazy Corner' in the Bridgegate . . . in great numbers, and learn the News of the day—the progress of the Rebels in 1715 and 1745; and the Events of the American War some time later."[95] George Gibson, or *Bell Geordie*, was the most famous of the city's town criers. A later writer remembered Gibson would signal his intent to share news with the ringing of a bell, which led "each house in the neighborhood . . . to dispatch a messenger to hear what he had to communicate."[96]

Printer's shops, like James Rivington's in New York City, often served as one of these public gathering points.[97] The Monrovian minister Ewald Schaukirk complained in his journal when Rivington broadcast news of a British military victory outside his shop on the Sabbath. "Our vain chief printer," he exclaimed, "had an account of it printed in hand-bills and cried about in the forenoon, while people were going to church—another catch-penny!"[98] In Halifax, it was "deemed a sufficient publication" by local officials if John Bushell, the town's first printer, had a recent law or news of an important event read aloud "on the Parade of Halifax, after Notice by beat of Drum."[99]

British subjects also resorted to their local taverns and coffeehouses to share newspapers and discuss the latest news from home and abroad (fig. 1.1).[100] Tavern keepers, in fact, regularly advertised the number of different papers they carried in order to attract patrons. In New York City, George Burns concluded an advertisement for his tavern by stating: *"And further to gratify his customers, he constantly takes in the* Boston, Philadelphia, *and* New-York *News-papers."*[101] John Adams, among many others, took advantage of coffeehouse newspaper subscriptions during a short stay in the city en route to Philadelphia for the meeting of the First Congress in 1774. He noted in his diary that he stopped at "the Coffee House which was full of Gentlemen, [and] read the News Papers."[102] Six years later, "QUIP" reported that while reading Rivington's paper at another of the city's many coffeehouses he "overlooked several persons in the neighbouring boxes who had other papers in their hands reading aloud to their acquaintance, such articles of Advertisements or intelligence as struck them."[103]

The same was true in Glasgow, where as early as 1717, "Mrs. Shiells of the Coffee House" paid £14 annually for subscriptions to several London newspapers, which arrived by way of the Edinburgh post office.[104] Later in the century, the city's Tontine Coffee Room was often the scene of chaos and excitement as Glaswegians fought to get their hands on the latest gazettes. One local antiquarian recalled a "densely crowded" room "anxiously waiting the delivery of the newspapers." When they arrived ("generally about sixty in number" at that time), the Room's waiter sorted them before "making a sudden rush into the middle of the room [where] he then tossed up the whole lot of newspapers as high as the ceiling of the room. Now came the grand rush and scramble . . . every one darting forward to lay hold of a falling newspaper, pushing and driving each other about without mercy."[105] Once patrons had finished reading the various publications, the worn pages were sent down the street to Thomas Durie, owner of the Swann Inn, for even more of the city's residents to peruse.[106]

Haligonians regularly gathered at the Great Pontac Inn to read the latest news. Standing three stories tall, the building dominated the Halifax skyline, and its location near the major dock in the harbor made it the hub of commercial and information networks within and beyond the town.[107] Rich and poor Kingstonians also gathered in their local taverns and coffeehouses. One of the most popular was the Old British and American Coffee-house, owned

FIGURE 1.1. *Interior of a London Coffee House* (1690–1700 circa). This anonymous print of a London coffeehouse captures the public nature of reading newspapers at the turn of the eighteenth century, an act replicated over the following decades in coffeehouses and taverns throughout Britain's Atlantic empire. Gentlemen sip coffee and smoke clay pipes while reading and debating the many stories published in the various newspapers scattered across the tables. ©*The Trustees of the British Museum. All rights reserved.*

by Alexander Robertson, printer of the *Jamaica Mercury*, who advertised it as the hub of the city's print and information network.[108] During his brief stay in the city, William Hickey recalled spending two hours every morning making "the round of coffee houses and taverns, reading the newspapers and conversing on the general topics."[109]

It was so common to read aloud in British society that sometimes subjects forgot who else might be listening. In 1776, white Jamaicans foiled a planned slave revolt that was caused, in part, by dinner conversations concerning the latest news from the rebellion in the northern colonies. Reverend John Lindsay wrote from Spanish Town shortly after the plot was discovered that "our late constant disputes at our tables (where by the by every Person has his own waiting man behind him) we have I am afraid been too careless of Expressions, especially when the topic of American rebellion has been by the Disaffected amongst us, dwelt upon and brandished of with the strains of Virtuous Heroism."[110]

Britons everywhere in the latter half of the eighteenth century engaged in a robust print world, regardless of rank or location. Thanks, in part, to the emergence of vast multilayered communication networks, news traveled with increasing speed and consistency to all corners of the empire. Though far from perfect, these networks delivered news of all kind to communities in the British mainland, in North America, and throughout the Caribbean. By ship, boat, horse, and foot, news entered a local communication infrastructure of taverns, coffeehouses, public spaces, and subscription networks that increased accessibility and satisfied people's curiosity of the world around them. Britons were encouraged to see themselves as part of an imagined community of subjects stretching the length and width of the North Atlantic. They increasingly came to believe, just as Daniel Fowle argued, that their "particular Welfare is in many Respects blended with the whole."[111]

This understanding of community, of what it meant to be British, which was defined over and over again in the pages of British Atlantic newspapers, emerged out of the many wars the British nation found itself in during the first half of the eighteenth century. As these wars expanded to all corners of the empire, a growing number of Britons were forced to take up arms, and pens, in defense of their state. From Kingston to New York City and Halifax to Glasgow, Britons fought and wrote about battles lost and won and shared those stories in their local gazettes, which were carried across these many webs of communication layered atop the North Atlantic. Out of this arose a narrative of nationhood—of Britishness—that was capable, to some degree, of transcending deep-rooted local and regional differences that had divided communities within the empire.

Popular understandings of what it meant to be British rested on the real, and sometimes imagined, threat of Catholicism to the empire. While rooted in religious differences—Protestantism versus Catholicism—stretching back a century or more, this language of British loyalty and patriotism centered mostly on the alleged threat the Catholic faith posed to British political and economic liberties. A vast majority of mid-eighteenth-century Britons believed their Protestant nation was founded in such a moment of crisis, when a Catholic king, James II, envisioned an absolutist empire drawn from his own religious convictions. Even after their revolution, Britons never lost sight of these dangers, thanks in large part to a political culture saturated with anti-Catholic rhetoric and imagery. Widely read books like John Foxe's *Book of Martyrs*, songs like "Rule Britannia" and "God Save the King," popular prints such as those of William Hogarth, and an elaborate festive culture that included celebrations of Pope's Day and royal birthdays and anniversaries, drew Britons of all rank into a Protestant national political culture defined almost singularly against the perceived danger of Catholic tyranny.[112]

The simplicity of this popular brand of loyalty and patriotism appealed to the nation's diverse inhabitants. Britons in all corners of the empire linked

Catholic political rule with the perceived absolutism, tyranny, and brutality of the religion. In turn, Britons believed such rule produced a population of backward and subordinate subjects who lacked the ability to think and reason. This characterization, of course, stood in stark contrast to the celebrated British constitution and government, which, many argued, was a product of a Protestant revolution against Catholic religious and political tyranny. The British political system favored a balanced, representative government that promoted economic prosperity, personal liberty, and religious toleration. British subjects believed their religious beliefs and political ideals had created a learned, prosperous, and free society envied throughout Europe.[113] The sheer simplicity of this ideology, what we might call Protestant Whig Loyalism, enabled Britons to identify themselves against their enemies in broad sociopolitical terms that overcame, to some degree, the many distinct local or regional identities that dotted the British Atlantic.

No war had a more profound impact on the formation and expression of this ideology than the Seven Years' War. Historians of the American Revolution rightly emphasize the importance of this war in the subsequent imperial crises of the 1760s and 1770s.[114] But the war also, ironically, strengthened shared transatlantic understandings of Loyalism in ways never before seen in the nation's short history. Part of this had to do with the geographical reach of the conflict. Battles were fought on land and at sea across the Atlantic and beyond. Britons everywhere felt this war in real and meaningful ways. Fears of invasion were commonplace in Halifax, Kingston, New York City, and Glasgow, pushing subjects to arm themselves in defense of both their community and nation.

But such actions required explanation. Britons needed stories that justified their sacrifice and made it possible for them to see their participation in the war as part of a broader empire-wide effort to defeat Britain's European foes and their allies. The Seven Years' War, not the later imperial crises of the 1760s and 1770s, marked the first real test of the printing industry's ability to provide such stories, to create a British common cause.[115] Samuel Johnson certainly understood this, writing in the midst of this war that it was the job of news-writers, whom he called the "weekly historian," to construct narratives of battles, "in which we and our friends, whether conquering or conquered, did all, and our enemies did nothing." He was especially aware of the value of "tale[s] of cruelty" in uniting the broader British public, ones that described "how the enemies murdered children and ravished virgins; and, if the scene of action be somewhat distant, scalps half the inhabitants of a province."[116]

Over and over again in British Atlantic newspapers, writers did just this, describing the French as cruel despots, attributes that they believed occurred naturally in those devoted to the Catholic faith. "Decius," for instance, writing in a 1755 issue of the *Glasgow Courant*, exclaimed that "our Enemies on the Continent are a People whose Religion is principally Maintained by forgery, and Falsehood: repugnant to the Laws of Nature, and Nations . . . [and] keeping its deluded Votaries in Blindness, and ignorance of God! and real Goodness."[117] James Parker devoted almost an entire page of a January 1757 issue of his *New-York Gazette* to a history of the atrocities committed by the French church and the nation's previous monarchs so as "to keep alive a just Indignation against the treacherous bloody Religion of France." He concluded with an appeal to his readers: "What do you think of it, that *America* should become the Scene of such Barbarities? The Thought must fire you into Heroes, and rouse all the *Man* within you, to keep such a cruel murderous Power far from your Borders."[118]

New Yorker William Livingston also authored an essay on the danger of *"our neighbouring Enemies the French"* with hopes of convincing readers "upon the whole *British* Continent of *America*, to rise as one Man" and to enter into a union "against *these* our faithless, usurping, insolent Enemies." His essay traveled across regional communication networks, reaching Halifax in February 1755 (no doubt delayed by seasonal weather), and also boarded ships in the harbor destined for mainland Britain, with at least one copy arriving in Glasgow in January. He described "scenes of horror and distress" should Britons not lay aside their differences and prepare for war against France. "The sacking of a city, by a cruel and merciless enemy! . . . our fighting men slaughtered or subdued! our streets streaming with blood! our houses in a blaze! our aged trampled under foot! our wives a prey to lust! our virgins ravished! our infants tore from their fond mother's breast, and inhumanely dashed against the walls! these are the heartbreaking calamities which we may suffer from a French fleet and army."[119]

Similar reports and editorials flooded British Atlantic newspapers in the latter half of the 1750s. Readers in New York City and Halifax were regularly made to believe that barbaric French soldiers, joined by their allegedly even more savage Indian allies, intended to wipe Protestant British subjects from the continent.[120] "Think you see the Infant tore from the unavailing Struggles of the distracted Mother," one such widely circulated report went, "the Daughters ravished before the Eyes of their wretched Parents; and then, with Cruelty and insult, butcher'd and scalped."[121] These stories also traveled across the Atlantic to cities like Glasgow, where they fit within a broader narrative of the cruelty of Britain's enemies.[122]

Kingstonians feared a French and Spanish invasion, too, especially in the last years of the war when the island lacked an adequate defense. They regularly read of enemy sailors in neighboring islands raiding Jamaican plantations to capture slaves and, worse yet, attacking British civilians and soldiers. One report from the fall of 1759 claimed the crew of a French privateer slaughtered unarmed sailors on board the recently captured ship *Britannia*. "How many such Monsters these French Colonies will produce," the writer concluded, "Time must shew; but we hope some of our brave British Seamen may find some Way to retaliate the many Injuries received by their defenceless Countrymen."[123]

The island's white residents faced even greater internal threats occasioned by the war. Tacky's Rebellion in 1760, the largest and deadliest slave rebellion in the Caribbean before the Haitian Revolution thirty years later, occurred, in part, because British troops stationed on the island were transported to the recently captured French colony of Guadeloupe.[124] Others believed France and Spain played a more direct role in the events that transpired. Edward Long, in his popular history of the island written just a decade later, reported that "some persons surmised, that [slaves] were privately encouraged, and furnished with arms and ammunition, by the French and Spaniards, whose piccaroons were often seen hovering near the coast."[125] Beginning in April, thousands of Coromantee slaves from the Gold Coast revolted, aiming at "the entire extirpation of the white inhabitants" and the establishment of "small principalities in the African mode; to be distributed among their leaders and head men."[126] The rebellion lasted more than a year and came dangerously close to consuming both Spanish Town and Kingston. It also resulted in the death of at least sixty white colonists, sixty free blacks, and at least five hundred slaves, as well as the forced deportation of hundreds more.[127] Over the summer months, the heads of executed conspirators were placed on stakes in towns across the island to warn the slave population of the dangers of rebellion. Such horrific displays also reminded white Jamaicans of the perils of war with France and Spain.[128]

Britain's enemies in the middle of the eighteenth century were repeatedly described as barbarous monsters, attached to a bloody, oppressive faith and willing to butcher, scalp, rape, and pillage innocent white Protestant Britons. It is hardly surprising, then, that many subjects found this narrative of the war so compelling. This was not just a war for empire, it was understood as a war of good versus evil, of civility versus savagery, of freedom versus tyranny. Such battles, such enemies, defined and discussed over and over again in the many newspapers circulating the British Atlantic, made it easy for Britons everywhere to lay aside their differences and come together in defense of their nation.

Nothing better captures this emphatic embrace of Britishness than Benjamin West's monumental painting *The Death of General Wolfe*, perhaps the most important work of history painting in eighteenth-century Britain (fig. 1.2).[129]

When we think of Wolfe dying on the Plains of Abraham, in fact, we see West's painting. But crucially, what we do not see is all the print that came before and prepared the British public. Printed stories made that painting resonate. They not only amplified its status at the time, but they also reinforced, in striking ways, a particular transatlantic white Protestant national identity, which was brought to life by West's brushstrokes.

When the painting went on display in London's Royal Academy galleries in 1771, thousands lined the streets to catch a glimpse, including many of the nation's nobility.[130] The popularity of West's painting spurred an entire industry of cheap reproductions, in print and even on household objects, which traveled across both regional and transatlantic communication networks into homes, shops, taverns, and coffeehouses everywhere.[131] The painting also joined a larger transatlantic chorus of praise for the fallen general, who, since his death more than ten years earlier, had been celebrated in paintings, toasts, songs, plays, and verse in newspapers on both sides of the ocean.[132] Wolfe, or rather his dead body, emerged as the most potent symbol of British loyalty and patriotism in the empire at the very moment the nation descended into political crisis and rebellion.

West's massive painting overwhelmed the viewer's senses. The famed artist presented a scene rich in symbolism and emotion, drawing on the seemingly eternal contest between Protestantism and Catholicism. He adopted the classic lamentation of Christ scene, but traded Christ for the dying general, replaced the cross with an unfurled British flag, and inserted soldiers in place of mourning disciples. He defined Britishness as a religion, replete with symbols, rituals, and sacrifice. Wolfe's death, like that of Christ, was both a cause to mourn and to celebrate. For in this moment of sorrow, viewers were also witnessing the glorious birth of Britain's Protestant Empire. This was an empire backed by God no less, evidenced by Wolfe's longing gaze up toward the heavens, which shone brightly across his face. Behind him, the dark, menacing clouds of Catholic popery that had hung low over the capital of French Canada for more than a century gave way to the bright, clear skies of Protestantism.[133]

West's painting also portrayed a diverse empire, evidenced by the many grieving men surrounding the hero Wolfe, most of whom were not actually present on the occasion. There are foot soldiers and elite generals, a servant and a provincial ranger standing alongside future members of Parliament. West included several Englishmen, like Robert Monckton, second in command to Wolfe at Quebec and himself injured hours before the general's death, and Hervey Smith, Wolfe's aide-de-camp, who is pictured holding the general's arm as he expires. To the right of the wounded Monckton (holding a handkerchief to his chest) is Simon Fraser, a former Scottish Jacobite and chief of the Clan

Fraser, who fought against the Crown in the '45 Rebellion, was pardoned in 1750, and went on to have a prominent career in the British military. Also present is Irishman Isaac Barré, the son of a Huguenot linen dealer from Dublin, who became an influential member of Parliament and outspoken critic of the Stamp Act. In the foreground stands an American colonist, dressed in buckskin pants and a green wool jacket, the unit colors of Robert Rogers's famed provincial rangers.[134] Finally, the Indian kneeling before the general represented both the distance and perhaps foreignness of this new empire, but his contemplative pose also suggests something of its power and authority. After years of treacherous French Catholic rule, Wolfe had finally unshackled the Indian from the chains of popery and drew him toward a freer, more prosperous British Empire.[135]

West's painting captured the popular imagining of British loyalty and patriotism—Fowle's "Body Politic"—circulating in British Atlantic newspapers on the eve of the American Revolution. This narrative proved capable of uniting subjects across a broad geographical and social spectrum, of civilizing the noble savage, and most importantly of defeating Catholic tyranny. Britons came to believe that their nation was of the future, no longer beholden to classical Greece or Rome, and without a contemporary rival in Europe.

Figure 1.2. Benjamin West, *The Death of General Wolfe* (1770). West's painting resonated with Britons on both sides of the Atlantic, in part because it so wonderfully captured popular mid-eighteenth-century understandings of Britishness. *William L. Clements Library, University of Michigan.*

Underneath this bluster of nationhood, however, there existed an uncomfortable reality. The success of West's painting—of mid-eighteenth-century popular definitions of Britishness more generally—depended less on the sacrifice of men like Wolfe and more on those turbulent clouds of Catholic popery. In their absence, Fraser's tartan kilt, the ranger's wool green jacket, Monckton's distinctive red coat, and the scantily clad Indian suddenly appear at odds with one another. The columns of the many newspapers crisscrossing the North Atlantic would have also been empty without the stories of Catholic cruelty that had taught Britons how to make sense of their nation and their place within it.

Ironically, as we will see in the following chapters, Britain's ultimate victory in the Seven Years' War created such a moment. For the first time in many years, Britons were at peace with their European rivals. But the costs of this victory strained the imperial economy and left the government in London buried in debt. To overcome this, imperial officials pursued a series of legislative measures aimed at gaining a greater degree of control over all of their North Atlantic colonies. These policies proved especially unpopular in British North America, where subjects crafted a narrative of tyranny steeped in British Protestant Whig tradition. As the situation escalated, and the crisis turned to rebellion and war, subjects throughout the empire struggled to make sense of a conflict absent (initially) those dark clouds of Catholic popery. If victory in the Seven Years' War expanded and strengthened an understanding of Protestant British superiority, then the American Revolution and the War for Independence represented a far greater and more profound assault on that imperial British identity.

CHAPTER 2

Liberty Triumphant

The Stamp Act Crisis in the British Atlantic

In early June 1766, William Weyman's *New York Gazette* carried an account of Londoners celebrating the repeal of the widely unpopular Stamp Act. Weyman's readers were likely not surprised by this news, for New Yorkers had read of similar celebrations over the preceding weeks and months from cities across the North Atlantic. But this account from London differed from these others. Desperate to make sense of a domestic political crisis that had shaken the loyalty of Britain's colonial subjects, the writer chose to frame the day's festivities in London as a victory for a broader, familiar language of Protestant British loyalty popular among the empire's diverse inhabitants. The story began by describing the thousands of Londoners who lined the streets of that city as George III processed to Parliament "to put the finishing hand to the bill for repealing the American stamp-act." His actions, proclaimed the writer, "sufficiently testify how grateful it is to the nation, and how glorious for the Monarch who accomplished it." They also offered "a very striking contrast" to the "conduct of the King of France," which, according to the writer, was "pleasing surely to every Briton, and what ought to make his heart exult in that name."[1]

As it turns out, at nearly the same moment crowds were cheering on George III, his rival in Paris, Louis XV, was embroiled in a dispute with several regional French high courts, or Parlements. Their members represented the nobility and held considerable legal authority in their respective jurisdictions, but recently they had claimed that they were one collective unit and shared power with the monarch to legislate for the kingdom. On the morning of March 3, 1766, just two weeks before George III repealed the dreaded Stamp Act, Louis XV surrounded himself with soldiers as he made an unannounced visit to the Palais de Justice, home to the Parlement of Paris. Speaking to the surprised audience, the king reasserted his absolute authority. "I will not allow an association to be formed in my kingdom that would pervert the natural ties of duty and obligation into a confederation of resistance," he warned the nervous onlookers, "nor an imaginary body to be introduced into the Monarchy to disturb its harmony." He was not finished. "The magistrates are my officers," he asserted, "charged with the truly royal duty of rendering justice to my subjects [and it is] in my person [that] the sovereign power rest."[2]

These two episodes struck at the heart of how mid-eighteenth-century Britons had come to understand the advantages of their Protestant nation and empire over that of their Catholic rivals. George III processed alongside his fellow subjects on his way to Parliament to repeal an unpopular tax, while his counterpart in Paris surrounded himself with soldiers as he scolded his government for not recognizing that he alone was the voice of the nation. The writer in Weyman's gazette certainly understood the significance of the moment. "Our King goes to his Parliament amidst the acclamations of a free people," he declared, "to repeal an act, that was found grievous to one part of his subjects, and fatal to the wealth and prosperity of the rest. The King of France," by contrast, "sends for his Parliament amidst the sighs and silent murmurings of a subjected people, to chastise them for daring [to add] here to the few privileges that still remain with them. The one consents to undo an act legal and constitutional in itself," the writer concluded, "but found by experience inconsistent with the well-being of his people. The other arbitrarily confirms an ordinance issued contrary to law, and the good of his kingdom, and punishes his Parliament for remonstrating against it.—Britons, hear and rejoice."[3]

The Stamp Act Crisis features prominently in the history of the American Revolution. It raised important questions about ideas of consent and representation, and ultimately the very sovereignty of Parliament in Britain's Atlantic colonies—questions that grew in significance over the following decade. Additionally, the loosely formed methods of resistance adopted by colonists, which included calls for boycotts, violent rioting, and the use of the press to spread ideas and create unity, played a decisive role in colonial opposition to imperial policies in the years to come. For some, the dispute also led to a crisis of identity. The arbitrary actions of Parliament began to cast doubt on the very meaning of British loyalty in the American colonies, which some colonists were ultimately able to resolve only by declaring their independence. For many historians, popular opposition to the Stamp Act was the opening act in a political debate that ultimately ended in rebellion. According to its most famous chroniclers, the Stamp Act Crisis was the "prologue to revolution."[4]

The report in Weyman's gazette, however, offers a different way of thinking about the Stamp Act Crisis. It suggests that for Britons living in the spring of 1766, the crisis did not portend a future of political strife, rebellion, and war, but rather demonstrated the strength and resilience of their constitution and the virtue of their monarch. The crisis was, in some ways, a victory for Protestant British liberty, not a threat to it.[5] The report also hints at the larger geographic reach of the crisis. The thousands of subjects parading that day lived in London, not in a colonial American town or city (though residents of those places did their share of parading). Similar celebrations also occurred in many other port cities dotting the British Atlantic. The dispute over the tax was not contained within the thirteen American colonies. It generated conversations across the empire and among Britons of all rank in society. Finally, that the writer framed this victory for Britishness in relation to the continued tyranny of Catholic France demonstrates the enduring importance of a transatlantic language of Protestant Whig Loyalism.

But this report suggests as well that Britons found it difficult to make sense of a political crisis absent their traditional Catholic foes. Never before on this scale had subjects argued with one another over the nature of liberty and tyranny, and the rights of Britain's colonial subjects. Moreover, though many were against the tax, not all subjects agreed on how to oppose it. Of the four communities in this study, only New Yorkers took to the streets to resist the implementation of the Stamp Act. Haligonians and Kingstonians paid the tax, despite their alleged opposition to it.[6] Forms of colonial protest, or the complete absence of them, also invited new and decidedly more contentious debates over the meaning and practice of these shared political beliefs. For some on both sides of the Atlantic, rioting was a necessary response to an assault on colonists' liberty and fit within a broader political culture that supported the right of subjects to check those in power. Others, however, believed such actions spoke to a more popular, republican notion of consent, which threatened the loss of personal liberty and constituted government. These Britons instead advocated for formal channels of protest, which could effectively address colonial grievances without challenging the natural order of society. Finally, some colonial subjects did nothing, despite their opposition to the tax. They were ridiculed by Britons elsewhere in the North Atlantic, but their inaction was, in part, the result of particular local conditions that suppressed political dissent.

Divisions over methods of resistance ultimately overshadowed the widespread popular opposition to the Stamp Act, leaving Britons to make sense of a crisis that was capable of both uniting and dividing their nation. In such circumstances, Britons did what they knew best: they framed the crisis in relation to Catholic French tyranny. In this instance, the writer in Weyman's gazette hoped to shift that conversation toward a more familiar narrative of loyalty, one that was perhaps capable of smoothing over the cracks formed during the preceding several months.

These cracks were relatively minor in comparison with what was to come. Britons across the North Atlantic, including those living in the four cities in this study, roundly criticized the Stamp Act. Reports, essays, editorials, songs, and poems exchanged in newspapers celebrated ideals like liberty and virtue and railed against the legislative tyranny of Parliament. This was certainly true in New York City, but it was also the case in Halifax and Kingston, cities in colonies where residents reluctantly paid the tax. Most Glaswegians also opposed the legislation, viewing the tax as dangerous to liberty and their profitable Atlantic trade. The crisis then, to some degree, revealed the strength of British Atlantic communication networks and the resilience of Protestant Whig beliefs. The popular celebrations surrounding the repeal of the tax in the spring of 1766 also evidenced a nation committed to a defense of liberty and convinced of the superiority of their political system, especially when contrasted with their Catholic rivals in Europe. It is more accurate then to think of the language of Britishness elicited by the crisis as more closely related to 1763 than to 1776. The Stamp Act Crisis marked not the opening salvo of a future rebellion but, rather, the final moments of a united British Atlantic.

The British government faced enormous challenges in the aftermath of the Seven Years' War. Nearly six decades of conflict, financed primarily through a system of credit, had left the government deeply in debt.[7] Britain also now governed an immense empire that extended across the North Atlantic and Caribbean and into Africa, India, and Southeast Asia. This empire was a source of great pride for many, evidence of the immeasurable success of their nation in wars against their European rivals. But it also cost a great deal of money. Estimated annual expenses for maintaining a small military force of ten thousand soldiers in the North American colonies (to say nothing of the soldiers and sailors needed in the Caribbean colonies) exceeded £200,000, which the government could not afford.[8]

Other problems also confronted members of Parliament. The decision to return a majority of France and Spain's Caribbean colonies captured in the Seven Years' War left Britain's most valuable colonial possession, Jamaica, vulnerable to invasion. That colony's dependence on slave labor also led to persistent fears of insurrections, like Tacky's Revolt in 1760, which might be encouraged by Spanish and French invaders. To the north, Haligonians continued to face a hostile Indian population, allied with the small number of Acadians still living in the remote regions of the province. Local officials also relied on annual financial grants from London for the basic functioning of their government and depended on the British military for protection from their many enemies. New Yorkers, on the other hand, were part of a growing population of North American colonists who recognized their region's commercial importance to the empire and pushed for greater, and freer, access to their nation's profitable Atlantic trade. Years of salutary neglect had also allowed for the development of political institutions that operated independently from imperial rule and a political culture that demanded colonial subjects enjoy the same rights as their mainland British counterparts.[9] In Glasgow, merchants and laborers alike recognized that the city's prosperity depended on a well-regulated mercantile economy that protected their lucrative Atlantic tobacco trade. Meanwhile, many in London and elsewhere in the North Atlantic were suspicious of the growing influence of Scots, believing that they still harbored Jacobite sympathies that threatened the growth and stability of the nation.[10]

Such challenges plagued imperial officials and pushed the Grenville ministry toward a series of political and economic reforms intended to consolidate power in London and bring greater stability to their empire. They hoped to achieve this by tightening their control of the colonial trade, establishing a military presence in the colonies, and using taxes to make colonists more dependent on the Crown and more accountable for the costs of governing their colonies.[11] Initially, these officials targeted existing mercantile policies, like the tax on sugar, the results of which revealed the difficulties of administering an empire with so many competing interests.[12] The 1765 Stamp Act, however, differed from previous mercantile reforms. It was passed specifically for the purpose of raising revenue (not regulating trade) and was the first attempt by Parliament to directly tax British colonists.[13] The act, which listed fifty-four duties on everything from attorney licenses to newspapers, was passed in March but did not go into effect until November 1.[14]

During these intervening months (and also after its implementation), Britons everywhere spoke out against the Stamp Act, even in places where the tax did not apply and where residents were not able to resist its implementation. In fact, that the Stamp Act Crisis sits so squarely in the history of America's founding obscures this wider British Atlantic importance. While other mercantile reforms tended to divide subjects by favoring the interests of one group or region of the empire over another, opposition to the stamp tax drew together a large population of Britons. From the summer of 1765, subjects everywhere framed their opposition to the legislation in the context of a shared commitment to Whig ideals, including the right to representative government, defense of a free press, and protection of personal property. Many also argued that the legislation demonstrated the inherent dangers of political authority, the extension of which might cause even inhabitants of a free, Protestant nation to succumb to the kind of tyranny notorious to Catholic countries. The Stamp Act was not an inconsequential tax on printed items; rather, it portended a dark future, where British political and economic liberties were subjected to the whims of arbitrary politicians with unchecked authority over their people.[15]

This transatlantic narrative constructed in opposition to the Stamp Act, or what one contemporary Scottish writer referred to as "their common cause," demonstrates just how fearful Britons were of political tyranny.[16] Within a matter of weeks and months following its passage, thousands rioted in cities and towns across the North Atlantic, others wrote and read essays denouncing the tax, while still more agreed to boycotts and adopted formal resolutions. The scale of popular mobilization surpassed any other event in the history of the British Atlantic.

Subjects everywhere despised the tax because it challenged a fundamental right of all Britons, that government could not dispossess its subjects of their personal property without their consent. Many described the tax as a form of enslavement, capable of stealing away the property of free Britons by denying them their constitutional rights. Rhode Island Governor Stephen Hopkins understood this view. In his pamphlet, *The Grievances of the American Colonists Candidly Examined*, which was widely read in the colonies, and even excerpted in the December issue of the *Scots Magazine*, Hopkins warned that "they who are taxed at pleasure by others, cannot possibly have any property, can have nothing to be called their own; they who have no property can have no freedom, but are indeed reduced to the most abject slavery."[17]

These ideas, in fact, were fairly ubiquitous in mid-eighteenth century British political culture, and subjects of all rank were quick to draw a connection between the tax and the threat it posed to their liberty and property. In the fall, for example, New Yorkers, Haligonians, and Glaswegians all read of an attack on a stamp distributor in Hartford, Connecticut who, after resigning from office, was forced by a crowd to shout "the Words LIBERTY and PROPERTY, three times, which having done, the whole Body gave three Huzzas."[18] In December, the New York City printer, John Holt, published a broadside against the tax signed by "Britannus Americanus" that included an ornate copy of the city's seal at the top, along with a banner that read, "LIBERTY, PROPERTY, and no STAMPS."[19]

The timing of the Stamp Act also stoked popular fears of political and economic tyranny. Residents of the four communities in this study suffered from a crippling postwar recession felt across all of society. The recent passage of the Sugar and Currency Acts, and the shortage of hard currency, only exacerbated the situation. In October, a New Yorker lamented that residents were "exerting every nerve, to free ourselves from the wretched condition, to which our debts to Great Britain have reduc'd us," while the government desires "to plunge [us] deep in ruin,—never to rise again."[20] Halifax printer Anthony Henry was more candid in his gazette (which was printed on stamped paper after November 1): "Trade is dull, Money scarce, and to complete our Misfortunes we must be STAMP'D.—Qure, *Is this right?*"[21] Kingstonians grieved as well the loss of the Spanish bullion trade, which had provided a market for surplus British goods and injected much-needed hard currency into Britain's Atlantic economy.[22] During debates over the tax in February 1765, Rose Fuller, brother to Stephen Fuller, Jamaica's agent in London, petitioned Parliament arguing that "the inhabitants of the said island are in general distress in their circumstances," and that "the Publick as well as private Credit of the Island is at the utmost stretch."[23]

Mainland British merchants were deeply concerned with the financial implications of the stamp tax, as well, and feared a further decline in their trade. Indeed, if nothing else, the Stamp Act Crisis demonstrated just how much residents of mainland port cities like Glasgow viewed access to colonial markets as a defining characteristic of their attachment to the empire. Rumors and reports regularly circulated in the Scottish press of the suffering of colonists, many of whom were indebted to British merchants and manufacturers. A letter from a New Yorker in September claimed "trade in this part of the world is come to so wretched a pass . . . on account of a proposed stamp duty," and it was possibly "still worse at Philadelphia."[24] The same was true in Kingston, where Scots read in October that "upwards of 1500 persons had lately been rendered insolvent, by the general stagnation of trade."[25] Many of these debts, especially in the Chesapeake, were to Glasgow's tobacco merchants, who looked on cautiously as the crisis unfolded in the summer and fall of 1765.

Increasingly over the fall months, Scots also read of efforts by some colonists to begin to manufacture their own goods, rather than rely on British imports they could no longer afford. In a letter from Philadelphia, a writer cautioned readers that "the taxation of the colonies, and the restraining their trade, (however popular it may be in England) was certainly the worst scheme that could be thought of; for when a people becomes poor, it naturally looks within itself for resources."[26] By September, Scots (and Haligonians) read that New Yorkers were producing a wide variety of locally made goods that they sold at a "Homespun Market" at the Exchange.[27] At the end of October, "*upwards of Two Hundred principal Merchants*" had also agreed to a boycott of British goods, which was followed by Philadelphians and Bostonians over the following two months.[28] Even in Halifax, local tailors asked for "the Prayers of all good People that the Stamp Act may be repealed, as most of their Customers have declared they will have no new Clothes made, until such Time as said Act is repealed.—*A noble Resolution!*"[29]

Boycotts and homespun helped to create unity throughout the American colonies by eroding social distinctions and emphasizing virtue, frugality, and commitment to a political cause that demanded the repeal of an unpopular tax.[30] But unpaid debts, bankruptcies, and threats of dismantling Britain's once prosperous Atlantic trade, also drew some mainland Britons to the colonists' cause. Glaswegians were especially dependent on a robust Atlantic economy, where colonial subjects avidly consumed British goods and produced raw materials needed to sustain manufactories. The Stamp Act threatened to undermine what Glaswegians believed to be a mutually beneficial relationship. "SIMPLICIUS," writing in an October issue of the *Caledonian Mercury*, believed that the tax revealed a decline in virtue among government officials at the cost of their country's once prosperous colonial trade. Previously, the writer argued, selfish merchants were responsible for oppressive colonial debts, but the current crisis was in consequence of "Ministers of state . . . [whose] injurious schemes of commerce . . . [have] promoted the interest of individuals to the prejudice of the community."[31]

This growing "common cause" also included the right of subjects to be heard and to have a say in how they were governed. The Stamp Act deprived British colonists of this cherished right because it had been passed without their consent as they lacked representation in Parliament. John Morin Scott, writing as "Freeman" in the *New-York Gazette*, referred to the right of subjects to be taxed *"only by our own consent given by our representatives"* as *"the sacred badge of liberty"* and bemoaned any legislation that directly challenged that right. "Was there ever a more monstrous absurdity to be found in the practice of the most barbarous nations upon earth? how is our glory fallen!"[32] The anonymous author of the essay, "On the privileges of the Americans," which appeared in the *Scots Magazine*, warned readers that "wherever the governed have no share in either [branches of government], there is no public liberty; and consequently such a government, with respect to them, must necessarily be an arbitrary one."[33] Similar sentiments could be found among white Jamaicans like Charles Price Sr., a prominent sugar planter and member of the island assembly, who considered consent and representation to be "a Bulwark essential to the very existence of a British Constitution." To raise taxes "in any other manner," he argued, "would be destructive of this most essential Privilege of a Briton."[34]

Scots were also staunch defenders of such rights. Since the 1707 union, they had come to embrace English constitutional history, and in the fall of 1765, some had sought the repeal of their nation's longstanding entail laws for reasons that closely paralleled American opposition to the Stamp Act.[35] One anonymous writer in the *Scots Magazine* believed that curbing hereditary land rights and expanding land ownership would improve the nation's domestic economy and expand political liberty to a greater swath of Scottish society. "It is the privilege of a British subject to be taxed by his own consent, or at least with the consent of his representative in parliament," the author argued. "And the person who pays the tax ought to have a vote in the choice of the member who is to lay it on. Accordingly, to enlarge this privilege as much as possible, and to destroy that dependence which vassalage naturally creates," would promote liberty by making government more accountable to a larger portion of the population.[36]

For some, the Stamp Act was so dangerous to eighteenth-century conceptions of Britishness that they believed the two simply could not coexist. They claimed that submission to the tax would make a free Briton into a slave, by which they meant not just those from Africa, but also Catholics and Muslims in Europe. A New Yorker, for example, warned that to obey the tax would be to say that "there is no difference between absolute power and limited government, between Englishmen and Frenchmen, between law and despotism, *freedom and vassalage, tyranny and justice.*" In such circumstances, he feared, colonial subjects could be reduced to "the bondage of Frenchmen; or rather to the beastly servitude of Turks."[37] In a poem published first in New York City and then in Halifax, the writer declared "'Tis virtual the same to stay here or go there, To breath a free British or some other Air; A Freeman in London, or a Vassal at Bender, In Effect are the same—the Masculine Gender."[38] This was not just a tax on printed items. Many subjects in these four communities believed it was capable of destroying their Protestant empire, of turning once free Britons into a foreign people, enslaved to a tyrant.

Opposition to the new tax, though widespread, did not lead inevitably to open resistance. Despite fears of impending tyranny, only New Yorkers joined with other communities in aggressively and violently resisting the implementation of the Stamp Act. Both Haligonians and Kingstonians paid the tax, if reluctantly. Glasgow's influential tobacco merchants waited until the following February before petitioning for the repeal of legislation, despite its unpopularity among many of that city's inhabitants. This divide between opposition and resistance—between believing the Stamp Act to be oppressive and arbitrary and being willing (or able) to resist its implementation—suggests that for historians there is another way of thinking about the Stamp Act Crisis. Resistance required buying into a narrative where action was necessary and where even certain kinds of violence were deemed acceptable. This narrative, of course, drew from broader ideas of liberty and tyranny elevated by the crisis over the tax but also, crucially, required particular local conditions and political cultures that made defying the tax possible.

This kind of resistance rested on a republican conception of consent that was widely popular in the mid-eighteenth-century British Empire. Many Britons, though loyal to the Crown and constitution, believed they enjoyed the right to collectively assemble, to have a say in politics, and to speak out against corrupt officials or arbitrary legislation. These ideas drew from an abundance of English and Scottish Commonwealth writings, such as those of Algernon Sidney and John Locke and especially the more recent works of Joseph Addison, John Trenchard, and Thomas Gordon. These writers warned of the possible corruption of power and celebrated ideas of virtue and individual liberty.[39]

Their works regularly appeared in London taverns and coffeehouses, but they also found their way into colonial American bookshops, like Hugh Gaine's in New York, and even into the hands of purportedly more moderate Britons in Glasgow.[40] During disputes over the stamp tax, the famed Glaswegian printers Andrew and Robert Foulis reprinted Addison's enormously popular 1712 play, *Cato: A Tragedy*, which recounted Cato's famous struggle against the tyranny and corruption of Julius Caesar.[41] In late October, a 1722 essay by Trenchard appeared in the *Caledonian Mercury*, which the printer believed spoke to "the present melancholy situation of affairs with respect to the American colonies." Trenchard warned in the letter that if the British government resorted to arbitrary violence to control their colonial subjects, they would likely push those colonists toward independence and destroy the nation's Atlantic economy in the process.[42]

Yet as much as Britons understood and generally shared in this republican notion of popular consent, it remained a fairly ambiguous idea, without clearly defined parameters. Subjects recognized the rights of others to assemble, to protest, to write and march in defense of their liberties, but they were less certain when such methods were necessary and how far protests could go. Even the practitioners of this ideology failed to provide clear guidelines for action. John Locke famously argued that resistance, or even rebellion, was justified when subjects were "made miserable, and find themselves exposed to the ill-usage of arbitrary power."[43] But who decided when that was the case? Were colonists "miserable" as a result of the stamp tax? Did the legislation represent an "ill-usage of arbitrary power"? Most Britons throughout the North Atlantic agreed that it was a dangerous and unconstitutional piece of legislation, but they were less sure about the sort of response it warranted.

Subjects also disagreed on the exact relationship between popular consent and political authority. Radicals on both sides of the Atlantic increasingly argued that officials derived their authority from the consent of those they governed. Moderates, on the other hand, maintained that popular consent operated within a political structure where authority remained in the hands of those in power. These debates are often thought to relate to emerging class divisions in British society, given that they played out most often in a rapidly expanding market economy where questions of fairness and equality butted heads with profit and self-interest.[44] But these disagreements also had to do with how Britons thought about political stability, constituted authority, and the broader relationship between liberty and power. While some argued that popular consent was a necessary check to political authority, others believed that violent crowds and subversive writings were an abuse of liberty and could lead to chaos and anarchy. Even when particular communities felt justified in taking to the streets and adhered to established traditions of crowd behavior, as so many colonial communities did in the fall of 1765, it did not necessarily follow that subjects elsewhere believed their actions to be legitimate. Popular consent, it turns out, was both well understood and endlessly divisive.[45]

The Stamp Act Crisis also revealed divisions over the relationship between popular consent and a free and open press. Some subjects viewed the press as the greatest bulwark against political tyranny and feared the stamp tax would destroy the printing industry by driving up the price of newspapers, or in some cases, force printers out of business. At least five printers, from South Carolina to Quebec, closed shop temporarily during the crisis. Many others complained that the tax would ruin them financially. Some decorated their papers with black borders and other symbols of mourning to signify the approaching death of liberty.[46] In late October, Hugh Gaine notified readers of his *New-York Mercury* that *"It must now cease for some Time; and the Period of its Resurrection uncertain."*[47] Haligonians continued to read their local newspaper throughout the crisis (with the nameplate outlined in thick, black ink), but discovered in November that the *Maryland Gazette* had "expired . . . in *uncertain* Hopes of Resurrection to Life again," and the same was true for Gaine's "New-York Mercury . . . [and] the Philadelphia papers."[48] Anthony Henry also reprinted essays that defended a free press because "the chief of the blessings which we now enjoy" depend on the "public Knowledge and public Freedom" that a free press promoted.[49]

Yet, for some printers, the colonial press actually became considerably less free during the Stamp Act Crisis. Opponents of the tax, especially newly formed Sons of Liberty groups in northern port cities like New York City, took steps to ensure certain printers favorable to their cause remained open during the crisis. In November, a group of New Yorkers warned the radical Whig printer John Holt that if he "shut up the press, and basely desert us, depend on it, your house, person and effects, will be in eminent danger."[50] At the same time, some began to argue for violence toward any colonist who wrote or spoke in favor of the tax. In the fall and winter of 1765–66, printers on both sides of the Atlantic exchanged copies of the Virginia House of Burgesses' resolutions against the Stamp Act and included an unpassed resolution that warned "any person who shall, by speaking or writing" show support for the Act "shall be deemed an enemy to this his Majesty's colony."[51] Jefferson later remarked that Virginians rejected this last resolve, because "no mind was then prepared" for such action.[52] But these threats of violence toward printers and proponents of the tax suggested that republican notions of consent might not apply to everyone. Some colonists were willing to argue that defending their liberty required suppressing the liberty of others.

The suffering of some printers, however, did not deter the majority of colonists from expressing their right to be heard (so long as they were against the tax), which they believed to be essential to their sense of loyalty and Britishness. John Morin Scott warned readers that their silence implied acceptance of the tax. "Would not our silence at this time imply a criminal insensibility, or indifference, about the possession of one of the most valuable gifts of God, and shew us to be unworthy to enjoy it?"[53] Haligonians also cherished the idea of popular consent, even if a powerful political and military class made it difficult to act on such beliefs. In December, Henry reprinted (on stamped paper) an essay from London, which argued that every Briton should be inculcated from birth in the importance of virtue and liberty, and should be prepared at all times to speak out against any "sycophant" who sought to trample on "the sacred liberties of mankind."[54]

Britons disagreed, though, on how far subjects could go in checking the authority of those in power. This was especially true when colonists rioted against the implementation of the tax, but it was also the case when it came to speaking and writing against the unpopular legislation. The notion of popular consent—the belief that power and authority answered, to some degree, to the voice and actions of subjects—divided moderate and radical Whigs across the North Atlantic, despite their shared dislike of the tax.

A majority of New Yorkers united in opposition to the stamp tax in the fall of 1765, but they did not agree on the forms of resistance. Moderates within the De Lancey and Livingston factions believed that violent protests threatened to undo the natural political order of society and instead advocated for peaceful, nonviolent methods of resistance. They encouraged city and colony officials to petition Parliament for a repeal of the legislation, backed resolutions adopted by the Stamp Act Congress in October, and were behind efforts to establish a boycott of British goods.[55] But these moderates faced increasing pressure from a growing population of radicals in the city. Middling merchants and artisans, such as Isaac Sears, John Lamb, and Alexander McDougall, organized protests and took to local newspapers to advocate for a far more aggressive opposition to the tax.[56] Scott's "Freeman" essays, for example, went so far as to argue that colonists had the right to rebel against a government that had succumb to tyranny. "If the welfare of the mother country necessarily requires a sacrifice of the most natural rights of the colonies . . . ," he warned, "then the connexion between them ought to cease."[57]

Colonists began to resist in August 1765, targeting the appointed stamp distributors who had come to symbolize the tyranny of the legislation. Bostonians were the first to act when, on the night of August 14, thousands of residents paraded an effigy of Andrew Oliver through the town and then destroyed his home and the building intended to house the stamps. News of his resignation the following day traveled quickly across the British Atlantic.[58]

The events of August 14 are often thought of in relation to another more violent riot that occurred in Boston two weeks later, which revealed internal divisions over class and politics in that northern port city.[59] But the attack on Oliver and his property also had a kind of ripple effect across the North Atlantic, shaping initial attitudes toward stamp distributors and raising questions about the right of colonists to resist the enforcement of the stamp tax. Glaswegians, for example, read of the assault on Oliver and his property alongside similar violent attacks against other stamp distributors throughout Britain's Atlantic colonies.[60] While sympathetic to the plight of their fellow subjects, they abhorred the crowd violence, which they believed encouraged political instability and upended the natural order of society. In their October issue, the editors of the *Scots Magazine* revealingly titled a section on the August 14 riot, "Insurrections in North America." Scots also began to attribute the worst of the violent behavior to radical New Englanders and increasingly believed their political culture differed significantly from other regions of the empire. In November, an inaccurate report circulated of Virginia's stamp distributor, George Mercer, having been invited to a ball after arriving in the colony. He was treated "with the utmost politeness" at the event but was told he should leave the colony immediately, "lest his life should be endangered by his staying there another day." "Observe the difference between the people of Virginia and New-England," reported the writer in the *Caledonian Mercury*. "The one, outrages, threatens with destruction the person appointed to an office that was odious; the other, feasts and dismisses him."[61]

Radicals in New York City, on the other hand, eagerly read of the riot in Boston, which appeared alongside other reports encouraging violent resistance to the tax. "CATO," writing in the same issue of Gaine's *Mercury* that carried news from Boston, complained of the inaction of New Yorkers "whose only Fortitude is in the Tongue and Pen." He also warned other stamp distributors "to look for Nothing but the Hatred and Detestation of all the Good and Virtuous."[62] Oliver's demise and warnings from writers like "CATO" were enough to convince James McEvers, a local merchant who had been appointed as the city's stamp distributor in early July, to resign from the post.[63]

McEvers's resignation strengthened the radical cause in New York City. In October, they asked residents to form "an ASSOCIATION of ALL who are not already SLAVES, in OPPOSITION to all ATTEMPTS to make them so."[64] Local writers urged residents to refuse stamped paper, while the city's newspapers exchanged reports from across the colonies boasting of stamp distributors being forced to resign their offices. The growing unity of radical Whigs frustrated moderates and imperial officials. General Thomas Gage, stationed in New York City throughout the crisis, wrote to Lieutenant Governor Colden shortly after McEvers's resignation that every loyal Briton must feel "the greatest Pain and Anxiety to see the Public Papers crammed with Treason, the Minds of the People disturbed, excited and encouraged to revolt against the Government, to subvert the Constitution, and trample upon the laws."[65] It was one thing to oppose a bad policy, but it was another to encourage attacks on others and their property.

Radicals kept writing, however, capturing the growing spirit of resistance spreading across the continent. From September, a majority of colonial newspapers shared reports and editorials calling for greater opposition to the tax. Resistance was especially widespread from Charleston to Boston. Virtually every stamp distributor resigned his office, which was reported in newspapers on both sides of the Atlantic.[66] "Caesariensis," writing in Gaine's newspaper, believed that the entire cause depended first on the resignation of these despised men. "The conduct of the stamp officer will give the true political complexion of every colony," the writer argued. "If the stamp officer cannot execute his office with any degree of comfort and reputation, and thereupon resigns, then it will be evident that the inhabitants of that colony are sensible of the imposition, and spurn it."[67]

"Caesariensis's" calculation did not bode well for residents of Halifax or Kingston. Neither city's residents were able to force their stamp distributors to resign, despite the public's opposition to the tax. They did try, however. On the night of October 12, some Haligonians targeted the colony's appointed distributor, Archibald Hinshelwood.[68] The crowd hanged an effigy of the despised "Stampman" alongside an image of the devil and "a Boot," a symbol for the unpopular Scot and alleged Jacobite, Lord Bute, believed by many to be behind the tax. Someone in the crowd also pinned a short poem to the effigy that appeared in several colonial American newspapers. It described Hinshelwood's crimes to all those in attendance ("it was for the Sake of Gain I took this Place . . .") and threatened violence toward anyone who defended him: "Whoever carries this away is an Enemy to his Country. What greater Glory can this Country see, Than a Stamp-master hanging on a Tree."[69]

But Haligonians, unlike their New York City counterparts, lacked the necessary social structure and political culture to sustain such a resistance movement. Whereas New Yorkers increasingly depended on the participation of a broad swath of society, the merchant and political elite in Halifax were reluctant to challenge Parliamentary legislation given their continued dependence on annual financial assistance from London. The city was also a garrison town, home to hundreds of British soldiers and seamen, limiting the ability of residents to assemble en masse or to confront those who supported the unpopular tax.[70] These particular local circumstances likely explain why the protest against Hinshelwood was absent any sort of grand procession or crowds threating violence against the stamp distributor, his property, or any other government official in town. Haligonians, unlike their southern neighbors, were unable to remove him from office in October.

The report of the effigy incident exchanged in other colonial newspapers even admitted to the challenges faced by residents of the northern port city. The writer explained that Haligonians hoped others would "believe that nothing but their dependent situation prevents us from heartily and sincerely opposing a tax unconstitutional in its nature, and of so destructive a tendency as must infallibly entail poverty and beggary on us and our posterity, if carried into action."[71] Another Haligonian reported to a friend in New York City that "the Spirit of Liberty and British Freedom reigns in the Hearts of the People of Halifax, though as an Infant dependent Colony, it is not prudent, or even in their Power to exert themselves in Opposition to oppressive Government."[72]

This narrative—of a community wanting but unable to resist an arbitrary tax—came to define how others viewed Halifax during the Stamp Act Crisis. John Adams believed Haligonians were "kept in fear by a Fleet and an Army," while Captain John Montresor observed from New York City that that "the singular advantage of troops and fleets to enforce his Majesty's orders are here plainly demonstrated."[73] Even as far south as Charleston, colonists praised the widespread resistance to the Stamp Act but excused "Canada, Nova Scotia, and the two Floridas, which being, in some sort, military governments, of course no opposition could be expected from them."[74] Others took a more pessimistic view of what was happening in Halifax, fearing that it might serve as blueprint for the future oppression of the remaining colonies. The stamps were "forced upon the inhabitants of . . . *Nova Scotia* . . . where a sufficient Military Force is maintain'd to enslave the Inhabitants," argued one writer, before concluding with a "Remark of a Writer in 1697": "In all ages and parts of the world, a Standing-Army has been the never-failing Instrument of enslaving a nation."[75]

A week after the failed protests against Hinshelwood, John Howell arrived in Kingston as Jamaica's newly appointed stamp distributor.[76] His first days in the city were anything but peaceful. In a letter to Secretary of State Henry Conway, Howell complained that he had faced "repeated Threats of Violence, Torrents of Personal abuse and many other very disagreeable Circumstances."[77] He decided quickly (and wisely) to move his office and the stamped paper to nearby Spanish Town, where there was less resistance to the tax. "This expedient," he argued, "put an Intire stop to the violences threatened, [and] the Existence of the Stamp office is Intirely owing to it."[78]

We do not know for certain what motivated Kingstonians to threaten Howell. Many of the city's inhabitants were directly involved in the Atlantic trade and would have certainly felt the effects of the tax. It is possible, too, that they were influenced by the events occurring in the North American colonies, which were likely covered extensively in the island's newspapers, though no copies from this period survive today. Later, in May 1766, Howell admitted to the influence of the local press when he wrote that Jamaicans would have paid more of the tax had they not believed it would be repealed, "which they inferred from the conduct of the N. Americans."[79]

Like Haligonians, Kingstonians faced particular local circumstances that made resistance difficult. They, too, lived among a large population of British soldiers and seamen, there to protect the white inhabitants from slave revolts or French or Spanish invasions. Subjects elsewhere appeared to understand this, with one writer complaining that "Stamps have been . . . crouded upon the people of Jamaica . . . who were kept in awe by a military power."[80] The colony's white inhabitants were vastly outnumbered by slaves as well, and many feared widespread rioting might offer opportunities for slaves to revolt against their masters. One Jamaican, writing at the time of Howell's arrival, hinted at the challenges of resisting imperial legislation in the British Caribbean. "Great are the murmurings against the stamp-law," suggested the writer, "but we dare not proceed to such violences as the people of Boston and Virginia."[81] Moderation was thus a pragmatic decision, made necessary by particular conditions on the island, and was not necessarily evidence of a desertion of Whig principles.

Back in New York City, the arrival of ships carrying stamped paper in late October exacerbated tensions between officials and colonists. As many as two thousand New Yorkers gathered at the docks on October 22 to protest the ships' arrival, while a writer in Gaine's *Mercury* reported that McEvers wanted "nothing to do with them."[82] The situation worsened the following evening when word got out that Lieutenant Governor Colden had stashed the stamped paper at the fort. Notices were posted throughout the city warning that "the First Man that either distributes or makes Use of Stampt Paper, let Him take care of His House, Person, & Effects."[83]

Radicals in New York City were emboldened by the arrival of the stamped paper, which they believed portended a dark future absent liberty. On October 31, just a day before the tax went into effect, a crowd gathered on a rumor of a funeral procession for "Liberty," while two hundred and fifty merchants met at Burn's Tavern to agree to a boycott of British goods.[84] Everywhere, the city appeared in a state of grief and inactivity. In the evening, a still larger crowd roamed the streets, chanting "Liberty," breaking windows and street lamps, and warning supposed supporters of the tax "that they would the next night pull down their Houses." They even threatened to bury alive Major Thomas James, who had earlier claimed "he would cram down the Stamp Act upon them with a hundred men."[85]

The following night, the crowd targeted Lieutenant Governor Colden for having supposedly declared his intention to distribute the stamps against the will of the people. They stole his carriage and hanged the reviled governor in effigy attaching a label to his jacket that read, "The Rebel Drummer in the Year 1715." The quote referenced a rumor running through the city that Colden had served as a drummer in the Old Pretender's army during the first Jacobite Rebellion. In the absence of real French Catholic enemies—the greatest threat to Protestant British liberty—New Yorkers were left with having to turn their governor into a secret Jacobite.

Colden was more than just a rebel drummer, however. When a crowd gathered at the fort's gate later that evening, someone passed to a guard a note addressed to Colden. It warned the lieutenant governor that if he attempted to distribute the stamps, he would "be Hang'd, like Porteis, upon a sign-post as a Memento to all wicked Governors."[86] *Porteis* referred to Captain John Porteous of the Edinburgh City Guard, who was called to put down a riot in 1736, during which he ordered his men to fire on the crowd, killing seven and wounding at least twenty people. Afterward, he was found guilty of murder but given a stay of execution, which incited the crowd to take justice into its own hands. The following day the crowd stormed the prison, dragged Porteous through the streets, and hanged him by his neck on a signpost.[87] Linking Colden to the infamous Porteous not only revealed the city's deep ties to a radical transatlantic political culture but also served to transform the unpopular governor into something far more heinous and threatening. Colden was both a disguised Jacobite and cruel military official, both of which were antithetical to mid-eighteenth-century understandings of Britishness. Writers over the previous several months had warned that accepting the tax would turn Britons into dangerous foreigners. Colden revealed this warning to be true.

Though the stamped paper remained at the fort the following day, tensions continued to rise in the city, made worse by the approaching Pope's Day celebration.[88] On November 2, rumors spread of a possible siege of the fort, prompting Colden to order all of the guns in the city to be spiked.[89] Meanwhile, more moderate New Yorkers desperately sought to bring calm to the streets of the city but struggled to find support for fear the crowd might turn on anyone who opposed them. Colden finally agreed three days later to turn the stamps over to the City Council in order "to prevent the Effusion of blood and the Calamities of a Civil War." That evening, nearly five thousand New Yorkers, perhaps the largest crowd ever to gather in New York City, watched as seven boxes of stamps were transported to City Hall.[90]

There were no riots in Halifax or Kingston in the first week of November, nor did crowds force officials to move stamped paper to secure locations. In both places, colonists paid the stamp tax, which was administered by the distributors they were unable to remove from office. Haligonians lived in a colony that received only £1,609 worth of stamped paper (the least of any colony), and they appear to have purchased all of it by the following February. Jamaicans received £15,781 worth of stamped paper (the most of any colony), despite having a white population of fewer than eighteen thousand. By the following March, they had paid just over £2,000, more than any colony that administered the tax, but just a fraction of the amount they were consigned. Nova Scotia and Jamaica produced more tax revenue than any of the other British colonies.[91]

These numbers tell only part of the story, though. Haligonians and Kingstonians continued to speak out against the tax even as they paid for it. In a letter to a friend in New York City (penned on Pope's Day, no less), one Haligonian described the Stamp Act as an "American Hydra," inverting popular references to the mythical ancient Greek serpent monster.[92] Britons were the true heirs of Herculean power and order, claimed the writer, and needed to stand up to a government "threatening a general devastation . . . over all the provinces on the continent."[93] In late November, Isaiah Thomas wrote in Henry's gazette that "the Stamp Works are going forward, though much against the Inclination of the People in general, who wait with great Impatience to hear the *happy News* of the STAMP-ACT being repealed, which would fill the Breast of every loyal Subject, and Friends of LIBERTY, with Joy and Gladness!"[94]

Similar accounts emerged from Kingston as well, with one resident reporting that "the People here are in a perfect phrenzy on account of the stamp-act, and declare they will sooner forfeit their lives than those privileges, the foundations of which were laid in the blood of their ancestors, namely the right to tax themselves!"[95]

During the winter months, Hinshelwood was subjected to repeated abuse from locals. In January, he wrote to the Board of Trade that his acceptance of the position had "brought upon me the whole Indignation of the people upon the Continent," and included a letter he had recently received from a group of men who threatened his ruin "if you don't resign that damnable Office of Stamp Man for this Province."[96] Other reports exchanged in newspapers across the North Atlantic supported Hinshelwood's claims. In December, colonists read that the unpopular official was "guarded by a party of soldiers night and day, lest he should fall a victim to the justly enraged people."[97] False reports even circulated in January that Hinshelwood had resigned "his detestable office as he is held in the utmost abhorrence and his life is in great danger."[98]

Henry regularly filled his gazette with detailed coverage of events occurring in the American colonies, reprinting reports of rioting and editorials that denounced the tax.[99] The stamped paper also became a form of protest. In the December 19 issue, he outlined the masthead in thick black lines and replaced the stamp mark with an image of a skull and crossbones and the word "America" across the top. In the February 13 issue he printed the image of the Devil with pitchfork in hand stabbing the stamp mark along with the inscription: "Behold me the scorn and contempt of AMERICA, pitching down to Destruction. D[evi]ls clear the Way for B[ut]es and STAMPS"[100] (figs. 2.1 and 2.2).

News from Halifax, however, was not all devils and pitchforks in the early months of 1766. During the first weeks of January, reports began to circulate in newspapers from Boston to Williamsburg, and across the Atlantic to Scotland, that Hinshelwood was no longer enforcing the tax on transactions related to the city's trading interests. "It gives us great Pleasure to find the Port again opening," claimed one Haligonian, "The Vessels are admitted to an Entry here as usual, without exacting the Penalty of ten Pounds as prescribed in the—Stamp Act."[101] Weeks later, Henry happily reported that "as all the Stampt Paper for this gazette is used up, and no more to be had."[102] Three months after their southern neighbors had driven stamp distributors from their colonies and refused to abide by the legislation, Haligonians finally rid themselves of the despised tax.

Similar reports emerged from Kingston of officials either outright ignoring the use of stamps in business transactions, or at the very least allowing ships to enter their port without stamped paper.[103] Several ship captains confirmed

FIGURE 2.1. The *Halifax Gazette*, December 19, 1765. In the absence of crowds protesting the Stamp Act, Thomas used his newspaper to express opposition to the unpopular tax. He likely found inspiration for the design of this issue from the more popular October 31 issue of William Bradford's *Pennsylvania Journal*, which was made to look like a tombstone marking the death of a free press. *Courtesy, American Antiquarian Society.*

these reports, adding that Kingstonians "greatly approve of the conduct of the North-Americans, in opposing the Stamp Law."[104] The decision to favor trade over stamps was likely motivated by the dependence of the island's white inhabitants on slave labor. Rumors of boycotts threatened the loss of North American markets, which supplied the basic necessities to sustain the colony's nearly two hundred thousand slaves. Previously, food shortages, which slaves always felt more acutely, often contributed to increased tensions on the island and sometimes led to violence and rebellion. In late November, just as the tax

The text visible within the woodcut image reads:

> corn and con-
> tempt of A-
> MERICA, it
> ing down
> Deſtruction
> four
>
> ... them. There they found
> ... given Eo, two thouſand to
> ... nothing at all. Now for
> ... into a violent paſſion, and
> ... "You are to obſerve, he has uſed me ve-
> ... in not giving me three times as much, and
> ... I won't go into mourning for him."
> ... ſaid, "I don't think myſelf at all obliged
> to him." Poor Reo ſighed ; "We had none
> ... of us any right to a ſhilling, ſaid he ; in his life
> ... time he was very good to us all, but one thou-
> ... pounds would have made me quite happy."
> ... ſuppoſed corpſe had heard enough ; out he
> ... ed from a cloſet. tweak'd Eo by the ...

FIGURE 2.2.   The *Halifax Gazette*, February 13, 1766. Thomas's woodcut of the devil stabbing the stamp is one of the more iconic images from the Stamp Act Crisis, which is remarkable given that it appeared in a newspaper published in a colony that actually paid the tax. Two weeks after its publication, the *Halifax Gazette* returned to being printed on unstamped paper. *Courtesy, American Antiquarian Society.*

went into effect, an uprising in St. Mary's parish northeast of Kingston resulted in the death of "several of the Planters there." "Our Negroes are politicians enough to know," reported one resident, "that while all public business is at a stand in the island, when there is said to be no money in the Treasury, and no assembly . . . likely to be called to raise supplies, such is the most favourable time for them to succeed in any attempts against the white people."[105]

The willingness of Kingstonians to otherwise pay the tax, however, did not go unnoticed by other colonial subjects. Some blamed the inaction of the island colonists to having been nurtured in a slave society where ideas of freedom and liberty were best understood only in relation to the enslavement of others. John Adams described Jamaicans as "sordid, stupid Creatures, below Contempt, below Pity" and believed the only thing capable of awakening their sense of liberty was, ironically, their rebellious slaves. "I could wish that some of their Blacks had been appointed Distributors and Inspectors &c. over their Masters," he proclaimed, "this would have but a little aggravated the Indignity."[106]

Over the winter of 1765–66, Kingstonians were also embroiled in a local political crisis, in which the rights and liberties of the local assembly were set against the authority of the royal governor, Henry Lyttleton. The controversy, which concluded in favor of the assembly and led to the recall of Lyttleton, possibly forced larger imperial issues like the Stamp Act into the background.[107] Kingstonians suffered from geographic isolation, as well. It took as long as four to six weeks to travel between the Caribbean port city and centers of resistance in North America, a distance that delayed communication and hampered efforts to effectively plan resistance. The difficulty posed by geographic isolation was evident as early as the summer of 1765, when the Massachusetts Assembly called for a Stamp Act Congress to meet in New York City but extended the offer only to mainland colonial assemblies.[108] The following spring, Sons of Liberty groups excluded Jamaicans and Nova Scotians from efforts to coordinate opposition to the tax, likely in consequence of their colonies' failure to resist the legislation.[109]

New Yorkers did not face the same challenges to resisting the Stamp Act as residents of Kingston and Halifax. Instead, the crisis actually expanded and strengthened popular notions of consent and representation and convinced a growing number of the city's inhabitants that loyalty demanded an active citizenry. By the end of 1765, New Yorkers talked less of why they opposed the stamp tax and more of how they had successfully resisted its implementation in their city. John Morin Scott believed New Yorkers had "lately sustained the most violent attack that has ever been made upon *British* Liberty," but through it all, they had "hitherto withstood the united efforts of force and cunning. Though dishonoured, injured and oppressed," he proclaimed, "we are still FREE."[110]

Moderates in the city certainly felt the growing political strength of New Yorkers and desperately sought to check their continued efforts to violently resist the tax. In December, several merchants refused to submit to the demands of the Sons of Liberty to repeal the boycott and allow merchants to trade without using stamped paper. These merchants also courted relationships with radical leaders like Isaac Sears in hopes of preserving order in the city.

But there was no discounting the growing influence of the Sons of Liberty and their supporters, who had begun to embrace far more radical, republican notions of loyalty and Loyalism. In early January, the Sons of Liberty drafted a set of resolutions "for the Preservation and Security of the English Constitution, and the Rights and Privileges of the Subject, in America," which numbered five in total and were published in newspapers throughout British North America. The authors were committed to defending their "Lives and Fortunes" and declared that anyone who used stamped paper "shall incur the highest

Resentment of this Society, and be branded with everlasting Infamy." They also assumed police-like duties in their city, offering to protect anyone "who carry on Business . . . on unstamped Paper" and publishing the names of any "Promoters of the said Act." A month later, as the authors began to push for greater unity across the thirteen American colonies, they added a sixth resolve, which expressed their commitment to "a firm union of the whole . . . [and] to repel every attempt that may be made, to subvert or endanger the liberties of America."[111] For these and many other New Yorkers, resistance was no longer just about defending one's own liberty but also protecting the rights and freedom of Britain's American subjects.

Throughout the winter and spring of 1765–66, Scots read of the events unfolding in the American colonies and expressed shock at the level of violence, the threats to personal property, the attacks on political and military officials, and the many essays and editorials that spoke of the right of subjects to overthrow government. Though not adverse to traditional forms of popular protest, Scots worried that colonial crowds had acted beyond the limits of what they deemed acceptable behavior. In late December, Thomas Reid, professor of philosophy at the University of Glasgow, wrote that some Glaswegians considered the conduct of the American colonists "as an open rebellion, and an avowed claim to independence." He went on to describe these colonists as "a dastardly, pusillanimous race, and that a British fleet and army would soon reduce them to such terms as would secure their future dependence upon the mother country."[112]

As the crisis unfolded, Glaswegians became less concerned with broader questions of consent and representation, and more with how the instability in the colonies would impact their profitable Atlantic tobacco trade. This concern was especially evident after January 1, when the several colonial boycotts went into effect. Glasgow merchants believed that if the situation worsened, they risked losing access to colonial markets and might never recover their many outstanding debts in the Chesapeake colonies. Archibald Henderson wrote to Edmund Burke in early February that "the merchants of Glasgow (under the greatest concern for their depending property in North America) had authorized Mr. Glassford, Mr. M'Call, and myself" to petition Parliament on their behalf. Henderson and his friends in Glasgow (fifty-eight in total) were especially concerned with the Virginia and Maryland tobacco trade and claimed "the debts due to them, from those provinces alone, to be above half a million sterling."[113] In the petition, they complained that "a stop has been put to the administration of Justice since the first of November" so that "none of their Debtors can now be compelled to pay [their] Debts." Facing "such unhappy circumstances," they joined with their colonial counterparts in asking Parliament to repeal the unpopular legislation.[114]

Resistance to the Stamp Act revealed deep ideological divisions in the British Atlantic. For many New Yorkers, the crisis made them more aware of the need to be vigilant in protecting their freedom from those in power. In print and on the streets of that city, subjects gradually, if unevenly, began to articulate a refined understanding of loyalty that remained committed to monarchy and constituted government but also demanded that individuals actively defend their liberty. The crisis had solidified the importance of ideas like popular consent and Whig fears of encroaching tyranny, while also demonstrating the capacity of subjects to effect change within their community and empire. Kingstonians and Haligonians expressed a similar defiant sense of patriotism, but the crisis also revealed just how significant particular local conditions were to shaping each city's political culture. In some ways, the ability of colonists to resist the Stamp Act had acted as sort of litmus test, drawing clearer lines of distinction between the empire's diverse inhabitants and communities.

Finally, Glaswegians watched from a distance as the crisis unfolded in Britain's Atlantic colonies. Local writers were largely sympathetic to the colonists' plight and shared their view that the tax was oppressive and dangerous to British liberty. But colonial forms of resistance frightened the city's merchant elite. They were concerned that rioting, boycotts, and rebellious rhetoric might undo their profitable Atlantic economy, in which Glaswegians of all rank were intimately involved. Glaswegians' push for repeal early in 1766 was greeted with cheers in colonial port cities, but it masked deeper divisions emerging in the empire around competing definitions of loyalty and patriotism.

After a series of contentious debates, Parliament agreed to a repeal of the Stamp Act in early March 1766, but not before also agreeing to the passage of a Declaratory Act, which reasserted the sovereignty of Parliament in the nation's Atlantic colonies.[115] Two weeks later, on March 18, George III gave his royal assent to the repeal amid the cheers of thousands of Londoners who lined the streets of the city. Feux de joie ensued everywhere as news spread across the British mainland and then traveled by ship to ports dotting the North Atlantic. Britons paraded, drank, sang, and toasted in celebration of their king and constitution. The Stamp Act Crisis, which had threatened the political and economic stability of the empire throughout the fall and winter of 1765–66, now brought about perhaps the largest and loudest acclamations of joy in the nation's brief history. These repeal celebrations demonstrated the strength and resilience of Protestant Whig ideals—the right of the people to confront tyranny and the willingness of those in power to listen—but they also revealed how the crisis had meant something different to Britons throughout the North Atlantic. Weyman's account of the parade in London hinted at these differences: "Our King goes to his Parliament," proclaimed the writer, "amidst the acclamations of a free people to repeal an act, that was found grievous to one part of his subjects, and fatal to the wealth and prosperity of the rest."[116]

Glaswegians were the first of these four communities to learn of the repeal, which they interpreted first and foremost as a victory for the city's trading interests. On March 2, Messrs. Glassford, McCall, and Henderson, the three tobacco merchants who had traveled to London to deliver the city's petition, returned to Glasgow with "the agreeable news." There were "great Rejoicings" throughout the city and "all concerned in the trade and manufactures of this place who are so deeply interested in the *prosperity of the colonies* expressed a more than common joy and satisfaction."[117] Rather than marching in parades or lighting bonfires, however, the city's residents loaded cargo and completed ship manifests.[118] For many, the repeal represented economic opportunity as much as, if not more than, a defense of political liberty.

Letters from the city that appeared in colonial newspapers emphasized the economic advantages of the repeal and made no mention of the broader constitutional crisis occasioned by the tax. In one letter the writer praised colonists for having opposed the tax, not because they were defending their rights as British subjects, but rather because "had [the tax] been enforced, it would certainly have occasioned some confusion in your trade."[119] Another Scot reported that "in the capital towns in Scotland . . . great rejoicings were made by the Manufactures" on account of the repeal.[120] For Glaswegians, the crisis did not so much awaken a spirited defense of their political liberties as much as it strengthened their attachment to the nation's mercantile economy.

Haligonians were almost certainly pleased to learn of the repeal of the Stamp Act, news of which arrived in May. Yet, by all accounts, there were no popular celebrations in the city. It is possible a gathering of some kind did occur (no copies of the *Halifax Gazette* survive for this period), but reports of such an event would have been exchanged in other British newspapers. Residents of the nearby town of Liverpool assembled on June 3 for a "Day of rejoicing" on account of the repeal, but it was an isolated event and was not even recognized by officials in Halifax.[121]

It is likely that local officials in the colony's largest port city wanted to restrain crowd activity so as to present the city as a loyal, orderly, and law-abiding community, unlike their neighbors to the south. Such an appearance could help the officials curry favor with the government, upon which they still relied upon for annual financial grants and military protection. They had already taken steps in March to curtail the influence of Henry's gazette on the colony's inhabitants. On the nineteenth of that month, they forced Henry's partner, Isaiah Thomas, to leave after just "5 months, 3 weeks, and 3 days" in the city.[122] And the following August, they replaced Henry as the king's printer for the colony with a recently arrived Englishman named Andrew Fletcher who was far more submissive to local authority.

The governor and colonial assembly also went to great pains to express their support of the Crown and submission to Parliament in the aftermath of the crisis. In late July, members of the assembly sent an address to the king declaring that "we most humbly offer our most dutiful thanks and acknowledgments for the repeal of the act for granting certain stamp duties in America."[123] Acting Governor Benjamin Green added in a letter to Secretary Conway that the passage of the Declaratory Act with the repeal was "the most Expressive means of Exciting their most Dutifull Sentiments of Gratitude."[124] Three months later, the new governor, Michael Francklin, wrote to the assembly congratulating them on their conduct "during the late commotions in America," which, he reported, "had obtained His Majesty's highest approbations."[125]

The absence of popular celebrations set Halifax apart from most places in the empire. The preceding year's crisis did little to wrest power from the hands of the few wealthy merchants and politicians in the city and only further highlighted the limits of popular politics in the remote garrison town. But Haligonians had found subtle, if unsuccessful, ways to protest the Stamp Act, which were suggestive of the community's commitment to Whig principles. Officials repeatedly stymied efforts to join in the resistance movement unfolding to the south, but they were incapable of completely squashing such sentiments.

The situation was very different in Kingston. Residents responded to news of the repeal with a lavish celebration that belied the city's submission to the tax over the preceding four months. When the news arrived, "the whole town was illuminated" in the evening, "the ships in the harbour displayed their colours, and the spirt of LIBERTY diffused itself thro' all ranks of people." Three days later, a more extravagant event unfolded, which involved the entire community—local citizens and soldiers, and free and enslaved blacks—and was replete with parades, toasts, bonfires, and effigies.

The evening began with the magistrates and principal merchants gathering at the courthouse, while various regiments fired several vollies to mark the occasion. Meanwhile, soldiers constructed an effigy of Grenville, affixed with a label that read, "A Stamp," which was carted through town by a group of slaves. Their presence signified his and the legislation's low standing in the community and the continued importance of slavery to white subjects' understanding of liberty. The solider leading the procession carried a flag that depicted Lady Liberty standing on the ace of spades, "on which was wrote, *Obitt*, 1766," while scattering flowers. An image of the stamp distributor, "with a large pair of goat's horns on his head," stood alongside her trying to catch the flowers while "at the same time dropping a stamp he held in his hand." A second effigy of John Howell followed closely behind and appeared alongside "the figure of a goat hanging . . . in loving forgiveness for his many notorious oppressions." The effigies, according to one resident, with "the great number of lights carried by the negroes, and the illuminations in the houses, added to the brilliancy of the procession." They were temporarily hung up at the London coffeehouse (likely the place where most Kingstonians had read news of the repeal) before "being cut down [and] receiv[ing] an incredible number of stabs from bayonets." They were then burned in a bonfire amid "the great joy and pleasure of an incredible number of spectators."[126]

It is difficult to know what to make of this celebration. It suggests that Kingstonians cared a great deal about the unpopular tax, and that that they believed it to be a genuine danger to their freedom as British subjects. The images of a devilish stamp distributor unable to hold on to stamps while he caught Liberty's flowers, of Liberty trouncing on the dreaded ace of spades, and of the tax's main culprits—Grenville and Howell—roasted in effigy reveal a community that thought of the crisis in stark terms, as a dangerous contest between liberty and tyranny. Perhaps that had always been the case, but, as in Halifax, particular local conditions had simply made resistance impossible. The use of slaves in the procession might have been intended to show both the cause of Kingstonians' inaction (fears of slave revolts) and their ultimate victory over the combined threats to their most cherished of freedoms, the right to self-rule and ownership of other humans. A list of toasts delivered later that evening confirmed Kingstonians' continued loyalty to the Crown and Parliament but also suggested that they saw themselves as part of a broader political cause stretching across the western Atlantic. Gathered around a table, they drank to "the King," but also to "Mr. Pitt, Mr. Secretary Conway, [and] the NOBLE NORTH-AMERICANS."[127]

New Yorkers were certainly included in those "NOBLE NORTH-AMERICANS." Nearly the entire city turned out to celebrate the repeal of the despised tax, which they learned of at nearly the same moment as Kingstonians did. Hugh Gaine had the news published as a broadside with the words, "Joy to AMERICA!," written across the top.[128] One resident described how "a sudden Joy . . . immediately diffused thro' all Ranks of People in the whole City. Neighbours ran to congratulate each other, and all the Bells in Town were set to ringing, which continued till late at Night, and began again early next morning."[129] On the Commons, crowds hoisted "a large Board" atop a flagstaff, which bore the inscription, "George 3rd, Pitt—and Liberty." In the evening, there were also two large bonfires and "a Grand illumination throughout the city." The "Night ended in Drunkeness," according to one resident, with revelers "throwing . . . Squibbs, Crackers, firing [their] muskets and pistols, breaking some windows and forcing off the Knockers off the Doors."[130] These were no random acts of mob violence. Residents had escaped from a devastating sense of pending tyranny that had hovered over their city for nearly a year.

The Sons of Liberty played a crucial role in the day's festivities. They assumed positions typically reserved for the political and military elite, demonstrating their increasing influence on city politics. In the morning, they met with the rector of Trinity Church to decide on the sermon to be preached for the occasion, before returning to the Commons, which they had dubbed "the Field of Liberty." Once there they ordered a royal salute to be fired and then processed to "their usual House of publick Resort, where an elegant Entertainment was prepared [and] attended with a Band of Musick." Afterwards, they delivered a series of toasts, published in local newspapers, to the king and his family, "Mr. PITT, the Guardian of AMERICA," and lastly to "All true Sons of Liberty in AMERICA."[131]

A few weeks later, New Yorkers combined their joy over the repeal of the Stamp Act with celebrations of the king's birthday. "Two oxen were roasted" on the day, "which, together with a quantity of Beer, with Bread and Bisket was given to the People assembled, they constantly shouting a return of Thanks for the late Repeal on the 18th of March 1766." The ships in the harbor, which six months earlier flew their flags at half-mast on account of the arrival of the Stamp Act, were now decorated for the joyous occasion, and the "many Houses paid the same Compliment to the Day with Flags, Streamers, &c." The celebration continued into the evening with "Illuminations, Fire Works, Representations of Personages, Crowns, Coat of Arms, &c."[132] Several weeks later, the general assembly also agreed to erect an equestrian statue of George III along with a statue of William Pitt, the staunch Whig who had declared the Stamp Act unconstitutional and repeatedly defended colonial rights. The two statues together identified the city as both loyal to the Crown and committed to defending residents' political liberties.

These celebrations, which had stretched for almost three weeks and involved nearly everyone in the city, also revealed a community transformed by the crisis. The growing number of radical New Yorkers believed their actions—the justifiable threats of violence and intimidation, the numerous essays and editorials, the efforts to combine with an expanding radical transatlantic political culture—played a significant role in defeating the Stamp Act. Increasingly, these New Yorkers expressed an understanding of loyalty that continued to celebrate monarchy and good government but was just as, if not more, committed to a defense of the rights of British subjects. William Weyman understood this, writing in his gazette that the victory did not prove that the people had "gained an ascendency over the British Parliament." It did show, however, that the government had agreed "to re-consider the operation of that most destructive ACT, from a consciousness that it had a tendency to alienate the affections of many loyal subjects, and eventually destroy the usefulness of these colonies to the British empire." Parliament enjoyed the right to legislate for the empire, in other words, but was expected to do so in ways that promoted the liberty of the nation's diverse subjects.[133]

The Stamp Act Crisis is remarkable in that it was capable of simultaneously uniting and dividing the British Atlantic. The inhabitants of these four communities shared in a political culture that believed the tax was unconstitutional because it deprived subjects of their liberty and property, ignored certain cherished rights like consent and representation (however ill-defined), and threatened to ruin Britain's profitable Atlantic trade. From New York City to Glasgow, and Halifax to Kingston, subjects railed against the unpopular legislation in reports and editorials exchanged in newspapers across both regional and wider North Atlantic communication networks. Even in the absence of their traditional Catholic French enemies, Britons were able to construct a shared cause precisely because the Stamp Act offended so many commonly held political beliefs.

But the act of resistance, or even submission, threatened to weaken common shared understandings of loyalty across the empire. It generated new narratives of the crisis that centered on whether, or to what extent, Britons were able to deny imperial legislation and what that denial said about a particular people or community. Subjects on both sides of the ocean held different views of popular consent, which informed their understanding of the crisis as it unfolded. Glaswegians were sympathetic to colonial grievances, but believed violent protests and subversive writings were evidence of a broader movement to denounce the authority of Parliament and perhaps even overthrow British rule. Glaswegians were also dependent on those colonies for their economic livelihood and ultimately called for a repeal of the tax to protect their prosperous Atlantic trade.

In colonial communities like New York City, many subjects embraced a more radical republican definition of Britishness, which called for checking the authority of those in power and tolerated the use of violence in some circumstances. Printers and writers encouraged these attitudes by describing the implications of the tax in conspiratorial terms, as the first act in a broader plan to enslave the empire's colonial subjects. Events mattered, too, both as evidence of these shared beliefs and for their ability to push participants into embracing a far more radical political culture. New Yorkers removed their stamp distributor from office, refused the use of stamped paper, and even threatened violence against their governor. Such actions were possible, New Yorkers argued, precisely because of their willingness to commit to a radical defense of their rights, to sacrifice their own interests in the name of preserving liberty, and to collectively organize among themselves and with colonists elsewhere.

Haligonians and Kingstonians, however, were unable to resist the tax despite sharing in this growing radical political culture. They threatened their stamp distributors and complained of the disastrous impact of the tax on their community, but they failed to stop its implementation. Their submission to the tax led to new narratives elsewhere, which blamed particular local circumstances for these communities' political shortcomings. The presence of soldiers and seamen, financial dependence, an oppressive ruling oligarchy, geographic isolation, and a large slave population accounted for why residents paid the tax. Such explanations suggested a frightening possibility for the inhabitants of these two cities: if they could not resist a law they deemed a betrayal of their Britishness, perhaps it was not possible to be British.

There were no lines drawn in 1766. Everyone, in fact, was a Loyalist, even if the crisis had raised more precise questions as to exactly what that meant. The repeal of the Stamp Act convinced (if temporarily) a majority of Britons of the superiority of their monarchy and constitution. It produced widespread acclamations of joy in communities across the North Atlantic and reminded subjects of the benefits of being a part of a free Protestant empire. Weyman's account of George III processing through the streets of London, while his adversary in Paris scolded his subjects, demonstrated this very point. But the need for such stories that contrasted Protestant Loyalism with Catholic tyranny, even at times of crisis that were absent those foes, suggests that beneath the joy over the repeal there existed widespread discontent and division in the empire. It was far easier for Britons in the summer of 1766 to look to France, and not to themselves, to understand who they were as people.

CHAPTER 3

In Search of Common Happiness
A Divided British Atlantic on the Eve of Rebellion

In the late fall of 1773, John Vardill, a professor of natural philosophy at Kings College in New York City and known to his peers as "uniformly and steadily loyal" to the Crown, sat down to pen a letter in defense of the East India Company. To do so was dangerous given the public's outrage over the company's monopoly of the tea trade. The situation had worsened in recent weeks with news that company ships were headed toward ports in North America laden with chests of that "noxious weed."[1] Perhaps recognizing the seriousness of the situation, Vardill took the wise step of publishing anonymously under the pseudonym "Poplicola."[2]

Vardill's letter, addressed "TO THE Worthy Inhabitants of the City of NEW-YORK," argued that colonists' opposition to the East India Company's monopoly over the tea trade was an affront to a natural and benevolent brand of patriotism that he believed bound together Britain's vast Atlantic empire.[3] "Every good citizen," he began his essay, "will be inclined from duty as well as interest, to love his country" and the "man who makes the general interests of society, of which he is a member, the prevailing object of his actions, justly merits the honourable title of a patriot." Yet those who sought selfish gains over *common happiness*," as he called it, lacked the magnanimity and virtue of loyal British subjects. "With what countenance, then, fellow citizens," he asked, "can they assume the character of patriots, who endeavour to separate (what in nature can never be disjoined) the good of particular branches of the community from the good of the community itself?"

Of course, for Vardill and many other Britons in the latter half of the eighteenth-century loyalty and patriotism were closely tied to Britain's *"commercial advantages,"* which included a near domination of the Atlantic trade. Yet for some, colonial boycotts of East India Company tea reflected the colonists' failure to see beyond their own petty self-interest. Even worse, it suggested at least tacit support for Britain's European rivals. "You love your country, and this affection is your duty, your honour; but remember that not this, or any other province, is your country, but the *whole British empire.* Its strength and superiority over its rival neighbours, are the strength and glory of every part of its dominions, and its injuries, the injuries of us all." At a moment in which we are accustomed to thinking of colonists beginning to rally around a nascent *common cause* that celebrated virtue and unity in the face of oppressive British imperial policies, Vardill instead branded their actions as provincial and self-serving.[4]

Vardill blamed the absence of public virtue on "the fluctuating and capricious decisions of a giddy cabal." Many of the city's prominent merchants benefited from an unlawful trade with the Dutch, he reasoned, so they played upon long-standing fears of political tyranny to encourage discontent among their "deluded dependents."[5] These *"illicit traders,"* Vardill declared, "sacrificed their consciences for their pocketbooks," and in doing so, abandoned law and order for violent crowds and illegal committees. It was self-interested merchants, not imperial bureaucrats or East Indian Company traders, who posed the real threat to colonists' freedom. "But among US," Vardill declared, "the crude decrees of a small cabal, who are actuated by self interest, are to be binding on the whole community; and whoever ventures to contradict them, or even express a doubt of their validity and propriety, must be exposed to violence, and, unheard, without a tryal, must be condemned to infamy and disgrace." In the essay's final, foreboding sentence Vardill warned readers, "While we are watchful against *external* attacks on our freedom, let us be on our guard, lest we become *enslaved* by *dangerous* tyrants within."[6]

Vardill and his readers were unaware that they stood on the precipice of a nearly decade old imperial crisis. Just a month later, Bostonians would destroy more than £10,000 worth of East Indian Company tea. Parliament reacted to the news by effectively shutting down Massachusetts's economy and government while also extending the boundaries of neighboring Quebec and guaranteeing religious toleration to the French Catholic population. In response, the following fall, just nine months after Rivington published Vardill's essay, representatives from twelve of the thirteen colonies gathered in Philadelphia at the First Continental Congress, where they began to assume political and economic authority in the colonies. In November 1773, however, New Yorkers were unsure what the future held. Vardill's address offered an alternative path for responding to the ongoing imperial crisis and for understanding what it meant to be British. He did not view the Tea Act as the latest and most egregious instance in a long list of oppressive imperial policies. He instead claimed his opponents were actuated by selfish material gain, had deceived New Yorkers, promoted trade with Britain's rivals, and preferred mob violence to legitimate constitutional law.

The existence of another path also suggests, perhaps obviously, that by the fall of 1773 New Yorkers were divided over the patriotic identity of their community. The joy and unanimity occasioned by Parliament's repeal of the despised Stamp Act in 1766 had given way to a fractured political culture, with competing definitions of Britishness expressed both in print and on the streets of the city. Parliament's attempt to raise revenue by reimagining long-held mercantilist policies played a critical role in this process, but so too did far more local concerns, such as a depressed economy, violent encounters between soldiers and citizens, a contentious boycott, and rumors of the establishment of an Anglican episcopacy in the colonies.

In the absence of a shared discourse of Loyalism, Britons elsewhere in the Atlantic were also confronted with a similar crisis of identity in the late 1760s and early 1770s. Glaswegians grew to oppose colonial protests, which they increasingly associated with the intensely Scotophobic Wilkes and Liberty movement. In doing so, they began to adopt a far more moderate and inclusive definition of Loyalism that celebrated political authority, constituted government, and support for a mercantile-based Atlantic economy. Meanwhile, Kingstonians faced a series of legislative decisions, like the 1766 Sugar and Free Port Acts, which threatened to ruin the city and colony's economy. Additionally, rumors of a war with France and Spain, along with several attempted slave revolts, led Kingstonians to recast their patriotic attachment to the empire in far more moderate terms, professing a support for political and military authority on the island. Finally, Haligonians, though sympathetic to the sufferings of their southern neighbors, were unable to join in popular protests and movements to boycott British goods. They were also exposed to attacks from enemy Mi'kmaq and Acadians after the departure of the troops to Boston in the fall of 1768. Local officials were forced to engage with their long-standing foes through diplomacy and appeasement, which tested the Protestant loyalties of the province's inhabitants.

It is worthwhile to think of the critical years of 1766 to 1773 as creating a series of possible paths toward making sense of the growing crisis. These were not paths that ended in 1776, but rather ones that began in 1766. Envisioning a series of possible paths requires abandoning a narrative of inevitability, which emphasizes only certain events, such as the Townshend duties, colonial boycotts, the massacre, or the Tea Act, for their role in moving American colonists closer to rebellion. These and many other incidents carried multiple meanings and importance and were part of a broader British Atlantic political culture that was just as crucial in shaping popular understandings of loyalty and Loyalism.

Additionally, this multiple paths approach requires reimagining the geographical contours of the potential rebellion. Britons were reared in a shared political culture that regularly framed political controversies as a struggle between popish tyranny and Protestant liberty. This was certainly true during celebrations of the repeal of the unpopular Stamp Act, which many perceived as detrimental to the political and economic well-being of their empire. But by 1773, the inhabitants of New York City, Glasgow, Kingston, and Halifax had begun to pursue different and often competing paths in the ongoing crisis, which demonstrated the tenuous nature of popular British loyalty in the latter half of the eighteenth century. In the absence of a common shared enemy, these same subjects reverted to far more local and conflicting understandings of Britishness, which were defined most crucially by events that directly concerned their communities.

We are accustomed to viewing the crisis over the 1767 Townshend duties as the next major political dispute to divide the empire. The taxes ignited new rounds of protests that drew sharper lines of difference in communities across Britain's North American colonies. Yet this perspective ignores both the wider Atlantic context of Parliament's struggle to govern its expanding empire and the continued importance of local events and conditions in shaping popular expressions of loyalty. In the immediate aftermath of the Stamp Act Crisis, new problems emerged in these distant Atlantic outposts, which required Britons to rethink the meaning and importance of their empire and their place within it.

This was certainly true in Kingston in the fall of 1766, where new domestic and imperial crises once again revived concerns among the city's inhabitants of the loss of their political and economic liberties. The first of these was the recently passed Sugar and Free Port Acts, which have largely been ignored by historians of the Revolution. The revised Sugar Act sought to counter the illicit sugar trade carried on by North American merchants. Under the new bill, a committee of West Indian and North American merchants and planters agreed to reduce the import duty on foreign molasses from three pennies to one penny per gallon, believing that the lower duty would make smuggling unprofitable. This agreement upset merchants and planters in Jamaica who counted on their profitable monopoly of the sugar market, which had all but vanished over the previous three years. The famed absentee planter and Whig MP William Beckford and Jamaica's agent in London Stephen Fuller opposed the revised bill and were able to convince the committee to approve a similar one penny tax on molasses imported from the British Caribbean. They also got Parliament to agree to classify all sugar (domestic and foreign) entering ports in Great Britain as foreign in an effort to dissuade North American merchants from claiming that cargoes of cheaper foreign sugar were British.[7]

Of greater concern to Jamaicans, however, was the loss of the profitable Spanish trade in bullion over the previous decade. Though illegal, imperial officials had long turned a blind eye to this trade. They understood that Britain's Atlantic economy depended on regular injections of Spanish hard currency, while Spanish Caribbean markets provided a necessary outlet for a surplus of British goods. Edward Long, who resided in Jamaica during the 1760s, wrote in his three-volume history of the island that "the act of navigation [regarding trade in Spanish bullion] . . . was never rigorously observed here; because it appeared repugnant (so far as regarded these imports) to the spirit of commerce, and the plain interest of Britain."[8] Such attitudes revealed the degree to which Kingstonians associated their loyalty with the right to trade freely with Britain's longtime enemies. That their government encouraged such behavior by not enforcing laws against the Spanish trade led residents to believe their actions were justified.

This changed with the passage of the 1764 Sugar Act, which led to a greater regulation of the Caribbean economy by effectively turning British naval patrols into revenue offices. In May 1766, the Society of Merchants of Kingston in Jamaica reported that these patrols, alongside corrupt naval officers who regularly "extorted and received various high and illegal fees" from Spanish merchants, "are great discouragements to the said *Spaniards* from importing bullion here, and highly detrimental to the commerce of this island."[9] Glaswegians, who certainly had a vested interest in a prosperous Caribbean trade, read in a local newspaper of the dismal economic conditions of Jamaica at that time: "Our trade with the spaniards is asmost [sic] totally lost, our country destitute of currency to support the internal commerce thereof, our treasure long empty, and in consequence, our gaols filled with unhappy sufferers."[10] In 1765 and 1766, virtually every major British Atlantic port city sent petitions and memorials to Parliament expressing similar concerns about the decline of the Spanish trade.[11]

To remedy this problem, early in 1766 members of Parliament pushed for the creation of free ports in the British Caribbean at the same time they were revising the Sugar Act and discussing the repeal of the Stamp Act.[12] Charles Townshend, whose unpopularity in Britain's Atlantic colonies preceded his more famous 1767 duties bill, played a central role in devising this legislation.[13] One witness went so far as to claim that the future chancellor defended "the Free Port in particular, in framing which I should imagine he had a principle hand."[14] Initially, Townshend and other imperial officials targeted ports in the former French colony of Dominica obtained by Britain in the aftermath of the Seven Years' War. These officials hoped the ports, like the revised Sugar Act, would lure illicit North American traders away from foreign ports in the area. Their approach reflected a common, if contentious, mercantilist view that trade among the nations of Europe was a zero-sum game, and it was essential for states to use such protectionist policies to encourage their own country's commercial success.[15]

Imperial officials' turn toward free ports, however, frustrated both Jamaican merchants and planters, who believed that their greedy North American neighbors would actually use these ports to openly trade with European rivals at the cost of Britain's Caribbean interests. One report from London warned that Parliament "will not be made the dupes of those gentlemen [Dominica merchants and planters], and of the cunning North American smugglers, who alone will be gainers, to the ruin of our sugar Islands, and to the making of the French Islands."[16] In response, Townshend and the administration agreed in early May 1766 to also establish four free ports in Jamaica, at Kingston, Savannah-la-Mar, St. Lucea, and Montego Bay.[17]

This news might have appealed to the commercial interests of Kingstonians were it not for the fact that influential absentee planters in London negotiated for substantial restrictions on the island's free ports.[18] The act, which received the king's assent in June, stated that Jamaican merchants could not import from foreign vessels any goods that were grown or produced on the island, nor could merchants purchase foreign manufactures over those produced in Britain. Without access to these goods, which British suppliers could not always provide, Jamaican merchants found it nearly impossible to reignite the profitable Spanish trade. They also objected to the ban on foreign sugar, particularly that produced in French colonies. If Kingstonians could import this commodity, Long later argued, illicit traders from North America who coveted French sugar would come to Jamaica rather "than run the hazard of getting them clandestinely from Hispaniola."[19] Officials hoped to defray the costs of the new legislation by including a duty on African slaves sold to foreign buyers, which threatened one of Kingston's most profitable industries.[20] These restrictions, along with the loss of a monopoly on the sugar trade, frustrated Kingstonians, many of whom depended on the port city's lucrative Atlantic trade. Such protectionist policies, they concluded, appeared to protect the interest of some at the cost of others' commercial well-being.

Both the revised Sugar and Free Port Acts were due to go into effect on November 1, 1766, around which time Kingstonians also learned about Townshend's promotion to chancellor of the exchequer and the determination of the newly appointed Chatham ministry to assert Parliament's authority over the colonies. The city's inhabitants were also embroiled in yet another local dispute with leading planters in Spanish Town. During a contentious election for speaker of the island's assembly in November, Charles Price Sr., the prominent planter and politician despised by Kingstonians, threatened to revisit the 1758 County Act, which had divided the island into three counties—Middlesex, Surrey, and Cornwall—and established justices of assize and oyer and terminer in each.[21]

The County Act was the culmination of a four-year dispute in the 1750s over the place of the capital city on the island, which is often framed as another example of the contested nature of colonial and imperial politics in Britain's most prosperous Atlantic colony.[22] But for Kingstonians, the capital controversy had less to do with questions of royal prerogative and more to do with the competing interests of planters and merchants. Residents of the port city had argued for a relocation of the government and courts to Kingston based solely on their commercial interests, insisting in a 1754 petition to the Board of Trade that the distance of the island's courts from their city delayed business and increased costs.[23] Their cause enjoyed widespread support in port cities throughout the British Atlantic, suggesting that others also shared in an imperial identity that emphasized the government's role in both protecting and promoting their nation's commercial success.[24]

For a brief period during the crisis the capital moved to Kingston, but in the fall of 1758 planter influence in London forced the recall of Governor Knowles and the removal of the capital back to Spanish Town. The decision appeared to represent a victory for planter interests, and yet another example of the supremacy of the island's assembly. But as a concession to Kingston's merchant community, the Board of Trade also agreed to establish Kingston, Savanna-la-Mar, Montego Bay, and Port Antonio as legal ports of entry and clearance for ships on the island, which relieved ship captains of making the arduous and costly trip to Spanish Town. At the same time, Price Sr. and the island's assembly passed the County Act, which gave Kingstonians control over local legal proceedings, particularly those involving their commercial dealings.

In November 1766, however, Price Sr. discussed revisiting the 1758 County Act as a ploy to get a planter ally of his elected as the next speaker of the island's assembly.[25] In response to this and the recent implementation of Townshend's pro-planter Sugar and Free Port Acts, Kingstonians took to the streets in late November, burning both men in effigy. They began by marching the effigies of Townshend and Price Sr. through the city's major streets before returning to the courthouse where the crowd assumed the role of judge and jury, sentencing the two men (and a third effigy of the devil) to death for their crimes. Afterward, the condemned effigies were slowly carted to the gallows to the sound of muffled drums and "illuminated by a great number of candles and flambeaux," which surely made an impressive if haunting display against the dark nighttime sky. The three were then executed before a large crowd of Kingstonians, with the Devil exclaiming:

"What! C—, T—, and my old friend P—,
You're welcome to me; we're at hell in a trice."

The whole affair, the report concluded, was enjoyed by "an incredible number of spectators, perhaps the greatest ever assembled in this town."[26]

The elaborate burning in effigy of Price Sr. and Townshend revealed the influence of domestic and imperial economic interests on the loyalty of white Kingstonians. Concerns over Price Sr. reconsidering the 1758 County Act, which proved beneficial to the commercial dealings of Kingstonians, coincided with Townshend's broader imperial plan to reimagine Britain's profitable Caribbean trade in ways that threatened the interests of Kingston merchants and traders. But their protest, though resembling in some ways the sort of street theater so common in the North American colonies over the previous year, was absent the more sporadic bouts of crowd violence and challenges to authority that had occurred in places like New York City. It is likely the event in Kingston was sanctioned (and organized) by the local elite, and the inclusion of a broad swath of the city's inhabitants was intended to emphasis the widespread dislike of both of these men and their policies.[27] Kingstonians were voicing their opposition to legislation they feared would weaken their city's economy (and their attachment to the empire); they were not challenging the existing social and political order in their community.

Kingstonians also found few friends elsewhere in the empire for their cause. Their crisis ultimately mattered little to North American colonists, who celebrated the repeal of the stamp tax, enjoyed the further lowering of the duty on foreign sugar (even if they now had to pay a small tax on British sugar), and stood to benefit from access to Caribbean free ports, particularly those in Dominica.[28] As a result, the Sugar and Free Port Acts failed to enter the lexicon of colonial American grievances against the British government despite popular opposition to the legislation in Kingston.

The apparent joy and unanimity occasioned by the Stamp Act repeal was similarly short-lived in New York City. In the fall of 1766, New Yorkers also returned to the streets in protest of the nearly fifteen hundred British regulars stationed in their city. Over the previous several months, drunken and rowdy soldiers had repeatedly brawled with locals, destroyed public and private property, and frequented the many brothels and bawdy houses in the city.[29] Off-duty soldiers often took on laboring jobs at lower wages that would have otherwise gone to poorer residents in the city. In response, more and more New Yorkers began to draw upon long-standing fears that associated the use of a standing army in times of peace with political and economic tyranny.[30] When the assembly refused to comply with the 1765 Quartering Act, which required colonists to pay for the billeting of British soldiers, one writer reminded New Yorkers that "a Standing Army is dangerous to Liberty . . . and that it is kept here to over-awe them into a Tame and blind Submission to all Ministerial Mandates."[31]

Tensions between soldiers and citizens surfaced in a four-year dispute over the liberty pole on the city's Commons, raised in May 1766 during the Stamp Act repeal celebrations. Liberty poles and liberty trees held an important place in eighteenth-century British popular political culture. As visual symbols of the political identity of a community, they were important tools of political expression for residents who lacked access to more formal channels of representation.[32] Though New Yorkers built theirs to memorialize their successful resistance to the Stamp Act, the large wooden mast came to symbolize their broader defense of British rights and liberties. Over the next few years, New Yorkers regularly gathered at the pole to protest imperial policies and to punish suspected opponents.

However, twice in August 1766, just months before Kingstonians burned Price Sr. and Townshend in effigy, a group of soldiers cut down the popular pole. These soldiers had come to believe that the pole was encouraging New Yorkers to subvert government authority in a baseless defense of protecting their liberty. The first incident led to a brawl between soldiers and citizens. Local printed accounts sided with the citizens, whom writers described as defenseless, patriotic New Yorkers being attacked by soldiers, "bayonets in their Hands . . . cutting and slashing everyone that fell in their way."[33] The second pole, erected by the Sons of Liberty two days later, featured a flag at the top with the words, "George, Pitt and Liberty," a symbol of the community's continued commitment to an imperial identity that equated support for the king with a defense of their liberty.[34]

In late September, a group of soldiers again cut down the newly erected liberty pole, but a third one was raised the following day.[35] Things quieted in the city until March 1767, when during the anniversary of the Stamp Act repeal, soldiers returned to the Commons and demolished the pole. New Yorkers responded by erecting a fourth pole, this time encasing the fifty-foot-tall mast in iron girders up to eight feet from the base.[36] Over the following several weeks, soldiers made repeated attempts to destroy this pole and regularly fought with residents until finally local magistrates and military officials worked together to calm the situation. The fourth pole stood unmolested on the Commons for the following three years.

The disputes over the liberty pole mattered little to Kingstonians, who depended on British military protection against rival nations and rebellious slaves. They were also far more concerned in the spring and summer of 1767 with the state of their island's economy in consequence of the Free Port Act, which both Spain and France actively engaged in undermining. The Spanish government doubled the number of naval patrols, or *guarda costas*, in the region with strict orders to seize any ship attempting trade at a free port. They did so indiscriminately, but effectively, acting with "a spirit of jealousy" toward their enemies.[37] The presence of the patrols weakened the island's economy while strengthening that of its rivals. Spanish traders, fearing violence and possible imprisonment, shifted their trade toward Danish and French free ports in the region.[38] One resident reported in a letter exchanged in newspapers on both sides of the Atlantic that very few Spanish traders "have been bold enough to run the risk of coming here" and had instead been trading with the French, "where they meet with great encouragement."[39]

The extent to which Spain's activities hurt the island's economy is unclear. Two years later, in the fall of 1769, a report suggested Jamaica's valuable slave trade with the Spanish had "fallen into the hands of the French and Dutch, to the amount of about five hundred thousand pounds sterling loss to Great Britain."[40] Kingstonians were certainly aware of the damage their rivals were causing to the local economy. Governor Dalling later wrote that residents often complained of "the loss of the Spanish Trade," which "has been particularly experienced since the opening of the Free Ports."[41] Edward Long lamented as well that "instead of being served by it [the Free Port Act] . . . Jamaica-traders . . . have lost what perhaps may never be retrieved."[42]

From the summer of 1767 on, Spanish opposition to the Free Port Act led to a besieged mentality among the island's residents. Kingstonians, in particular, resented the passage of the legislation, but they were even more alarmed by the presence of Spanish naval boats along their coastlines. This threat reignited a marital spirit of patriotism, while also reminding the city's white residents of their need for military protection. In October, while New Yorkers openly questioned whether soldiers should be stationed in their city, the Jamaican assembly instead "cheerfully agreed to provide . . . for the troops sent them for the protection of that island."[43]

Tensions also ran high in Glasgow in the spring and summer of 1767, just as Parliament approved of Townshend's plan for raising duties in Britain's Atlantic colonies. Glaswegians were consumed, not with news of pending taxes or marauding Spanish sailors, but with the results of what was popularly known as the Douglas Cause. The Cause was a civil suit between the Douglas and Hamilton families over who were the rightful heirs to the famed Douglas estate.[44] The Douglases were the preeminent noble family in all of Scotland, having played a prominent role in Scottish, English, and even European politics over the preceding four centuries. Though proudly Scottish, they were also staunch defenders of the Protestant British state, having defended the Act of Union, fought against Catholic conspirators in the '15 and '45 Rebellions, and openly declared their support for the Hanoverian succession.[45]

Their family also represented something of the complicated and messy nature of noble families in this period, what with excessive titles, internal rivalries, and, perhaps most important, competing lines of inheritance. This was especially so after the family split in the middle of the seventeenth century when William Douglas married twice, producing two separate lines: the Douglases and the Hamiltons. The situation grew more complicated in the early 1760s when the heir to the estate, Archibald Douglas, died. He left the estate to his thirteen-year-old nephew, Archy Douglas, whom many, including the Hamiltons, believed was illegitimate.[46] For the next six years, lawyers for both families gathered evidence to support their claims to the inheritance, leaving the public unsure of what would happen to the estate.

In July 1767, the case went before the High Court in Edinburgh, captivating Scots of all rank in society, most of whom sided with Archy and the Douglas family. One contemporary in Edinburgh noted that the Cause "has been the prevailing topic of conversation. . . . High and low, young and old, male and female, have interested themselves in this cause with a warmth equally unprecedented and unaccountable."[47] Reports also circulated that in Scotland alone "no less than £100,000" had been wagered on "the Great Cause," mostly in favor of Archy.[48] James Boswell, a friend to the Douglas family, took particular interest in the case and began to write regularly in London newspapers and magazines in defense of Archy's claim to the inheritance.[49]

The public's interest in the case rested, in part, on the popular appeal of noble families, which remained a constant feature of eighteenth-century British society. But Scots also saw in the Douglas Cause a defense of their proud Scottish history, which took on added meaning in the face of an intensely Scotophobic Wilkes and Liberty movement that shaped British Atlantic political culture in the late 1760s. The printer turned politician John Wilkes emerged as the living symbol of British liberty, an image he cultivated by regularly deriding Scots. He and his followers believed their northern countrymen were all backward-thinking Jacobites plotting to expand the authority of the Crown over the rights and liberties of Protestant British subjects.[50]

But the Wilkite cause also proved especially important in shaping popular Scottish Loyalism in the 1760s, which celebrated a moderate, order, and hierarchical political society. Writers regularly complained of the licentiousness and disorder of Wilkite crowds, which under the false pretense of defending liberty actually promoted tyranny and violence. One Scot claimed Wilkes lacked the virtuous character associated with popular definitions of Britishness and was instead motivated by personal ambition and partisan interests. Readers were cautioned that the "true spirit of liberty" was not in the *"mobs, huzzas, and triumphs: in Jack Boots, petticoats, and Wilkes for ever!* For these . . . are only snares thrown out to gain your attention, while your real liberties and properties are attacked with impunity: avarice and ambition are at the foundation of the whole." The writer played upon popular anti-Catholic rhetoric, arguing that Wilkite publications falsely promoted a popish idolatry of liberty, "the darling deity of every Englishman," which had turned Britons into "the very QUIDNUNCS of the nation, and running like hounds, to the music of their own notes, have mistaken LIBERTY *for a licence to do what they please.*"[51]

Other Scottish writers leveled similar complaints at Wilkes and his supporters. An anonymous author of a pamphlet published in Glasgow declared Wilkes a "false patriot" fueled by "Luceferian passions." Wilkes was ridiculed for his use of newspapers "to support and promote sedition, by which means the multitude are incensed, and the number of their readers are increased." The consequences were devastating, according to the writer, for Wilkite rhetoric had caused subjects to lose faith in their king, who was "truly virtuous, truly patriotic, and endowed with every fit disposition to make us a happy, prosperous, and a powerful people."[52] Another writer best summarized Scottish attitudes toward the alleged Patriot, claiming that when he "heard the bells ringing for King Wilkes's birthday, every peal sounded in my ears like the doleful clank of manacles and fetters."[53]

The Douglas Cause offered Scots an opportunity to publicly reject Wilkite radicalism by, of all things, celebrating their country's most important noble family. Archy's victory in the civil suit could counter a pervasive Scotophobic political culture because it would suggest that Scottishness could still exist within a broader British imperial identity. Yet to the shock of most everyone, the court in Edinburgh decided in favor of the Hamiltons, thus taking the estate from Archy and the Douglas family. News of the verdict nearly caused rioting in cities throughout Scotland, and angry Douglas supporters twice threatened the life of Robert Dundas, lord president of the court. One writer even warned Dundas that residents of Edinburgh would "make a Captain Portus of You," just as New Yorkers had said to Cadwallader Colden a year earlier.[54] Meanwhile, Archy's lawyers immediately filed an appeal, which sent the case to London to be heard before the House of Lords.

Britain's Atlantic empire was anything but calm in the months between the Stamp Act repeal celebrations and the passage of the Townshend duties. New crises emerged in these distant port cities, caused both by broader imperial policy making and by far more local concerns and interests. Kingstonians and New Yorkers were drawn further toward a radical defense of their rights in the face of unfair policies, hostile European navies, and unruly British soldiers. Meanwhile Glaswegians (and other Scots) protested in defense of a moderate, more inclusive brand of British Loyalism, which the initial decision in a popular civil suit failed to uphold. In the absence of a shared enemy and language of nationhood, subjects on both sides of the Atlantic divided over questions of what it meant to be British, what rights subjects enjoyed, and how imperial officials were to govern their empire.

In May 1767, Townshend, now in the role of chancellor of the exchequer, pushed through Parliament a new duties bill on five commonly imported British goods: paper, paint, lead, glass, and tea. He also decided the revenue would not go to covering military costs, as originally intended, but would rather be used to pay the salaries of colonial officials. To enforce the duties, Townshend created a highly contentious colonial Customs Board and three new vice-admiralty courts at Boston, Philadelphia, and Charleston with the power to try suspected tax evaders and smugglers.

Like the Stamp Act, many North American colonists viewed the new duties as a threat to their constitutional rights as British subjects. The most vocal critic of the new legislation was a Philadelphia lawyer, John Dickinson, who authored a dozen letters under the guise of "a Farmer in Pennsylvania." His letters were an instant sensation among radical Whigs in New York City and throughout the Atlantic, and did more than any other piece of writing to shape colonial attitudes in the late 1760s and early 1770s toward the new tax scheme and the authority of parliament more generally. The letters appeared in virtually every British North American newspaper between December 1767 and March 1768, and later in 1768 several printers on both sides of the Atlantic reprinted them as a pamphlet.[55] Until the publication of Thomas Paine's *Common Sense* in 1776, John Dickinson's *Letters from a Farmer in Pennsylvania* were the most widely read critique of British imperial policies.[56]

Historians often celebrate Dickinson for his moderate, reasoned response to Townshend's tax scheme, which he defended with an impressively erudite understanding of English constitutional law.[57] But Dickinson also framed his opposition to the duties bill within the context of long-standing British fears of Catholic tyranny, which appeared to always be hiding just around the corner. In many ways, his writings echoed *and* amplified the far more radical and emotional defense of liberty made popular by the ongoing Wilkite cause.[58] In *Letter IV*, for instance, he cautioned readers to remain vigilant in detecting government conspiracies to deprive them of their liberty as had happened under the rule of *"James II*, when he meant to establish popery, talked of liberty of conscience, the most sacred of all liberties; and had thereby almost deceived the Dissenters into destruction."[59] Similarly, in *Letter II* he claimed that should colonists "admit that *Great-Britain* may lay duties upon her exportations to us" for the purpose of raising revenue, then "the tragedy of *American* liberty is finished. . . . We are as abject slaves as *France* and *Poland* can show in wooden shoes and with uncombed hair."[60] Dickinson's letters provided readers with examples of past political tyranny, which he often described in popish terms, to awaken them to the imminent threats posed by the Townshend duties.

In New York City and throughout Britain's North American colonies, "the Farmer" emerged as a potent symbol of colonial rights against the perceived tyranny of the state. The printers Hugh Gaine, James Parker, and John Holt published all twelve letters in serial format in their newspapers, providing New Yorkers with three opportunities each week to read and revel in Dickinson's writings. In virtually every popular celebration in the late 1760s and early 1770s, New Yorkers toasted Dickinson often as the lone American alongside both past and present radical political figures.[61] For example, when the Sons of Liberty gathered in March 1770 to celebrate the Stamp Act repeal anniversary, they toasted "the Farmer" beside such transatlantic radical luminaries as "Alderman Wilks," "General Paoli," "Algernon Sidney, Esq," "John Hampden, Esq," and "the celebrated Female Historian Mrs. M'Auley."[62] These New Yorkers did not view Dickinson's letters as moderate in tone and meaning, but as part of a broader radical transatlantic movement intended to inspire subjects to oppose the dangerous tendencies of those in power.

New Yorkers were especially receptive to this narrative. The threat of imperial taxes in early 1768 combined with factional local politics, a depressed economy, angry British soldiers, and an ongoing religious dispute over the establishment of an Anglican episcopacy in the colonies to produce a far more radical political culture defined by increasing fears of political tyranny.[63] Virtually every direction New Yorkers looked in the last years of the decade, they saw a conspiracy of oppression and imagined a need to take action. Elite merchants feared the growing influence of these radicals and were initially reluctant to commit to defending their rights at the cost of their livelihoods. But in April merchants agreed to adopt a nonimportation agreement, effective the following October, which encouraged radicals to be more vigilant in opposing the duties bill by confronting those who continued to trade with Great Britain.[64]

Glaswegians, in contrast, feared colonial boycotts, which threatened to undo the city's prosperous Atlantic trade, so critical to their understandings of loyalty and empire. They rejected as well Dickinson's writings, which one writer described as "seditious in its principles, superficial in its execution, and tending to the perdition of the country for which the author is so furious an advocate."[65] Glaswegians began to take a different path in the growing imperial crisis, gradually associating the language and actions of colonial resistance with the radical Wilkes and Liberty movement. They believed both causes sought to undermine legitimate constituted authority by playing upon the common fears and prejudices of Protestant Britons. A writer in the popular *Scots Magazine*, for example, claimed a Boston radical and supporter of the city's boycott opened a public meeting by reading Wilkite newspapers like the *Whisperer* that had sprung up in London during the late 1760s.[66] "When he finds his audience sufficiently inflamed, [he] proceeds to the business of the day," which often involved assaulting their political opponents. "Thus is the life, liberty, and property, of every loyal subject who chuses to pay obedience to the laws of his country," concluded the writer, "left at the mercy of an enraged populace, spirited up by a few factious demagogues to commit every kind of violence and outrage; and this, in the language of Boston, is LIBERTY and PATRIOTISM."[67] Of course, many Scots had previously drawn similar conclusions of colonial opposition to the Stamp Act, but now they saw a growing transatlantic crisis unfolding. Radicals on both sides of the ocean were promoting disloyalty to the Crown and government and appeared intent on destroying the growth and prosperity of the empire and the freedoms of its subjects.

The situation was different in Halifax, where residents appeared to embrace this radical transatlantic political culture. In the pages of their local newspaper, they closely followed the mounting tensions between soldiers and citizens in New York City and regularly heard of their southern neighbors celebrating "the Farmer."[68] Haligonians also read in some detail about the tumult overtaking London in the late 1760s as a result of the Wilkes and Liberty movement.[69] Their narrative of the political crises of this period mirrored that of other radical communities across the British Atlantic.

Yet the streets of the northern port city remained virtually silent during this period. So too did the city's newspaper when it came to reporting on local news or giving space to locally-written editorials and essays supportive of colonial resistance efforts. For many, Halifax remained an occupied city, with residents forced to accept a more conservative understanding of loyalty that favored order, hierarchy, and the rule of law. This was especially apparent in the government's response to the February 1768 Massachusetts Circular Letter, which asked other colonies to join in opposition to the Townshend duties.[70] The letter had shocked imperial officials in London. Lord Hillsborough, secretary of state for the colonies, ordered Governor Bernard to dissolve the assembly unless the representatives rescinded it. They refused in July, on a vote of 92–17, leading Bernard to take action. With tensions mounting, General Gage ordered several regiments stationed in Halifax to Boston to bring order to the streets of that city.

William Nesbitt, the speaker of the Nova Scotia Assembly, received the circular letter from Massachusetts officials in March and immediately showed it to the then acting governor, Michael Francklin. The two men decided against introducing it to the assembly, perhaps a sign that there was at least some opposition to the duties among the colony's representatives. Francklin admitted to such fears but promised that "no temptation, however great will lead the inhabitants of this colony to show the lest inclination to oppose acts of the British Parliament."[71] At the same time, Hillsborough wrote to the governor expressing his gratitude to the Nova Scotia Assembly for their "reverence and respect for the laws" and "faithful attachment to the constitution" during these difficult times. But he also ordered Francklin to dissolve the assembly should they consider "this seditious paper."[72]

When the assembly met in June and July, several colonies had already expressed their support for the letter, and the number 92 emerged alongside the number 45 as a potent symbol of a defense of British liberty.[73] Throughout the summer, Haligonians continued to take part in a radical transatlantic print culture that celebrated popular opposition to the Townshend duties, reveled in Wilkes's victory in the spring Middlesex elections, and lamented his subsequent arrest on charges of seditious libel.[74] Nearly an entire issue of the local gazette was devoted to coverage of the St. George's Field massacre, with reports mourning the deaths of Londoners at the hands of the British military.[75] Haligonians also read accounts of rioting in Boston after customs officials seized John Hancock's sloop *Liberty* on smuggling charges.[76] For avid readers of the *Nova-Scotia Gazette*, the British Atlantic was awash in a sea of violent protests, parades, and public toasts as Britons rightfully took to the streets to defend their constitutional liberties against the increasingly abusive tendencies of their government.

As a result, Francklin had every reason to be concerned over the assembly's handling of the circular letter. But according to the governor, it was not read in the assembly and not a single representative made mention of it. "The most perfect harmony prevailed," he reported to Hillsborough afterward. "The people of this province have the highest reverence and respect for all acts of the British legislature."[77] Of course, that Francklin and others felt compelled to withhold the letter from the assembly disproves such an assessment. In fact, the crisis surrounding the Massachusetts Circular Letter demonstrates, more than anything, the divide in Halifax's political culture. While many Haligonians might have wanted to follow the path of a growing, radical transatlantic political culture, they lacked support from those in positions of power, most of whom remained politically and economically dependent on the government in London.

Local officials may have emerged victorious in the circular letter dispute, but they were unable to control the rapidly deteriorating situation in nearby Boston. By September 1768, Gage had ordered soldiers from Halifax to Boston to quiet the streets of that port city. Scholars are well aware of the significance of this move in the broader narrative of the Revolution. The British occupation of Boston led to an increasingly hostile relationship between soldiers and citizens that culminated in the March 1770 massacre, the first deadly act of violence committed in the ongoing imperial crisis.

But Gage's decision also held enormous consequences for popular understandings of loyalty in Halifax. Unlike their southern neighbors, Haligonians depended on the British military establishment. Soldiers and seamen made for good customers, especially because they injected the local economy with hard cash, a rarity in Nova Scotia at the time, and much in need during the postwar recession.[78] The province's annual Parliamentary grant was also in decline, from £50,000 a decade earlier to just £5,000 in the late 1760s. With decreasing funds, local officials struggled to maintain or improve the province's already frail infrastructure, leaving sparsely populated interior settlements isolated from Halifax. The decline in the planter migration from New England, hastened by the opening of the Ohio Country after the signing of the 1768 Treaty of Fort Stanwix, also contributed to the weakening of the local Nova Scotian economy at the very moment Gage and thousands of British soldiers departed for Boston.[79]

The absence of soldiers, some feared, might also encourage the Mi'kmaq to combine with the few Acadians left in the region to attack isolated British settlements scattered across the interior of the province.[80] Local officials worried as well that the growing number of Irish Catholics would join with their old allies to topple the provincial government.[81] There was some truth to such concerns, especially with regard to the Mi'kmaq. In spite of the 1760 and 1761 treaties, the rival nations remained at odds with one another. Reports regularly circulated in the early 1760s of an intended Mi'kmaq and Acadian attack on Nova Scotian settlements. Even as recently as 1766 rumors abounded that the Mi'kmaq were combining with the small number of French settlers at nearby St. Pierre and Miquelon to retake their former lands. Far from being a defeated nation, the Mi'kmaq occupied the attention of colonial and imperial officials throughout the 1760s. They also inspired an ongoing narrative in the minds of some Haligonians of the threat posed by the fabled skulking Indian, who many continued to believe was waiting to ambush defenseless settlements in their province.[82]

The fall of 1768 presented such an opportunity, in part the result of the province's declining population, poor infrastructure, and the removal of troops to Boston. Governor William Campbell anxiously wrote to Hillsborough in September that "the removal of these Troops . . . would expose the thinly in-habited settlements to attack from the Indians."[83] A month later he worried that a small number of Mi'kmaq "would be able . . . to bring fire and Destruc-tion to the very entrance of this Town."[84] Haligonians expressed similar fears in letters published in North American newspapers. One resident believed that there was nothing "to prevent a small body of enemies . . . from taking pos-session" of well-stocked garrisons once the soldiers left.[85] Another spread a rumor that the Mi'kmaq "have lately killed several People in the Settlements at the Back of Louisbourg."[86] Like Kingstonians, residents of Halifax pleaded with imperial officials in the late 1760s for more British soldiers at the very same time Bostonians and New Yorkers complained of their presence.

Rather than initiate a war, the Mi'kmaq instead seized the opportunity to demand better trade relations and greater access to land. They also ordered the British to fulfill a request first made in 1763 to employ a Catholic priest for their people living in the St. John River valley.[87] This was an especially dif-ficult demand for officials in Halifax given that the province was founded as a Protestant bulwark against the perceived encroachments of French Catholics in Canada.[88] But local officials also recognized the defenseless state of their province and worried that if they did not supply the priest, the French would, and that might lead to renewed hostilities between the two countries. In July, even before Gage's departure, acting Governor Francklin reported the arrival of the Catholic missionary, Charles François Bailly de Messein, from neigh-boring Quebec.[89] "He seems to be a man of liberal education and a good sub-ject," claimed Francklin, "and his influence may have a good effect on the Canadians." In October, Bailly was provided with an annual salary, though he was "to officiate only to Acadians and Indians."[90] He took up residence with John Breynton, rector of the town's Anglican St. Paul's Church, who hoped that Bailly's presence in the province would lead the Indians to "live peace-ably under the Government."[91]

While local officials spoke of the "good effect of the presence of Baillie the missionary," reports from Halifax in colonial newspapers suggested residents were less than enthusiastic about his appointment.[92] One Haligonian claimed that "the popish priest" was stealing away recent Protestant converts, and "rebaptized [them] into the Holy Church."[93] Another described the activities of Bailly among the Indians, before lamenting that the "Mi[nist]ry at Home, I suppose have not so bad an Opinion of that infamous Religion that you and I have."[94] The public's outrage peaked in July 1771, when Bailly was brought before the grand jury at Halifax for having broken the 1758 statue in administering his faith "against the Peace of our said Lord the King," though nothing appears to have come of the case.[95] Haligonians had reluctantly accepted the salaried priest, likely because he represented their best chances of remaining at peace with the Mi'kmaq. Their Protestant loyalties were tempered by the realities of living in an impoverished, remote, and defenseless province.

In New York City, Bailly's appointment bolstered a growing radical Whig narrative, echoed by the likes of Dickinson and Wilkes, that played on long-standing anti-Catholic sentiment. In December 1769, John Holt's *New-York Journal* carried a report entitled "The SIGN of the TIMES," which excited reader's fears of the spread of popery in their empire. After the British abandoned Corsica, the writer lamented, "the French [were] suffered to enslave a free people," while "the Pretender [was] emerging at Rome out of his obscurity." At home, the government had pardoned "Popish officers engaged in the late rebellion," reversed "the act of settlement . . . by admitting papists into office," and "professed Jacobites and papists extolling every party coloured administration . . . [while] execrating the name of Mr. Wilkes." Finally, the bishop in Canada had ordained "a missionary for Halifax in Nova-Scotia . . . [with] a salary of 100l. sterling from the government." All the while, concluded the writer, "Americans, haters of the tyrant Stuarts, aggrieved, pleading for the rights of Englishmen, and desiring to be heard."[96]

These crises over taxes, boycotts, and Catholic missionaries mattered little to Glaswegians and Scots more generally. They were instead consumed again by news of the Douglas Cause, which was heard before the House of Lords in the early months of 1769. In their final ruling, the Lords reversed the Scottish court decision and ruled in favor of Archy Douglas. The decision ignited widespread celebrations throughout all of Scotland, which "exceeded any Thing of the Kind that has happened there in the Memory of the oldest Man living."[97] There were so many bonfires lit for the occasion, one correspondent noted, that the "whole country was one universal blaze."[98]

When Glaswegians learned of the verdict "at least forty bonfires were lighted up" across the city, and at night many residents illuminated their homes. The following day, friends of the Douglas family who had gathered at the famed Saracen's Head Inn to celebrate the decision "had fourteen carts of coals made into a bonfire before the door," while a "band of Chelsea pensioners drank before it." In the evening, crowds of Glaswegians enjoyed as "much porter as they could swallow." According to one resident, "Such [day] and night of mirth, festivity, and joy, was never seen in Glasgow."[99] Over the following week, English and Scottish newspapers were littered with accounts of similar festivities occurring across the country. Even several colonial newspapers reported on the widespread jubilation throughout much of Scotland.[100]

For Glaswegians, and Scots more generally, Archy's victory symbolized a broader defense of Scottishness, not as independent from, but as part of an emerging British national identity. Since the 1707 Union, Scots had appeared to outsiders as reluctant to embrace a new British imperial identity even as they played an integral role in the political, military, and commercial expansion of the empire. These beliefs gathered steam with the Wilkes-inspired Scotophobia of the 1760s, which portrayed Scots as dangerous foreigners, incapable of ever fully integrating themselves into a new British political and cultural identity. That image had even crossed the Atlantic, where Scots in the colonies were regularly derided for their supposed absolutist beliefs. But the success of the Douglas Cause, vindicated by Britain's highest court, radically altered this narrative, making it possible for Scots to embrace a more inclusive understanding Britishness that could account for Scotland's rich national heritage.[101]

This reimagining of Loyalism in Scotland was best captured in a supposed conversation about the verdict that took place between two old women in the small village of Lochwinnoch, located just south and west of Glasgow. The exchange appeared in a letter from an anonymous resident of the village and was printed in several English and Scottish newspapers. That it was written in Scots dialect highlighted—even celebrated—the Scottishness of the two ladies. The conversation began with Elspeth noticing that a "lozen," or pane, of her window was broken, a common occurrence during times of rioting and revelry. "What can a' this mean?" she asked herself. "The bell fa'n a ringen! The drum fa'n a beaten! The pipes fa'n a playen! The colours flyen, and a' the folk, young and auld, rinnen with their guns!" She listed several possible reasons, all of which confirmed her community's Protestant British loyalties. "It canna be the King o' France and Pretender landed again; for the folk's are a' in a joyfou mood.—It man be some rejoicings about the King o' Prussia.—It canna be that neither; for it's lang sin we heard ought about him.—Pauli may ha'e beat the French: or eablens, Wilkes, that sinfou fallow, has hanged himself."

Just then, Elspeth's friend Janet entered the house complaining that her son had gotten off with her whiskey, which she had intended "to drink the Parliament, and *Douglas* wha has win his plea." The news shocked Elspeth, who responded in total disbelief, "Say ye me sae? Say ye me sae, woman? Has *Douglas* win his plea! . . . An' ha'e we yet a DOUGLAS!" She broke down weeping, "Fair fa them! Fair fa them, Janet! . . . O Janet, Janet, Janet!" With both women now in tears, Janet paused to reflect, if only briefly, on how much her country had changed over the course of their long lives. "You and I ha'e seen auld times! Monny, monny changes! Monny changes!" Suddenly, they heard a volley fired from the center of town confirming the glorious news. Elspeth exclaimed, "The guns!—Huzza—huzza—huzza—The drums!—Thank Heaven, there's still a *Douglas* in our land! O how I like the King, the Parliament, and the gallant name o' *Douglas*." She turned to Janet, "But come, cast awa your cards, and let's ha'e a pint to the King, Parliament, and *noble* name o' *Douglas* . . . Huzza—huzza—huzza.—Three huzzas, Janet. Bless their honest sauls!—A's right now!" Elspeth concluded with a remark that captured exactly what the Douglas Cause had come to mean to so many Scots. "This kintry will yet stand!" she declared, "I now forge'e [forgive] the very Union itself!"[102]

Though it is unclear whether this conversation actually took place, it nonetheless captured the significance of the Douglas Case for popular understandings of British patriotism in Scotland. Janet and Elspeth represented two ordinary Scots who over the past half-century were forced to embrace a new British imperial identity at the cost of their former Scottishness. "Monny, monny changes!" as Janet said. But Douglas's victory, secured in the highest court in the kingdom, now made it possible for people like Janet and Elspeth to celebrate their Britishness without having to abandon their Scottish roots (fig. 3.1).

New Yorkers read of the celebrations surrounding the Douglas Cause just as they were forming committees to enforce the boycott that had been recently agreed on. Efforts to promote frugality and local manufactory had already been going on for the previous year as a result of the recession, but now they combined with the politically motivated boycott to weaken residents' social and cultural ties to Britain.[103] The boycott also inspired a more vigilant, and often violent, community. Over the following several years, New Yorkers were regularly tested by opponents of the agreement, which played an important role in encouraging community solidarity and political allegiance. Crowds, sometimes but not always under the guidance of the Sons of Liberty, assumed police-like powers over their city, threatening to report anyone who dared to import British goods. Such notorious offenders thus served as crucial conduits for a burgeoning radical political culture that took meaning from the day-to-day, face-to-face experiences of New Yorkers. They did not have to imagine Dickinson's bogeyman. He regularly appeared in the streets of their city during this period.

In July 1769, a local shopkeeper named Simon Cooley experienced firsthand this radical shift in the city's political culture. In the span of several days, Cooley

FIGURE 3.1.   *The Honorable Archibald Douglas* (1770). This popular print commemorates Douglas's victory over the Duke of Hamilton. The figure of Justice is depicted trampling on Calumny while holding the famed Scot's portrait, which stands atop a plinth carved with images of two of the leading judges on the case, Lords Camden and Mansfield. ©*The Trustees of the British Museum. All rights reserved.*

was accused of having twice broken the boycott, but according to local reports he remained obstinate to the demands of the committee. Shortly thereafter, an advertisement appeared in shop windows that described Cooley as a "vile Ingrate," whose "knavish, jesuitical Intentions" threatened to "defeat the united virtuous Efforts in the Support of so righteous a Cause, not only of this City, but of the whole Continent." According to Cooley, the broadside also asked that New Yorkers meet at the famed liberty pole the following evening "to consult what death I should die."[104] He was ultimately saved by Major Pulline and the 16th regiment, but he was later required to renounce his opposition to the agreement in front of "several Thousands of the Inhabitants."[105] Cooley was just one of a number of local New Yorkers assaulted by crowds for having supposedly put their economic interests above those of the community and the American colonies more broadly.[106]

Increasingly, the actions of radicals in New York City reflected a broader reimagining of Loyalism among some residents in their city, which began to emphasize a more serious commitment to republican-held beliefs. In November 1769, New Yorkers gathered at Montayne's tavern to celebrate the anniversary of the Stamp Act, a day they had "nobly determined not to surrender their Rights to arbitrary Power." A series of toasts delivered on the occasion began, not with a customary praise of the king and royal family, but rather with "may the North American Colonies fully enjoy the British Constitution." Those gathered also applauded various colonial assemblies for opposing standing armies and supporting boycotts, and they drank to "the Liberty of the Press," "honest Supporters of the Bill of Rights," and finally, "a total Extinction of implicit Belief," a likely stab at the Anglican Church and the ongoing bishop controversy. Their toasts also drew them into a broader transatlantic coalition of radical Britons, with calls out to "the Farmer of Pennsylvania, or the American Cicero," "the Authors of the Boston Journal of Occurrences," "John Wilkes, Esq.," "Mr. Bingley," "Doctor Lucas, the celebrated Patriot of Ireland," "Paschal Paoli and his honest Countrymen," and finally, to "the real Friends of Liberty thro'out the World."[107]

That coalition did not take hold in Glasgow, however, where residents were increasingly critical of the violent nature of colonial boycotts, which they continued to associate with the Wilkite cause. While New Yorkers toasted radicals, in fact, Glaswegians learned of Simon Cooley's sufferings. After he had escaped to London, the former merchant and tradesman published his own account of what had transpired, a version of which appeared in several Scottish newspapers. Cooley claimed that on two separate occasions, leading proponents of the boycott refused to allow him to import several goods. They then proceeded to incite New Yorkers to act against him, first by publishing "an advertisement" listing his supposed crimes, then by calling for a public meeting at the liberty pole where they provoked a large crowd to attack the now infamous shopkeeper. (The irony of using both the press and the liberty pole as tools of tyranny and coercion certainly would not have been lost on readers in Glasgow.) Cooley escaped to the fort with the help of several British soldiers and stayed there for five days, fearing that he "should have been murdered in the street." Finally, Cooley agreed to "bow my neck to their Liberty-pole" just to quiet his angry neighbors.[108] Cooley's account portrayed the city's radicals, not as acting in the defense of British liberty, but as politically manipulative and tending toward violence to promote their own selfish designs at the cost of others' freedom.

The contentious events of the late 1760s led to new understandings of loyalty and Loyalism in these four British Atlantic communities. Many New Yorkers began to embrace a more determined defense of liberty, which condoned the policing of the local economy and encouraged residents to more aggressively challenge political authority. Haligonians appeared sympathetic to this narrative, but were denied opportunities to join in colonial protests by a ruling elite with a vested interest in maintaining close ties to the empire. The loss of troops to Boston, itself a consequence of these protests, also left the city and colony vulnerable to Indian and Acadian attacks, which forced Haligonians to imagine an imperial identity capable of tolerating the paid employment of a Catholic missionary in their province. In the midst of all of this, Glaswegians of all rank took to their streets to revel in a more inclusive brand of British Loyalism that recognized Scots as loyal participants in an expanding British Empire. They did so by rejecting the violent and seditious political culture coming from North America and London, and toasting the success of Scotland's most famous noble family.

These multiple narratives of the ever-growing number of crises spreading across the Atlantic in the late 1760s revealed the increasing divisions within the British Empire. Competing political and economic interests not only divided subjects in these communities, they reshaped local political cultures, which began to describe new and differing understandings of loyalty and Loyalism. Britons began to view their attachment to the Crown and empire from particular local contexts, often without reference to traditional shared enemies and ideologies. These crises led to a fracturing of empire, not just between the government in London and the colonists but within and among the many inhabitants of the British Atlantic.

The situation worsened in New York City in the winter of 1769–70 when the assembly agreed to finally provide funds for the billeting of troops. Local Sons of Liberty member Alexander McDougall railed against the decision, which he tied to Parliament's broader plan to raise revenue in the colonies. He referred to members of both governments as "minions of tyranny and despotism" and believed the funds would be used for soldiers "to enslave us." Even worse, he argued the assembly's decision ultimately meant that "all the checks resulting from the form of our happy constitution are destroyed."[109] His essay not only shocked colonial administrators but also renewed tensions between soldiers and citizens over the city's liberty pole.[110] In January, angry soldiers blew up the famed pole, hacked it to pieces, and piled the remains at the doorstep of Montayne's tavern, a popular gathering place for the city's radicals.[111] Shortly thereafter, thousands of New Yorkers gathered at the site of the downed pole and publicly swore not do business with the soldiers, who they declared were "Enemies to the Peace and good Order of this City."[112]

Days later, an encounter between two well-known radicals and several soldiers provoked another confrontation between soldiers and citizens that spiraled into a violent, bloody conflict known as the Battle of Golden Hill.[113] For the better part of two days both sides fought it out in the streets of New York, while local officials and military officers desperately tried to maintain order in the city. "An Impartial Citizen," whose account of the event was exchanged in newspapers from Georgia to Massachusetts, claimed that unarmed, peaceful New Yorkers were brutally assaulted in a premeditated attack by British regulars stationed in the city.[114] Though no one died in the conflict, the battle presaged the deadlier Boston massacre by nearly two months, suggesting the extent of New York City's radical political culture.

The Battle of Golden Hill altered the radical consciousness of many New Yorkers, who found even greater cause for concern with the sobering news of a massacre in Boston six weeks later.[115] Dickinson had warned of the impending doom of British imperial policies. In the early spring of 1770, several New Yorkers now bore the physical scars of that threat. To make matters still worse (if that were possible), McDougall was arrested on February 9 for publishing the broadside that sparked the recent violence. Taking note of the political climate, he refused to pay bail and instead rejoiced in being "the first Sufferer for Liberty since the Commencement of our glorious Struggles."[116] Almost overnight, he emerged as the "Wilkes of America" and enjoyed widespread popularity in the city and throughout the American colonies.[117] McDougall's cause drew together and expanded the city's radical Whig community, which continued to derive strength and meaning from the political, religious, and economic crises affecting their city.

In February, radical New Yorkers also erected a fifth (and final) liberty pole, which they deemed *"sacred to Constitutional Liberty"* (fig. 3.2). The massive fifty-six-foot-tall pine mast was carried through the streets by six horses, with "3 Flags flying, with the Words Liberty and Property, and attended by several Thousands of the Inhabitants . . . while the French Horns played God save the King." The procession resembled those given to arriving political and military officials, suggesting the pole's sacred place in New York City's political culture. Leaders also affixed an enormous twenty-two-foot-long mast atop the pole with a gilt vane inscribed only "with the Word LIBERTY."[118] But they also buried the pole eleven feet beneath the ground and surrounded it with an indestructible encasement of "Iron Bars" and "Iron Hoops." This act certainly signified the residents' indefatigable defense of their rights, but it also sym-

FIGURE 3.2. *Raising the Liberty Pole in New York City* (1770). Many New Yorkers interpreted the four-year dispute over the liberty pole as evidence of the increasing tyranny of the British state. In this drawing, done by the Swiss-born artist Pierre-Eugène du Simitière, members of the Sons of Liberty appear in the windows of the city's jail gazing across the Commons at the recently re-erected liberty pole. The pole remarks that it is unable to help the men because it is "encompas'd with a Ton and half of Iron." One of the jailed New Yorkers is likely Alexander McDougall, or the "Wilkes of America," given the reference to the number 45 and the ribbon leading to the jail reading, "Road to Libel Hall." Meanwhile, a British soldier stands, with sword drawn, in the doorway of a small building across the field, declaring the sight of the iron-clad liberty pole "a fine Prospect of Liberty." *The Library Company of Philadelphia.*

bolized the precarious state of their freedom in the early spring of 1770. The only way to protect it was to lock it behind bars.

Kingstonians, in contrast, showed little interest in the escalating military presence in northern port cities or in the notorious Townshend duties. The island's unique political conditions and greater influence on imperial politics shielded residents from the worst of the legislation. Jamaican lobbyists were able to convince lawmakers to exempt the island's inhabitants from the unpopular vice-admiralty courts. The island assembly also enjoyed greater control over the governor's salary, which made the assembly less concerned about the intended use of the tax revenue.[119]

Jamaicans were also distracted by more pressing issues, which had little to do with the North American crisis. They were bracing for a Spanish and French invasion of their island in consequence of those countries' opposition to the Free Port Act, and also because of a much larger controversy involving the

Falkland Islands in the South Atlantic. The British had established an outpost (Port Egmont) on the islands in 1765 as part of a broader plan to dominate both ends of the Atlantic and gain a foothold in the Pacific Ocean. The Bourbon powers recognized the threat and, in the summer of 1770, Spanish forces at Buenos Aires attacked and captured the settlement.[120]

As news spread of the unwarranted invasion (at least according to the British), Britons throughout the empire readied for war. In fact, many looked forward to the conflict, believing Spain's attack on Port Egmont and France's recent conquest of Corsica had tested Britain's dominance of both Europe and the Atlantic. When the North ministry initially dragged its feet, appealing for compromise over conflict, the famed British patriot William Pitt delivered a scathing speech in defense of Britain's immense Protestant empire.[121] Parliament responded by rapidly mobilizing the navy, which at full strength outnumbered the combined navies of France and Spain.[122] One writer saw opportunity in the impending conflict to bring together a nation so bitterly divided from the political disputes of the previous five years. "The late hostile Blow struck by the Spaniards . . ." the writer lamented, "and the warlike Preparations making by France and Spain, hath alarmed this nation, and even aroused the Ministry from their Lethargy." With "a constant Din of War in our Ears . . . A Union amongst ourselves is now allowed to be our true Interest, and the Colonies are spoken of by Courtiers in less invidious Terms."[123] Wars, especially those fought against their old nemeses, France and Spain, encouraged Britons to put aside political differences and regional interests and to see themselves as part of a larger Protestant empire. The Falklands Crisis presented such an opportunity.

Most British observers believed the war would be fought in the Caribbean and that their enemies would target the empire's crown jewel, Jamaica. Reports began to circulate as early as December 1769—even before the assault on Port Egmont—that Spain planned to capture the island. In one widely exchanged account, Britons read that the Irish-born Spanish general Alejandro O'Reilly, who became famous months earlier for violently putting down a French Creole revolt in Louisiana, now intended to invade Jamaica.[124] To make matters worse, slaves on the island attempted to revolt, likely motivated by the distractions caused by the rumored war. Only months earlier, Kingstonians discovered "a Conspiracy . . . among the Negroes, to set Fire to the Town . . . in several Places at once, and in the general Confusion to cut the Throats of the Inhabitants."[125] These foreign and domestic threats led another writer to conclude, "If the Spanish squadron . . . should be destined against Jamaica, the worst consequences may be dreaded, from the present disposition of the negroes on that island."[126]

Though an invasion never materialized, reports continued to flow in from Jamaica of an increased Spanish naval presence around the island.[127] At the same time, white Jamaicans foiled yet another attempted slave revolt, where slaves intended "to poison every white person in the country." Recognizing the seriousness of the situation, local officials resorted to gruesome methods to murder the supposed ringleaders: "some of them hanged, some burnt, and others beheaded, after being first strangled: their heads are fixed on poles along the high roads, as a warning to the rest."[128] From 1769 to at least the spring of 1771, persistent fears of domestic and foreign attacks overwhelmed Kingstonians who had already suffered a great deal from Spanish opposition to the Free Port Act.

Rather than recoil from such threats, Jamaicans armed themselves in defense of their island. One resident wrote that if Spain were to attempt an invasion Jamaicans would "muster at least fifteen thousand white people, who have been regularly trained in arms." There was also two regiments stationed on the island, and if necessary, they could "arm from fifty to a hundred thousand negroes."[129] "We are prepared for them," another of the island's inhabitants warned, "our men are stout and healthy, the fortifications on every part of the island in good repair, our militia under good discipline, several men of war stationed here, and we are at peace amongst ourselves."[130] The threat of war was so palpable that the island's assembly petitioned Parliament for more troops and the governor declared martial law at the same moment Britons elsewhere in the Atlantic complained of standing armies and arbitrary governments.[131] The island's residents did not see such a move as threatening to their rights and liberties, reportedly accepting military rule "with the greatest Chearfulness and Vigilance."[132] The crisis ended the following year, after France and Spain both arranged to return Port Egmont to the British in exchange for a secret agreement from Britain that they would eventually abandon the settlement.

Haligonians were also on edge, fearful of Indian and Acadian attacks on their community despite the work of the missionary Bailly. In the last years of the decade, some of the town's residents sought to calm the situation by reviving the Mi'kmaq's annual Festival of St. Aspinquid. The event took place in Halifax seven days after the first moon in May and coincided with the Mi'kmaq celebration of the spring feast. As a testament to its growing significance, one resident declared that "the Festival of this eminent Saint" should be listed "in red Letters" in the colony's almanac alongside other royal anniversary dates.[133]

Little has been written on the Festival of St. Aspinquid, likely because the origins of the event are obscure. Most agree that St. Aspinquid was a popular sachem who converted to the Catholic faith at some point in his life and desperately tried to avoid the European and Indian wars that ravaged New England in the late seventeenth century. During King William's War in 1696, however, the English murdered the future saint at Fort Pemaquid, after luring him and eleven other tribal leaders there on "pretense of treaty." Afterward, a Jesuit missionary declared him a saint, apparently without the official support of the Catholic Church. In the years that followed, Mi'kmaq from across the region gathered annually during their spring feast to celebrate the newly anointed St. Aspinquid, stopping only after the British created a permanent settlement at Halifax.[134]

Why, in light of this history, would Haligonians revive a festival devoted to a martyred Catholic sachem at the very moment some feared Bailly's growing influence on the Mi'kmaq population? Apparently, contemporaries needed an answer to this question as well, prompting Robert Fletcher to provide readers of his gazette with "a true account of the *Festival of Saint* ASPINQUID." His version departs considerably from the narrative just related by insisting, instead, that Aspinquid was a friend to the British and a celebrated proponent of religious toleration. The "renowned Saint," was actually born a British patriot "in the Year 1588 . . . recorded in the Annals of *Britain* for the most heroic Acts of shining Virtues." Though educated in "Pagan Superstition," the famed sachem converted to Christianity in his forties and spent the remainder of his life as "a zealous Preacher of the Religion he had now embrac'd." Contrary to popularly held British views of Catholicism, the writer claimed the Indian sachem professed a faith that "was zealous without Bigotry, and religious without Frenzy." When he died, not at the hands of the English, but only as a "Victim to the universal Tyrant," he was buried atop Mount Agamenticus, north of Portsmouth in present-day Maine.[135]

This reimagining of St. Aspinquid as a friend to the British, a former Protestant, and afterward a tolerant and peaceful Catholic, provided both Mi'kmaq and Haligonians with a historical symbol that stood for peace and friendship at an especially tenuous moment in their relationship. The festival also reminded Haligonians that despite claims to the land their friendship with the Mi'kmaq relied on constant negotiation and compromise. In May 1770, several Haligonians gathered at the homes of two fisherman along the town's harbor where they drank "many loyal Toasts . . . in Honour of the Day." They also paid tribute to the "twelve Sachems Chiefs, of the twelve Tribes, "who were General Friends and Allies to the English."[136] During a later celebration, Henry published a list of toasts given by the sachems drawn from various peace treaties that included these: "our good Friend and Brother the English King," "My good Friend the Governor I bury the Hatchet," "Englishman my brother all one me," and "Me fight for my brothers the English when War."[137] Such toasts likely comforted Haligonians in the midst of a crisis caused by the withdrawal of British troops to the south to quell their unruly neighbors.

Beyond its obvious diplomatic importance, however, the revival of the Festival of St. Aspinquid also says a great deal about the loyalty of Haligonians at this key moment in the imperial conflict. While some residents viewed Bailly's presence in their province as an assault on their Protestant loyalties, followers of St. Aspinquid celebrated religious tolerance as a benchmark of their imperial identity. Of course, to do so was no small matter in a transatlantic political culture that still depended on age-old stereotypes of Catholics and other non-Protestant people. To push the boundaries of a traditional definition of Britishness perhaps exposed the isolated nature of life in the remote province. One's identity remained far more malleable, despite the continued influence of a vibrant, transatlantic Protestant print culture.

Looked at another way, there might also be something far more radical about these celebrations. Participants not only paid tribute to a Catholic Indian saint, something unimaginable to most Britons, but also perceived of this event as uniquely American. Hints of this perception appear in Fletcher's history of St. Aspinquid. There is a sense throughout the description of his life that the sachem represented something only possible in North America, a celebrated union of several distinct identities long thought to be at odds with one another. He was an Indian, taken in by Puritan New Englanders, before joining with French Jesuit missionaries; according to the writer, that history is what made him worthy of commemoration. One Haligonian suggested that the event was most popular among the New Englanders (or "Americans" as he called them) in Halifax, who represented nearly a majority of the town's population.[138] Another writer in Henry's gazette referred to the famed Indian sachem as "our American Saint." The writer also boasted of the multiethnic and religious makeup of the participants, which included Protestants of all sorts, Catholics, and Jews, in addition to the several Indian sachems present for the festivities.[139]

Such an eclectic mix of participants might also suggest that the festival's popularity was in reaction to the growing influence of the Anglican Church (and the Society for the Propagation of the Gospel) in Nova Scotia. Despite Anglicans being in the minority, the church had enjoyed legal status since the early 1760s, and missionaries worked tirelessly to make converts from among the dissenting New England migrant population.[140] Meanwhile, Nova Scotian tradition also suggested that the celebration carried subversive political principles. A later antiquarian history of the town claimed that when Haligonians gathered to commemorate the famed saint during the American War for Independence, "the wine having been circulated freely, the Union Jack was suddenly hauled down and replaced by the Stars and Stripes." As was always the case in Halifax, however, "those persons who

held public offices" immediately removed the flag and forbade future celebrations of the Festival of St. Aspinquid.[141]

Until the late 1760s, the success of a shared transatlantic understanding of Loyalism depended to a great degree on the presence of a common enemy. For the
better part of the century to that point, France, and to a lesser extent, Spain,
played that role with astonishing levels of success, convincing Britons everywhere
to defend their Protestant empire against the perceived spread of popery. This
national narrative, constructed in an increasingly vibrant and accessible print
culture, united a disparate population and drove Britons to see themselves as
members of a larger empire. Even during the previous Stamp Act Crisis, British
subjects on both sides of the Atlantic shared in a Protestant political culture that
described the policy as misguided and arbitrary. Many had taken to the streets to
celebrate its repeal, an act that demonstrated the greatness of their political system and the rights they enjoyed as members of a free Protestant empire.

The political and economic crises of the late 1760s and early 1770s, however, drove a wedge in this shared notion of Loyalism. Attempts by officials in
London to regulate Britain's complex Atlantic economy raised important questions regarding the authority of Parliament and the political and economic
liberties of Britons everywhere. Just as significant, these attempts at regulation revealed the role of economic self-interest in popular understandings of
British loyalty. In places like New York City and Kingston, residents were confronted with a series of legislative decisions that threatened to undo previous
commercial advantages gained through the illicit trade with Britain's enemies.
In both cities, Britons argued against such protectionist policies, believing that
the success of the empire required that government allow for a greater degree
of free trade throughout the Atlantic. Glaswegians, on the other hand, depended on a robust colonial trade and supported these mercantile policies as
the surest way to protect their own economic livelihoods. They also spoke out
against colonial boycotts, which were motivated, Glasgow residents argued,
by petty self-interest; but, of course, so too was Glaswegians' opposition to
the boycotts. Finally, Haligonians' continued reliance on Parliament's financial support and commercial protections undermined a local political culture
that appeared sympathetic to colonial grievances.

In a political culture fractured by often competing political and economic
interests, local conditions factored more largely in how subjects defended their
actions and defined their loyalties. One of the more remarkable aspects about
this period is the near absence of a shared British Atlantic political culture, the
consequences of which were devastating. The growing number of radical
Whigs in New York City, for instance, not only opposed the Townshend du-

ties but also drew meaning from a relentless series of local disputes involving British soldiers, Anglican ministers, and obstinate merchants. The combined force of these crises profoundly altered how many New Yorkers perceived their loyal attachment to Great Britain, leading to calls for a far more aggressive and violent resistance to British imperial rule and those who supported it.

Haligonians shared with many New Yorkers a commitment to these radical Whig principles but lacked the political and economic independence to act on these beliefs. Kingstonians also likely sympathized with their northern colonial neighbors, but the city's white resident's were consumed by both domestic and foreign threats that reinforced their dependence on the British government and military. Finally, Glaswegians understood that the domestic and imperial crises of the late 1760s threatened their commercial interests and raised questions about their political loyalties. Consequently, residents turned to a far more moderate defense of Britishness that supported British mercantilism, celebrated the Crown and constituted government, and championed the loyalty of Scots to the British state.

Even the threat of popery, long thought of as capable of diminishing these local and regional differences, proved especially divisive in these four British Atlantic communities during this period. New Yorkers, for instance, drew from a radical Wilkite political culture in London that regularly labeled political opponents as espousing arbitrary, papist appearances. Dickinson's hugely popular *Letters from a Farmer in Pennsylvania* drew from this long-standing Protestant Whig political tradition to defend colonial rights. The effect was to drive many New Yorkers toward a far more radical political culture that increasingly, if unevenly, described their government in unfamiliar, foreign terms.

In Kingston, however, illicit French traders and Spanish *guarda costas*, alongside the possibility of a war with France and Spain in 1770, pushed many Kingstonians toward a more loyal political culture that celebrated British military valor and defended the authority of government. In Glasgow, Wilkes's claims that all Scots were Jacobites drove Glaswegians toward a greater defense of their Protestant loyalties, expressed most profoundly in the public celebrations around Archy Douglas's legal victory in 1769. Meanwhile, defenseless Haligonians, left exposed by the departure of British soldiers to Boston in 1768, were forced to reconcile their loyalty with the need to protect themselves from the perceived threat of Indian and Acadian enemies. For some, such a reconciliation proved impossible, especially when the government appointed a Catholic missionary to the province in 1768. But others seemed to embrace a new political identity that was both multiethnic and multireligious, though it is unclear whether they believed such an identity could fit within a broader, transatlantic definition of Britishness.

Still, amid all of these crises—indeed, in consequence of them—some Britons also began to voice another competing definition of loyalty that opposed the growing influence of radical Whigs on both sides of the Atlantic. These Britons instead embraced a more moderate political culture that praised order, authority, and virtue, which they contrasted with the tyranny and self-interest of colonial protests and Wilkite mobs. Hints of this perspective had emerged among critics of the rioting during the Stamp Act Crisis, but it grew in significance in the late 1760s, especially among anti-Wilkite writers in Glasgow and across Scotland. This narrative began to forge a new path, slowly and unevenly, in communities across the British Atlantic. It linked some Britons to a conception of Loyalism every bit as committed to a defense of personal liberty but did so by distancing itself from the growing turbulence in the American colonies.

Some New Yorkers began to express these attitudes in the summer of 1770 when Parliament repealed the Townshend duties, except the one on tea.[142] But this narrative of the crisis, this new understanding of Loyalism, emerged more forcefully three years later, amid colonial resistance to the Tea Act. Some had grown tired of the riots and protests and saw in the budding Patriot movement corrupt and self-interested motives. These New Yorkers—John Vardill among them—increasingly described their loyalty in far more moderate terms. Like Glaswegians, they celebrated order, the rule of law, and a respect for authority against the backdrop of violent subversive crowds and illegal committees. It also helped that beginning in the spring of 1773, the bookseller turned printer James Rivington began to publish his gazette, which provided greater opportunities for these moderate Whigs to publicly express their views.

Supporters of the government wrote incessantly in late 1773 to expose readers to the base designs of radical leaders in their community, who, they contended, were misleading the public in their pursuit of wealth and power.[143] In December, Vardill responded to his many critics in another essay by systematically refuting their various arguments, before concluding with the most profound statement of loyal British thinking to date.[144] "Examine, Fellow-Citizens!" he began, "the Conduct of the men, who would revive our fatal Dissensions; and you can be no longer deceived. Their Positions have already been proved subversive of LIBERTY; their Measures introductive of the most imperious TYRANNY." Vardill was astonished that radical Whigs had effectively, if temporarily, assumed control of the city. "Whence did THEY derive the *Authority* to treat with the Commissioners, as AMBASSADORS for the venerable *Body of Merchants*, the *Mechanics*, and *landed Interest* of this COLONY?" He then turned radical Whig rhetoric on its head, asking readers, "If to be *governed without our Consent*, given either immediately, or by our Representatives, is SLAVERY, then, Fellow-Citizens! [we] have been treated *as* SLAVES."

Vardill preempted his critics who might have thought such rash maneuvers on the part of the Sons of Liberty were necessary in the city's fast-moving political climate. "But what marks of Public-Spirit have they discovered?" he asked. "If the *illicit* Trade is fatal to our Country; why have they not *renounced* it? This is the surest Proof they can give of disinterestedness . . . '*Perish* the noxious Commodity, (would be the voice of every good Citizen) rather than debase the dernier Resort of Government . . . or support the Interest of a foreign Country, in opposition to our *own*!'" The authority assumed by radical leaders not only lacked political legitimacy, reasoned Vardill, it was also absent a principled, reasoned argument.

Vardill concluded with a spirited attack on these imagined defenders of British liberty, whom he characterized as having tossed aside law and order and their love of the country for their own material gain. "That genuine *Liberty* can only be found in *civil society*," he cautioned, "that without *laws, civil society* cannot *stand*;—that *laws* are of no benefit, if they may be *transgressed at pleasure*;—that if *one part* of the community transgress them, *another* may also;—that where *all are free from the restraint of law*, there is no SECURITY for ANY."[145] Vardill had effectively stolen from his opponent's playbook, which perhaps explains why he acquired so many critics. He, too, saw the disregard of constitutional law and the enslavement of Britons as the result of the corrupting influence of self-interest. His villains, however, were not imperial officials or opponents of boycotts, but rather an increasingly influential set of radical Whig leaders who, he believed, fomented riot and discord to promote their own infernal designs.

That Vardill and his supporters in New York City and across the Atlantic came to the defense of Parliament and the empire in the winter of 1773 demonstrates, perhaps more than anything, the contingent nature of Loyalist discourse during a period of increasing political instability. In the absence of a common shared enemy, Britons reverted to local explanations of both domestic and imperial crises. This led to the emergence of competing transatlantic understandings of Loyalism, which often sat at odds with one another. Thus far, however, no one was yet calling for rebellion or for a war against perceived rebels. Despite such rigid divisions, most Britons in these four communities still professed an allegiance to the British Crown even if they questioned the legitimacy of those in power. This shared allegiance was to change over the course of the following year, when a political culture of fear and violence engulfed the empire, leading some to finally reject their loyalty to the monarch while others adopted a more inflexible defense of their king and government.

CHAPTER 4

King-Killing Republicans
Rebellion and the Making of a British Common Cause

In October 1774, John Holt's *New York Journal* carried an anonymous letter from Montreal, which was then exchanged in newspapers across North America and on the British mainland over the following month. The letter described the recent arrival of the province's governor, Sir Guy Carleton, who had been in London helping members of Parliament craft the controversial Quebec Act. Welcoming ceremonies for governors, whether arriving for the first time or returning from a long trip, were common occurrences in the eighteenth-century British Atlantic and were regularly covered in newspapers. Such events played a crucial role in reinforcing ideas of civic authority, political allegiance, social harmony, and more broadly national identity and patriotism. At times, however, these events could also bring to the surface latent political and social tensions within the community, region, or even empire.[1]

This was true of Carleton's arrival in Montreal, which, according to the writer, received little of the fanfare usually associated with such an event. There was no mention of soldiers parading, bells ringing, public toasts, or fireworks illuminating the nighttime sky. Instead, the author reported only that Carleton and his family were met by Lieutenant Governor Hector Theophilus de Cramahé, "all of the French Clergy," and the colony's bishop, Jean-Olivier Briand. Local citizens, whose presence writers typically noted to confirm the authority of the governor and the widespread loyalty of the community, were conspicuously absent from the ceremony.

Their absence, and the apparent solemnity of what should have been a celebratory occasion, is perhaps best explained by what happened next. After the initial greetings from de Cramahé and the clergy, the writer alleged that Carleton "had the Honour to be kissed by the Bishop, and afterward very genteelly introduced to Popery." From there, Briand invited Carleton to join him in his chaise as they made their way to the castle. Seduced by the bishop's kiss, Carleton, a former war hero who had served under James Wolfe in Britain's glorious victory at Quebec in 1759, had now embraced popish rule within moments of stepping foot in the colony he helped secure for his country a mere fifteen years earlier.[2] Over the following several days, according to the writer, the governor was "visited by every Frenchman, down to the meanest People in the Place:— But very little by the *beggarly English* (as we hear he has been pleased to call them)." The writer explained that the English colonists were "incensed against [Carleton] . . . on Account of the detestable Quebec Act, which is wholly ascribed to him, and said to have been framed under his Direction."[3] Even worse, claimed the author, "the French have said, *'That now all of their Laws will be made by the General, and the Bishop'*—and in Fact, if the General was a Roman Catholick, he could not shew them more Respect than he does."

Holt included two pieces of intelligence at the end of the letter to force readers to imagine the broader implications of one governor's embrace of popery. First, they were told that ten days earlier a "few English Merchants" in Montreal—those *"beggarly English"* whom Carleton was now ignoring—had collected one thousand bushels of wheat to be sent to Boston to aid those suffering under the recently passed Coercive Acts. Readers also learned that Carleton recently received letters from officials in New York asking him to have several regiments "in Readiness, to embark at an Hour's Warning: We expect every Moment to hear of Vessels being taken up to carry them to Boston."[4] Such intelligence likely shocked New Yorkers and subjects elsewhere in the British Atlantic: Carleton and his Catholic allies were now prepared to use the army to further subdue Bostonians. Meanwhile, the few remaining Protestants in Montreal desperately sought to retain their Britishness by, of all things, opposing British rule in favor of their American brethren.

Stories such as this—and there were many more—left loyal Britons in a precarious position at a crucial juncture in the imperial crisis. Over the previous several years, as we have seen, British attitudes toward their nation and empire were often shaped by competing political and economic interests, made more obvious when Parliament sought greater control over their Atlantic colonies.

Out of these imperial disputes there had emerged conflicting understandings of Loyalism that also often and necessarily drew from a myriad of contentious local disputes. Absent a shared narrative, Britons instead created enemies out of other Britons who, truth be told, shared in a similar definition of Britishness. These divisions often led to moments of violent conflict in communities throughout the British Atlantic, but ultimately neither side was able to make their enemies anything more than political adversaries. There was no single path toward resolving the growing imperial crisis.

The situation was different when Carleton arrived in Montreal in the fall of 1774. Not since the Stamp Act Crisis of 1765–66 were Britons throughout the empire so directly engaged in the imperial conflict. The nation now found itself on the verge of a civil war that called into question the very Protestant Whig ideals that were so fundamental to popular definitions of Loyalism. In response, Britons on all sides of the Atlantic were forced to formulate answers to larger questions of national identity and popular expressions of Britishness. What did it mean to be British? And, more crucially, why would it eventually become necessary for Britons to take up arms against their own brethren or to support such a conflict? To make this leap required constructing a narrative of war—a common cause—that made dangerous enemies out of former countrymen.

For a nascent American Patriot movement, this leap was made possible, in part, because at a key moment in the conflict the British government chose to do the unthinkable: tolerate Catholicism in the empire. In the spring of 1774, the British government passed the Quebec Act, just months after the destruction of tea in Boston and on the heels of the unpopular Coercive Acts.[5] The Quebec Act simplified the complicated ideological debates of the previous decade by recasting political divisions in the far more familiar and frightening terms of popery. To do so was to reimagine supporters of such policies, not merely as political opponents, but as dangerous and foreign, as real enemies to the rights and liberties of Britons everywhere. Lord Shelburne recognized as much in the fall of 1775, declaring before his peers that since the Stamp Act Crisis colonists had "seen a uniform lurking spirit of despotism pervade every Administration . . . that has accumulated oppression upon oppression since, till at length it has openly established, by the *Quebeck* Bill, Popery, and arbitrary power over half *America*."[6]

Worse yet, in the days and months following fighting at Lexington and Concord, their government also made alliances with many Indian societies and agreed to arm runaway African American slaves.[7] *Catholics, Indians,* and *slaves*: such enemies terrified and excited colonial subjects, who both understood and derived meaning from the threat that such groups posed to their cherished rights and liberty, their Britishness. Loyal Britons were thus faced with a Herculean task. They had to support a nation who counted among its allies the most feared inhabitants in all of British North America, while opposing a revolution based on a Protestant Whig explanation of political and economic tyranny.

Despite this difficulty, many Britons across the Atlantic remained loyal in the early months of 1775. A significant minority of New Yorkers, in fact, opted for loyalty over rebellion. They took to the streets and turned to Rivington's press to construct a persuasive pro-British narrative of the crisis that enjoyed support in mainland British cities like Glasgow and even among some Britons in colonial port cities like Halifax and Kingston. This narrative—Britain's *common cause*—was, to some extent, defensive and reactive, for it depended mostly on refuting an emerging Patriot cause. Not surprisingly, supporters lauded the supremacy of monarchy and legitimate government and believed the Crown and Parliament offered the surest path toward resolving the near decade-long crisis. But their cause was proactive, too. Loyalist writers took particular aim at the newly formed Continental Congress and the various local committees created to enforce the Continental Association, which they declared were illegitimate, unrepresentative, and resembled popish tyranny. These Britons, like their Patriot counterparts, were committed to basic Protestant Whig ideals that celebrated political liberty and economic freedom; Loyalists just believed that Congress and the committees represented the greatest threat to those rights.

The problem, however, was that this British common cause failed to articulate a clearly defined enemy at a crucial moment in the conflict. Instead, loyal Britons relied on a narrative that described delegates to Congress and local committee members as misleading, deluding, cajoling, and duping colonists into support for the Patriot cause. Loyalists desperately tried to frame the rebellion as unnatural, guided by motives at odds with popular conceptions of British Whig patriotism. But such language did little more than reveal the most troubling aspect of the British cause: their enemies were still Britons, if misguided ones.

The Quebec Act devastated a shared discourse of Loyalism that previously permeated communities throughout Britain's vast Atlantic empire. When shots rang out in Lexington in the early hours of April 19, 1775, none of the four communities in this study clearly backed the British cause. New York City's Patriot leaders used the start of the war (and the threat of popery) to take control of the city, despite the presence of a substantial and vocal minority of pro-British subjects. Many Haligonians appeared to support the Patriot cause in the face of ongoing efforts by the ruling elite to silence such sentiment. Kingstonians, too, showed at least tacit support for rebellious Americans in the spring of 1775, but they also understood that particular local circumstances made it all but impossible to join their cause. Finally, even in Glasgow some residents harbored pro-American views, while most of the city's prominent merchants opted for neutrality in hopes the war would end quickly and their valuable Atlantic trade would be saved.

The British common cause—a new, shared understanding of Loyalism constructed by Loyalist writers in the winter and spring of 1774–75—struggled to convince a majority of Britons that the Patriot cause was dangerous and that Patriot leaders and their supporters were a legitimate threat to the nation. The absence of a shared narrative of British patriotism, distinguishable from that of the rebellious colonists, further fractured the empire and left loyal Britons to question what it meant to be British.

In September 1774, delegates to the First Continental Congress met in Philadelphia. Claiming to represent the interests of subjects from Nova Scotia to Georgia, their expressed purpose was to find a peaceful solution to the increasing tensions between colonists and imperial officials.[8] Over the previous spring and summer, communities across the Eastern Seaboard of British North America reacted to news of Parliament's decision to punish Bostonians for the destruction of tea by pushing for new boycotts and forming extralegal committees to aid their New England brethren. The Coercive Acts, intended to make an example of the Massachusetts colony, instead excited the fears of colonists everywhere that similar forms of tyranny might visit their own towns and villages should they not make a stand.

Radical Whigs in New York City formed a committee in August to help Bostonians. When a false rumor spread through the city the following month that Gage had burned Boston to the ground, crowds threatened merchants, ship owners, and artificers not to aid Gage and his soldiers in that town.[9] Some Haligonians also took a stand. In July, residents attempted, unsuccessfully, to stop the landing of East India Company tea in the city.[10] The colony's obstinate new governor, Francis Legge, arrested the alleged ringleaders and ordered a ban on unlawful assemblies that "promote illegal Confederacies, Combinations, public Disorders and the highest Contempt of Government."[11] Apparently, not all Haligonians listened, as reports circulated that "subscriptions are opened" in Halifax to send relief to Bostonians.[12] On the eve of the delegates meeting in Philadelphia, Holt reported in his *Journal* that "the provinces of New York, Philadelphia, South and North Carolina, Nova Scotia, and Halifax, have heartily entered into the American cause."[13]

Colonists turned out in number to aid Bostonians, while members of Congress expressed their disproval of the new legislation. The Coercive Acts deprived Massachusetts colonists of those rights cherished most by subjects

everywhere. Crucially, though, these new laws did little to change the radical
Whig narrative of the previous decade, which continued to frame Parliament
as corrupt and prone to tyranny.

The Quebec Act, on the other hand, was of even greater concern to many
colonial subjects. In the months before the beginning of the war, Patriot writers from Virginia to Massachusetts fashioned a new narrative of the now
decade-long imperial crisis by turning to a very old rhetorical weapon.[14] Tyranny now was not some abstract Dickinsonian concept, the consequence of
corrupt officials or a faltering political system, but rather the product of a government that had succumbed to popery and was now conspiring with Catholics to destroy the freedoms of British subjects. Even more than the shutting
down of Massachusetts's government and economy, the Quebec Act encouraged Britons across the Atlantic to embrace a nascent common cause that
found meaning in their shared fears of popish tyranny.

Moderates and radicals in Congress wrote incessantly against the destructive consequences of the Quebec Act, despite the fact that the Act did not directly affect the fourteen colonies they purportedly represented.[15] John Adams,
along with many other members of Congress, loathed the legislation, scrib-
bling in the margins of his diary the dire consequences if colonists—and
Congress—did not make a stand.

> Proof of Depth of Abilities, and Wickedness of Heart.
> Precedent. Lords refusal of perpetual Imprisonment.
> Prerogative to give any Government to a conquered People.
> Romish Religion.
> Feudal Government.
> Union of feudal Law and Romish Superstition.
> Knights of Malta. Orders of military Monks.
> Goths and Vandals—overthrew the roman Empire.
> Danger to us all. An House on fire.[16]

In their various petitions and address, many of which made their way into
the pages of newspapers across the empire, members of Congress repeatedly
claimed that the ultimate purpose of the legislation was to use French Catholics as a "fit instrument" to violently suppress the rights and liberties of American colonists. The *Memorial to the Inhabitants of the British Colonies* warned
readers "that the [French Canadians], deprived of liberty and artfully provoked
against those of another religion, will be proper instruments for assisting in
the oppression of such as differ from them in modes of government and
faith."[17] The radical *Suffolk Resolves*, endorsed by Congress in September, argued
for the arming of citizens because, among other things, the Quebec Act "is

dangerous in an extreme degree to the Protestant religion and to the civil rights and liberties of all America."[18] New York delegate John Jay wrote in an *Address to the People of Great Britain* that Canada was "daily swelling with Catholic emigrants from Europe . . . [who] might become formidable to us, and on occasion, be fit instruments in the hands of power, to reduce the ancient free Protestant Colonies to the same state of slavery with themselves."[19] Delegates to Congress defended their adoption of the Continental Association, which created extralegal committees in every city in the colonies to enforce their new boycott, by arguing that the Quebec Act encouraged French Canadians "to act with hostility against the free Protestant Colonies, whenever a wicked Ministry shall choose so to direct them."[20] Perhaps Adams's diary scribbles were not hyperbole, for delegates warned colonists that the Quebec Act really could set *their* houses on fire.

These petitions and addresses helped to generate (as delegates had hoped) the incipient beginnings of a shared narrative—a common cause—among the growing number of opponents to British policies. The Quebec Act was crucial to this emerging narrative. Congress's message, that the bill was to be used as "fit instrument" to bring death and destruction upon innocent American colonists, was repeated over and over again in reports that circulated throughout the British Atlantic press in the months before Lexington and Concord.

This narrative played particularly well in New York City and Halifax, where residents lived in such close proximity to their old enemies. Late in 1774, for instance, when Carleton was supposedly "kissed by the Bishop," New Yorkers read a short soliloquy allegedly written by Lord North, who believed his best hope of restoring order rested on raising a "Popish army" in Canada that would be "glad to cut the throats of those heretics, the Bostonians."[21] Another widely shared report claimed Carleton had actually received orders *"to embody thirty thousand Roman Catholic Canadians immediately as a militia,"* who are to act *"under the same military law as regular troops."*[22]

Worse yet, still more reports began to appear that the Quebec Act—and the alleged arming of Catholic Canadians—was part of an even more sinister plot to reinstate the Stuart dynasty to the throne. "The Chevalier seems to derive some Hopes from the Discontent which this new Doctrine may create," Holt reported in early November, "nor will he refuse to take the Coronation Oath to gain a Kingdom he so highly longs to govern." Holt also included a letter from a Parisian who claimed that "a great English Peer" was making his way to that city to meet with the Young Pretender, Charles Stuart, "and there are Whispers here, that certain Engagements made in the Year 1745, are to be the chief Subject" of conversation.[23] For some colonists then, the decision to mobilize in defense of their rights and liberties was inspired, in part, out of a fear of a potential third Jacobite rebellion.

If the Quebec bill appealed to colonists' innermost fears—the spread of pop- ery—it also drew upon their more reasoned sensibilities. In giving assent to a bill that promoted Catholicism within the empire, George III betrayed one of his most important responsibilities as king: to act as the protector of the Protes- tant faith.[24] Doing so was a breach of his coronation oath and, according to some colonists, a legal justification to absolve their allegiance to the monarch. Though Congress avoided making such claims, Patriot writers frequently de- nounced the king's actions in "giving his royal assent to the obnoxious Quebec bill, and thereby breaking his coronation oath."[25] In October, New Yorkers read an "EPIGRAM, on the QUEBEC BILL" that placed George III alongside two notorious British monarchs, whose support of Catholic policies cost them the throne, implicitly suggesting that the former deserved a similar fate:

COULD James the Second leave his Grave,
Or Charles peep up, without his Head,
How the two royal Knaves would rave
To find a Parliament so bread!
To join the King, and the Religion own,
For which one lost his Head, and one his Crown![26]

The threat posed by the Quebec Act did not replace decade-long concerns over the increasingly arbitrary policies of Parliament. But it did shift the conver- sation away from the corruption of government officials to another, more dan- gerous narrative: Parliament, and perhaps even the king, were no longer British. Tradition gave this narrative its heft. It was steeped in a century of British preju- dice. Anti-Catholicism resonated because of how deeply it was embedded in the very notion of what it meant to be British in the eighteenth century. Long before Thomas Paine's *Common Sense*, some Britons were beginning to consider that their political opponents were no longer like them and their system of govern- ment had given in to a form of tyranny that could not be negotiated with.

In New York City, radical Whigs grew in strength and numbers in the weeks and months after the meeting of the First Congress, motivated in part by the many declarations against the Quebec Act. In November, one resident called for the raising of an army after having read repeated "accounts of orders be- ing sent to Canada, for embodying the militia, who, in conjunction with the Indians, are to cooperate with a Roman catholic General . . . to rob, enslave and murder their fellow subjects."[27] At the same time, the moderate Commit- tee of Fifty-One, formed in the spring to respond to the Coercive Acts, gave way to a more radical Committee of Sixty that began to aggressively enforce Congress's Association. Between December 1774 and February 1775, the committee confiscated the cargoes of twenty-one vessels and threatened public humiliation and violence to anyone caught breaking the boycott.[28]

Yet moderates in the city—many of whom would come to identify as Loyalists over the following several months—fought back, though with limited success. The colonial assembly refused to recognize the resolutions passed by Congress in October, some merchants tried to import British goods in spite of the Association, and others in the city and surrounding region remained obstinate in the face of the growing number of Patriot committees and crowds. The city boasted the largest urban population of pro-British subjects in the colonies on the eve of fighting in Massachusetts, while moderates and Loyalists in some neighboring communities formed a substantial majority over their radical Patriot counterparts.[29] Between a fifth and a third of the entire white colonial population remained loyal during the rebellion; in New York City and the surrounding region, that proportion doubled.[30]

Historians have largely ignored the possibility that these Loyalists, like their Patriot counterparts, were attracted to a shared cause, instead pinning Loyalists' political allegiances on a diverse range of personal interests that often predated the imperial crisis.[31] Some historians also argue, as Patriot writers did at the time, that these Loyalists lacked a political identity altogether. They were instead dependent ministerial tools or, worse yet, cowards, who lacked the courage and conviction to stand up for their rights and liberties.[32]

But these interpretations underestimate the extent to which a vibrant Loyalist press, like its opponents, could mobilize a populace. This was especially evident in New York City, home to the influential Loyalist printer James Rivington. He was likely the most widely read printer in all of Britain's North American colonies, at least until the spring of 1775.[33] Through his press, Loyalist writers gave meaning to a transatlantic political culture of Loyalism. This British common cause was no less committed to eighteenth-century Whig ideals that celebrated political liberty, economic freedom, and Protestant virtue, which these writers framed against the dangerous, and at times popish, tendencies of their political opponents. Their writings described a moderate form of Loyalism that echoed Scottish authors of the late 1760s who railed against the licentiousness and disorder of the Wilkite cause and those New Yorkers in the early 1770s who were critical of the violent tactics used to enforce colonial boycotts. On the eve of war, these Britons publicly celebrated their shared attachment to the king and constituted authority, whom they believed were most capable in protecting their rights and liberties as British subjects.

This cause was reactive, however. It took form only after October 1774 and in response to the words and actions of the First Congress and its supporters. According to one local Patriot, "a club of Tories" began to meet every Wednesday and Saturday evening at Rivington's print shop "to examine the newspapers, and direct him what paragraphs to reprint." "The Club," as the writer dubbed it, likely included several outspoken Anglican ministers such as Samuel Seabury, Myles Cooper, Charles Inglis, and Thomas Chandler, along with "some officers" stationed in the city.[34] According to Seabury, their objective "was to watch all publications either in News papers or pamphlets and to obviate the evil influence of such as appeared to have a bad tendency by the speediest means."[35]

For about six months—between the first meeting of Congress and the beginning of fighting in Massachusetts—these and other Loyalist writers produced perhaps the most voluminous literature in favor of Great Britain during the entire conflict. Well over a dozen Loyalist pamphlets appeared in the streets of New York City, all of which were published by Rivington, before boarding ships bound for communities scattered across the British Atlantic, including the three other cities in this study.[36] We are accustomed to viewing this period from the perspective of a nascent Patriot cause, because we know how this story will play out. But British subjects at the time did not. This was equally a Loyalist moment. Just as Patriot writers began to draw lines and define enemies, so too did Loyalist writers begin to construct a transatlantic narrative of the crisis that attempted to distance loyal Britons from the radical and subversive actions of their opponents. These Loyalist writings were effective—and dangerous.

Unlike their opponents, however, Rivington and his "Club" of writers struggled to articulate a unifying narrative capable of turning their opponents into dangerous enemies. This struggle is especially evident in their unsuccessful attempts to defend the enormously unpopular Quebec Act. Some writers tried to argue that it would help to bring peace and stability to a region of the empire in crisis. In October, Rivington published Lord Lyttelton's response to William Pitt's attack on the Quebec Act, in which Lyttleton maintained that religious toleration was the surest way to secure the political loyalty of former enemies. He did so by playing on the very same age-old fears of lurking Catholics (and their Indian allies) employed by Patriot writers. He asked Pitt what was the point of acquiring Canada, "but that France might not have at her command a body of men, either to attack our American settlements in time of war, or harass them in time of peace, by inciting the native Indians to invade them?" Even worse, he feared that should Parliament have "to *coerce*

America; do you wish in that melancholy event, to combine the Canadian with that of the Bostonian?"[37] Thomas Chandler agreed in a pamphlet Rivington published in November arguing that to deprive these subjects of their faith "would probably have increased the number of his Majesty's disaffected American subjects; which appears to be too great without them."[38]

Writers also tried to shift the label of popery on to their opponents, demonstrating the importance of Protestant Whig rhetoric to the emerging conflict. Lyttleton, in the same published letter to Pitt, went so far as to argue that to deny the conquered French Canadians a right to a free exercise of their religion was a clearer sign of popery than to tolerate the Catholic faith in the empire. "No true Protestant," he declared, "can harbour any such idea as that of establishing religion by force. Is the Spaniard in Mexico to be an example for a Protestant legislature?"[39]

In other instances, supporters of the British cause frequently framed Congress and Patriot committees as a popish organizations that sought to deprive loyal Britons of their most cherished rights and liberties. In *The Congress Canvassed*, Samuel Seabury likened the Association to a *"Popish* inquisition. No proofs, no evidences are called for. The committee may judge from *appearances* if they please—for when it shall be made appear to a majority of any committee that the Association is violated, they may proceed to punishment, and *appearances*, you know, are easily *made*."[40] "Mary V. V." turned to rhyme in a pamphlet addressed "to the Married Ladies of *America*," to admonish her husband, a delegate to Congress who supported the creation of extralegal committees to enforce the Association:

> Consider one Moment, your Courts of Inspection:
> Could the Inquisition, Venice, Rome, or Japan,
> Have derived, so horrid, so wicked a Plan?
> In all the Records, of the most slavish Nation,
> You'll not find an Instance, of such Usurpations.[41]

In other, more innocuous ways, Loyalist writers tried to use the language and symbols of popery to make sense of their political enemies. "BELLISARIUS," writing in Rivington's newspaper, lamented that Patriots "have made themselves idols, viz. liberty Trees, News-papers and Congresses, which by blindly worshipping, have so engrossed their minds, that they give not the least attention to their several occupations, but attend at taverns, where they talk politicks, get drunk, damn King, Ministers and Taxes; and *vow* they will follow any measures proposed to them by their demagogues, however repugnant to religion, reason and common sense."[42] Such claims sought to reimagine cherished symbols of

Protestant British liberty—the press, liberty trees or poles, and (supposedly) representative assemblies—as images of Catholic tyranny.

Even New Englanders were susceptible to accusations of popery. Early in 1775, Rivington published John Lind's *An Englishman's Answer, to the Address from the Delegates to the People of Great-Britain*, which portrayed Puritan New Englanders—the supposed ringleaders of colonial resistance—as not all that dissimilar from their French counterparts. Lind cautioned readers that in the last century they had "shed blood of the sovereign, and dispersed impiety, bigotry, superstition, hypocrisy, persecution, murder, and rebellion through every part of the empire!"[43] Lind's choice of descriptors was intentional. He sought to recast Patriot leaders as no longer British by likening them to the puritanical fanaticism of the Cromwellian era. Yet he did so by quoting from Congress's description of Catholics in its *Address to the People of Great Britain*. As the colonies descended toward rebellion, both American Patriots and British Loyalists sought desperately to affix popish labels to their enemies to show that they themselves were the true defenders of Protestant British patriotism. If the king could become a papist, so too could Oliver Cromwell.[44]

Even absent direct accusations of popery, Loyalist writers believed the words and actions of Congress and committees threatened to undermine legitimate, constituted authority and would lead to a far greater assault on personal liberty than the policies of the previous ten years. These writers were especially troubled by the methods used by radicals to elect delegates to their various extralegal bodies. In *The Congress Canvassed*, Seabury questioned the representative nature of these newly formed committees, a claim that struck at the foundation of colonial grievances over the past decade: that government derived its authority from the consent of the governed. He argued that delegates were not chosen by their colonial assemblies, but rather by ad hoc committees formed only by men who were most hostile toward the Crown and Parliament. "No delegate," he argued, "can in any *true* sense be called the *representative of a province*, unless they be appointed by the joint act of the whole legislature of the province." To claim otherwise, as Congress had done, was "a piece of impudence which was never equaled since the world began."[45]

Other writers derided an election process rigged in favor of Patriot interests. The anonymous author of *The Triumph of the Whigs* joked that representatives of the "illustrious, grand, Continental Congress" were *rightfully* elected by the "rule of *false position*." That is when, he argued, "the blue-skins [Patriots] outvote the loyalists, there the minority is included in the majority, and ought, in honour, and conscience submit: But where the loyalists out-vote the blue-skins, there the majority is included in the minority, and ought to be governed by it."[46]

"AGRICOLA" questioned the right of the city's leading Patriots to speak for the broader public. "Who is *the Public*? If by this expression a majority of the inhabitants is understood, I will take upon me to say that nine tenths of them, never heard of the *application* which gave birth to this *noble refusal*. . . . Dreadful indeed, would be the situation of *American freedom*," he concluded, "if it were only to be preserved by setting up one body of men to tyrannize over the rest."[47]

Seabury pushed these ideas even further, arguing that Congress was a foreign government because it ruled over a people without their consent. In one instance, he claimed some colonists had agreed to the introduction of "a *foreign* power, and [made] it an instrument of *injustice* and *oppression*."[48] In *An Alarm*, he warned New Yorkers that "a *foreign power* is brought in to *govern this province*. Laws made at *Philadelphia*, by factious men from *New England, New-Jersey, Pennsylvania, Maryland, Virginia*, and the *Carolinas*, are imposed upon us by the most *imperious menaces*."[49] Such criticism differed little in rhetoric from claims made about Parliament over the previous decade, but now these critiques were leveled against Congress and the burgeoning Patriot cause.

Loyalist writers also went to great pains to describe how Congress and Patriot committees suppressed dissent and denied loyal subjects their most basic freedoms. If a colonist were to break the boycott, Seabury warned, "they shall be considered as Out-laws, unworthy of the protection of civil society, and delivered over to the vengeance of a lawless, outrageous mob, to be tarred, feathered, hanged, drawn, quartered, and burnt.—O rare American Freedom!" His readers had two choices, he concluded, act like Englishmen or "bow, and cringe, and tremble and quake.—fall down and worship our sovereign Lord the Mob."[50] In another of his pamphlets, Seabury referred to Association committees as a "*committorial* inquisition" and was astonished that colonists who "have blustered, and bellowed, and swaggered, and bragged, that no British Parliament should dispose of a penny of your money without your leave," could now so willing suffer themselves "to be *bullied* by a *Congress*, and *cowed* by a COMMITTEE."[51]

In the critical months of the winter of 1774–75, a growing number of Loyalist writers constructed an alternative path toward the imperial conflict by playing upon popular definitions of British loyalty and patriotism. Tyranny, according to these writers, came not from the actions of British imperial officials, but rather from an extralegal and unrepresentative Congress. Though no less committed to a Whig defense of personal liberty, the crisis had encouraged these writers and their readers to adopt a more moderate view of Loyalism. They celebrated the rule of law and legitimate, constituted authority in the face of violent, subversive committees and crowds.[52] Their writings also turned political labels—ones that have endured to this very day—on their heads by

claiming that it was Patriots who favored popish submission to political authority (an illegitimate one no less) over a defense of one's rights and liberties.

In the early days of 1775, as the crisis approached rebellion, these two narratives came to dominate the British Atlantic press. A burgeoning Patriot cause
drew from the declarations of the First Congress, which sought support and
unity by declaiming against the popish leanings of Parliament and the king.
Conversely, an emerging British cause responded to the words and actions of
Congress by constructing a narrative of the crisis that described American Patriots as acting the part of popish tyrants. As these two divergent appeals to a
common cause circulated the Atlantic in the winter and spring of 1774–75, Britons living in New York City, Halifax, Glasgow, and Kingston were forced to
choose sides. As in previous years, they did so both in reaction to these broader
imperial debates and in the context of particular local interests and attitudes.

Choosing sides was not easy, however. Britons in these four communities were
unable to collectively and openly support a cause. These emerging narratives of
loyalty and rebellion collided with local political and economic interests that often were at odds with both causes. Additionally, though each of these two sides
drew from a rich political vocabulary that celebrated Protestantism and liberty,
each side also, according to their opponents, acted the part of the oppressor.
Loyal Britons were troubled by a budding Patriot cause that had absconded formal, constituted government for extralegal committees and associations, and
relied on violence and intimidation to ensure support for their cause. While
American Patriots questioned how loyal subjects could still support a king and
government willing to promote the spread of Catholicism in the empire, which
contradicted the very foundation of eighteenth-century British Loyalism.

This was certainly true in Halifax, where locals failed to overwhelmingly
support either cause in the months leading up to the outbreak of the war. Of
the four communities, Halifax was the only one not to send a petition of any
kind to Parliament over these winter months. There were also no major demonstrations or riots in the city, and residents appear to have not followed
through on their promise in the fall to raise goods and supplies for distressed
Bostonians. Part of this lack of activity had to do with Governor Legge's ban
on public meetings, which made it difficult for the town's residents to act in
accord with their southern neighbors.[53] The continued presence of British soldiers and sailors also likely limited opportunities for Haligonians to join with
other New Englanders, though such threats did not intimidate rural Massachusetts colonists.

Despite the apparent inaction of Haligonians, Henry's gazette continued
to stoke reader's fears of the dangerous designs of the Quebec Act. He printed

every one of Congress's declarations alongside various other rumors and reports evidencing that the king and government had abandoned their Britishness.[54] This narrative played well in a local political culture shaped in recent years by fears of invading Indians and their Catholic allies.[55] The paid appointment of the Catholic missionary Charles Bailly renewed tensions between a population who defined themselves as both Protestant and British and a local government that appeared willing to accommodate Catholicism. Now, in the winter of 1774–75, their own king and Parliament seemed capable of employing French Canadians to suppress popular opposition to imperial policies.

But Haligonians also stood to benefit from Congress's planned boycott, which would push New England merchants out of the North Atlantic and open up Halifax to the lucrative Caribbean trade.[56] Legge recognized the opportunity in November when he repealed a tax on rum, a move intended to weaken the political influence of local distillers and encourage the exportation of goods to the Caribbean, where residents could no longer depend on trade with the thirteen American colonies. Legge also petitioned the government in London, unsuccessfully, to give Nova Scotia complete control over the North Atlantic fishing industry. By March 1775, however, Parliament passed the New England Restraining Act, which excluded the rebellious New Englanders from access to the fisheries, and officials extended these restrictions the following month to the remaining American colonies. The Association, long thought to have played a crucial role in drawing together colonists in opposition to British policies, likely tempered the radical Whig interests of some Haligonians. They were forced to reconcile their political leanings with a desire to expand their colony's commercial interests.[57]

Legge's attempt to reform the colony's fledgling economy, however, angered many of the city and colony's leading merchants and assemblymen. For the previous decade or more, men like Joshua Mauger, Michael Francklin, Jonathan Binney, and John Day had used trade policies and monopolies to establish a near dominance over Nova Scotia's economy and government.[58] Legge recognized as much, complaining to Lord Dartmouth in the fall of 1774 that the influence of these men was so great that "there is at present scarce a Merchant, Shop keeper, Tradesman, Retailer of Spirituous Liquors, and all other Labourers and low Macanicks but entirely have their dependance on this Party."[59]

These local tensions—between assemblymen and councilmen, and their governor—divided residents at a critical moment in the imperial crisis. Many Haligonians embraced a British imperial identity that celebrated access to a prosperous Atlantic economy, which might expand further as a result of both local and imperial reforms and colonial boycotts. Others saw in the burgeoning crisis an assault on their more basic political rights as British subjects, ones that guaranteed a degree of self-government and the removal of oppressive and unnecessary taxes. Neither cause, however, appears to have garnered enough support to draw together the divided community at a moment when Halifax's neighbors to the south were moving toward rebellion.

Even news of fighting at Lexington and Concord, which arrived in the port city in the first days of May, failed to push a majority of residents to one side or the other. Anonymous supporters of the Patriot cause allegedly set two fires, one targeting the warehouses of local merchant and assemblyman Joseph Fairbanks, who had agreed to send a large quantity of hay to Gage's army in Boston, and the other the home of Richard Morris, a local justice of the peace and ally of Governor Legge.[60] News of these fires excited Patriots in New York City, but Henry's gazette included only a brief report that was critical of both incidents and did not publish any additional essays or editorials.[61] Afterward, Legge responded by offering a reward for the capture of the culprits, and a week later he ordered recent immigrants from "any Parts of *America*" be required to give a public oath "to their Fidelity and Allegiance to his Majesty's Sacred Person and Government."[62] Halifax and the colony of Nova Scotia were to remain loyal to Great Britain, by force if necessary.

Surprisingly, Glaswegians expressed virtually no opposition to the toleration of Catholicism in North America, in spite of the city's strong ties to the radical Popular Party within the Church of Scotland. Its members were loyal supporters of the Protestant Hanoverian succession and believed strongly in the constitutional liberties guaranteed to all subjects.[63] Additionally, Glaswegians were aware of many Britons' ongoing suspicions that Scots still harbored Jacobite sympathies, and reports in the fall of 1774 even linked the ill-fated Quebec Act with alleged Scottish Jacobites, like Lord Bute.[64] Local newspapers and the popular *Scots Magazine* reprinted virtually every petition and address against the legislation, although unlike in New York City or Halifax, they did not publish editorials that questioned the legitimacy of the king.[65] Glaswegians also did not directly comment on the Quebec Act in their local newspapers. There were no essays lamenting the spread of Catholicism in the empire, nor did residents petition Parliament for repeal of the legislation.

One reason for their seeming indifference may have been that the bill did not directly affect them. In October 1774, editors of the *Scots Magazine* reprinted an excerpt from Samuel Johnson's pamphlet, *The Patriot: Addressed to the Electors of Great Britain*, in which he reasoned that mainland Britons should not fear the bill, because "Quebec is on the other side of the Atlantic, at too great a distance to do much good or harm to the European world." Johnson also shared the view of Loyalist writers in New York City that "the inhabitants being French, were always Papists, who are certainly more dangerous as enemies than as subjects."[66] Such observations reflected an increasingly popular and pragmatic attitude in mainland Britain toward the governing of an expansive and far more diverse Atlantic empire.

These observations also played well in Glasgow, where residents were deeply connected to the American trade and desperate to find a peaceful resolution to the growing conflict.[67] Even though debates in the colonies were beginning to shift toward questioning the very legitimacy of the Crown, Glaswegians continued to view the crisis in economic terms. They agreed with the argument of Seabury (and Vardill and others before him) that "this bustle about Non-importation, &c. has its rise, not from Patriotism, but selfishness," and believed colonists relied too heavily on the Atlantic trade to ever commit to such a boycott.[68] "MERCATOR AMERICANUS," writing in the *Caledonian Mercury* in January, referred to the previous boycott in the late 1760s, claiming that the "very people who first proposed it, were the first who broke it." He was especially skeptical of the southern colonists "whose produce is raised by negroes." Not only did these colonists need the trade to pay for the costs of their slaves, but the loss of such an economy would inevitably lead to insurrections on their plantations. "The richer they are in negroes," he concluded, "the more precipitate will be their ruin."[69] For many Glaswegians, colonial boycotts, as much as failed imperial policies, represented an affront to one of the core tenets of Protestant British Loyalism: access to Britain's profitable Atlantic economy.

Writers were especially quick to criticize colonists who saw opportunity in the conflict to absolve themselves of long-standing debts to Glasgow tobacco merchants.[70] Seabury understood this aspect as well, writing that "I have heard it confidently asserted, that the single province of Virginia, owes the single city of Glasgow, at this very time, no less than two hundred thousand pounds sterling. To get rid of their enormous debt, at a stroke, may be the grand reason why the Virginians are so ready to embrace any scheme that promises exemption from the British government."[71] As such, Scots were likely not surprised to learn in a letter from Virginia published in the *Caledonian Mercury* that "the people are come to a resolution of putting every Scotch merchant on board of vessels, with all their goods, and send them off to England; but are determined to burn all their accompt-books."[72] Nor would they have been shocked to discover that a Scotsman living in Virginia in November 1774 was "in danger of his life ([or] at least of being tarred and feathered) if he says a word that does not please them."[73]

David Wardrobe learned of this danger firsthand. In November, he was hauled before the Westmoreland County Committee for having written a letter to a friend in Glasgow critical of the boycott. His friend liked what he read and had the letter published in the *Glasgow Journal*, a copy of which arrived in Virginia months later.[74] In consequence, the committee declared Wardrobe's letter "false, scandalous, and inimical to America" and labeled Wardrobe "a wicked enemy to America." Fearing the loss of his property and possibly his life, Wardrobe relented to the demands of the committee, which appeared to him every bit the popish inquisition described by Loyalist writers. He publicly admitted what was, in fact, not true: that his letter contained "falshoods and misrepresentations, which may be of fatal consequence to the rights and liberty of America"[75] (fig. 4.1).

Faced with the possible loss of their Atlantic tobacco trade, which played such an essential role in defining their attachment to the empire, Glasgow merchants and traders decided to petition Parliament in the early days of 1775. They were not alone; similar petitions arrived from Bristol, Birmingham, Norwich, and North American merchants in London.[76] Thought of by some historians as at least a tacit recognition of the legitimacy of colonial grievances, the Glasgow petition more accurately revealed a community who feared that colonists' resistance to imperial taxes would ultimately ruin their city's economy.[77]

This petition stood in stark contrast to the one from nearly a decade earlier, when the city's tobacco merchants railed against the Stamp Act and demanded

FIGURE 4.1. *The Alternative of Williams-burg* (1775). Loyal Britons were especially critical of members of Patriot committees, whom they ridiculed for using violence and intimidation in their supposed defense of American liberty. In this popular print, a motley crowd of colonists wielding knives and wooden bats force two Loyalists to sign the Continental Association while a bag of feathers and a barrel of tar hang from a scaffold in the background. Glaswegians would have been especially upset with the inscription on the barrel of tobacco, which was to be a gift for the anti-Scot John Wilkes. *Library of Congress, Prints and Photographs Division, Cartoon Prints, British.*

its repeal. This time they declared that they were "deeply interested in the Trade to *North America*" and that they had "Debts due to them . . . to the Amount of One Million and upwards." But they stopped short of questioning the arbitrariness of the Coercive Acts, observing instead that recent acts of Parliament "have created Fears and Jealousies, and raised much Dissatisfaction, in the Minds of His Majesty's *American* Subjects, who have been induced to enter into Resolves to interrupt the Commerce between *Great Britain* and the Colonies." They also trusted Parliament, something many Americans were less inclined to do in early 1775, "to bring about a happy Reconciliation between *Great Britain* and the Colonies."[78]

Fears, jealousies, induced: these words suggest less a defense of colonial rights, and more a critique of the nascent Patriot cause. To some extent, they mirror the writing of Seabury and others who saw, in the escalating conflict, not principled men defending their just claims to the rights of British subjects but rather a set of radicals playing upon the public's base emotions to excite the people against their government. Yet they also reveal the distance from which Glaswegians still viewed the growing conflict in Britain's American colonies. While colonists were beginning to choose sides and trying to make enemies, Glaswegians still cared more about their city's profitable Atlantic trade and believed Parliament remained capable of solving the dispute.

For the first time since the Stamp Act Crisis, the conflict brewing in the colonies garnered the full attention of Kingstonians. Recent legislation, and the colonists' response, had put the island's residents in a precarious position in the winter of 1774–75. While the Coercive Acts and the Quebec Act challenged popular Whig beliefs in the city and colony, the Association threatened to ruin their local economy and perhaps even jeopardize the tenuous hold white residents enjoyed over the enslaved black population. Ongoing rumors of foreign invasions, possibly inspired by the increasing turmoil in the northern colonies, and planned slave insurrections regularly reminded residents of the importance of British military protection. Such local circumstances also continued to shape the inhabitant's loyalties, which were defined as much by a commitment to liberty as they were by a sense of security and stability provided by the British state.

Loyalist writers in New York City were quick to remind readers that the Association sought to unify American colonists by harming other Britons within the empire. Seabury warned that the boycott would anger Britons living in Ireland and the Caribbean who depended on the American trade and would push his colony's profitable Indian trade north to Canada. "Good God!" he lamented, "can we look forward to the ruin, destruction, and desolation of the whole British Empire, without one relenting thought?"[79] In January,

Rivington printed an address signed by *"A Native of the British* WEST-INDIES," which reminded North American colonists that their Caribbean neighbors depended on the intracolonial trade for their basic necessities. The author pleaded with readers, "surely you will not doom them to Bankruptcy, to Nakedness and Famine! Shall Men who so nobly combat Oppression, be themselves oppressive. . . . Shall unoffending Thousands be plunged into Want and Wretchedness, by the Means for punishing the supposed Venality of a few Individuals?"[80] Such comments suggest something about the boundaries of the imperial crisis. If Britons living in Jamaica were supportive of North American political grievances, then why had Congress marked them as enemies to their cause? It was a stern reminder that constructing a common cause was as much about drawing people toward your interests as it was about pushing others away.

Even worse, letters from Jamaica printed in British Atlantic newspapers suggested that American merchants who supported the boycott were carrying on an illicit trade with the Dutch, French, and Spanish to the detriment of Kingston merchants and traders. As early as August 1774, Londoners read that a recently captured New York vessel arrived at Port Royal, "on board of which were found sufficient testimonies to condemn her for carrying on a clandestine trade in the French and Dutch islands by means of false entries."[81] The following spring, *"an eminent planter in Jamaica"* writing in an Edinburgh newspaper suggested that the best way to end the crisis in North America was for absentee planters in London to petition "to put a stop to the North American trade with the French islands."[82] Simon Taylor, writing from Kingston in June 1775, lamented the efforts of American colonists to "Smuggle into America" Spanish molasses and coffee "to the ruin of our Colonies."[83]

It was not just the hypocrisy of American Patriots that angered Jamaicans. They worried that the recent increase in the number of attempted slave revolts on the island was the result of the loss of the food and provisions trade with the North American colonies. The Association might actually kill them. In August, a planned slave revolt in Westmoreland Parish was averted only after an enslaved woman revealed the plot to officials. There were also reports of a maroon uprising at Port Antonio and another at Old Harbour, a small settlement a little more than twenty miles west of Kingston, which caused "a general Alarm throughout the Island."[84] Worse yet, in December five slaves were arrested for having murdered their master near Halfway Tree on the outskirts of Kingston. Dick, the slave who delivered the fatal blow, was sentenced to be gibbeted alive. His co-conspirator, Anthony, was burned at the stake, while Frank "was immediately hanged, his head afterwards cut off, and fixed on a pole" to scare off would be rebels.[85] Such events reminded white Kingstonians that the growing hostilities in

Britain's North American colonies threatened to deprive them of their most sacred liberty: the right to own other human beings.

Rumors of planned French and Spanish invasions of the island also grew in number in the winter of 1774–75 as the British government transferred more of the colony's soldiers north to deal with the growing tensions. Early reports were vague, but suggested that Spanish warships were gathering in Havana in preparation for an attack on Jamaica. In September, London newspapers carried a letter from Jamaica in which the writer complained that "the Spaniards are daily committing outrages upon our trading vessles . . . some they take, others they plunder."[86] In December, several American printers informed readers that they had received a series of letters from Jamaica suggesting that "a fleet of the royal navy of Spain, with a well appointed army of land forces, are assembled at the Havanna, which occasions very serious apprehensions to the inhabitants of that island."[87]

By the early spring, official intelligence reported in newspapers linked Spanish activities in the Caribbean to the budding rebellion in the colonies. In one letter, from Cork, Ireland, the writer testified that France was planning to attack Ireland "as soon as the forces are sent from thence to America, and that the Spaniards have a large fleet ready to attack some of the western islands, but it is generally believed that Jamaica is their principal object."[88] A few weeks later, "letters from Spain [revealed that] it is no longer a secret, that the court of Madrid have ordered a very considerable fleet to the West-Indies . . . as soon as our troops are engaged with the Bostonians."[89]

Despite these internal and external threats, the island assembly was dominated by Kingston merchants who had a vested interest in protecting the intracolonial trade and decided to petition the king in favor of their colonial neighbors. The petition, drafted in late December, offers perhaps the most comprehensive account of how Kingstonians understood the escalating conflict and their loyalty to the empire in the months before the war began.[90]

The assemblymen began by admitting that particular local circumstances prevented their involvement in the conflict. "That weak and feeble as this Colony is, from its very small number of white inhabitants, and its peculiar situation from the incumbrance of more than two hundred thousand slaves," they asserted, "it cannot be supposed that we now intend, or ever could have intended, resistance to *Great Britain*." Yet they felt compelled at this critical moment, "with the approaching horrours of an unnatural contest between *Great Britain* and her Colonies," to express their views so as to possibly "heal those disorders which may otherwise terminate in the destruction of the Empire."

Despite growing fears of slave revolts and foreign invasions, the petitioners sided with the colonists on virtually every legislative crisis of the preceding decade. They reminded the king in no uncertain terms that colonists "were a part of the *English* people, in every respect equal to them, and possessed of every privilege at the time of their emigration." They conceded that Parliament had always enjoyed the right to regulate trade in the empire, but they did not "confer on them a power of legislating for us, far less than destroying us and our children by devesting us of all rights and property." They feared Parliament had a plan in place, "almost carried into execution, for enslaving the Colonies," and believed the Quebec Act sought to reduce the colonists "to an abject state of slavery, by having an arbitrary Government established in the colonies," and by establishing the "Popish Religion . . . which by treaty was only to be tolerated."[91]

News of this petition spread like wildfire throughout Britain's Atlantic empire. Imperial officials in London feared the effect such a statement would have on the crisis, given the critical importance of the island. Lord Dartmouth expressed frustration at the "indecent, not to say criminal, Conduct of the Assembly," while government officials decided against debating the petition to keep it from reaching the general public.[92] Nearly two hundred West Indian merchants and absentee planters gathered in London in January to draft a more moderate alternative. They avoided the political dispute for the most part, instead reminding officials that colonial boycotts posed a threat to the lucrative West Indian islands because of their "necessary dependence on external support."[93]

American Patriots, on the other hand, applauded the spirited defense of colonial rights exhibited in the assembly's petition. From late February to early March, virtually every newspaper from Nova Scotia to Virginia printed the entire petition, usually on the front page so that it could double as a broadside (fig. 4.2).[94] A letter "from a worthy Gentleman in Kingston" suggested that genuine political convictions, not selfish economic interests, motivated the assembly's radical turn: "I find the many excellent publications from the continent have had a wonderful effect in softening the minds of our opponents, enlightening those who were uninstructed, and confirming the faithful." The author felt the person who deserved the most recognition was "the sexton who tolled the bell at the church of the late excellent Dr. Sherlock," a likely reference to a town crier for Robert Sherlock's *Saint Jago Intelligencer*, a popular Spanish Town newspaper.[95] It is impossible to know which "excellent publications" he was referring to, but it might have been the many recent letters and addresses from Congress, which probably arrived in Jamaica just weeks before the assembly drafted the petition.[96]

In late March, delegates to both the Virginia Convention and the Connecticut House of Representatives voted an "Address of Thanks" to the Jamaica

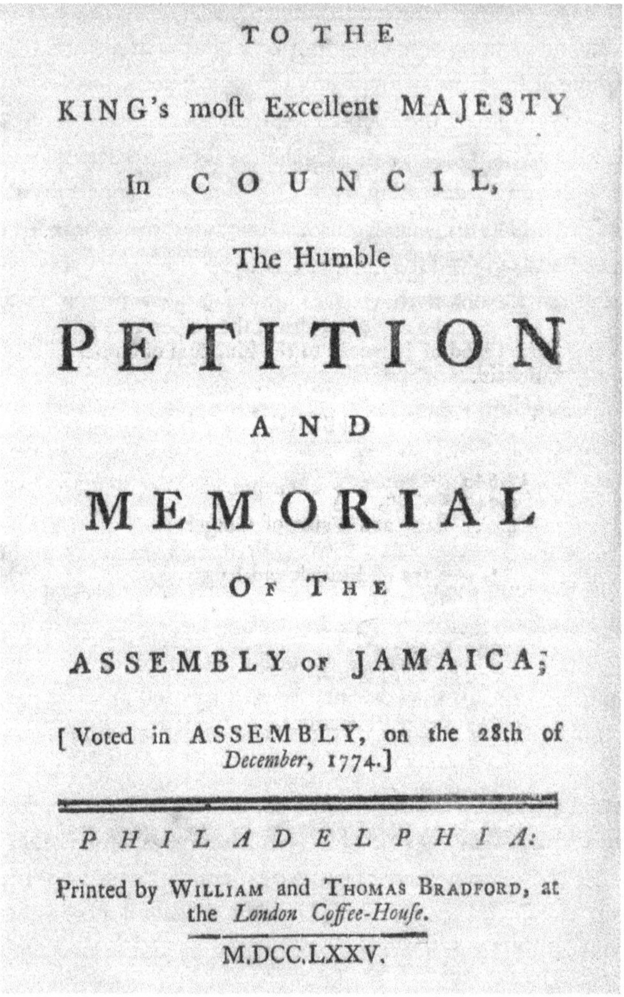

TO THE

KING's moſt Excellent MAJESTY

In C O U N C I L,

The Humble

PETITION

A N D

MEMORIAL

Oғ Tне

ASSEMBLY oᴙ **JAMAICA;**

[Voted in ASSEMBLY, on the 28th of
December, 1774.]

P H I L A D E L P H I A:

Printed by Wɪʟʟɪᴀᴍ and Tнoмᴀs Bʀᴀᴅғoʀᴅ, at
the *London Coffee-Houſe.*

M.DCC.LXXV.

FIGURE 4.2. *Jamaica Assembly Petition to the King* (1775). The Jamaica Assembly's petition was wildly popular among American Patriots, who viewed it as further evidence that their growing cause enjoyed the broad support of communities across Britain's Atlantic empire. While printers along the Eastern Seaboard of North America reprinted the petition in their weekly gazettes, Philadelphia printer, William Bradford, who was also the official printer for the Congress, had it published as a short eight-page pamphlet. *The Library Company of Philadelphia.*

Assembly "for their kind and seasonable Mediation in favour of the Colonies on this Continent." The Connecticut representatives went so far as to invite the Jamaicans to create a Committee of Correspondence, "or a similar Method of mutually communicating such Intelligence," which was a curious offer, given the assembly's admission that the large number of slaves on the island precluded Jamaican participation in the conflict.[97] Yet the offer also says something about how American Patriots viewed their fellow Caribbean colonists in the weeks before the outbreak of the war. Connecticut representatives briefly considered the imperial crisis in broader geographic terms, in part because they believed both regions feared the consequences of the recently passed Quebec Act.[98]

The situation was deteriorating quickly in New York City in the winter and early spring of 1775. Patriot leaders were increasingly able to wrest control of the city and colony, but loyal Britons remained obstinate in their defense of the British cause. Much of this had to do again with the reach and influence of Rivington's print shop, which continued to broadcast a British narrative of the conflict. The famed printer reveled in the success of his newspaper, announcing in an October 1774 issue that "the weekly impression of this Gazetteer is lately increased to Three Thousand Six Hundred, a number far beyond the most Sanguine expectation of the Printer's warmest friends." Copies of his gazette traveled the length and width of the North Atlantic as well, which, if he is to be believed, made it one of the most widely read newspapers in all of the empire: "The paper is constantly distributed thro' every colony of North-America, most of the English, French, Spanish, Dutch, and Danish West-Indian islands, the principle cities and towns of Great-Britain, France, Ireland, and in the Mediterranean."[99] Newspapers carried stories that created narratives and defined enemies to encourage support for a cause, and on the eve of the war no printer outside of London likely enjoyed a larger audience than James Rivington.

Little wonder patriot leaders from South Carolina to Massachusetts took increasingly aggressive steps to silence the popular printer and his allies.[100] They recognized the danger. Beginning as early as September 1774, delegates to the First Continental Congress worked to encourage a public boycott of Rivington's press.[101] As winter approached, communities began to label Rivington and his newspaper as the greatest threat to their rights and liberties. One writer declared the infamous printer "an unsavory, high flying, Jacobite priest," while the Committee of Observation in Elizabethtown, New Jersey, called Rivington "a vile Ministerial Hireling, employed to disunite the Colonies" and ordered all the town's residents to cancel their subscriptions.[102] In early January, the Morristown, New Jersey, Committee of Correspondence branded Rivington "an enemy to his country" for publishing Seabury's pamphlets, which contained "many falsehoods, wickedly calculated to divide the Colonies, to deceive the ignorant, and to cause a base submission to the unconstitutional measures of the *British* Parliament for enslaving the Colonies."[103] Between December and April, at least fifteen communities in New York, New Jersey, Connecticut, and Massachusetts, alongside several others in Pennsylvania, Maryland, Virginia, and South Carolina, publicly displayed their support for the Patriot cause by vilifying Rivington and suppressing dissenting views in their communities.[104]

Patriots also found other, more violent ways to stop the spread of Loyalist publications for fear that they might win over support to the British cause. Crowds in and around New York City publicly burned copies of Loyalist pamphlets and shamed those who hawked them, while residents of nearby Freehold, New Jersey, tarred and feathered a bundle of Samuel Seabury's *Free Thoughts*.[105] Further afield in Newport, Rhode Island, a crowd used copies of Rivington's newspaper, along with "divers other ingredients" to burn 300 pounds of tea.[106] Such occasions fostered unity and support for the Patriot cause, but they also revealed Patriots' fears about the influence of a pro-British political culture in the colonies. Rather than engage with a persuasive Loyalist narrative, Patriot leaders instead tried desperately to keep it from being read.

American Patriots also threatened violence against Rivington for publishing essays and editorials in defense of the British government. Several subscribers in Baltimore warned of tar and feathers if he did not stop printing his newspaper, while Philadelphians decided Rivington and his cast of writers "deserve not to live among us."[107] At one point, John Jay and Phillip Livingston, members of New York City's Committee of Observation, threatened harm against Rivington at his print shop for publishing a report that purportedly questioned the decisions of their committee.[108] Even James Madison wrote in the weeks before the start of the war that he wished Rivington "& his ministerial Gazetteers" were in Virginia for just a day, where "they would meet with adequate punishment."[109]

In response, Loyalists acted the part of victims in this print war, labeling such attacks on the press as further evidence of the popish tyranny of Congress and local committees. Thomas Chandler likened their actions to the "old popish way" of pre-Reformation Europe and advised Loyalists to take cover "when these burning zealots assemble together, in order to hold an *Auto de Fe.*"[110] Major Benjamin Floyd of Brookhaven on Long Island confronted members of the local Patriot committee: "Do you really mean to immure the colonies in Popish darkness, by suppressing the vehicles of light, truth and liberty? Are none to speak, write or print, but by your permission? . . . A free press," he concluded, "has been the honour and glory of Englishmen. . . . But we are become the degenerate plants of a new and strange vine; and now it seems, ignorance must be the mother of both devotion and politics."[111] When looking back at this moment years later, the Loyalist judge and historian Thomas Jones saw the hypocrisy in Patriot attempts to suppress the writings of their opponents: "These were the people contending for *liberty*. They engrossed the whole to themselves and allowed not a little to their opponents, they published whatever they pleased, and threatened destruction to any printer who should dare to print an answer to any of their inflammatory, detestable publications."[112]

Historians have often marveled at the ability of the Continental Congress and local committees to create unity and cohesion without resorting to the sort of excess violence and disorder that typically characterized rebellions of this and earlier periods.[113] Yet Patriot opposition toward Loyalists and their writings contradicts this argument. In the months before armed conflict in the Massachusetts countryside, at the very moment colonists were forced, for the first time, to take sides, Patriot leaders purged their communities of a competing narrative of the imperial crisis. They burned, hanged, and tarred and feathered influential pamphlets; threatened Loyalist writers and printers; and increasingly countenanced violence against anyone who opposed their views. Patriot leaders did their level best to destroy the competing narrative of a British common cause. It is a remarkable and largely forgotten point that before colonists raised their bayonets in defense of their rights and liberties, as they argued, they drew first blood in the war over words.

The impact of these Patriot attacks on the press, on the lives of loyal Britons, and on the authority and legitimacy of their king, drew many subjects in and around New York City toward a more resolute defense of their monarch in the early months of 1775. Rather than accede to intimidating Patriot committees and crowds, loyal New Yorkers instead publicly declared, often at great risk to their lives, their loyalty to the Crown and constituted authority. These pronouncements contradict a long-standing characterization of Loyalists as lacking the sort of political fortitude and ideological commitment of their rivals. That portrayal underestimates the extent to which a Loyalist political culture drew from, and gave meaning to, a transatlantic language of moderate Whig patriotism. For a decade, loyal Britons had opposed the violence and subversive nature of the radical Wilkite cause and were critical of the tactics colonists used to resist imperial legislation. Now, in the spring of 1775, these Britons were committed to defending a British political system they believed to be capable of securing their rights and liberties, rather than submit to a new, unrepresentative political order that, to their mind, acted every bit the tyrant.

At the center of this renewed sense of Britishness was an absolute defense of George III. This both stemmed from the long-standing belief in the ability of the monarch to bring order and stability to the empire and also responded to a radical Whig political culture that had begun to denounce the king as a papist.[114] Before the fighting at Lexington and Concord, Loyalists were regularly forced to defend their allegiance to a king no longer trusted by a growing number of American colonists. In March 1775, William Cunningham was beaten and robbed by a crowd for defiantly proclaiming, "God bless King George," rather than going "down on his knees and damn his Popish King George."[115] Weeks later in New Haven, Connecticut, a "loyal Constitutional-ist" was "interrogated after the manner of the *Spanish* and *Portugal* inquisi-tions" for refusing to "damn the King" and publicly criticizing Congress. "To this complexion is *American* liberty," claimed the writer, "through the influ-ence of the King-killing Republicans, already arrived."[116]

John Case experienced something similar in January 1775 when Alexander McDougall and Isaac Sears invited him to a New York City tavern "to con-verse . . . on politicks." Case, a known Loyalist from nearby Long Island, frus-trated all of McDougall's attempts to prove his error in thinking. Sears then asked him point blank "whether the King had not violated his coronation oath?" (Yet another example of Patriot hostility toward the Quebec Act.) Case "thought he had not." Incensed, Sears labeled the old man a "Tory, and told him, that if he was in Connecticut government he would be put to death." He then asked Case "whether, if Bostonians were to take up arms, he would fight for the King?" Case said he would, "as he conceived King George to be his lawful Sovereign." Growing angrier, Sears ordered Case to sit in a chair "in the chimney corner" and "a Negro boy, who belonged to the house . . . to sit along with him." The boy "had too much understanding to comply," but Case remained in the corner for the remainder of the evening, while Sears and Mc-Dougall "ordered the rest not to drink with a Tory."[117] Given the descent into violence that Loyalists all over the American colonies endured in these months before the war, Case—though socially humiliated—got off lucky.

In the early months of 1775, Loyalists living in nearly two dozen communi-ties around New York City, and even as far away as North Carolina and Geor-gia, took to Rivington and Hugh Gaine's newspapers to proclaim their loyalty to George III. These declarations differed in length and purpose but shared several important characteristics: an absolute defense of the king, support for the constitution and legal representative assemblies, and a willingness to risk their lives in defense of Britain.[118] None of the declarations, it is worth not-ing, commented on the decade-long political dispute. They did not question the right of colonists to defend their liberties against arbitrary tax policies or trade restrictions, issues that many Loyalists also grieved.[119] They criticized, instead, the methods by which some American colonists had chosen to op-pose Parliamentary authority. No doubt influenced by the Loyalist writings of the previous months, these Britons believed Congress and its growing network of committees and associations were arbitrary, encouraged licentiousness, and unnecessarily provoked the inhabitants to disavow their loyal attachment to the king and government.[120]

Some might consider these addresses as declarations of dependence, because they confirmed the signer's devotion to the existing British political system. But it makes more sense to think of them as the first declarations of independence in this worsening imperial crisis, preceding by a year the many other, smaller American declarations that emerged in Patriot-controlled communities across the colonies.[121] The Loyalist declarations announced a willingness on the part of some loyal colonists to break from the tyranny of an emerging political authority—Congress—and to turn to their king and Parliament to safeguard their cherished rights and liberties.

Virtually every one of them included a statement of loyalty to the king. Several residents of Ulster County declared that "we have lived [and] we are resolved to die, in true and faithful allegiance to his most gracious majesty, King GEORGE the THIRD." Loyalists in Dutchess County avowed "that our sovereign lord king George the third, is the only sovereign to whom the British American may, can, or ought to owe and bear true and faithful allegiance." One hundred and forty-one subscribers to an address from Reading publicly professed their "due obedience to his most gracious Majesty King George the third." Nearly four hundred residents of Westchester County, led by Seabury himself, "declared their determined Resolution to continue steadfast in their Allegiance to their gracious and merciful Sovereign King George, the Third," and concluded by signing, "with a loyal Enthusiasm, the grand and animating Song of, *God save great George our King, Long live our noble King, &c.*"[122]

Despite the crises of the previous decade, these subjects remained convinced of the durability of a constitutional-based Anglo-American empire that began with the monarch and extended down to their representative colonial assemblies. In Newtown on Long Island, fifty-seven residents declared they did not "acknowledge any other representatives but the *Members of the General Assembly of the province of* NEW-YORK." In Dutchess Country, "a great number of the inhabitants" proclaimed "that our representatives in General Assembly convened, are the only guardians of our rights and liberties; that without them no laws can here be made to bind us, and that they only are the channel through which our grievances can properly be represented for redress." At a town meeting in Hampstead, residents praised their local assembly for "petitioning his most gracious Majesty, [sending] a memorial to the House of Lords, [and addressing] a remonstrance to the House of Commons."

Several hundred residents of Cortlandt Manor north of the city argued that "we have a Governor, Council and Assembly, to represent our grievances to the KING, LORDS, and COMMONS; we are assured that we shall be heard."[123]

Not surprisingly, many of the subscribers were also critical of the violence they associated with the Patriot cause. Loyalists in Reading believed Congress's resolutions "appear to us immediately ca'culated to widen the present unhappy breach," while Hampstead residents believed support for Congress had "diffus[ed] a spirit of Sedition among the people, destroy[ed] the authority of constitutional Assemblies, and otherwise introduce[ed] many heavy and oppressive grievances." Ulster County residents complained of "all treasonable associations, unlawful combinations, seditious meetings, tumultuous assemblies, and execrable mobs; and of all measures that have a tendency to alienate the affections of the people from their rightful sovereign, or lessen their regard for our most excellent constitution."[124]

Others targeted Congress's use of the Quebec Act to deceive colonists into abandoning their attachment to the king. The "friends of government" in Ulster County lamented the violent tactics used by their opponents to win the support of "the ignorant, credulous multitude." The most egregious example, they argued, was the claim that in passing the Quebec Act the king "had established the Romish religion in America, and thereby broken his coronation oath; whereby the people were discharged from their allegiance, and were justifiable in associating to make proper provision for their common safety."[125] John Case could have used these arguments—and these friends—in his January debate with Sears and McDougall.

Finally, in virtually every one of these declarations, the signers announced their willingness to defend their loyalty even at the cost of their lives. These were Britain's minutemen, thousands of colonists who in the spring of 1775 believed the threat of Congressional tyranny was so great that they countenanced violence against their former friends and neighbors. Dutchess county residents agreed "to promote, encourage, and when called to, enforce obedience to the rightful authority of our most gracious sovereign king George the third." Loyalists in Reading declared it their "indispensible duty . . . to defend, maintain, and preserve, at the risk of our lives and property, the prerogative of the crown, and the privileges of the subject from all attacks, by any rebellious body of men, any committees of inspection, correspondence, &c." Loyalists in Ridgefield announced that "we will to the utmost of our power, support his throne and dignity, against every combination in the universe."[126]

Ulster County Loyalists went further, erecting a seventy-five-foot-tall pole—a king pole to counter the colonists' many liberty poles—at the house of John Graham in late February. Atop their pole they fixed a royal standard along with a lengthy inscription that celebrated their loyalty to the king but also served as a call to arms in defense of their rights as British subjects:

And to make known to all Men,

That, We are ready, when properly called upon, at the hazard of our lives, and of every thing dear to us; to defend the KING, support the magistrates in the execution of the laws, and maintain the just rights and constitutional liberties of freeborn Englishmen (fig. 4.3).[127]

Such declarations complicate the popular and long-held narrative that celebrated the common New England farmer as the ultimate symbol of personal sacrifice in the cause of freedom and liberty. In this instance, loyal Britons expressed a similar willingness to put their lives on the line but did so in the face of what they believed to be the tyranny of crowds, committees, associations, and an illegal Congress.

The targeting of Loyalist printing presses (and writers) paid important dividends in keeping these statements from reaching a wide colonial audience. Printers far from the reach of Patriot committees, however, included Loyalist declarations in their columns, though not a single one appeared in the pages of Henry's *Nova Scotia Gazette*. In the spring and early summer of 1775, virtually every London newspaper carried several of these provincial testaments of loyalty.[128] They were also exchanged in many provincial English and Scottish newspapers over the following days and weeks.[129] In doing so, loyal New Yorkers began to draw new connections, ones that linked their support for the Crown with loyal Britons elsewhere in the Atlantic. These declarations, and the many pro-British essays and editorials that appeared in Rivington's gazette throughout the winter and spring of 1774–75, shaped public opinion in mainland Britain of the crisis going on in North America. New York City was the Boston of the British cause.

Despite the broad appeal of the British cause, loyal New Yorkers were still unable to make their opponents into anything other than misguided subjects. Meanwhile, the larger Patriot population began to take control of the city in the early spring of 1775, in part because of their continued dependence on anti-Catholic rhetoric. When moderates threatened to block attempts by radicals to elect like-minded delegates to the Second Continental Congress in March 1775, the "Friends of Freedom" marched from the liberty pole to the city's exchange to ensure their victory in the contest.[130] According to a report of the incident widely circulated in colonial newspapers, they were "attended by Music; and two Standard Bearers carried a large Union Flag, with a blue Field, on which were the following Inscriptions: On one Side, GEORGE III.

FIGURE 4.3. *Rivington's Gazette,* March 2, 1775, reproduction of the royal standard. For Rivington's Loyalist readers, the royal standard atop the Ulster County king pole, an image of which adorned the front page of his popular gazette, symbolized a far greater commitment to liberty than the notorious Patriot's pole that stood on the Commons. *Courtesy, American Antiquarian Society.*

REX AND THE LIBERTIES OF AMERICA. NO POPERY. On the other, THE UNION OF THE COLONIES, AND THE MEASURES OF THE CONGRESS."[131] The words, "No popery," in this case, played the part of the villain. They threatened to deprive New Yorkers of their liberties and their loyalty should they not join with the other colonies in supporting the decisions of their Congress.

In early April, Holt carried several rumors from Boston that Gage planned to march his army south to New York and that additional regiments in England and Ireland were preparing to embark for the city. Other reports suggested that France and Spain were "waiting [for] a favourable opportunity to dismember America from England" and that even the Young Pretender was again making plans for an invasion.[132] Days later, the city's Committee of One Hundred received several anonymous letters from London warning of a plot by some Loyalists to hand over the city to British soldiers upon their arrival. One letter writer claimed Gage was then going to call on the "Assistance of Quebeck to rule with a Rod of Iron all the Slaves of America."[133]

A week later, New Yorkers were shocked to read of the fighting at Lexington and Concord. For nearly a week, the city found itself under quasi-military rule. John Case's tormentor, Isaac Sears, and other members of the Sons of Liberty "formed themselves into a Voluntary Corps and assumed the Government of the City." They raided the arsenal for weapons and ammunition and captured two supply ships intended for General Gage's army in Boston. They also ordered the disarming of known Loyalists, while Patriot crowds harassed and threatened their former friends. One merchant recalled Loyalists being dragged to the liberty pole—"the darling deity" of the Patriot cause—where they were "insulted and beaten in a Cruel manner if they refused to kneel down and Curse the King and his Government."[134] Sears and his friends forced Rivington to publicly rescind his views and to promise to "conduct my Press upon such Principles as shall not give Offence to the Inhabitants of the Colonies in general, and of this City in particular."[135] Rev. Myles Cooper and Rev. Thomas Chandler, two of Rivington's "Club" of writers, refused to bow to Congress and instead fled the city for England.[136] Colden lamented the "unfortunate situation of the City . . . the people were assembled, and that scene of disorder and violence begun, which has entirely prostrated the Powers of Government, and produced an association by which this Province has solemnly united with the others in resisting the Acts of Parliament."[137]

With the city teetering on the edge of rebellion, Isaac Low, then still joined with the Patriot cause, called a public meeting to announce the creation of a local association that would effectively turn control of the city over to the General Committee, which he chaired. Speaking in front of thousands of New York Patriots who gathered that day, Low "damned the King, [and] cursed the Ministry," before launching into a tirade against George III intended to inspire the crowd to action. He declared, of all things, "that the Ministry were in the interest of the pretender," and worse yet, "the King was a Roman Catholic, nay, a Roman Catholic tyrant; that he had broken his coronation oath, had established the popish religion in Canada, which was shortly to be extended to all the other colonies."[138] Fears of a popish king and army, not surprisingly, marked New York City's entry into armed conflict with Great Britain.

The beginning of the war, the moment when Britons began to kill one another, raised important questions about the meaning of popular eighteenth-century definitions of Britishness. For more than three-quarters of a century, anti-Catholicism drew together disparate Britons from across the empire, providing them with a popular language of Loyalism that softened local and regional distinctions and gave meaning to the rights and liberties they enjoyed. But in the spring of 1775, anti-Catholic rhetoric divided the empire. Both Patriot and Loyalist writers turned classic Protestant Whig language against itself, fashioning narratives of the approaching conflict that sought to transform their former friends into dangerous enemies. Patriots took advantage of the Quebec Act to denounce their king and government (and their supporters) and promote rebellion, while loyal Britons framed Congress and the Association as popish institutions. For the first time in the nation's history, Protestant Britons were engaged in a war in which popish narratives were waged against their own people.

Consequently, Britons everywhere were left to make sense of a war that contradicted the basic tenets of eighteenth-century Britishness. Their king's tolerance of Catholicism in the province of Quebec not only raised questions about the legitimacy of his rule but also led to rumors that forty thousand French Canadians were planning to invade the thirteen American colonies. On the other hand, the formation of a Continental Congress and extralegal and seemingly arbitrary committees and associations deprived innocent subjects of their right to trade, representative government, and the ability to speak and write freely. To choose sides in the spring of 1775 was to call into question a critical aspect of one's Protestant loyalties.

Britons in these four communities filtered these competing ideologies through their own distinct local circumstances. Kingstonians rallied in support of their American brethren in the winter of 1774–75. They petitioned against the absolute sovereignty of Parliament, they opposed restrictions placed on colonial trade under the Coercive Acts, and they feared the "abject state of slavery" brought about by the recently passed Quebec Act. But they also understood the limits of their opposition. Outnumbered by their slaves, and surrounded on all sides by their European enemies, Kingstonians knew rebellion was not an option. They also recognized that Congress's boycott, which outlawed the African slave trade, potentially threatened their labor system and social structure. Glaswegians also understood the dangerous consequences of tolerating Catholicism in the empire, but they relied too heavily on the colonial trade to not see in the crisis a threat to their city's economic prosperity.

Reports of Patriot crowds attacking Chesapeake tobacco factors, and Congress's planned boycott of all British goods, convinced most Glaswegians of the dangerous consequences of the Patriot cause. Even then, though, the city's merchant community continued to walk a fine line, declaring early in 1775 their opposition to oppressive imperial policies but also believing that Parliament could still bring peace and prosperity to the empire.

These competing causes especially divided New Yorkers and Haligonians, with both their cities on the front lines of the approaching conflict. Fears of Catholic tyranny, coming from both Quebec and London, lived alongside a growing Patriot movement that suppressed political expression and replaced constituted government with extralegal and unrepresentative committees and associations. This division led to a considerable amount of violence in New York City and the surrounding region, where both causes enjoyed wide circulation in a vibrant local print culture. In Halifax, however, residents made little effort to join the Patriot cause, despite their many cultural ties to New England and a largely pro-Patriot print culture. This inaction had to do in part with the possible economic benefits the city and colony might enjoy on account of Congress's boycott, and also with the arrival of a new governor whose political and economic reforms divided residents. As the crisis shifted to war and rebellion, Britons from Halifax to Kingston, and from New York City to Glasgow, divided over the meaning and importance of the conflict and their own understandings of Loyalism.

CHAPTER 5

The Madness of these Deluded People
Independence and the American Enemy

In late October 1776, nearly a thousand loyal New Yorkers signed their names to a declaration addressed to General William Howe and Admiral Richard Howe. The brothers had recently captured the beleaguered city from Washington's occupying army. The victory was more of a rout and occurred just weeks after news of Congress declaring independence had spread across the empire. For loyal Britons, the Howes' taking of New York City signaled a brighter future, and raised their hopes that the rebellion would soon be defeated.

The address aimed at restoring civil government in the city, a step the signers believed would demonstrate the willingness of British officials to defend the liberties of their loyal subjects. To convince the Howes, the signers returned to a narrative of the conflict constructed in the months before the war began—a British common cause—which celebrated monarchy and constituted government and renounced the violence of the Patriot cause. They declared their absolute "allegiance, to our Sovereign GEORGE the Third," and affirmed the "constitutional supremacy of Great-Britain over these colonies," which they believed to be "essential to the Union, Security and Welfare of the whole Empire." They also recalled the personal sufferings of many of their countrymen, lamenting the many "loyal Citizens [who] have been driven away by the calamities of war, and the spirit of persecution which lately prevailed."[1]

Weeks later, more than five hundred refugees signed a second, longer declaration to the Howes that asked again for a restoration of civil government. The signers spoke out "against the strong tide of oppression and tyranny, which has almost overwhelmed this Land" and described the war as "the most unnatural, unprovoked Rebellion, that ever disgraced the annuls of Time." They also continued to attest to their "unshaken fidelity . . . to His Majesty," expressed a continued willingness "to preserve and support the Constitutional Supremacy of Great Britain over the Colonies," and prayed "for a speedy restoration of that union between them."[2]

It would have surprised no one in the fall of 1776 to hear loyal New Yorkers declare their "unshaken fidelity" and describe the war as an "unnatural, unprovoked Rebellion." Since the winter of 1774–75, they had borne witness to, and written incessantly about, the devastating consequences of the crisis and rebellion, more than residents in any of the other three communities in this study. Patriot crowds and committees—former friends and fellow Britons—had stolen Loyalists' property, driven them from their homes, ruined their livelihoods, and used violence and intimidation to deny them their most basic rights. The American Revolution promised for them, not their right to "life, liberty, and the pursuit of happiness," but rather a life of terror, oppression, and displacement.

A return to civil government offered these Britons a chance to renew their commitment to an empire they still believed capable of promoting liberty and freedom. Over the previous year, in fact, they had embraced a cause that sought to reconstruct a political society dependent on order and hierarchy. They believed a benevolent monarch, alongside a legitimate, representative government, was most capable of extending freedom and promoting prosperity, which had been lost to the tyranny of extralegal and unrepresentative committees and associations. This narrative, Britain's common cause, fit perfectly with Loyalists' calls for restoring civil government in the occupied city.

Unfortunately, however, they were unable to persuade either of the Howe brothers. Even worse, their cause had failed to counter a growing Patriot narrative of the conflict that described the king and his government as having succumbed to the sort of corruption and tyranny previously believed to be found only in Catholic countries. Patriot writers and delegates to Congress, in fact, had imagined their own narrative of the crisis, which framed their former countrymen as dangerous enemies because of the friends they kept. Initially, Catholic French Canadians had acted in this part, but Patriot leaders shied away from such rhetoric after they invaded Canada in the fall of 1775 and began to court an alliance with France.[3] Instead they turned to other common fears that pervaded colonial American society: British-inspired slave revolts—made real after the publication of Lord Dunmore's proclamation in the fall of 1775—and British alliances with the "merciless Indian savages," as Jefferson stated in the Declaration of Independence. Such dreaded enemies drew together desperate Patriot communities who came to associate British tyranny and foreignness with their African and Indian allies.[4] The need for such a narrative that relied on proxies to recast British subjects as dangerous foes revealed just how difficult it was to separate friends from enemies in a civil war.

Loyal New Yorkers, and others across the empire, were unable to make rebellious Americans into similarly feared enemies. Popish labels applied to committees and associations, or even delegates to Congress, had failed to stick in the face of a rival political culture that had far greater claims to fears of popery. Instead, loyal subjects constructed a narrative of war that described rebellious Americans as being deceived, duped, or misled by a few factional, self-interested colonists. Repeated claims, both by contemporary Loyalists (like those who signed the New York declarations) and subsequent historians, that the war was an "unnatural, unprovoked rebellion," that it was absent reason and legitimacy, underlined the fact that loyal Britons were simply unable to make sense of their purported enemies.[5] In this failure lay the loss of America. Perhaps a total military victory might have kept the colonies in the empire, but this inability to make the British cause "common" jeopardized those chances from the start.

In the first years of the war, Britons in each of these four communities were unable to collectively come to terms with who and why they were fighting and what this meant for their understandings of loyalty and empire. In such circumstances, local events and interests assumed greater importance than a shared commitment to a broader imperial cause. White Kingstonians, for example, filtered news of independence and war through the lens of their island's dependence on slavery, which required the support of the British military. A failed slave rebellion in the fall of 1776, caused in part by the war in North America, convinced many that their rights and liberties—particularly that of owning another human being—required remaining loyal to Great Britain. Haligonians remained divided over the rebellion, which appealed to many of the colonists' Protestant Whig ideals but also threatened to ruin the colony's economy and lead to war with the nearby Indian and Acadian populations. Glaswegians continued to view the rebellion from the standpoint of their city's profitable Atlantic economy. From the beginning, they refused opportunities to publicly express their support for the war for fear that it would anger colonial planters. But they also saw economic opportunity in the conflict, which required the transportation of a growing number of men and supplies that Glaswegians were perfectly suited to provide.

The first two years of the American War for Independence regularly elicit stories of struggle and sacrifice, of crushing losses and miraculous victories. Patriot leaders and writers often and necessarily framed the events of this period around questions of sacrifice and morale—"these are the times that try men's souls," Paine famously observed—and historians tend to describe them as the prelude to the final years of the conflict when the alliance with France, and then Spain, dramatically changed the complexion of the war.[6] But for loyal Britons across the North Atlantic, the start of the war lacked a similar narrative. The first years of the rebellion were marked, not by a growing sense of unity and a shared understanding of nation, but by divisions over what it meant to be British and who and why they were fighting.

In the early years of the war Kingstonians embraced a nascent British common cause, which defended monarchy and constituted government as the surest safeguards of liberty. Crucially, however, white residents came to see the value of those institutions in relation to their right to own slaves. From the start of the conflict, Kingstonians recognized the inherit dangers of supporting a rebellion in a colony where rumors of invasions and insurrections were commonplace. But the war also left them in a difficult situation, given their limited resources and particular interests. Should they choose to support their North American counterparts, Kingstonians risked losing the protection of the royal army and navy. If they remained loyal to Great Britain, they would likely see a precipitous decline in the profitable intracolonial trade.

This much was understood by the delegates to the Second Continental Congress who met in Philadelphia in July 1775. They drafted a second address to the Jamaica Assembly that was as much an expression of gratitude for their "pathetic mediation in our behalf with the crown" the previous December as it was recognition of their parting of ways. The delegates described the present crisis as a civil war in which the "treasure and blood of Britons [has been] spilt and wasted in the execrable design of spreading slavery over British America." Yet they also recognized, paradoxically, that slavery, or as they euphemistically termed it, "the peculiar situation of your island," prevented Jamaica from joining their cause. "But we have your good wishes," they concluded, "From the good wishes of the friends of liberty and mankind, we shall always derive consolation."[7]

Kingstonians were reminded again of the "peculiar situation" of their island the following summer, when they foiled yet another slave rebellion motivated in part by the crisis in Britain's northern colonies.[8] Just as they had feared, slaves on the island suffered under the colonial boycott; a succession of severe droughts only exacerbated the problem.[9] Shortly after Congress declared independence, the assembly petitioned Governor Basil Keith that many parts of the island were "labouring under the distresses of Famine," which particularly affected the majority slave population.[10] Indeed, one such slave, Pontack, complained that the slaves "were angry too much with the white people, because they had taken from them their bread."[11]

Other reports suggested that the language of revolution coming from the northern colonies encouraged some slaves to revolt. Rev. John Lindsay wrote to Dr. William Robertson in Edinburgh in August 1776 that "dear Liberty has rang in the heart of every *House-bred Slave*, in one form or other, for these Ten years past—While we only talk'd about it, they went no farther than their private reflections upon us & it: but as soon as we came to blows, we find them fast at our heels. Such has been the seeds sown in the minds of our Domestics by our Wise-Acre Patriots."[12] It was later discovered the revolt was to occur after soldiers on the island departed for the war in the northern colonies, and while British naval vessels were busy protecting merchant ships from American privateers. One resident complained weeks before the planned revolt that "the rebels have carried matters to so great a length, encouraged by foreign powers, that their privateers cruise publicly around this island."[13]

The foiled slave revolt might have clarified for some white Jamaicans in the summer of 1776 the dangers of supporting a rebellion in the thirteen American colonies, but most had already drawn such conclusions. Though they were just as committed to ideas of Protestantism, free trade, and self-government as their neighbors to the north, they had come to believe that the British government (and military) offered them the best chance to enjoy those ideals. They needed a stable system of government that promoted order and hierarchy, and a professional army and navy capable of protecting them from the many threats of domestic slave revolts and foreign invasions. This had been true since white subjects first inhabited the island, and it was especially the case over the previous decade when virtually every imperial crisis had led to rumors of revolts and invasions. Their liberty, they had come to know all too well, was intimately tied to the enslavement of others. That the rebellion in British North America worked to the benefit of their opponents—African slaves and Catholic Europeans—only strengthened the loyalty of the island's white inhabitants.

Glaswegians approached the early years of the war hesitantly, fearing that openly supporting one side or the other would jeopardize their profitable Atlantic trade economy. Congress's boycott had initially led to a glut in the tobacco market, driving prices up and giving the city's tobacco merchants control of the European market. It also helped that 1775 produced a bumper crop of tobacco, filling warehouses at Port Glasgow and Greenock on the eve of the boycott. Finally, concerns over the loss of debt receded in importance, given that the large tobacco companies operated at a size and scale that did not require immediate debt recovery.[14] Such factors contributed to a momentary boost in the city's economy, leaving one resident to remark in the spring of 1776 that "the demands for all our manufactures still continue brisker than when the American trade was open."[15]

This situation left Glasgow's ruling merchant class, and the many city inhabitants who depended on the Atlantic tobacco trade, in a precarious position. While they remained a loyal people, committed to the Union and vocal defenders of their Protestant Whig heritage, they understood that a prolonged war was bad for their pocketbooks. The city's merchant elite also did not want to anger Chesapeake planters on whom they counted for annual supplies of tobacco. In the fall of 1775, these merchants blocked attempts by the local magistrates to submit an address of loyalty to the king for fear that it would upset colonial planters and possibly ruin their lucrative trade with the colonies. Glasgow, in fact, was the only burgh in all of Scotland that did not send a customary address of loyalty to the king at this critical juncture in the conflict.[16]

Scottish tobacco factors living in the Chesapeake also tried to declare their neutrality in the conflict in hopes of preserving their home country's trade. Virginian planters recognized their efforts, with one writing that "no part of the *British* Nation have exerted themselves with greater warmth . . . than the Merchants of *Glasgow*, for a restoration of that happy union so ardently wished for by every true friend to *America* or *Great Britain*."[17] Glaswegians, both at home and abroad, were aware of the vital role American markets played in the success and prosperity of their local community. They did not want to jeopardize their economic interests in the colonies.

Three months later, however, in January 1776, "members of the Trades House of the City of Glasgow" agreed to a loyalty address to the king. It shared a great deal in common with the Loyalist declarations produced in and around New York City in the spring of 1775. The signers railed against the "unproved and unnatural rebellion" and proclaimed their willingness to "defend your Majestys persons and government" by helping return "the rebellious colonys to a due submission to the laws and government of Great Britain."[18]

While the Trades House did not represent the city's merchants, most of whom still remained quiet about the war, their address did reflect the influence of the British common cause in the city, which framed the rebellion as a threat to the order and stability of monarchical government. Additionally, Glaswegians were certain to benefit from the financial opportunities provided by wars fought in the outer reaches of the empire. Throughout the winter and spring of 1776 reports circulated that Glasgow merchants and tradesmen were securing military contracts to supply the British army and navy in the colonies. A writer in the *Scots Magazine* informed readers in February that a "government-agent contracted with some merchants of Glasgow and Greenock for upwards of 7000 tons of shipping, to carry troops to America, and for bedding, water-casks, butcher-meat, &c."[19] Though they were immersed in a political culture largely critical of the Patriot cause and supportive of the Crown, Glaswegians also understood that the wealth and prestige of their city depended on access to colonial markets, which had grown more precarious in the early years of the conflict.

During the first year of the war, Haligonians were embroiled in a local political dispute that did more than broader narratives to frame how residents understood the conflict. The unpopular governor, Francis Legge, refused to concede power to the merchant-dominated assembly and began to take aggressive steps to silence those residents who remained sympathetic to the American cause. The summer and fall months of 1775 were especially divisive, as war waged around Boston and Congress planned an invasion of Quebec. In June, the Halifax-dominated assembly sent an address to Parliament that affirmed their loyalty "at this dreadful and alarming crisis, when civil discord, and its melancholy consequences, are impending over all British America." Like Glasgow merchants, they recognized Parliament's sovereignty, a point few, if any, American Patriots were willing to concede. Yet they also worried that Legge's attempt to impose new taxes on the colonists and divide the assembly threatened to weaken their loyal attachment to the empire. In response, members of the assembly laid out a new plan of imperial-colonial relations that gave colonial assemblies a greater degree of control over taxation and limited the authority of royally appointed governors and their councils, which the assemblymen believed would "preserve the inhabitants of this Province in duty and allegiance to our King."[20]

Their address met with approval in London, though it was never formally adopted. But it angered Legge, who wrote to Dartmouth that it "contains some projection for the Alteration of Government upon the American System of Popularity."[21] Legge had reason to be concerned as rumors continued to circulate in the colony that American sympathizers were attempting to aid their southern neighbors. In July, he prohibited Nova Scotians from "exporting gunpowder, arms, and ammunition, or Salt Petre out of the colony," and from aiding or abetting any rebel colonist.[22] The situation was so dire by August that he ordered all the small arms and gunpowder in town to be moved to vessels in the harbor.[23] He also asked officials to open negotiations with local Indian peoples and the Acadians for their support "during the present Rebellion [in] America," a move made possible by the work of Father Bailly and the revival of the Festival of St. Aspinquid over the previous half decade.[24]

It is not surprising that some Haligonians found the Patriot narrative of the war appealing. Fears of popery running roughshod over Britain's Protestant colonies likely resonated with many of the city's residents who enjoyed close religious and cultural ties with their New England neighbors. This was true of Timothy Houghton, a New Englander by birth and veteran of the Seven Years' War. In August 1775, he objected to Legge's proclamation that every resident had to swear allegiance to the king because, according to Houghton, George III "had broke his Coronation Oath by establishing the Roman Catholic Religion at Quebec and that he could not in Conscience serve his Majesty." A friend and neighbor, William Harrison, claimed as well that Houghton had refused "to supply the King's troops then at Boston with any kind of relief or necessaries."[25] Another resident said that Houghton swore he could no longer serve as the town's magistrate, because "the King was a Papist," and his adviser, Lord Bute, was a "Stewart," a term commonly used to describe a Jacobite. To prove his point, Houghton referred to a law book that showed "that no Protestant was bound in Allegiance to the King any longer than he continued protestant."[26] Such accusations were not tolerated by officials in Halifax, however. Houghton was found guilty on charges of treason, ordered to pay a £50 fine and serve six months in jail, and stripped of his government position.[27]

Others in the city questioned the assembly's loyalty address to Parliament in June, which one resident argued was written by a "few ministerial hirelings," and represented the views of only "about one-thousandth" of the colony's inhabitants. The resident contended that the assembly's aim was to curry favor with the London government in its dispute with Governor Legge, but the assembly's address had actually led most Haligonians to declare "themselves Friends to the Cause in which the whole Continent of America are engaged." As evidence of this, when a ship arrived in September carrying "two Tons of Tea from Bristol," the town's "Liberty Boys . . . caused [it] to be committed to the water Element to make Tea for the Fish."[28]

It is difficult to say whether or not Haligonians participated in their own tea party. There are no reports of such an event in either Henry's gazette or Patriot newspapers, nor is it mentioned in any government correspondence. But things were certainly not calm in the city and colony in the fall of 1775. In September, Henry published Chief Justice Jonathan Belcher's charge to the colony's grand jury, in which Belcher denounced the rebellion and affirmed the colony's loyal attachment to the Crown. He reminded jury members and readers of Henry's gazette that the purpose of government is to protect "civil rights and interests, in security and preservation of the lives, liberties and properties of every member of consequence." However, "when this fabric is once demolished," as it had been in the thirteen colonies over the previous year, "all laws, all justice [and] common safety, will be [lost] in the ruins." He pressed jury members to seek out "every design & attempt to weaken . . . [or] to dissolve [government] authority & when detected present the bold defenders" for trial and punishment. He also reminded them "to give all heed for preserving inviolate the allegiance due to his sacred Majesty, our most gracious Sovereign King George the third, whose Royal Heart, inclinations, nature, Soul Virtues, & Religion, all combine to fix him truly the continual tender Father of his people."[29]

In response to Belcher's charge, "near four hundred" Haligonians (which definitely did not include Timothy Houghton), "excited by the deepest lamentation for the melancholy scenes of disallegiance and delusions in America," signed an association to defend their "rightful and most gracious Sovereign his Majesty King George the third." They also agreed, "at the peril of our lives and properties," to oppose all "traiterous and rebellious conspiracies & attempts whatsoever" to overthrow British rule in their colony.[30] Belcher's charge and the subsequent association oath gave voice in Halifax to a British common cause first narrated in the many similar proclamations published in New York City the previous spring. Both criticized the subversion of constituted authority in the colonies, celebrated a renewed defense of monarchy, and expressed a willingness to go to war against their former brethren.

But loyalty in the northern port city continued to be defined as much by the ongoing rebellion as it was by popular antipathy toward their governor. In the fall, Legge pushed through, then repealed, extremely unpopular militia and tax bills. Each placed an enormous strain on communities outside of Halifax and led some to petition for neutrality in the already unpopular conflict.[31] In December, Legge declared martial law after learning that Congress was considering an invasion of the Bay of Fundy on the north side of the colony, and in response to American privateers harassing local ships bound for mainland British and Caribbean markets.[32] His efforts to form a volunteer regiment in the fall to defend against such an invasion failed miserably, despite promises of substantial land grants to officers and generous pay to soldiers. One local remarked in a letter to Gage that "it is strange that Government should be so far imposed upon as to make them believe that" a regiment could be raised in a colony where there are only "2500 fit to bear arms and the two thirds of them Notorious Rebells in their hearts."[33]

In light of Legge's actions, "the Principle Gentlemen and Inhabitants" of the colony—many of whom had signed the Association months earlier—petitioned the king early in 1776 for their governor's removal. They argued on personal terms that he had insulted "the Old Officers of Government and others of respectable and worthy Character," while attaching himself to men "universally known to be obnoxious to the inhabitants." In the current political climate, the petitioners feared such actions might also portend larger, more dreadful consequences, claiming that "this your Majestys valuable province may be irrecoverably lost, unless Governor Legge be Speedily removed."[34] The petition revealed the tenuous state of loyalty in the northern port city in the early years of the war. Unpopular governors—though common in the years before the rebellion—could now represent the difference between peace and war, loyalty and rebellion.

Halifax and Nova Scotia remained on the brink of rebellion in the spring of 1776, even after William Howe arrived from Boston with roughly one thousand Loyalist refugees and many more soldiers in tow. One of these refugees, former Massachusetts governor Thomas Oliver, said they were "anxious to get away" from Halifax as soon as possible, because they were "so much exposed to an Incursion or Descent of the Rebels, who are not without their [support] among the Inhabitants."[35] In the late spring, north of Halifax, near Fort Cumberland, Jonathan Eddy solicited the support of Patriot leaders in Boston and the American Congress to invade the colony. While his rebellion ultimately failed—he was defeated the following November—the extent of support he received from rural Nova Scotians evidenced a dangerous divide in loyalties among the colony's inhabitants.[36]

In July, officials in London recalled Legge, but even that decision did little to allay fears of rebellion in the city and colony.[37] Later in the month, the new governor, Mariot Arbuthnot, stopped Anthony Henry from printing the Declaration of Independence, because of concern that "it may gain over to them (the Rebels) many converts, and inflame the minds of his Majesty's loyal and faithful subjects of the Province of *Nova Scotia*."[38] His executive council agreed, stating that "the Publication thereof being deem'd of most dangerous Consequences, and directly tending to inflame the minds of the Kings Subjects in this Province and to Seduce them from their duty and Allegiance by Asserting the most Malignant falsehoods, and misrepresentations." Arbuthnot responded with yet another proclamation, this time "forbidding all persons whatsoever to utter, publish or print . . . any such Traiterous and Treasonable papers" that would upset "the good Order and Peace of this Government."[39] In doing so, Arbuthnot and Nova Scotia officials acted the part of Patriot crowds and committees in the winter of 1774–75. They encouraged unity by threatening punishment to anyone who spoke out against their cause.

The fact remained, however, that in the first years of the war, Haligonians were divided over their loyalties. Wartime narratives—competing causes—mattered to some, who saw in the conflict either a popish king be-traying his (and the nation's) Protestant identity or a self-interested Congress employing a vast network of ruthless committees to deny opponents their most basic rights and liberties. Others turned to local disputes with an unpop-ular governor, or their continued economic dependence on Parliament and the rum trade, to define their loyalties and frame their understanding of the rebellion and war. In the end, Halifax, and the colony of Nova Scotia, remained a part of the British Empire, but these divisions highlighted a troubling aspect of British Loyalism at the start of the war. As in Kingston and Glasgow, popu-lar expressions of Britishness continued to defend basic Protestant Whig val-ues, but the absence of a common shared enemy left the inhabitants without cause to commit to the war.

The same was not true in New York City, where the start of the war neces-sarily drew more entrenched lines between neighbors and friends. Beginning in May, Isaac Sears and the Sons of Liberty began to patrol the city, took con-trol of the Customs House and port, attempted to capture the city's royal ar-tillery, and actively disarmed known Loyalists. By the fall, the Provincial Congress formalized such proceedings, ordering the arrest of known conspir-ators, and in the spring of 1776 required residents to take an oath of alle-giance to the Patriot cause.[40] Patriot leaders also continued to wage an effective print war that sought to create unity around a shared cause, while silencing their most vocal critic, James Rivington.

But Rivington and others not only stood up to such threats, they used them as evidence of the continued Patriot assault on long-cherished Protestant Brit-ish liberties. In late April, a crowd in nearby New Brunswick burned the unpopular Rivington in effigy, but he responded by printing a satirical image of his hanging. Alongside the image he included a fabricated report of the in-cident that framed Patriot crowds as driven by popish motives. "A number of Bacchanalians, at Brunswick," he declared, "flushed with the inebriating draught, not of the juice of the Vine, but of New-England Rum, have lately sacrificed him to the *Idol of Licentiousness*." He reminded readers that "he al-ways heard the LIBERTY OF THE PRESS represented as the great security of freedom," but his opponents aimed "to establish a most cruel tyranny" rather than live under "the GOOD OLD LAWS AND CONSTITUTION" of Great Britain.[41]

For a short time Rivington resisted these intimidating crowds, even after he was forced to seek refuge on a British naval ship stationed in the harbor. But in November, Sears and about eighty Connecticut Sons of Liberty marched into the city to the tune of "Yankee Doodle" and attacked and destroyed Riv-ington's print shop. Fearing for his life, the famed printer and his family escaped to London. He would not return for almost two years.[42] The loss of Rivington's press—the single most influential pro-British newspaper in the empire at the start of the war—devastated the British cause, which was now unable to counter the Patriot narrative of the rebellion. One loyal New Yorker recognized as much, reporting to a friend that "the Presses are now all shut up against publications in favour of Government Poor Rivingtons was the last . . . The Violence of the People is incredible and the leading men, have taken effectual means that nothing shall be said or wrote to open the Eyes of the Populace."[43]

Yet the influence of Rivington's press in shaping a nascent British common cause lingered on in the city, even after his forced departure. While as many as ten thousand New Yorkers escaped the city after the arrival of Washington's army in the spring and amid reports of a British invasion, others refused to concede to the repeated threats of rebel crowds and committees.[44] A butcher named George Birks, for instance, was imprisoned three times for his loyal sentiments before finally being banished in June 1776. In July, John Lewis, a milkman by trade, was jailed at city hall "for his Drinking healths to King George and Success to his Fleet and Manifesting his intention to Join the Said fleet or the Army of the Enemy, against the Continental Army." James Deas, a hairdresser and perfumer, suffered at the hands of a "Riotous & Tumultuous Mob . . . with[ou]t any other provocation than his persisting in his Loyalty and Attachm[t] to his Sovereign and the British Constitution."[45] All the while, local Patriots reveled in the violence, apparently embracing Seabury's definition of "American Freedom" as the need for residents to "fall down and worship our sovereign Lord the Mob."[46] After an especially violent week in which several loyal New Yorkers were "handeld verry Roughly," one rebel colonist happily boasted to a friend that "There is hardly a toory face to be seen this morning."[47]

Though outnumbered, some loyal New Yorkers continued to write in defense of the Crown and government. In March 1776, Charles Inglis, one of the few members of Rivington's Club still in the city, penned a response to Thomas Paine's enormously popular pamphlet, *Common Sense*, which had railed against monarchy, for "in every instance [it] is the popery of government."[48] Inglis's attack on Paine mirrored previous Loyalist claims that Patriot leaders sought to mislead colonists into war against Great Britain (the original title of Inglis's pamphlet was *The Deceiver Unmasked*). Even worse, Inglis contended that Paine's embrace of republicanism now threatened to throw society into chaos and anarchy. When New York Patriots learned that the printer, Samuel Loudon, intended to publish Inglis's response, members of the Committee of Mechanicks confronted Loudon, demanding to unmask the author. Others in their group went to his print shop and "nailed and sealed up the printed sheets in boxes." The following evening, a group of forty men forced their way into his shop and "took away the whole impression of said pamphlets, being about fifteen hundred," which they proceeded to burn on the Commons.[49] Loudon and Inglis, like Rivington, Seabury, and others before them, understood that narratives mattered as much as battles and that the American Patriots were more willing to silence their critics than to confront their arguments.

Despite these attacks on Loyalists, Patriots in New York City continued to depend on Protestant Whig language and symbolism to make their case for rebellion. When Jefferson and Congress called for independence in July—a decision motivated, in part, by Whig fears of a king who had turned against his own Britishness by arming slaves and Indians, and using Quebec as "a fit instrument for introducing the same absolute rule into these states"—New Yorkers tore down the equestrian statue of George III in an act of symbolic regicide that was repeated in communities throughout British North America.[50] Thereafter, the crowd reportedly melted the remains of their fallen king into 42,088 bullets, "to assimilate with the brain of our infatuated adversaries."[51] The numbers forty-two and eighty-eight harkened back to the years 1642 and 1688, when the pro-Catholic policies of previous British monarchs had also cost them the allegiance of their people. Just as important, though, these dates referred to moments when Englishmen overcame their popish oppressors in defense of their Protestant Whig beliefs. In other words, Patriots in New York marked their turn toward independence by, of all things, acting the part of loyal defenders of Protestant Whig liberty. They had not become American; their king had abandoned his Britishness.

Independence, however, did little to alter a British common cause constructed in the months before Lexington and Concord. Loyal Britons in New York City and across the empire continued to believe that colonists were misled into rebellion, and now independence, by a small cabal of Patriot leaders. But the colonists remained British subjects, capable of seeing through the dark designs of their leaders if only Loyalist writers could break through the silence. When Ambrose Serle learned of the Declaration of Independence from the deck of a British naval ship stationed in New York harbor, he wrote that it revealed "the Villainy & the Madness of these deluded People."[52] Similar language prevailed in Halifax, where, as we have seen, officials believed the publication of the Declaration would *inflame* people's minds and possibly *seduce* them into accepting independence. The same was true across the Atlantic, where editors of the *Scots Magazine* published the Declaration in their August 1776 issue, but concluded it with the Latin phrase: "*Quos Deus vult perdere, prius dementat*" (those whom a god wishes to destroy, he first drives mad).[53]

Formal critiques of the Declaration echoed such sentiments. John Lind's painstaking, 132-page assault on Jefferson's list of grievances was motivated, in part, "to induce this deluded people to listen to a voice of reason; to abandon a set of men who are making them *stilts* to their own private ambition."[54] Thomas Hutchinson agreed in his own shorter censure of the Declaration, writing that "many thousands of people who were before good and loyal subjects, have been deluded, and by degrees induced to rebel against the best of Princes, and the mildest of Governments."[55]

British efforts to regain their colonies—to awaken American rebels from their deluded slumber—began with the taking of New York City in late September 1776, which the British held to the end of the war. During these years, that city emerged as the center of British Loyalism in the colonies. But it was a shell of its former self. Retreating Patriots burned nearly a quarter of the city in September, and the thousands of often unruly British and Hessian soldiers competed with residents for housing, food, and basic necessities.[56] One returning resident "found it a most dirty, desolate and wretched Place," while a British general lamented that "the Houses were destitute of Inhabitants." At one point, Ambrose Serle wandered into Rivington's abandoned print shop "to look at some of his books," which had likely collected some dust since his forced departure nearly a year earlier. In the moment, Serle was left to ponder the famed printer's fate and the role of the press in the unfolding rebellion. He lamented how men had devoured "the inflammatory Publications of the Faction in England," some of which could still be found on Rivington's shelves, and then spread those ideas like a virus to their neighbors and friends. "Thus the Influenza affected almost the whole Country," Serle concluded, "and, through the Rage of the principal men, who at least should have acted with Calmness, there was no Possibility of circulating or administering an antidote."[57]

But for Loyalists living in and around New York City, and elsewhere in the empire for that matter, these misled colonists had accomplished the unthinkable. They had dramatically and emphatically killed their king. Of course, they had to for independence to be possible. Tearing down statues, destroying images and symbols of monarchy, worked to sever rebel colonists' political and culture ties to the empire. Crucially, however, the destruction of monarchy also strengthened the bonds of affection loyal Britons felt for their king, especially—indeed, almost exclusively—in places where he and his supporters suffered the most.

This was especially true in New York City, where residents embraced an even more determined defense of monarchy, despite many still believing their enemies could be redeemed. When soldiers processed through the streets after taking the city in September, "joy and gladness seemed to appear in all countenances, and persons who had been strangers . . . were now very sociable together, and friendly."[58] Returning Loyalists, who decorated their hats with red ribbons as show of support for the crown, paraded soldiers around the city while a group of women climbed to the top of Fort George, tore down the rebel standard, and proudly hoisted His Majesty's flag.[59] A month later, when the remaining British and Hessian soldiers disembarked from the ships in the harbor, crowds gathered along the water's edge "chearing their Military Brethren and other Spectators on Shore, and making the Hills resound with Trumpets, French Horns, Drums and Fifes, accompanied by the Harmony of their Voices."[60]

Thousands more responded by joining Loyalist regiments in the city (despite only tepid support from British officials), while others put their name to a slew of declarations, petitions, and oaths of loyalty published throughout the fall.[61] These included the two addressed to the Howe brothers signed by hundreds of New Yorkers, but also several others from communities outside of the city.[62] Their calls for loyalty mirrored those declarations penned in the early months of 1775, which proclaimed allegiance to the monarchy, defended constituted government, and decried the violence and destruction caused by rebellious Americans.

Historians suggest it was the French Revolution, not the American, that elevated George III in the minds of the British public.[63] But in the streets of New York City in 1776 and 1777, the embattled monarch experienced something of an apotheosis among the thousands of Loyalist refugees. Popular expressions of patriotism centered on an unremitting love of monarchy and a belief that George III was capable of saving oppressed colonists from the destruction caused by this unnatural civil war. Royal anniversary days, in particular, assumed enormous significance in the city's political calendar. During Accession Day celebrations in October 1776, nearly five hundred ships in the harbor hoisted the king's standard and fired a twenty-one-gun salute, "which echoed over the Water and Hills with a kind of pleasing Terror." One writer reported that "so noble an Appearance, and so grand a Salute, were never known in this Port before." Crowds of loyal New Yorkers also destroyed the liberty pole, "a monument of insult to the Government, and of licentiousness to the people." Liberty, to them, was expressed in their allegiance to the monarch and constituted government, not to *a Stick of Wood.*"[64]

In late January, residents gathered to celebrate Queen Charlotte's birthday, during which "a very fine Piece of Fire-work . . . was played off upon the Occasion; and a vast Concourse of People, considering the Place and its Circumstances, were assembled to see it. To most of them it seemed a most wonderful Phoenomenon."[65] New Yorkers crowded the streets again in June to celebrate George III's birthday, which, according to Hugh Gaine, "was kept in a different Manner from last Year, and every Face in Town seemed joyful."⁶⁶ At noon, more than four hundred ships in the harbor fired a feu de joie in honor of the day: "One could hear a continuous thunder and roar of the cannon, and there must have been over three or four thousand cannon shots."⁶⁷ During Coronation Day celebrations in September 1777, "many houses were illuminated" while the owners of the Loosley and Elms tavern produced a firework display unsurpassed in the city's history. The massive illumination, which depicted "the statue of his Majesty on horseback, crowned with laurels, standing on a pedestal, and several other figures, much surpassed any thing of the kind before exhibited."⁶⁸ Loyal New Yorkers had resurrected, if only for the night, the statue destroyed by rebel colonists a year earlier.

Just days after these festivities, the famed printer James Rivington returned to the city, igniting similar demonstrations of joy among loyal New Yorkers. Rivington received a hero's welcome, like that typically reserved for newly appointed governors or military officials. He processed through the city, while taverns and homes were illuminated "to testify the joy [of] *the true Sons of Freedom.*" Residents applauded his "unparalleled Fortitude" for having refused to publish "inflammatory Pieces, which might be productive of introducing Anarchy, instead of Constitutional Authority, into this once happy Country." For many, the popular printer embodied all the principles of the nation's most accomplished generals:

RIVINGTON is arriv'd—let ev'ry Man
This injur'd Person's Worth confess;
His loyal Heart abhor'd the Rebel's Plan,
And boldly dar'd them with his *Press.*⁶⁹

The first years of the war necessarily affected loyal New Yorkers in more profound ways than Britons living in Glasgow, Kingston, or even Halifax. Loyalist refugees suffered at the hands of Patriot crowds and associations, and arrived in New York City in the fall of 1776 having personally felt the consequences of rebellion and war. That they were more emphatic in their embrace of the king and government than subjects in the other three communities should come as little surprise. But loyal New Yorkers' continued reliance on a narrative of the conflict that only described their opponents as deluded or misled made it all but impossible for subjects elsewhere to empathize with the suffering of these refugees. Their enemies, despite having inflicted severe pain and suffering on many in the city, were just misguided subjects to others in the empire.

Wars, especially civil wars, are about making enemies out of friends. Pens, not swords, do this fighting, and rebel colonists won the decisive battles in the early stages of the war. They did so, in part, by denying Loyalists the ability to speak and write publicly. To protect their own liberty, Patriots denied it to others. At the same time, these Patriots built a narrative that relied on fear, recasting their political opponents as dangerous, threatening enemies. Their common cause turned loyal Britons into allies of perhaps the most feared inhabitants in all of British North America: French Catholics, "merciless Indian savages," and runaway slaves. Such a narrative captured the hearts and minds of many American colonists (and subjects elsewhere) at a crucial moment in the conflict. This understanding of the war shifted conversations away from questions of sovereignty, consent, and representation, and toward base emotions and sometimes irrational fears, both of which were critical to Patriot mobilization efforts.

Loyal Britons, however, struggled to strip rebellious Americans of their Britishness. Their counternarrative, a British common cause, was crafted in the days after the thunderclap that the First Continental Congress sounded all across the British Empire. Popular understandings of Loyalism celebrated a renewed defense of monarchy and legal government, and remained committed to basic Protestant Whig principles like free trade, political liberty, and religious freedom. But the promulgators of this cause also continued to argue that their opponents were nothing more than deceived subjects who were misled by a few self-interested colonists—mostly New Englanders—into war against their own nation. Loyal subjects thus failed to make rebellious Americans into dangerous enemies.

This failure presented real problems for loyal subjects across the North Atlantic. If American Patriots were just misguided Britons, then it stood to reason that the Patriot cause presented no real threat to popular understandings of Britishness. In part, this explains why so many loyal subjects were reluctant to support the war in the early years. They were not convinced that they faced an enemy worth fighting. Instead, many loyal Britons came to understand these years of the war from the point of view of particular local interests and occurrences. Kingstonians reluctantly but necessarily supported the Crown, because they came to believe that the American cause threatened their most cherished right as British subjects: the ability to own another person. Glaswegians remained committed to the Union and to Protestant Whig principles but waivered in their public support of the war for fear of disrupting the city's prosperous Atlantic economy. The war divided Haligonians, with some continuing to harbor pro-American sympathies, while others reaffirmed their attachment to the Crown. Only in New York City did there emerge a more entrenched defense of the British cause among the city's many loyal residents, though that too was mostly in consequence of the specific sufferings they had felt at the hands of their former friends and neighbors.

Things changed in the fall of 1777, when the American army achieved an unexpected victory at the Battle of Saratoga. For loyal Britons, the surrender of General Burgoyne's army was as surprising as it was embarrassing. But more important, it marked a crucial turning point in the war and in popular expressions of British Loyalism. The defeat awakened the British public to the realities of a civil war now more than two years old. Many had believed the conflict would be short-lived, that American colonists would come to their senses and recognize the value of membership in the British Empire. Not only was that belief a chimera, but months later, in the spring of 1778, Congress would reject Parliament's generous peace proposal while agreeing to a formal alliance with Britain's oldest enemy, France. The implications of the Franco-American alliance held enormous consequences for popular definitions of loyalty in the empire. The alliance also brought the war to the front doorsteps of Britons across the North Atlantic, including those living in New York City, Halifax, Kingston, and Glasgow.

CHAPTER 6

The British Lion Is Rouzed

The Franco-American Alliance and
a New British Common Cause

In the fall of 1780, Benedict Arnold conspired to hand over to the British the American arsenal at West Point. The famed American general had participated in the Patriot siege of Boston in the summer of 1775, later helped to capture the British fort at Ticonderoga, and played a crucial role in the American victory at Saratoga. Though not without his detractors, Arnold was a popular and successful American general who had, to that point, figured largely in many of the most important events of the war.[1]

But he had grown increasingly disillusioned with the Patriot cause by late 1778, both because of the failures of Congress and the army and because he believed he had not been properly recognized for his service. In the summer of 1779, while in Philadelphia, Arnold began spying for the British, sending encoded messages to Major John André in New York City. In August of the following year Arnold was appointed commander of the garrison at West Point and began to make plans to hand it over to the British. The fort, located north of New York City on the Hudson River, was the largest American arsenal and the Patriots' best defense against a British invasion of New England. The loss of West Point would have been a major blow to the Patriot cause, which had already suffered an embarrassing defeat at Charleston in May.

Unfortunately for Arnold, his plans were discovered when André was captured on the morning of September 23 just outside of Tarrytown, New York, carrying maps of the fort bearing the general's signature. André mistook three

rebel colonists for Loyalists, a decision emblematic of the difficulties of iden-
tifying loyalties in the midst of a civil war.[2] He was hanged for his crimes two
weeks later, but Washington failed to capture Arnold, who had escaped to New
York City. Patriot leaders nonetheless quickly set about erasing the public's
memory of one of their most successful generals, a process made necessary
by a war so dependent on establishing competing narratives and causes.[3] From
the fall of 1780, Benedict Arnold became the *Founding Traitor* of the American Revolution.

His defection also revealed the dangerous nature of political loyalties during a civil war, when even a successful military leader was capable of abandoning a cause in favor of the enemy. Once in New York City, Arnold took to
the press to defend his actions and to encourage rebel colonists to follow in
his footsteps. In early October, with the help of William Smith, he penned two
addresses, the first titled, "To the Inhabitants of America," and the second, a
recruitment advertisement, directed at "the officers and soldiers of the continental army." Both were published in Rivington's print shop, before spreading into Patriot-controlled territory and forcing Patriot writers to respond.[4]
The addresses also boarded ships bound for towns and cities throughout the
Atlantic, appearing in British newspapers from Jamaica to Nova Scotia and
across the ocean in Great Britain.[5]

Arnold's first address reads like a captivity letter. He sought to absolve himself of the crime of having ever abandoned his Britishness and hoped that his
story would awaken others to the duplicitous and deceitful nature of the Patriot cause. He claimed to have always seen the war in defensive terms, fought
only to redress colonial grievances in hopes of reuniting with Great Britain,
but that things had changed in the summer of 1778. In February of that year,
Lord North appointed a peace commission, led by the Earl of Carlisle, to negotiate directly with Congress for an end to hostilities. They arrived in the colonies in June with orders that satisfied virtually every colonial grievance over
the past decade, save independence.[6] Yet not only did Congress reject these
offerings outright, they also agreed to a formal alliance with Catholic France.

Arnold "lamented . . . the impolicy, tyranny, and injustice" of Congress for
having signed on to a treaty with Britain's eternal enemy, a move unimaginable at the outbreak of the war. He worried his countrymen had "been duped,
by a virtuous credulity, in the incautious moments of intemperate passion, to
give up their felicity to serve a nation [France] wanting both the will and the
power to protect us, and aiming at the destruction both of the mother country and the provinces." The alliance had convinced him (and hopefully others)
to return to the British rather "than to trust a [French] monarchy too feeble
to establish your independency, so perilous to her distant dominions; the enemy

of the Protestant faith and fraudulently avowing an affection for the liberties of mankind, while she holds her native sons in vassalage and chains."[7]

A week later, Arnold returned to this narrative of French Catholic tyranny in a recruitment advertisement for his newly formed Loyalist regiment. He believed the threat of popery offered the greatest possibility for luring colonists away from the Patriot cause. He implored Continental officers and soldiers, "who are determined to be no longer the tools and dupes of Congress, or of France . . . to share in the glory of rescuing our native country from the grasping hand of France." He also warned readers that he had witnessed a Catholic funeral procession in Philadelphia in May where he "saw your mean and profligate Congress at Mass for the soul of a Roman Catholic in Purgatory, and participating in the rites of a Church, against whose anti-christian corruptions your pious ancestors would have witnessed with their blood."[8] If Congress were lost to the French, he argued, so too was their once righteous cause.

Both of Arnold's addresses—his argument for defecting to the British and the reasons why others should join him—enjoyed such wide circulation across the British Atlantic precisely because they relied on a new narrative of the war dependent on older, popular understandings of Britishness. As news of Congress's alliance with France circled the Atlantic in the summer of 1778, Britons rallied around a renewed and more resolute defense of Protestant Whig Loyalism that helped to blur local and regional divisions by recasting their foes as political and religious enemies. They were shocked by the hypocrisy of a rebellion whose leaders had claimed a greater appreciation for personal liberty but were now allied with an oppressive and arbitrary Catholic nation. If, from the spring of 1775, runaway slaves and Indian warriors gave meaning and importance to a shared American common cause, then the image of Congress and rebellious colonists celebrating a union with Catholic France served similar purposes for a new, shared British common cause.

The alliance had also extended the geographic reach of the war, drawing Britons from all corners of the North Atlantic into the conflict. From the summer of 1778, residents of these four communities faced repeated threats of invasions and were required to commit a greater number of men and resources to the widening war. In consequence, the loyal British Atlantic experienced a sort of *rage militaire* that rivaled the arming of rebellious colonists three years earlier. It also encouraged Britons, for the first time, to think of their American counterparts as no longer British.

While the first years of the conflict were marked by division, apathy, and confusion among loyal subjects throughout the empire, the same cannot be said of the war after 1778. The Franco-American alliance consolidated popular definitions of Loyalism. Britons everywhere committed in greater numbers to a more robust defense of this new British common cause that depended on age-old fears of popery. For the first time, Britons in these four communities were able to see through a Patriot cause purportedly founded on a greater understanding of liberty. Arnold's case for defection was part of this broader recasting of the revolution and war as a defense of Britain's Protestant Whig supremacy, which was able to overcome, to some degree, the many local and regional divisions that had defined the early years of the conflict.

Burgoyne's humiliating defeat at Saratoga in November 1777 forced British subjects to confront the realities of a protracted war that few had aggressively supported to that point. Some, especially Opposition writers in London, believed the conflict could not be won and began to call for an end to hostilities. This defeatist attitude was, in part, the result of a misguided belief that the war would be short, that the Americans were no match for the British army and navy. But it also evidenced the failure of the British cause to effectively rally the public, to create a convincing narrative of the war that made rebellious colonists worth fighting. Now, in the wake of an embarrassing defeat, some hoped for an end to a war against a people most loyal subjects believed were just misled but nevertheless still British.[9]

Yet Burgoyne's surrender also spurred some Britons to action. Rather than acquiesce to defeat or succumb to political infighting, many subjects rallied to the flag. They believed instead that success in the field depended on a spirited, vigorous commitment to the war effort. In communities like Glasgow and New York City, and even in Kingston to some degree, a new narrative of the war began to emerge in the winter of 1777–78. This cause celebrated the courage, virtue, and sacrifice of British subjects, traits many believed had been absent in the early years of the war. "A proper spirit is now excited through the nation," reported one Londoner in a March issue of Rivington's newspaper. "The British Lion is rouzed [sic] in good earnest," and there is no doubt, "but the standards of Rebellion will shrink before him."[10]

This newfound martial spirit expressed itself most forcefully in the enlistment drives across England and Scotland early in 1778. Newspapers across the Atlantic reported on local efforts to enlist soldiers in cities like Manchester, Liverpool, Glasgow, and Edinburgh, as communities vied with one another in public displays of loyalty.[11] These reports were often accompanied by statements of loyalty, or more formal declarations, which mirrored the addresses made by loyal Britons in communities in and around New York City early in 1775. By the end of the year, as many as fifteen thousand Britons had enlisted while many more volunteered to defend their own communities against increased threats of invasion.[12]

The great militia encampments at Coxheath and Warley Common in southern England, covered extensively in London newspapers and the subject of repeated visits by the king and other nobility, are often held out as the most visible symbol of this newfound military spirit.[13] Yet Scottish recruitment efforts were possibly more impressive, especially among Glaswegians who were initially reluctant to support the war effort. In January 1778, government officials, leaders of various trades, and "other loyal Inhabitants of the City of Glasgow" sent an address to the king (for the first time in the war) declaring their "Attachment to constitutional Liberty and the Rights of Mankind," which were "still trampled upon by your rebellious Subjects in America." They promised to "raise a Regiment of Men . . . as a small proof of our Loyalty and attachment to your Majesty's Government" and "pray[ed] God that He will be pleased to put a speedy End to the Delusion of the Rebels, who, under the sacred Name of Liberty, are exercising every Act of Tyranny."[14]

Over the following several weeks, with rumors in the local press that "a war with France was . . . unavoidable," Glaswegians of all rank contributed an enormous sum of money—more than £9,000—to the formation of several local regiments.[15] Numerous reports, which appeared in newspapers on both sides of the Atlantic, made note of the contributions of the city's many trade incorporations, but they also highlighted the offerings of regular Glaswegians. The Hammermen, for instance, gave £200, but persons within that trade contributed another £355. The Incorporation of Maltmen gave £300, while individuals gave another £320. The list of contributors included Cordners, Taylors, Weavers, Bakers, Skinners, Coopers, and Barbers, and many others.[16] "It is with the greatest pleasure," one writer proclaimed, that "we inform the public of that generous spirit of loyalty which the Trades of Glasgow have shewn in this measure of national utility."[17] Such actions and attitudes differed significantly from a community who at the start of war refused to even send a declaration of loyalty to their king.

When military officials arrived in Glasgow at the end of January to fill the newly formed regiments with recruits, residents turned out in number to celebrate the occasion. And to enlist. "This city, ever remarkable for their steady attachment to his Majesty's person and government," reported one resident, "never displayed their loyalty more than they have this day." Town leaders processed through the city streets amid the sounds of drums and music, flags waving, and the loud "acclamations of a delighted people." At nightfall, bonfires lined the streets, "the bells [were] set aringing, and the windows grandly illuminated." A second procession began shortly thereafter, guided by "torch light with a fuller band of music, heightened by the universal acclamations of the people," during which recruits "flocked to the Loyal Standard. . . . In short," the writer concluded, "such a spirit of loyalty never appeared here; a stranger would imagine the whole inhabitants were going to engage themselves TO GO TO America."[18]

Burgoyne's defeat and a rumored war with France could have led to any number of new narratives in the Scottish press. The war had been unpopular from the start, and news of an embarrassing defeat, combined with a massively expanded and costly war, might have produced even greater calls for an end to the conflict. Glasgow's political and merchant elite might also have decided to remain quiet in hopes of not offending either side as they prayed for a return to a robust Atlantic trade. Instead, Scots rallied to the British flag, and in Glasgow, especially, residents embraced a martial spirit of patriotism—a willingness to risk their lives and fortunes in defense of the Crown and government—perhaps unparalleled in the more than seventy years since the Union. Later postwar histories of the city, in fact, tended to ignore the city's tepid response to the outbreak of the rebellion, instead focusing on these early months of 1778 to illustrate the loyalty of Glaswegians during the American Revolution.[19]

This *rage militaire* was contagious, spreading across the Atlantic to places like New York City and Kingston in the spring of 1778. In March, Rivington published reports of enlistment drives from across the British Isles and included the widely reprinted table listing the many contributions of the various trades in Glasgow. Burgoyne's surrender at Saratoga, according to one report from London, "has rouzed the rest of the Ministry, and the sleeping spirit of the nation in general, to make such an increase in the royal forces, as to finish the war with success in the ensuing campaign."[20] Another Londoner applauded the efforts of Britons who subscribed to these newly formed regiments. "For when once the nation is roused," he warned supporters of the American cause, "they may depend upon it, that the point will not be easily given up."[21] Such reports were reassuring to loyal New Yorkers, many of whom had suffered a great deal and had the most to lose in the conflict.

However, the many readers of Rivington's gazette were also confronted with a popular narrative of the war that blamed them for the lack of military ardor. British military failures—most notably Burgoyne's recent defeat north of the city—were the result of a colonial public loath to sacrifice their lives in defense of their nation.[22] "A Loyal Refugee," worried that after the start of the war "our resentment was lulled asleep," but hoped now that the spirit diffusing across Great Britain would find its way into the hearts of loyal New Yorkers and "awake and rouse us up, out of our lethargy, and excite us to embody ourselves forth . . . [and] break the neck of an obstinate rebellion."[23]

New Yorkers responded to these calls in the spring of 1778. Local newspapers were littered with enlistment advertisements targeting Loyalist refugees in the city, while some sought to persuade disaffected Patriots outside the lines.[24] Other advertisements were directed at the significant population of Scottish and Irish immigrants, which spoke to the capacity of the war to bridge old divides and draw subjects into a wider conception of loyalty and British-ness.[25] Nothing like the enlistment drives in Scotland occurred in New York City, but when Oliver De Lancey was ordered to raise three battalions of five hundred men to defend the city, "inhabitants of every town upon the island" contributed funds.[26] In February, General Tryon reviewed one of the newly formed regiments, during which the new recruits testified their loyalty to Brit-ain through "loud acclamations of joy, and other demonstrations." "What a pleasing sensation must this afford to every true friend of his King and coun-try," the writer concluded, "and at the same time animate others to imitate their laudable example."[27]

Kingstonians also rallied to the British standard in the early months of 1778, especially as rumors circulated of an impending war with France. Since the start of the rebellion, the island's residents had suffered from raids con-ducted by American privateers, who were acting on the orders of Congress to sell captured cargoes to the French at Martinique in exchange for weapons and gunpowder.[28] The numbers were staggering. Speaking before his peers in February 1778, the Duke of Richmond reported that 733 British ships were either taken or destroyed by American privateers since the commencement of hostilities, and about one-third of those traded with "the Island of Jamaica." He further estimated that the average value of the cargo on Jamaica-bound ships was "8,000 l. on her outward, and 10,000 l. on her homeward Voyage," putting merchant and planter losses in the hundreds of thousand pounds sterling.[29]

Jamaicans regularly complained of the disastrous consequences of these raids on their trade and were especially angered by the willingness of French officials to support rebel privateers. One resident described Martinique as "a nest of the greatest thieves that ever existed, and the governor and officers are at the head of the gang."[30] Jamaica's new governor, John Dalling, wrote to the French governor of Martinique, Comte D'Argout, to complain of the "Cloak [he] so kindly lent to that of our Rebels." He resented that Jamaica's largely unprotected coasts were "infested by such piratical Interlopers . . . manned, not with our European Subjects, not with those Rebels who were our Subjects, but totally with French Men, French Negroes and French Mulattoes; not fitted out in rebel Ports, but in French ones, not by American Rebels, but by French Mer-chants."[31] When the British captured the American privateer *Guest* in late 1777 they found that the ship was commissioned by Congress, but fitted out at Cape Francois, and "that her men were almost all French."[32] By March, reports were circulating in Britain that should there be a war with France, "Jamaica is their first object, they having had a long time an eye on that island."[33]

The immediate threat of American privateers, aided by French officials, played a greater role in spurring Jamaicans to action than news of Burgoyne's defeat. Early in 1778, the island's assembly, which just three years earlier petitioned the king in support of colonial grievances, now requested that he send more troops. The assembly complained of "the defenceless state of the commerce and sea coast of that island, which for some time past has been exposed to the insults of the American privateers," leaving "many parts of the island . . . much distressed, and the coasts exposed to continual alarm."[34] Jamaicans also began to muster militia units and enlist the island's inhabitants, including free blacks and mulattoes, into ranger units to patrol the coastlines.[35] "We are very apprehensive of a visit from the French," worried one resident, "and orders have . . . been issued by the Governor, to the Colonels in the different regiments of Militia to have every thing in readiness for an immediate call, in case of necessity."[36]

But some Kingstonians continued to harbor Patriot sympathies. They actively engaged in aiding enemy privateers even as others began to arm themselves in defense of the island.[37] Such actions, which apparently were tolerated in previous years, now became untenable as the war increasingly expanded into the British Caribbean. In March, "PLAIN TRUTH" took to the *Jamaica Gazette* to condemn the "small number of miscreants among us, who . . . hold communication with these hostile pillagers, and share with them the spoils of our planters and merchants, as a reward for the treacherous intelligence and assistance they give." The writer compared the practices of these men to that of the "New-England traitors" in the last war, who "sold to the common enemy, arms and ammunition, to shed the blood of those very men who were exposing their lives to save them from destruction."

The writer also disparaged the Patriot cause with language that drew from elements of the British common cause circulating around the North Atlantic. He argued that the rebellious Americans acted on "diabolical ambition," which had led to a level of "oppression, treachery and murder" previously unknown in the empire. He favored the martial spirt of loyal Britons to that of the Americans, who in repeated battles had displayed only "the ignominious marks of cowardice." He described their recent victory at Saratoga as an aberration that had actually awakened the British public. Britons, he declared, were now "roused to vengeance by the stings of ingratitude and unmerited reproach" of their enemy.[38] This call to arms mirrored similar efforts from across the British Atlantic, which depended on a new narrative of the conflict that demanded a renewed commitment to Britain's martial spirit.

Kingstonians apparently listened. Two days after the publication of the essay, residents gathered at the courthouse to draft an address to the king "offering their lives and fortunes in support of his crown and dignity, against the daring rebellion in North America." They also agreed to meet again the following Monday, "when it is thought a handsome subscription will be made, to raise money for his majesty's service. This true spirit of loyalty, I hope, will extend over all the island."[39] The following month, Rear Admiral Sir Peter Parker reported back to London "that the greatest harmony subsists among all degrees of People." Kingstonians were committed to preventing "Supplies or Intelligence from being sent to the Rebels, which I am told at the beginning of these disturbances . . . was carried on by a few Ill disposed Americans settled in this island."[40]

Haligonians failed to embrace this military zeal permeating communities throughout the British Atlantic. From the beginning of the crisis nearly fifteen years earlier, the majority New England émigré population vocally supported resistance to British policies and made life difficult for the ruling elite. Fears surrounding possible hostile Indian and Acadian populations also left officials on edge, while marauding Patriot privateers harassed the Nova Scotian coast and threatened Britain's hold on the valuable North Atlantic fishing industry.[41] The city and colony also lacked military protection. In December 1777, Governor Arbuthnot suggested there were no more than six hundred regulars in the colony, noting that the two militia units were "very young and very incomplete and I presume not be reckoned upon."[42]

Officials were now worried that "Burgoynes' misfortune has raised the spirit of the disaffected" and left the city and colony yet again on the brink of rebellion.[43] In March, nearly two dozen former inhabitants of Nova Scotia petitioned the Massachusetts state assembly to join with Congress and invade their former colony. They argued that at the start of the war only a "Tyrannical Government in Halifax" kept the colonists from rebelling, and now, in the spring of 1778, a majority remained "Friends to the Liberty of America."[44] Patriot newspapers reported on this petition, saying that "there will be a revolt in that Colony, all ranks of people seeming inclined in favour of the Americans except a few who hold places under the government."[45]

But local Halifax officials also understood the crucial role newspapers and narratives played in shaping popular attitudes toward the conflict, and none was more important than *Rivington's Gazette* in New York City. Beginning in early 1778, they made efforts to expand the influence of his newspaper in the region. Captain Alexander MacDonald of the Royal Highland Emigrants wrote to a friend in New York City that he would "be glad to have [Rivington's] paper by every Opportunity & will Endeavor to get more Customers from this place."[46] It is not clear what role he ultimately played in the endeavor, but by as early as 1780, and likely sooner, Haligonians could purchase subscriptions to Rivington's newspaper out of Anthony Henry's printing office.[47]

It was especially important in the spring of 1778 for officials to spread the British cause among Haligonians. The defeat and the rumor of war with France once again raised the specter of a French and Indian attack on the colony, which would now likely enjoy the support of Patriot sympathizers and even the American Congress. Arbuthnot reported that the city suffered daily from privateer raids, and "in case of a war with France there is every reason to apprehend mischief from the Indians and French Acadians."[48] In response, officials moved quickly in the spring to secure Mi'kmaq and Acadian loyalty. In April, Arbuthnot requested the appointment of another Catholic missionary, but this time he faced competition from Congress, who also coveted the support of Indian and Acadian populations in the region.

Arbuthnot's hopes for peace in the region rested on the shoulders of Joseph-Mathurin Bourg.[49] An Acadian by birth, Bourg had been exiled from Nova Scotia in 1755, lived for a short period in Virginia and then England, before settling back in France where he received his religious training. He was sent to Quebec in 1772, and a year later Bishop Briand appointed him to serve the few remaining Acadians throughout the region. He returned to Quebec in 1774 and was named vicar general for Acadia. He made sporadic trips to the region over the following years, but now, in the spring of 1778, officials in Halifax pleaded for his full-time residence in the region. Ironically, their hopes for peace rested on the shoulders of a Catholic priest their predecessors had exiled from the colony three decades earlier.[50]

Meanwhile, Michael Francklin, former governor and now superintendent of Indian affairs in the province, tried to negotiate alliances with the Mi'kmaq and Maliseet tribes along the St. John River (part of which involved the appointment of Bourg). But Francklin struggled in the face of similar efforts made by a Patriot emissary and former Nova Scotian, John Allan.[51] In early June, while officials were busy fortifying the harbor in case of a French attack, Francklin reported that he was struggling to obtain money and presents for the Indians, who were instead turning to Allan for gifts. If this were to continue, he feared "that [Mi'kmaq and Maliseet tribes] are going to break [the] alliance, and, if so, they may ruin the interior parts of the Province, reducing the capital to great distress."[52]

Negotiations continued over the summer months as Bourg arrived in the region and Francklin finally acquired the necessary gifts from the government. Their efforts paid off. In August, the new lieutenant governor, Sir Richard Hughes, secured a £100 salary for Bourg, the same received by Bailly a decade earlier. Haligonians did not complain this time, nor did American Patriots argue that a salaried missionary was evidence of the popish cruelties of their former government. Both had new enemies to deal with in 1778, and new friends to make.

In October, Henry was pleased to report that "the Indians of the district of St. John's, Pasmaquodie, and the several Tribes of all the Mickmack Indians" had agreed to "a treaty of Peace" with the British.[53] The timing could not have been better, for Hughes discovered that several of the tribe's Chiefs "had actually sent a declaration of war to Studholm [the British commander of Fort Howe on the St. John River]," but now they had "returned into the hands of Francklin the presents they had received from Washington to engage them to break their fidelity to the King."[54]

Haligonians' reluctance to take up arms in the spring of 1778, according to one scholar, demonstrated the city and colony's desire to remain neutral amid this "fratricidal strife."[55] But reports in local newspapers, and the letters of city officials, suggest that many Haligonians still favored the Patriot cause. Burgoyne's defeat and the initial rumors of a war with France, in fact, appear to have done little to alter popular attitudes toward the rebellion and might have actually encourage other non-Britons in the colony to join in the revolt. Fearful of a population that would welcome an American invasion, the government and military instead moved quickly to secure the loyalties of Indians and Acadians, and encourage the spread of pro-British publications. The British were having to fight a two-front war in Nova Scotia, against their nation's longstanding enemies and their own colonists.

The humiliating rout at Saratoga and the possibility of a French war awakened the greater British public to the realities of an entrenched and expanded conflict. This new war roused a majority to action, leading to a *rage militaire* that resonated across most of the British Atlantic. Competing political and economic interests, which previously divided Britons in these four communities, gave way to a martial spirit of loyalty that demanded action over complacency. In the span of just a few months in early 1778, subjects rallied to the British flag, inspired by this renewed commitment to the empire in the face of an ongoing civil war. But not all Britons felt this surge of martial patriotism. In distant port cities like Halifax, the loyalty of residents continued to rest precariously on local conditions and previous attachments. Elsewhere in the Atlantic, this burst of patriotism threatened to peter out in the absence of a new narrative of the war capable of making the Americans into enemies worth fighting.

For more than a decade, the crisis and rebellion had torn apart Britain's Atlantic empire. The American Patriot cause had turned a common language of

Protestant British Loyalism against the nation and its remaining loyal subjects. Loyal Britons struggled to make sense of who or why they were fighting, and their government appeared incapable of quickly squashing what many perceived to be an unnatural rebellion. "It is not our natural enemy, it is not French or Spaniards, nor rebel Scots, that we are contending with," proclaimed one of these many confused subjects early in 1776, "it is our friends, our brethren, with whom we have this unhappy and unnatural contest."[56] The crushing loss at Saratoga might have roused the public to action in some parts of the empire, but this collective embarrassment could hardly sustain a long-term war effort against an enemy many still believed to be British.

The Franco-American alliance provided answers to these troubling questions of identity and national belonging. It offered an opportunity for Britons to construct a new narrative of the conflict that was capable of bringing together an empire driven apart by a civil war. The alliance afforded subjects from across the Atlantic the chance to reclaim their Britishness from their opponents. The British common cause, which had suffered previously from an inability to make friends into enemies, could now turn toward a shared language of Loyalism that painted a far clearer image of who and why they were fighting. This was true of Benedict Arnold's defection in the fall of 1780, but there were many more Britons like him who finally grasped the meaning of the American war and their loyalty to Great Britain.[57]

In many ways, the Franco-American alliance actually confirmed what many loyal Britons had been saying since the start of the war: that it was an unnatural rebellion. Congress had first duped colonists into supporting a war out of self-interest and now had gone so far as to solicit the support of a Catholic nation at the cost of colonists' political and religious liberties. From the summer of 1778, loyal Britons regularly described this new friendship as an "unnatural alliance"—a phrase repeated over and over again in the British Atlantic press—formed not out of a shared set of beliefs and interests, but by a group of men willing to sell the colonies into abject poverty and arbitrary rule for their own material gain. Everywhere in the empire, reports, editorials, poems, songs, and even popular prints flooded local markets, recasting the war and rebellion in classic Whig terms as struggle between Protestant British liberty and Catholic French tyranny. "I blush, that the soil from whence I sprung," lamented one writer, "should have given birth to such unnatural feuds; and that the sons of America, should hold out the hand of friendship to ambitious France, while they are plunging their swords into their parent's breast."[58]

Loyal Britons were especially struck by the hypocrisy of a rebellion premised on an absolute defense of Protestant Whig liberty but now leagued with the Catholic French monarchy. Reports and editorials published on both sides of the

Atlantic linked the alliance with the Quebec Act, questioning how Congress could make friends with a nation whose people and faith were used just four years earlier to justify rebellion. "The time was when the bare *toleration* of the Roman Catholic religion in Canada," complained one writer, "was treated as a wicked attempt to *establish* 'a *sanguinary* faith, which had for ages filled the world with blood and slaughter!'" Now in the summer of 1778, "Congress are very willing to make us the instruments of weakening the best friends, and of strengthening the most powerful and ambitious enemies of the reformation . . . towards the universal re-establishment of Popery thro' all Christendom."[59]

When Congress published a manifesto in October defending their decision to ignore British peace offerings, a writer in Halifax responded by rewriting the proclamation, which they had "translated into TRUTH." Congress, the writer recalled, had previously described Catholicism "as impious cruel and bloody, in order to raise false terrors among our fellow citizens, at the very time [Congress] were courting the [French Canadians], to join [them] in rebellion, and to slaughter of those who are of the same religion [they] profess."[60]

It was not just that Congressmen were hypocrites, loyal Britons feared; it was that Congress's actions suggested they might actually be surrendering the colonies to the French. This was not an alliance, it was a French invasion, welcomed by the very men supposedly leading the fight for liberty. Glaswegians read late in 1778 that "the rebel soldiery say publicly, that . . . [Washington] and the Congress aim at absolute power, and mean to sell their country to the French."[61] "BRITANNICUS" warned readers that King Louis XVI had no intention "to establish you in that liberty, which he denies to his own subjects . . . he has made a better bargain for himself. Some part of America is undoubtedly to be his reward, and he will trust to accident and management to make himself master of the rest."[62] In Halifax, a writer cautioned that after "the Arrival of these Despotic Auxiliaries" their objective "will be to make a partition of the Provinces, the French the Northern, and the spaniard the Southern," and they "will take special care that Rebellion shall never again rear her head on this side of the Atlantic."[63] So pervasive was this rhetoric that a Spanish prisoner in Kingston found that most of the city's inhabitants were "anti-American," because they were convinced that if the Americans won the war Britain's former colonies in North America would "forever be subject to the influence of France."[64]

Loyal Britons came to believe that the deceptive nature of the Catholic faith, with its use of elaborate symbols and rituals, played a role in their securing the unnatural alliance with the Americans. In one widely exchanged story, Silas Deane, one of the American diplomats credited with having negotiated the alliance, allegedly handed over the city of Philadelphia to the French ambassador in a ceremony brimming with Catholic ritual and superstition: "Immediately on their setting foot [in the city], Mr. Deane cutting a piece of turf, formally delivered it to Monsieur Gerard, who received it with great solemnity, *applied it to his lips, and then crossed himself with much apparent devotion.*"[65] Something similar was said to have occurred when the French admiral Count d'Estaing arrived in Connecticut in July. In a report published in both New York City and Glasgow, he was alleged to have "solemnly took possession of it in the *name of the King his master,* and buried a stone to perpetuate his taking possession of it in form. This fact," the writer concluded, "together with the ceremony of the turf and twig, performed by the Count and M. Silas Dean, fully proves the designs of the court of France respecting America."[66]

Even members of Congress fell to the trappings of Catholicism. In one widely shared report—which appeared first in Rivington's newspaper, was reprinted in communities across the empire (including Halifax, Kingston, and Glasgow), and was later recounted in Benedict Arnold's recruitment advertisement—Patriot leaders knowingly participated in the rituals and practices of the once despised faith. According to Rivington, during a funeral ceremony in Philadelphia for a recently deceased Spanish diplomat, the officiating priest offered "the Holy Water to Mons. Lucerne [the French Ambassador], who, after sprinkling himself, presented it to Mr. Huntington, President in Congress." Samuel Huntington, a strict New England Calvinist, momentarily panicked, "but at length his affection for the great and good ally conquered all scruples of conscience, and he too besprinkled and sanctified himself with all the adroitness of a veteran Catholic." "Without hesitation," the rest of the willing congressmen "followed the righteous example of their proselyted President," while the crowded chapel grieved the loss of the Spaniard.

But before those attending the ceremony departed, "curiosity induced some persons to uncover the bier, when they were highly enraged at finding the whole a sham." They had been tricked by Luzerne, "there being no corpse under the cloth, the body of the Spanish gentleman having been several days before interred at Morris-Town. The bier was surrounded with wax-candles, and every member of this egregious Congress, now reconciled to the Popish communion, carried a taper in his hand."[67]

This episode, though likely the work of Rivington's pen, was remarkably similar to John Holt's narrative of Guy Carleton's arrival in Montreal in the fall of 1774, when he was said to have been "kissed by the Bishop" before delivering the colony over to French Catholics. In both instances, making friends with France, even if accidentally, portended future Catholic French aggression against Protestant Britons. It also enabled subjects to imagine their former friends as no longer British. In 1775, Patriots had painted George III and his supporters as papists in disguise; in 1778, loyal Britons made members of the American Congress into enemy Catholics.

Popular British prints from 1778 through the remainder of the war echoed this new narrative of the conflict. Previously, Frenchmen and Spaniards were often depicted in the background, plotting for the right moment to steal away Britain's valuable American colonies.[68] But these new prints positioned Britain's longtime enemies at the center of the conflict, as the greatest threat to Britain's Atlantic empire. In *The Family Compact*, the devil wears a papal crown while embracing a Spaniard and a Frenchman, who together stand as conquerors atop a map depicting several of Britain's American colonies (fig. 6.1). In other prints, the Americans (almost always represented as an Indian) recede in importance, often cowering behind their new allies. In *John Bull Triumphant*, the British bull, though restrained by a Highland Jacobite (old prejudices die hard), bucks a Spaniard before taking aim at a terrified Frenchman with the American hiding in his shadow (fig. 6.2). For many Britons, the rebellion was

FIGURE 6.1. *The Family Compact* (1779). Loyal Britons were convinced that France and Spain had no real interest in supporting American independence, but rather hoped that British defeat would allow their nations to conquer North America. *Courtesy of the John Carter Brown Library.*

FIGURE 6.2. *John Bull Triumphant* (1780). After 1778, Britons came to believe that the American war was really a European war, fought between Britain and their longtime Catholic enemies, France and Spain. The Americans, represented here as a cowering Indian hiding behind the Frenchman, were mere pawns in a more important conflict over who would control the North American continent. *Courtesy of the John Carter Brown Library.*

now a proxy war between Europe's most powerful nations, with the fate of the thirteen American colonies in balance.[69]

Others around the Atlantic turned to verse to explain this new war against Britain's old enemy. In August, the editors of the *Scots Magazine* published a poem titled "A FABLE, *addressed to the* AMERICANS, *upon their treaty with* FRANCE," which described the Americans as frogs; after declaring independence, "they went to work; First sign'd a treaty with King Stork." But after they secured the alliance, King Stork grew hungry, and "in his rage he to the marshes flies; And made a meal of his allies; Then he grew so fond of well-fed frogs, He made a larder of the bogs!" The poem ended with a warning to the Americans on the danger of making friends with Britain's eternal foe:

Say, *Yankies*, don't you feel compunction
At your unnat'ral, rash conjunction?
Can love for you in him take root,
Who's Catholic, and absolute?
I'll tell these croakers how he'll treat 'em;
Frenchmen, like Storks, love frogs—to eat 'em.[70]

In other ways, French Catholics appeared to be overtaking colonial American society, and there was little that delegates to Congress could do about it. Kingstonians read of a riot in Hampton, Virginia, between French and American seamen, which led to the deaths of five people. During the melee, a French officer reportedly encouraged his men "to continue the scene of bloodshed, using this very singular expression, *"That the King's marine troops should not be insulted with impunity by his* AMERICAN SUBJECTS."[71] Similarly, when French seamen arrived in Boston, reports circulated that they demanded "the free exercise of their religion in every port of the country." Days later, Bostonians purportedly granted their request, agreeing to turn over one of their Protestant churches to "a congregation, in communion with the church of Rome." This, the writer asserted, "ought to be ranked in the first class of the insults which distinguish the present era; as nothing can more elucidate the villainy and hypocrisy of these miscreant Puritans, than their preposterous coalition with the French Catholics."[72] Loyal refugees in New York were shocked by the news, with one resident recording in his diary that "these Enthusiastick Rebels in Boston have given Liberty to the French amongst them to sett up Mass in an English Church in that place. fine protestants indeed."[73]

British writers, especially those in the colonies, hoped their attacks on Congress would persuade deceived colonists (like Benedict Arnold) to return their allegiance to the British monarchy. This was especially true over the summer and early fall of 1778, when many loyal Britons believed that news of the alliance alongside British peace offerings might lead to popular revolt against leaders of the rebellion. Stories regularly circulated in the British Atlantic press that colonists were growing increasingly disturbed by Congress's willingness to make friends with Britain's natural enemy. "American Freeman," whose essay appeared in both New York and Scottish newspapers, believed many Patriots "now confess their apprehensions that their country is sold to the French King, and that all their boasted struggles for liberty, will end in wretched submission to French despotism, and popish superstition, should Great-Britain give up her colonies."[74] In November, Glaswegians read a letter from a New Yorker who reported that Congress's alliance with France had led to a "general clamour," and the writer believed "that before next spring, they [Congress] will be routed from their seats of tyranny, and that this season will finish the rebellion."[75]

Even alleged attempts to resist Congress's turn toward popery illustrated the violent, arbitrary nature of a body now in league with cruel European oppressors. In October, Rivington reported that an unnamed delegate to Congress declared that "our alliance with the French is unnatural, unprofitable, [and] absurd," and then demanded that Congress give up "this phantom of independence." Before he could finish, however, a messenger notified the Polish general, Count Pulaski, who "flew into the chamber . . . and with his sabre in an instant severed from his body the head of this honest delegate." Congress then ordered that the head be placed "on the top of the liberty pole of Philadelphia, as a perpetual monument of *freedom of debate* in the Continental Congress of the United States of America."[76]

Other writers pleaded with misled colonists to see through the cruelty and hypocrisy of their Congress and reaffirm their attachment to the British crown. "Rouse, then, my *infatuated countrymen!*" demanded "AN AMERICAN" in a June issue of *Rivington's Gazette*, "open your eyes. Be no longer cajoled, misguided and trepanned by wicked and designing men, who are laying your country waste, and, *are their selves*, bring Popery in your land." He also begged his former countrymen to not "lend France a helping hand, to overturn and pull down the *Protestant Church* to its ruins. Don't help the French King and the Congress, your best friends in *imagination*, but worst enemies in *reality*; don't, I say, help them to rob Great-Britain of her *dearly purchased colonies!*" The writer concluded with a final plea: "Act like *Englishmen*, like *Protestants*, like *Christians*. Be wise betimes, were *it be too late*. Be just, be loyal, be free, be happy."[77]

This was a proud affirmation of Protestant Whig Loyalism, but it also revealed the continued frustration loyal Britons felt as a result of a rebellion that had so thoroughly undermined their sense of identity and national belonging. To be just, free, and happy required being Protestant (and despising Catholicism), yet in the summer of 1778 loyal Britons found themselves desperately trying to convince tens of thousands of American colonists that this was still true. "MENTOR," writing in defense of the British constitution several months later, struggled with this same reality. "Americans . . . are of the same blood," the writer pleaded, "profess the same religion, speak the same language, and have in every respect a kindred interest." Yet they had chosen to rebel against "the only free nation in the world, enabled from its constitution and power to support the cause of liberty and toleration, and prevent the human race from being debased and rendered miserable by the tyranny of despotism or persecution of superstition."[78]

The Franco-American alliance, like the Quebec Act before it, revealed the degree to which this rebellion was a civil war even as the fighting expanded to all corners of the globe. Britons on both sides of the conflict were reared in a political culture of Britishness steeped in anti-Catholic language and rhetoric and had come to best understand their freedoms and liberties when framed against the tyranny of enemy Catholic states. At the start of the war, Patriot writers were cognizant of the challenge of making war against their own people and began to construct a common cause around the perceived spread of popery in their empire. Those stories—that narrative—cut across diverse regions and peoples, drawing together a broad swath of American colonists (and some Britons elsewhere) who shared little in common besides their mutual fear of Catholic tyranny.

Loyal Britons failed to find a similarly convincing narrative in the early years of the war. They instead defended legally constituted authority and celebrate their fidelity to the king, while they tried desperately to frame Congress and its various committees as illegal, unrepresentative, and prone to violence and tyranny. But now, in the summer of 1778, Loyalists were able to describe Congress as engaged in popish tyranny and were able to unravel a cause that had previously defied easy explanation. They could now see more clearly that popery was there from the start. Patriot leaders used violence to suppress dissent, created images and symbols to rally support, manipulated election results to create a false sense of consensus, and fabricated narratives intended to sow disloyalty and push colonists to their cause. Loyal Britons often described these actions as popish, common in arbitrary Catholic nations where one's freedom was regularly subjected to the fear and violence of state power. That Congress found a friend in France appeared the likely outcome for a political body bent, from the beginning, on achieving absolutist rule.

This new narrative—a British common cause built on the foundations of the one formed in 1775—consolidated popular opinion of the war and the nation. Britons across the empire who had begun to embrace a martial spirit in the wake of the embarrassing loss at Saratoga were now able to rally around an age-old shared sense of loyalty and Britishness. They championed a cause that was resolutely Protestant; devoutly committed to monarchy; and, perhaps most importantly, uninterested in the broader ideological disputes that previously characterized the conflict. Consent, representation, the sovereignty of Parliament, and even more general conversations about the basic rights and liberties of American colonists mattered less to the British public after 1778. Loyal Britons were more focused on winning a war against their old enemies. Previous divisions throughout the empire gave way to a far greater degree of consensus and unity toward their enemies, especially in the four communities in this study. From Glasgow to New York City, from Kingston to Halifax, Britons rallied in their support for the British Crown, which was now engaged in a war to stop the spread of popery within their empire.

These Britons also no longer struggled to see rebellious Americans as their foes. While some (especially Loyalist refugees) remained hopeful that these colonists would see through the dark clouds of popery hanging over their cause—as Arnold had done in 1780—others were increasingly convinced that the alliance revealed a people who were no longer British. Their cause, as such, was greater than it had previously been. Britons were no longer simply trying to extinguish a misguided rebellion, contrived in their eyes by a small cabal of self-interested men. They were fighting a war for empire and faced with a familiar opponent. If Burgoyne's defeat briefly awakened the public to the reality of a protracted war, Congress's alliance with France gave loyal Britons a reason—a cause—to fight. Refugee New Yorkers recognized as much in November when a group of twenty-three men from several provinces published an address affirming their commitment to the British cause. "The unnatural alliance, [Congress] have formed with the Court of France," proclaimed the authors, "which has ever been enmity with Great-Britain, must infallibly unite the whole empire in one common effort to render abortive a confederacy that threatens ruin to the civil and religious liberty of mankind."[79]

CHAPTER 7

In Defence of the Protestant Religion
Fighting Catholicism across the British Atlantic

On June 2, 1780, the Scottish MP Lord George Gordon and members of his Protestant Association gathered in St. George's Field in London to deliver a petition to Parliament against an English Catholic relief bill passed two years earlier. They were accompanied by between forty to sixty thousand Britons, as many as twenty thousand of whom hailed from Scotland. All were asked to wear "blue Cockades in their hats to distinguish themselves from the Papists, and those who approve of the late act in favour of Popery."[1] "It was a glorious and most affecting spectacle," one writer proclaimed, "to see such numbers of our fellow citizens advancing in the cause of Protestantism."[2]

The procession began peacefully, but when Parliament refused to review the petition, the crowd grew angry and began rioting through the streets of nation's capital city.[3] They initially targeted obvious symbols of Catholic influence. Catholic chapels and "Popish schools" throughout the city were ransacked and burned to the ground. Some assaulted prominent and ordinary Catholics, while others paraded through the streets burning effigies of the pope and declaring "Georg 3^d is a Roman Catholick . . . [and] he should lose his Head" to cheers of "No Popery!"[4]

Over the following days, rioters' attacks on symbols of Catholicism coincided with an increasing, and related, opposition toward representations of political and economic authority in the city. Drunken crowds ransacked the homes of many prominent politicians and leading government officials. Others broke open as many as eight debtors' prisons, demolished tollhouses, and dumped thousands of pounds of currency into the Thames.[5] An attempt was even made to storm the Bank of England, but British soldiers, led by John Wilkes of all people, held them back.

By Thursday, June 8, nearly a week after the rioting began, more than ten thousand British soldiers patrolled the streets of London with orders to fire on crowds that refused to disperse. The soldiers eventually gained control of the city, but not before at least 450 rioters and 210 soldiers perished, while dozens of city shops, homes, government offices, chapels, and prisons lay in ashes.[6] The level of devastation was astonishing. More people died in the streets of London in early June than in almost any single battle fought during the entire American war.[7]

The Gordon Riots, as the event came to be known, revealed another shocking reality: British Protestants had died fighting against their government's attempt to relieve Catholics while their nation was at war with France and Spain. In May 1778, as Britons rallied to the flag on news of the Franco-American alliance, Parliament passed the English Catholic Relief Act, and proposed similar bills for both Scotland and Ireland. The legislation repealed several longstanding penal laws against Catholic subjects so that they could fight in the expanded war. Like the American response to the Quebec Act four years earlier, the passage of pro-Catholic legislation (especially while the nation was at war with France) convinced many Britons that their government was conspiring to topple the Protestant nation they now so desperately sought to defend.

Historians have long thought of the Gordon Riots, and broader agitation against Catholic relief, in parochial terms, as having been the consequence of a particular political culture found only on the British mainland.[8] But these riots were part and parcel of a radical reimagining of British Loyalism occasioned by the Franco-American war that swept across the North Atlantic in the summer of 1778. The alliance upended previous British narratives of the rebellion. Britons now held a more entrenched view of their political rights and liberties, which they narrowly equated with their Protestant faith. This new understanding of the war, as we have seen, proved useful in the context of making enemies, but it was also just as capable of turning Britons against their own government.

This was especially true in Glasgow, where Gordon and his cause enjoyed widespread support and where residents twice resorted to violent (though less deadly) rioting in opposition to the proposed Catholic relief bill. In fact, the final years of the war in Glasgow were marked by a sustained degree of radicalism unmatched in the city's history within the empire. Glaswegians spoke, wrote, and took to the streets in opposition to their government's pro-Catholic policies, demanding the protection of their political and religious liberties. Their beliefs and actions resembled that of American Patriots in 1775, and they came dangerously close to starting their own rebellion in the last years of the conflict.

Elsewhere in the British Atlantic, subjects were less interested in the crisis over Catholic relief that was tearing apart the mainland. They were too concerned with their new enemies, France and, after June 1779, Spain. These long-standing Catholic foes had pushed the war into the farthest corners of the North Atlantic, exposing Britons to both foreign and domestic threats. These enemies also reignited a language of Protestant loyalty that produced a martial, retributive spirit in communities like Halifax, New York City, and Kingston. This was no longer a colonial rebellion, fought among former friends; it was a war for empire, which carried possibly devastating consequences for the inhabitants of the British Atlantic. For many, this was not the time to support violent protests or subversive rhetoric.

This new war also led to new explanations of loyalty and Britishness. Britons continued to depend on traditional fears of Catholic tyranny to make sense of the war, but they also expressed a greater commitment to popular understandings of Protestant Whig liberty. In fact, Congress's alliance with French Catholics, more than Jefferson's declaration two years earlier, sharpened loyal Britons' perceptions of their rights and liberties, and the need to defend them. It convinced many in these communities as well of the superiority of their nation and empire over that of their many opponents. Even after Cornwallis's devastating defeat at Yorktown in the fall of 1781, loyal Britons across the North Atlantic were more convinced than ever before that a Protestant monarchy and representative government offered the surest path to securing their freedom and prosperity.

On May 14, 1778, Parliament passed the English Catholic Relief Act, just as Britons began to react to official news of the Franco-American alliance. The bill stipulated that Catholics would still face imprisonment for holding mass, but removed the £100 reward for anyone who reported on them. Catholics were also permitted to teach at schools so long as they took an oath of allegiance to the king and renounced their belief in the pope's temporal powers within the British Empire. Finally, they were free to buy, sell, inherit, and bequeath land at any point in the future. Similar bills were proposed for Scotland and Ireland over the summer and fall, as well.[9]

Such legislation, though inimical to popular British attitudes toward Catholicism, was not entirely out of step with recent imperial approaches toward governing Catholics, and defining subjecthood, within an increasingly diverse empire.[10] The Irish and Scottish bills, like the Quebec Act passed four years earlier, sought to ensure the loyalty of Catholics in those countries at a time of increased fears of a French invasion. These bills were also a pragmatic decision on the part of government officials who were desperate to recruit more soldiers (even Catholic ones) to fight the Americans and their new allies.[11] Even after the success of the recruiting drives in early 1778, the British army and navy were still unprepared for a global war against their European and American enemies.

British officials could not have chosen a worse time for Catholic relief. The government's pro-Catholic policies during a war with France contradicted, even threatened, a resurgent Protestant British Loyalism spreading across the empire. By legislating in favor of Catholics, the king and Parliament risked betraying this identity, as they had done with Quebec in 1774. Their policies harkened back to previous monarchs who had threatened national security through pro-Catholic concessions. Their actions even led some to wonder whether Lord North's government was embracing the enemy's Catholic, absolutist form of rule in order to continue the war in America.

The situation was especially tense in Scotland amid constant rumors of a French invasion and in consequence of repeated attacks along the Scottish coastline by American privateers. The country also suffered from a shortage of oats in the spring of 1778, which had led to a series of violent food riots throughout the countryside. Lieutenant-General James Oughton, commander of British forces in Scotland, wrote in April that "the People complain that after having furnished near 12,000 Men to the Army and Navy they are exposed to the Insults of Mobs, and the Ravages of every insignificant Privateer."[12] In the fall, Oughton armed the citizens of Greenock, "being the Repository of the Shipping and Stores of the great Tradeing Town of Glasgow." He also ordered the foundry at nearby Carron to produce twelve cannons should that "Rebel [John Paul] Jones" make an attempt on the city.[13] The American War for Independence, long thought to be a defensive war against an overreaching government, now endangered the security of one the empire's most important mainland port cities.

Reports of a proposed Scottish Catholic relief bill shocked Glaswegians.[14] Many believed Parliament was subverting one of the core tenants of Protestant Whig Loyalism at an especially critical moment in the war. On October 13, the synod of Glasgow responded first to rumors of the proposed bill, just as reports were arriving of Congress rejecting Carlisle's peace proposal in favor of an alliance with France. Members of the synod declared that if they remained silent Scots would be "easy prey to Popish emissaries," and, like rebellious

Americans, be "seduced into that detestable superstition . . . which has often been drunk with the blood of the saints." The "astonishing progress of this detestable, cruel, and unjust superstition," they argued, threatened to destroy "the foundations of a Protestant state." As such, they agreed to create a committee to inform the lord advocate "of the spirit of the people in this part of the country." They also encouraged their ministers "to revise the study of the popish controversy, and preach frequently against it," appointing a day of public fasting in December "on account of the various evils which at present much abound."[15]

Glaswegians acted quickly on the fears engendered by the synod's proclamation. On the following Sunday, a crowd attacked the few known Catholics in their city who had gathered to worship at a house on High Street. The crowd allegedly "terrified the poor people to the highest degree," forced their way into what they now called "a Popish Chapel," and "demolished several pictures, that ornamented the room" that were believed to be "objects of their worship." Several "poor Highland women had their caps and cloaks torn off them, and were pelted with dirt and stones." In the evening, the crowd "broke all the windows of the house, breathing blood and slaughter to all Papists," before being dispersed by a town magistrate and several officers.[16] Though short-lived, the riot was reported in newspapers across Scotland and England amid growing concern of the government's pro-Catholic tendencies.

But Scots found few supporters for their "No Popery" cause elsewhere in the North Atlantic. Printers in Halifax, New York City, and Kingston did not carry news of the initial addresses against the bill, nor did they report on the Glasgow riot, despite the constant stream of news coming from the British mainland. It is likely some colonists actually agreed with the underlying motive for Catholic relief in the British Isles—the government desperately needed more soldiers and sailors—even as they rallied in defense of their nation in a war against their Catholic enemies. By the fall of 1778, in fact, there were already Irish and Scottish Catholics filling provincial regiments. Over the previous year, officials commissioned the Roman Catholic Volunteers in Philadelphia, Lord Rawdon formed an Irish-born provincial regiment in New York City, and it is likely the growing number of Catholic immigrants in Halifax and Kingston filled similar regiments and militia units.[17]

The inhabitants of these communities were also consumed by the war with France, which disrupted Atlantic trade routes and led to fears of invasion in their cities. Kingstonians regularly read of such rumors and worried, too, that their enemies might encourage the island's slaves to revolt. Rev. William Jones wrote that "all is tumult, hurry & confusion," and that there was "a general Murmur of discontent . . . buzzing thro' every part of Jamaica."[18] Local officials foiled another slave revolt in September, allegedly concocted by two disguised Spaniards who had secretly passed through plantations near Spanish Town providing guns to the slaves. Kingstonians believed the failed plot revealed the cruel tendencies of their European foes, who were now working with their American allies to incite slaves to murder white Britons on the island. "We are told," reported one resident, "that when the negroes should have begun their massacre the French and Americans were to come likewise, and so we were to be made a sacrifice amongst them."[19] These more immediate threats likely overshadowed any concerns Kingstonians might have had for Catholic toleration on the British mainland.

The war with France also reminded Haligonians of the dangerous loyalties of their colony's Catholic inhabitants, even with the salaried appointment of the priest Bourg. Fears of a combined French and American invasion in the fall convinced the provincial secretary and de facto governor, Richard Bulkeley, to double his efforts to ensure Indian and Acadian loyalty. In August, he directed Bourg to punish any person who refused to take the oath of allegiance and to be active in discounting those who favored "this unnatural Rebellion now Subsisting in America." Narratives also mattered to Bulkeley. He feared that Indian and Acadians might be "led astray . . . by Idle Rumours which are daily and frequently Spread . . . by His Majestys Deluded & Disaffected Subjects," and instructed Bourg to "Inculcate proper Sentiments of Morality & Subordination to His Majestys Government."[20] Haligonians were reminded again of the many competing loyalties of the colony's inhabitants, further complicated by France's arrival in the war.

Loyal refugees in New York City felt the effects of this new war more than residents of these other three North Atlantic port cities. In the summer, officials abandoned Philadelphia for New York City, and brought with them at least three thousand Loyalist refugees and seven thousand soldiers. Conditions in the city were already beyond deplorable, but the arrival of ten thousand soldiers and subjects drove it to near collapse. The situation worsened in early August when a second fire broke out in the city, destroying as many as sixty-four homes and stores, including the quarter-master-general's provision store. It was thought to have begun at the shop of a ship chandler, though a Hessian officer reported that "a few suspected persons, including Frenchmen, were arrested."[21] The destruction caused by the fire pressed the growing number of soldiers and citizens into tighter quarters and placed a greater demand on resources in the increasingly war-weary city.[22] It also raised people's suspicions that the city might fall, either by invasion or by insurrection.

At the same time, an increasing number of loyal New Yorkers began to abandon a narrative of the war that hoped for reconciliation for one that encouraged an almost bloodthirsty vengeance toward their former friends. The many published stories describing the horrors of the Franco-American alliance had led these residents to believe that rebellious colonists had abandoned a Protestant British political culture for one that was arbitrary and Catholic. France's entry into the war may have expanded the geographical reach of the conflict, but it also drove Loyalist thinking inward toward a more personal and vindictive language of British Loyalism.[23]

This was especially true in October, when the Carlisle Commission made a final direct appeal to the American public for an end to the war on generous terms. By now, Congress had not only rejected the commissioners' initial proposal but also undermined British efforts at reconciliation by reminding Americans of their opponents' willingness to employ slaves and Indians in the war.[24] Now in New York, the commissioners hoped to overturn Congress's common cause by appealing to the colonists' long-standing Protestant loyalties. If colonists refused to listen, however, they would suffer the consequences.

On October 3, just a little more than a week before Glaswegians rioted, Rivington published the Carlisle Commission's "Manifesto and Proclamation," which was then distributed through every colony in North America and carried on ships crossing the Atlantic. The commissioners warned rebellious colonists that only "the benevolence of Great Britain have thus far checked the extremes of war when they tended to distress a people still considered as our fellow-subjects. . . . But," they cautioned, "when that country professes the unnatural design, not only of estranging herself from us, but of mortgaging herself and her resources to our enemies, the whole contest is changed. . . . Under such circumstances," the commissioners concluded, "the laws of self-preservation must direct the conduct of Great Britain, and if the British colonies are to become an accession to France, will direct her to render that accession of as little avail as possible to her enemy."[25] The Americans' refusal to accept Britain's last overtures of peace might have demonstrated the strength and resilience of their cause, but their embrace of Catholic France had made efforts at reconciliation increasingly untenable.

Not surprisingly, Patriot leaders readily agreed to this challenge of a retributive war, which only further provoked loyal Britons. Congress responded to the commission's manifesto with its own call to action, which described the barbarous actions of the British army since the start of the war and declared that the Americans "will take such exemplary vengeance as shall deter others from a like conduct."[26] Newly formed state governments also increasingly agreed to legislation banishing known British sympathizers and confiscating their estates, which drove refugees in New York City to declare their former countrymen "avowed enemies" to Great Britain.[27]

New Yorkers, who by now counted among their number refugees from across the thirteen American colonies, understood the significance of this moment. "Edgar," writing in *Rivington's Gazette* a week after the publication of the manifesto, expressed shock at the "unnatural alliance your deceitful *tyrants* have entered into with the still more deceitful *Gaul*. . . . The horrors of war have hitherto till now been restrained," he warned, "but should you now refuse the offers of an indulgent mother . . . I shall glory in being one to execute the just vengeance of my King."[28] Another writer cautioned colonists that Britain will not stand idly by while "France is putting a yoke about your necks. . . . Great Britain is now roused and unanimous.—She is, must, and will be, by the blessing of God on her arms, triumphant over *all* her enemies."[29] Even two years later, Congress's fateful decision to ignore peace in favor of an alliance with France drove men like Benedict Arnold behind British lines.

This resurgent martial patriotism also cut across gender lines. Accounts of Loyalist women publicly acting or speaking in favor of the king rarely appeared in British newspapers during the war, the consequence of a conservative political culture that reinforced patriarchy and often criticized female Patriots who assumed overtly public roles.[30] But in January, "a number of the principle Loyal Ladies" in the city contributed funds to fit out a privateer ship called "THE FAIR AMERICAN." They claimed they were motivated by the queen and several other noble women in London, who had recently "equipped private ships of war . . . to assist in humbling the pride and perfidy of France, and in chastising the rebels of America." Their efforts, concluded the author of the report, "ought to be considered by the rebels as proof of the flagrancy of their own insolence and obstinacy, in rejecting, such generous offers of reconciliation, as to excite the indignation of the FAIR SEX."[31] A week later, "EXUL VIRGINIENSIS" turned to verse to celebrate these women for having equipped a privateer to fight against "the detested Rebel Corsairs, and their new Popish Allies, the base perfidious French." The poem, like many essays and editorials over the previous several months, described a new, vengeful war—and common cause—against Britain's combined enemies.

Brave loyal Tars, with Hearts of Oak, will vie,
For you to fight, to conquer, live or die;
By you inspir'd, they'll plead our common cause,
With vengeful Thunder, 'gainst the Congress laws;
Firm to sustain, and resolute to dare,
The Friends of GEORGE, no Gauls or Yankies fear;
With equal haste, the French and Rebels beat,
As if they rush'd your lovely lips to meet.[32]

Over the winter months, these more militant refugees condemned the military's handling of the war, spoke out against the peace offerings, and pushed Clinton to arm more of their people.[33] William Tryon was so infuriated by the Americans' resolve and the hesitancy of British military officials to aggressively arm refugees that he believed the British should enact a devastating war against their former countrymen. He outlined a plan that included offering substantial bounties for captured members of Congress and "usurping Governors," the drawing of Continental soldiers to the coast so that the British could "harass the Country," and worse still, encouraging "the Indians and Canadians to come down on the interior Frontiers. Women only to be saved."[34] In 1774–75, many colonists believed the latter tactic was the real motive for Parliament's passage of the Quebec Act. Now, in 1778–79, some Loyalists openly contemplated such a devastating war.

This new war demanded the attention of Loyalist refugees in New York City, who now understood that their lives depended on crushing a rebellion entirely at odds with Protestant Whig values and thinking. Others in the empire might have known this as well, but refugees in New York City had far more at stake. If Congress or their followers were unable to see fault in their friendship with France and to accept Parliament's generous offers of peace, then loyal Britons had no hope of ever regaining their former lives. In such circumstances, few New Yorkers had time to worry over a relief bill for Catholics living thousands of miles away.

While the British army celebrated the capture of Savannah in late December 1778, Scots remained focused on defeating the unpopular Catholic relief bill. In the same month, they formed committees of correspondence and associations, modeled on those created by the Americans during the 1760s, to coordinate and express the public's outrage. In Glasgow and the city's hinterland, members of trade incorporations, elite merchants, politicians, and prominent clergymen—many of whom had given generously toward raising regiments less than a year earlier—organized themselves as "the Eighty-five Private Societies in and about Glasgow."[35] By February 1779, more than three hundred and fifty petitions from churches, towns and villages, trade incorporations, and private societies throughout Scotland were published in local newspapers. In the Glasgow area alone organizers claimed to have collected more than eighty-eight thousand signatures.[36] If the Quebec Act was capable of driving American colonists toward rebellion, the Scottish response to the threat of Catholic relief offered similar possibilities.

In their various petitions, Scots argued that the oppressive nature of the Catholic faith would ultimately crush Scottish political and religious liberties, much as it appeared to be doing in the American colonies. The "Inhabitants of the Barony Parish of Glasgow," worried that "trafficking Papists, priests, and Jesuits, will be encouraged to settle among us . . . to exercise all their wicked arts, not only in seducing the ignorant, and corrupting the venal; but in spreading destruction amongst all those who oppose their designs."[37] Residents of nearby Gorbals were afraid that the time may come when "Christianity shall be banished [in] Britain for Popery, the Bible for the mass book; liberty, property, religion, happiness, changed into slavery, poverty, superstition and wickedness."[38]

Numerous petitioners also echoed claims made by American colonists four years earlier that toleration was a part of a larger popish plot to reinstate the Young Pretender to the throne. The Pollockshaws weavers believed the bill to be a "plot of Rome, hatched by Jacobites, carried on by Jesuits, and propagated by those who are practical enemies to his present Majesty's government." They reminded readers that "the establishment of Popery in Canada," not only caused a "general revolt in many of our colonies abroad," but ultimately led rebellious Americans to an alliance with those "under-handed, double-dealing, perfidious Papists, our natural enemies, THE FRENCH." The weavers thought the passage of a similar bill in Scotland might lead to equally "awful consequences."[39]

Scots also defended their opposition to Catholic relief by laying claim to the religious and political liberties guaranteed to them by the 1707 Act of Union. The "Trades of Hamilton" argued the legislation was "subversive of the present establishment, so solemnly secured to us by the Union," while the inhabitants of nearby Lanark described it as "dangerous to our constitution, civil and religious,—[and] a direct violation of the treaty of Union between the two kingdoms."[40] The "Glasgow Friendly Society" traced their rights back further to the Glorious Revolution, imploring readers to recall that their forefathers had "bled and died in defence of the Protestant religion, when a tyrannical prince introduced Popery, his favourite religion, into the politics of the state."[41] Members of the "Great Antiquity Society in Glasgow" agreed, while reminding readers, too, that their city had made "a distinguished appearance against the malevolent design of a popish Pretender, in the years 1715, and 1745."[42]

Unlike their American counterparts, however, Scottish petitioners were reluctant to question their allegiance to the king, though they were certain to remind him of his civic and religious obligations. In fact, many of the petitioners qualified their loyalty by listing a set of demands on their monarch. The "Journeymen Hammermen" in Glasgow were confident that their king "who is justly stiled, The Father of his people, will lend a paternal ear to the cries of his subjects" by refusing to give his royal assent to such a bill.[43] The Pollockshaws weavers were prepared to give their lives "in defense of our . . . Protestant Prince . . . who is bound, by his coronation oath, to defend [the] Presbytery in Scotland."[44] Residents of nearby Lanark claimed that toleration was "inconsistent with his Majesty's honor and interest, and destructive to the peace and security of his Majesty's best subjects, who have always reverenced his illustrious family."[45] A meeting in Glasgow of "many hundreds of the friends of the *Protestant Interest*" combined several of these themes into one rousing statement. They declared unanimously that Catholic relief "would be highly prejudicial to the interest of the Protestant religion in Scotland, dangerous to our constitution civil and religious, a direct violation of the treaty of Union, inconsistent with the King's honour, and destructive of the peace and security of his best subjects."[46]

The petitioners were more than willing to criticize Parliament for promoting Catholic relief and failing to successfully fight the war in North America. Members of the "Paisley and Ayrshire Society" scolded the ministers behind the bill who have done "every thing in their power for these four years past, to pursue measures that have been detrimental to the British interest in America; we fear, they have already lost America, by a course of blundering conduct."[47] Tradesmen in nearby Kilbirny prayed that Parliament would avoid such an unpopular bill when the country was "threatened with war, by our malicious and natural enemies, besides the lamentable rebellion in America."[48] Residents of Govan feared Parliament's support of Catholic relief would create "an unhappy spirit of distrust in the present Ministry . . . and marr the levies in Scotland, which . . . hath furnished twenty thousand men to his Majesty's army."[49]

The residents of the small of village of Carluke went further than others in their denunciation of Catholic relief. They feared a sinister plot was afoot to rob Britons of their liberty. "From the passing the Quebec bill to the present hour," they claimed, "the encouraging and tolerating this bloody religion seems to be the only *consistent*, and . . . *successful* measure which the present Ministry have adopted." Their nation had always been the great "bulwark of the Protestant cause," the petitioners argued, but in just a few years Parliament had done "what the united force of the Popish powers have attempted so often in vain.—They have lost America.—The West Indies in danger.— Trade and manufactures in a ruinous state.—Protestant alliances neglected or despised, while the Popish powers are closely united, and our internal safety thereby rendered very precarious."[50] Catholic relief, in other words, was part and parcel of a broader failure of government to effectively quell a rebellion and to hold in check their nation's European enemies. They believed their empire was collapsing before their very eyes and the government's toleration of Catholicism was their ultimate undoing.

Glaswegians reached a tipping point in early February, just a year removed from the widespread enlistment drives that evidenced the city's newfound loyal spirit. On a day originally set aside for public fasting, a large crowd "burnt and destroyed the houses of every Papists they could discover. One Bagnall [an English Catholic who held services at his home], I am afraid is totally ruined." Another witness to the rioting testified that there was "such a mob as was never seen here. The Papists are in a poor situation. A house beyond the East toll is entirely burnt, furniture and all. Our fencibles are drawn up, and every thing in confusion." The magistrates responded by ordering soldiers "to attack the Mob with clubbed Musquets; which they did so effectually as to clear the Streets of them, and they have been quiet ever since."[51]

At one level, Glaswegians had acted every bit the loyal subjects. They were deeply committed to defending their Protestant nation from the spread of popery. It was the government, they believed, not loyal Scots, whose actions were dangerous to the security of free Britons. But for some, Glaswegian's fears of Catholicism were irrational and out of step with an increasingly tolerant religious and political community in Great Britain. Neither explanation, however, accounts for the degree to which the American rebellion and renewed war with France provoked Scots toward a more inflexible understanding of their nation and what it stood for. Glaswegians were troubled by their government's inability to effectively wage war and grew even more alarmed after France joined the conflict. In such circumstances, it was entirely impossible for Glaswegians to accept the idea of toleration. That they formed extralegal committees and even resorted to violent rioting on several occasions—the very sort of behavior they had repeatedly condemned over the previous decade—also hinted at the broader influence of the revolution on popular conceptions of Britishness. Glaswegians might have lacked the "long train of abuses" complained of by American colonists in 1776, but their fear of popish tyranny, like that of their American counterparts, had left the city on the brink of rebellion.

Printers in Kingston, New York City, and Halifax either continued to ignore the growing opposition to Catholic relief in Scotland or derided protesters as crazed madmen whose backward thinking had led to chaos and violence throughout the country. In response to the riots, a writer in the *Jamaica Mercury* lamented "that, in this enlightened age, the barbarous spirit of Intolerance should so far prevail!"[52] Similar reports appeared in Halifax, where residents read in June that a mob of fanatical sailors and carpenters (not respectable inhabitants of the city) had laid waste to Edinburgh. "Such a scene has not happened here since John Knox's days," complained one writer.[53]

It is of little surprise that Haligonians were quick to criticize the protests and rioting in Scotland. The colony's officials abhorred such activity and had spent the better part of the previous decade trying to maintain order in Nova Scotia. It also appeared that an increasing number of Haligonians were beginning to throw their weight behind the British cause by the early months of 1779, influenced in no small way by the arrival of France in the war. Henry's gazette carried all kinds of writing critical of the alliance and regularly reprinted editorials from London and New York City newspapers that called for an unforgiving war against the French and Americans.[54]

Expressions of loyalty even briefly bled into local politics, offering a rare glimpse into how the events of the revolution and war shaped Halifax's local political culture. From March to May 1779, several candidates for the city's seat in the colonial assembly turned to Henry's newspaper to win over voters either by expressing support for the war or deriding their opponents as American sympathizers. In late March, Richard Gibbons argued that voters should consider his *"Loyalty to our Gracious Sovereign and Attachment to our Rights, and Privileges as British Subjects, and those of the Loyal Inhabitants of this Province in general"* in contrast to those "who openly avow or secretly possess Principles diametrically the reverse of mine and other his Majesty's *Loyal* Subjects." Richard Cunningham took the same approach, appealing to voters by expressing his "disinterested Uprightness of Conduct together with a constant Attention to the sentiments of my *Loyal Constituents*."[55] The following week, another writer took offense at Gibbons's accusations, believing that his "secretly possess" comment implied such a candidate supported the "principles of REBELLION." Candidates that "openly avow such principles," this writer argued, "ought . . . to be utterly rejected in a matter of such importance."[56]

While Haligonians sorted out their local politics, officials in Glasgow worked to restore order to their city. They were helped by the news that Parliament had decided against introducing a Catholic relief bill for their country, largely in consequence of the widespread petitioning over the previous several months.[57] Local magistrates, leading ministers, and members of the committee of correspondence publicly apologized for the violence and suggested that the city compensate Bagnall and others for the loss of their property. The small number of Catholics in both Glasgow and Edinburgh also petitioned Parliament for recompense and once again reiterated their loyalty to the Crown.[58]

Despite such overtures, Glaswegians, and Scots more generally, remained unflinching in their defense of Protestant Whig values. In the spring, leading figures in Glasgow and Edinburgh pushed the church's General Assembly to adopt resolutions opposing future attempts to relieve Catholics and protested efforts to reimburse abused Catholics. Hundreds of the city's weavers also destroyed an effigy of Lord North in March after news arrived that Parliament planned to repeal laws against the importation of French cambric into Great Britain. Glasgow was the nation's leading producer of the fabric, and the city's weavers saw in the bill yet another attempt by Parliament to favor French Catholics at the cost of their nation's well-being. One writer declared that "next to the Popish bill," it was "perhaps, the most effectual that could be devised to inflame the minds of the people of this country; the one struck deep at their spiritual, the present strikes equally so at their temporal welfare."[59]

Subjects across Scotland also turned their attention to Lord George Gordon's efforts in London to repeal the English relief bill, a movement that would ultimately culminate in the week-long riot in June 1780. Gordon first began to champion Scotland's No Popery cause early in 1779, when he spoke out against compensating Scottish Catholics and ridiculed their supposed displays of loyalty.[60] He also remained in regular contact with the various anti-Catholic associations and societies in Edinburgh and Glasgow. In late August, he toured the country, drawing enormous crowds and igniting the sort of parades and celebrations typically reserved for members of the royal family. His popularity frightened local officials who reported to London that Gordon "has gone about the Country to keep up the Flame."[61]

After returning from Scotland, Gordon continued to attack the North ministry for its defense of Catholic relief and for the protracted and costly war in America. Gordon and his growing number of followers also supported the county association movement, a radical cause pushing for major constitutional and economic reforms in Great Britain.[62] He continued to care about Scots too, complaining about the defenseless state of their country amid its lagging economy. In one speech before his peers, he warned that one hundred and twenty thousand Scots backed his cause and that he was prepared to deliver their sentiments to the "king and the Prince of Wales, that they may learn from them UPON WHAT TERMS THE SCOTCH WILL BE GOVERNED." He even went so far as to suggest that "most respectable people in Scotland" believed the North ministry was "following the same conduct for which the family of Steuart had been banished, and that . . . the King was a *Papist*."[63] Such charged language, which shared a great deal in common with the rebellious rhetoric of American Patriots in 1775, suggests that perhaps another rebellion was brewing in mainland Britain.

Scottish opposition to Catholic relief, which the Scots now voiced through their support of Gordon and the Protestant Association, demonstrated a profound shift in popular expressions of loyalty brought about by the ongoing crisis in North America. No longer voices of moderation, order, and stability, Glaswegians openly ridiculed the crown and Parliament, momentarily absconded formal government in favor of committees and associations, and even resorted to violence to defend their Protestant liberties. Scots were no longer arguing for inclusion and acceptance; they were acting the part of proud loyal Protestant Britons and were demanding that the king and members of Parliament join them or face the consequences.

But in the winter of 1779, Britain was at war against the combined Bourbon powers of France and Spain, a struggle that Glaswegians equated with their opposition to Catholic relief. In late December, the city's residents took to the streets to celebrate news of British forces having withstood a French and American siege of Savannah and captured Fort Omoa on the Bay of Honduras in Spanish America. The latter attack on Spain was organized by Jamaica's governor, John Dalling, who naively believed he could steal away Spain's valuable Central and South American colonies while Spaniards were distracted by events in North America.[64] Glasgow merchants were certainly interested in the success of this expedition, given their increasing involvement in the Caribbean sugar and slave trade.[65] The previous January, in fact, amid public calls for the repeal of the Catholic relief bill, forty-three Glasgow merchants petitioned the king for "a strong Naval Force to be employed in that Quarter of the Globe" to defend their nation's "valuable possessions" from their European foes.[66]

Near the end of 1779, Glaswegians also learned that the king had given his assent to Irish demands for free trade, a cause supported by Glasgow merchants and traders who already suffered from the loss of American markets.[67] "Public rejoicings [and] illuminations" occurred throughout the city, while the magistrates and "most respectable citizens" met at the town hall, where "several loyal toasts were drank."[68] Scots celebrated beneficial trade policies and victories over their Bourbon enemies for the same reason Scots violently opposed the spread of popery within their nation. They were defending a popular conception of Loyalism that celebrated economic prosperity and Protestant liberty, both of which were under threat at home and abroad.

The British victory at Omoa elicited similar expressions of joy in Kingston (if only momentarily), even as subjects in that city continued to know little of the growing popular agitation over Catholic relief in the British mainland.[69] But Dalling's expedition also drained the island of manpower, leaving Kingston vulnerable to attacks in the fall of 1779, especially now that Spain had joined the war.[70] By August, Dalling had once again declared martial law, which local merchants and planters initially supported despite the enormous financial burden.[71] Residents, who now were "under hourly apprehensions of being invaded by our old, inveterate, perfidious enemies the French," also asked Aikman and Douglass to keep them abreast of the state of other British Caribbean islands for fear that they all might fall like dominoes to the Bourbon powers.[72] Meanwhile, Spanish privateers continued to harass communities along the north coast of the island "with a view to carry off Negroes, and commit other depredations."[73]

In response, local militia units, numbering perhaps four thousand men in total, began patrolling coastal towns and villages. The governor and council moved their records and other valuables to the impenetrable mountain passes north of Kingston in the event that "the enemy had forced our works and routed the army."[74] They also reluctantly agreed to raise "a Corps of TRUSTY SLAVES" for the "DEFENCE OF THE ISLAND," and promised freedom to those who were "distinguished for their Courage and Fidelity."[75] Such an offer spoke directly to the revolutionary possibilities of the American war, but white Jamaicans were initially reluctant to consider such measures. There were certainly immediate dangers with arming slaves, and many feared military service would imbue slaves with a sense of independence and equality.[76] Others looked backward, as well, to a rebellion and war that had repeatedly affirmed the central importance of slavery to popular understandings of Loyalism among the island's white inhabitants. At the outbreak of hostilities, white Jamaicans' decision to remain loyal—their common cause—rested, in large part, on the realization that they depended on the British military to protect them from their slaves. Now the necessities of this new war forced them to reconsider such convictions, which some white Jamaicans struggled to accept.

This threat of invasion—as real a threat as Jamaicans had experienced since the start of the war—excited a martial spirit of patriotism among white Jamaicans that surpassed the brief *rage militaire* expressed in the aftermath of Burgoyne's defeat. Jamaicans showed a willingness for war, in fact, that had not been seen since the Falklands Crisis nearly a decade earlier and that matched the fury of loyal New Yorkers during the winter of 1778–79. Aikman and Douglass reported in August that in the course of just a week "above 1000 brave men . . . marched into Kingston," prepared to "sacrifice their lives in the defence of their country."[77]

One resident captured this resurgent Loyalism in a rousing address "To the MILITIA of JAMAICA." "For them, for our property, for our King, and in the defence of our civil and religious liberty," the writer declared, "we arm against these bold invaders, *and we will not bear the sword in vain.*" He reminded Jamaica's minutemen that they were descended "FROM BRITONS!—whose very *name*, in former times, has *blanched the faces of their foes with fear.*"[78] Jamaicans were not alone, either. Aikman and Douglass carried several reports from the British Isles expressing a similar widespread commitment to this new cause. A letter from a Londoner suggested "a spirit of loyalty, unknown, perhaps, before in the annals of Britain," had spread across the country, while in Ireland, "thousands are ready to take up arms" against "our most inveterate enemies the French."[79]

By October, fears of an invasion dissipated as reports suggested the French fleet had departed north for either Rhode Island or Halifax. But the momentary burst of loyalty in Kingston evidenced the power and pervasiveness of this new British common cause. Residents were roused to action by a narrative that could just as easily been lifted from any previous war fought during the eighteenth century. Perfidious Frenchmen, dangerous Spaniards—these were enemies loyal Britons were prepared to make war against. The French and Spanish were also the sort of common foes that excited subjects toward public declarations of loyalty to the Crown and empire. Just four years earlier, the island's assembly showed sympathy for the burgeoning American cause; now they were committed to a defense of Britishness in the face of their inveterate foes.

Gordon's movement to repeal the English Catholic relief bill gathered steam in the early days of 1780 as the war spread across Britain's Atlantic empire. His Protestant Association continued to depend on the support of Glaswegians and on the narrative of opposition they, and other Scots, constructed more than a year earlier. In February, Glasgow's Eighty-five Societies formally "resolved to join their brethren in England," and in March, they presented Gordon with a gold snuffbox for his "defence of the Protestant interests" in Great Britain.[80] By May, Gordon's Association described the movement in inclusive terms, imploring all "TRUE BRITONS" to unite against Popery: "if we unite, like one man, for the Honour of God, and the Liberties of the People, we may yet experience the blessing of Divine Providence on this Kingdom, and love and confidence may again be restored amongst Brethren."[81] Weeks later, Gordon and thousands of his supporters marched on Parliament, igniting six days of bloody, deadly violence in the nation's capital city.

News of the riots spread quickly across the empire. Britons everywhere read detailed accounts of the carnage in the streets of London, which often filled entire pages or more of their local gazettes.[82] Of course, such circumstance required explanation, but the scale of death and destruction was unprecedented. Over the previous two decades, the British Atlantic was racked by political violence that had often turned deadly. Yet events like the St. George's Field and Boston massacres paled in comparison with what had unfolded in London. Hundreds of Britons had lost their lives opposing their government's attempt to relieve Catholics while their nation was at war against both France and Spain. American colonists shuddered at the mere thought of Guy Carleton and tens of thousands of French Catholic soldiers descending on Boston in the winter of 1774–75, but Britons died in droves in the summer of 1780 at the hands of a government that appeared just as willing to strengthen Catholicism in the empire.

Yet, astonishingly, the transatlantic narrative constructed in the immediate aftermath of the riots offered not the least bit of sympathy toward the victims. Instead, they were variously described as crazed zealots, lawless ruffians, and deranged madmen, characterizations that persist even to this day.[83] Reports focused less on the original motives of many of the protesters—a defense of their Protestant Whig beliefs—and more on their attacks upon members of government, their destruction of debtors' prisons, and their attempted assault on the Bank of England. In one report, Gordon was said to have led an "army of assassins and incendiaries," while another argued that those who died "richly deserved it" and praised the soldiers for having shown "extreme humility" by not killing more "ruffians, thieves, incendiaries, [and] traitors."[84] Even popular prints, like James Gillray's *No Popery or Newgate Reformer,* disparaged the protesters as dirty, impoverished subjects who used the pretense of Catholic oppression to rob and steal from their betters. "Tho' He Says he's a Protestant," claimed the poem accompanying the image, "look at the Print, The Face and the Bludgeon will give you a hint, Religion he cries, in hopes to deceive, While his practice is only to burn and to thieve" (fig. 7.1).

Other reports pinned blame for the violence on outside agitators who hoped to use the dispute over Catholic relief to bring chaos to the nation's capital. Rivington published one report from London suggesting that "it is the Dissenters and Methodists who are secretly blowing up the flame," a claim that was rebuked a week later by New York's Methodist community.[85] There were even more accusations that secret Catholic and pro-American cells were operating in London, paying off rioters or plying them with alcohol to encourage more death and destruction. A letter from a Londoner reported that once the military arrived in the city "all this commotion of French, Americans, Spaniards and Puritans was subdued in two days."[86] In August, Kingstonians read that the "diabolical tumults . . . owe their contrivance and execution to foreign agents, assisted by seditious conspirators of our own country," while Glaswegians were led to believe that the "horrible riots" were "promoted by French money."[87] In subsequent issues, Jesuits were alleged to have been captured carrying large sums of money and lists of places to attack.[88] British enemies had infiltrated their capital city, threatening ruin to the British Empire at a critical moment in the war.

In the aftermath of the riots, many writers lashed out at the Opposition in Parliament and pro-American sympathizers, who these writers believed had

Down with the Bank!

No
POPERY

NO POPERY or NEWGATE REFORMER.

Tho' He Says he's a Protestant, look at the Print,
The Face and the Bludgeon, will give you a hint,
Religion he cries, in hopes to deceive,
While his practice is only to burn and to thieve.
Publish'd as the Act Directs, June 9, 1780 by J. Catch of Striker.

FIGURE 7.1. *No Popery or Newgate Reformer* (1780). In the aftermath of the Gordon Riots, British writers and artists were quick to characterize the protesters as dangerous and violent agitators motivated, not by principled beliefs, but by greed and self-interest. *Courtesy of The Lewis Walpole Library, Yale University.*

created a political climate ripe for such atrocities. They argued that supporting an American rebellion that cast off rank and distinction, favored extralegal committees and mob rule, and combined with both France and Spain had bred a similar culture of licentiousness and chaos in Great Britain. The riots were a manifestation of a political culture of disloyalty that had been allowed to fester for too long in the empire.

But after the defeat of these agitators—which was often described in newspaper reports as if the government had won a battle in the ongoing war—
British writers now believed the nation could come together. Like Burgoyne's
embarrassing loss nearly three years earlier, the government's victory over
Gordon and his supporters was sold as a victory for order and government.
"We shall grow up into more sociality," wrote a Londoner in letter published
in the *Scots Magazine*, "we shall value order more than anarchy; we shall look
upon it as madness to care only each for himself; we shall be less French and
less American, and less demoniacs than ever."[89] New Yorkers learned in September that residents of Britain's capital city were "more peaceable, more
unanimous, and more sensible of the blessings of a civil government. . . . In
short," the writer concluded, "this commotion . . . has, in my humble opinion been productive of more security and advantage to this country, than any
circumstance that has happened in [recent] memory."[90]

Published reports and letters also assured readers that the nation was still
committed to defeating the rebellion. "Impress this upon the minds of America," announced a Londoner in Rivington's newspaper, "her tyrants will hold
up the conflagrations and murders in the metropolis as symptoms of the ardor
and strength of their friends; it is so much the contrary, that the hardiest traitor
who has not taken flight to France, is compelled to skulk in holes and corners."[91] Weeks later, Haligonians learned in a report from New York City that a
fleet of British warships were destined for the coast of France to stop their enemies from sending troops and supplies to America. "Great-Britain," the writer
proclaimed, "like ancient Rome, never suffers her enemies to avail themselves
of her internal commotions, if the late tumultuous and riotous proceedings . . .
may be termed such."[92]

It was especially important for Glaswegians to demonstrate their loyal support for the Crown at this critical moment.[93] In August, the provost and city
council sent a loyalty address to the king that declared their "abhorrence &
Detestation of those Dreadful acts of violence and outrage." They also promised to "carefully watch over the Peace of the Community to which we belong, and oppose, with the utmost vigour, every attempt against the Dignity
of your Majestys Crown, and that Excellent Constitution of which you have
ever been the guardian."[94]

The city's ongoing support for the war also provided evidence of their loyalty. Such was the case when news of Clinton's victory at Charleston arrived
just days after the end of the riots. The British had captured more than five
thousand American soldiers and an entire arsenal of supplies and weaponry,
now possessed the most important port city in the southern colonies, and were
poised to march north toward Philadelphia. Glaswegians took to the streets

to celebrate the occasion, while published reports emphasized the peaceful-ness and order of the day's activities. Homes and places of business were il-luminated in "a most magnificent manner" and with "the utmost decency and decorum," while the "great bells were set a ringing" in the evening. Similar celebrations occurred throughout the west of Scotland, an area largely inhab-ited by zealous opponents of Catholic relief. Yet "there was not a town or vil-lage," concluded the report, "which did not feel the most heart-felt satisfaction at the success of his Majesty's arms, and express it in the most joyous and in-nocent manner that can possibly be conceived."[95]

In this way, Glaswegians shared a great deal in common with Britons else-where in the North Atlantic. Success in battle—and there were a slew of suc-cesses from the spring through the fall of 1780—led many to believe their nation was finally on the verge of victory. Kingstonians paraded in March on news of both Rodney's triumph over the Spanish at the Battle of Cape St. Vin-cent and premature reports of Clinton having captured Charleston from the French and Americans. Amid the celebrations, some "indulged their generous ardour" by enlisting in volunteer companies for a third (and ultimately disas-trous) assault on the Spanish Main. "The Genius of Britain, roused from her slumber, begins to pour down upon her valiant sons," who were winning at sea and on land against their combined Catholic and American enemies.[96]

New Yorkers and Haligonians also celebrated the taking of Charleston in late May with parades, bonfires, and general illuminations, even as Haligonians braced for a rumored French attack on their colony.[97] In August, residents of the northern port city read of Dalling's allegedly successful assault on the Span-ish Main, of crowds gathering in Charleston to toast the king's birthday, and of another naval victory at Martinique, again led by Rodney, whom one writer described as the *"Dread of France* and *Scourge of Spain!"*[98] A month later in New York City, on George III's coronation day and with the famed Rodney in at-tendance, the "City Militia, to a very great number, [and] the volunteer com-panies" paraded through town on account of Cornwallis's victory at the Battle of Camden.[99] British military success also led to growing rumors of widespread discord among Continental soldiers and more general American antipathy toward Congress and their allies.[100] It was then that Britons across the empire also heard of Arnold's defection to the British and subsequent calls for others to join him. Had the war ended differently, 1780 might have been remembered alongside 1759 as another *annus mirabilis* in the annals of British history.

This outburst of loyalty—this new British common cause—which crossed to all corners of Britain's vast Atlantic empire, ignored the previous ideologi-cal debates that drove a wedge in that empire. In the last years of the war, there were no discussions of taxes, consent, or sovereignty; no concerns over repre-

sentation and trade policies. This was a militant brand of Protestant Britishness that found meaning in British victories over Bourbon monarchs and their
less important American allies. Britons celebrated a commitment to popular
notions of Protestant British liberty, which they framed against the tyranny
of a Congress now beholden to French and Spanish Catholics. By the end of
1780, many had also come to believe that victory in the war was possible. They
were hopeful that rebellious colonists, once defeated, would see through the
deception of their Congress, abandon their alleged loyalty to a foreign monarch, and return their allegiance to the British Crown and empire.

The language of Protestant Loyalism, then, was capable of drawing together disparate subjects from across the empire, of rousing the British lion.
But it was also able to turn that lion against the government, especially in mainland Britain, where the specter of Catholic relief still haunted some subjects.
Despite repeated demonstrations of loyalty by local magistrates in the fall,
many Glaswegians refused to acquiesce to a narrative that sought to equate
opposition to Catholic relief with the violent riots in London. In November,
Scottish newspapers published the Protestant Association's resolves, which defended Gordon's role in the movement as he stood trial on charges of high
treason. They disavowed the violence "of the late horrid riots, which now, to
our joy, and that of all good Protestants and loyal subjects, are happily sub-
sided." But they also praised Gordon's "unshaken confidence" in defending
their faith against popery, "which the present family on the throne were called
to these kingdoms to protect and defend."[101]

A week later, the various societies and associations formed in Glasgow nearly
two years earlier met publicly to approve of the resolutions and "to appear in
behalf of the Protestant religion on every occasion."[102] In January 1781, several
trade incorporations, town councils, clubs, and societies in and around the
nearby town of Paisley published addresses in the *Glasgow Journal* in an effort
to rally public support for Gordon and the Protestant cause.[103] Officials were
so concerned by "the Enthusiastic Zeal of Thousands of Common People" in
southwest Scotland that they warned local military commanders and sheriffs to
be on guard should rioting occur.[104] As the trial approached, Scots appeared
once again on the verge of a Protestant rebellion against an arbitrary Crown and
government that sought to put to death the leader of their cause.

Gordon was acquitted the following month, however, and the news produced
widespread celebrations across Scotland. Reports from Glasgow and the surrounding region continued to emphasize Glaswegians' civility and peaceful-
ness—a necessity after the riots in London—but there was no mistaking the
joy this news brought to the general population. Gordon's friends in Glasgow

illuminated the city, while so many "bonfires [were] kindled in every street" that the city provost wrote to Edinburgh officials suggesting they "prohibit Such rejoicings" in the future for better "preserving the Public peace."[105] In other places, public toasts published in local newspapers equated Scottish opposition to Catholic relief with their support for the new British Common cause. In the southeast border town of Dunse, residents drank to the king, Gordon, and "the Protestant cause," while also toasting "Success to his Majesty's arms by sea and land, against all his enemies."[106] Gordon's acquittal excited larger and more elaborate celebrations throughout Scotland than any of the previous British military successes in the American war.

The No Popery cause—a movement precipitated by the crisis and rebellion in America—revealed a radical shift in how Glaswegians understood their place in the British Empire. Previously, Scottish subjects were susceptible to accusations of disloyalty and struggled to overcome the virulent Scotophobic rhetoric of the 1760s Wilkite cause. There were moments when Glaswegians collectively resisted such labels—as in the case of the Douglas Cause of the late 1760s—but their tepid support for the war in 1775 did little to mitigate these long-standing suspicions among their English peers. But beginning in 1778, Glaswegians turned to a cause that struck at the very foundation of eighteenth-century Protestant Whig Loyalism. Their violent opposition to Catholic relief, which derived greater meaning from the war against France, Spain, and America, evidenced a people no longer asking for inclusion. They were instead demanding that their king and government act in ways consistent with the nation's long-held Protestant political and religious obligations.

But Gordon's release from prison in February 1781 occurred at a moment when the war began to turn against Britain. British subjects learned early in the year that Dalling's hopes of capturing Spanish America had collapsed near Lake Nicaragua, where British forces died in staggering numbers from yellow fever and other tropical diseases. The expedition angered Kingstonians, who argued that Dalling's foolish plans had deprived their island of provisions and manpower and weakened their once prosperous trade.[107] At the same time, news spread of two devastating hurricanes having wrecked much of the north side of the island. They killed thousands, destroyed entire towns and villages, and once again left Jamaica susceptible to invasion.[108] In the late spring, Spanish forces were also able to wrest west Florida from British hands, while a combined Spanish and French siege of Gibraltar continued to drain British resources. Even victories caused problems for the nation. After Rodney captured the Dutch colony of St. Eustatius in February, he and General John Vaughn stayed behind to loot the local inhabitants, rather than pursue de Grasse's French fleet near Martinique, which left Jamaica vulnerable to attack.[109]

British operations in North America also began to falter. Officials overestimated the support of the rural Loyalist population in the south and struggled to retain territory taken from the Americans. Edward Cornwallis, in charge of the southern campaign, suffered a series of defeats in the spring, and by the summer months Patriot forces regained control of much of South Carolina and Georgia. Absent support, Cornwallis was forced to move his depleted army to the coast to be resupplied, first in Wilmington, North Carolina, and then again in Yorktown, Virginia, in the fall of 1781. British naval vessels from New York City attempted to reach Cornwallis in September, but by then de Grasse's fleet, freed to move north from the Caribbean while Rodney pillaged St. Eustatius, had blocked the entrance to the Chesapeake Bay. Meanwhile, Washington, who had planned to invade New York City in the fall, instead led his combined Franco-American army south to Virginia. There he joined with the Marquis de Lafayette's forces to lay siege to Yorktown. Without any possibility of being relieved, Cornwallis surrendered to the French and Americans on October 17.[110]

Britons everywhere recognized the enormity of this defeat. Loyalist refugees in New York City and Halifax were especially shocked. One New Yorker remarked that "general consternation and lamentation prevailed" throughout the city.[111] Myles Cooper felt their anxiety from across the ocean. The former member of Rivington's "Club" of writers who had fled to Edinburgh in the spring of 1775 wrote a friend in New York City that he had "never felt such anguish of Mind upon any Occasion. . . . I fear ye Cause is lost, I am tormented and distracted . . . I know not what Man can do for you."[112] Refugees were also angered by the articles of capitulation, which did not give immunity to captured Loyalists, many of whom served in New York regiments. William Smith recorded in his diary that the city's inhabitants were "vexed and despondent on the Fate of the Refugees left there to the Mercy of the Usurpers."[113]

Elsewhere, Britons lamented the state of the war in North America and worried things might get even worse. In Kingston, residents (correctly) feared that the defeat would trigger a French and Spanish attack on their island. One writer in the Cornwall Chronicle warned readers to be on "guard against any sudden attack or invasion . . . which nothing will be able to resist but manly fortitude, and a virtuous exertion."[114] News of the defeat also coincided with a fire that consumed a large portion of Kingston. It destroyed upward of one hundred homes and stores, leading some to speculate that lurking enemies were at fault. Over the following days, several more attempts were made to burn other parts of the city, prompting officials to arrest "all foreigners and other suspected persons" and to further restrict the movement of slaves.[115]

Glaswegians were devastated by news of the defeat, as well, but argued that it should not distract Britain from the more important war against France. One writer even believed that officials should abandon America: "turning the whole strength of our fleets and armies upon the French, through whose aid rebellion has flourished, seems to be the only means left for a renovation of our glory."[116] Though inconceivable to most Britons a year early, Cornwallis's defeat awakened subjects to a new reality. They had possibly lost their American colonies, most likely to the French, and were in danger of also losing their prized sugar colonies.

Loyal Britons in New York City, Kingston, and Halifax certainly understood the seriousness of the situation. In the days following Cornwallis's surrender they publicly declared their independence from the American Congress and hoped others would follow their lead. On November 17, Rivington published "A DECLARATION, &c.," which closely mirrored Jefferson's more famous declaration, except this one turned against Congress, not the king. According to the short introduction accompanying the piece, the asked that the declaration to be "circulated in the course of this winter through all parts of the continent," though that wish does not appear to have been fulfilled. Not a single Patriot newspaper carried the declaration, perhaps because they feared its influence, but also because they were too busy celebrating the victory at Yorktown. Instead, the declaration traveled to other loyal communities, arriving in both Halifax and Kingston in late January, not long after residents read of the tragedy at Yorktown.[117] Though intended for a colonial audience, the declaration also made its way across the North Atlantic to mainland Britain, though it does not appear to have been published in Glasgow.[118]

The declaration is a remarkable document on several accounts. First, and perhaps most obviously, it reveals the impact of Cornwallis's unexpected defeat on the British war effort. The devastating loss pushed aside previous conversations in which loyal Britons simply railed against Patriot leaders or complained of the hypocrisy of the French alliance. With the possibility of American victory in sight, Loyalists needed to formally sever ties with Congress, just as Patriots had done with their king in 1776. The declaration also demonstrates the civil nature of this now six-year-long war. When it came to declaring independence, loyal Britons turned to their enemy's own declaration. They defended their rebellion against Congress by using many of the same Protestant Whig ideas—a fear of tyranny and a love of liberty—that their former friends used to kill their king.[119]

But the ultimate importance of this document lay in the grievances. Like Jefferson's declaration, the anonymous writer needed evidence to justify separation. He had to prove to loyal Britons (and hopefully rebellious colonists) that Congress had not just made mistakes in the past, but that those mistakes portended a future rife with tyranny and widespread suffering. It is in the evidence—a list of nearly thirty grievances that filled more than two columns of Rivington's newspaper—that we find perhaps the most profound statement of the British common cause made during the entire war.

The grievances effectively blended both the 1775 and 1778 British common causes. The first, most forcefully argued by Rivington's "Club" of writers on the eve of the war, depended on an understanding of the crisis that was critical of congressional tyranny and crowd violence. The fifth grievance took Jefferson's accusation that the king had repeatedly dissolved representative assemblies and instead blamed Congress for having "by mobs and riots awed Representative Houses, repeatedly into a compliance with their resolutions, though destructive of the peace, liberty, and safety of the people." In the tenth grievance, the writer ridiculed Congress for having "raised a standing army . . . without any act of the legislature . . . [and] independent of the civil power." The sixteenth turned Jefferson's criticism of the Quebec Act onto the rebellious colonists, charging Congress with having "abolished the true system of the English constitution and laws . . . and established therein a weak and factious democracy." The writer also accused Britain's opponents of ending "all good order and government," driving loyal Britons "into exile" and confiscating their property, while also ruining "our trade" and destroying "our credit with all parts of the world." Rivington would have been especially moved by the twenty-seventh grievance: "We find them contending for liberty of speech," the writer argued, "and at the same time controlling the press, by means of a mob, and persecuting every one who ventures to hint his disapprobation of their proceedings."

A majority of the criticism leveled at Congress, however, drew from the 1778 common cause, which equated congressional tyranny with French Catholic despotism. The writer took Jefferson's claim that the king had joined with Parliament to subject colonists to laws "foreign to our constitution," and offered a far more damning accusation that Congress had "combined with France, the natural and hereditary enemy of our civil constitution, and religious faith, to render us dependant on and subservient to the views, of that foreign, ambitious, and despotic monarchy." Similarly, the writer challenged Jefferson's accusation that the king had used German soldiers "to compleat the works of death, desolation, and tyranny." He blamed Congress instead for having "invited over an army of foreign mercenaries" that prevented "an honorable peace and accommodation with our ancient friend and parent" under the terms of the Carlisle Commission.

The writer ended with a flourish, targeting the hypocrisy of the Franco-American alliance. Much as in Jefferson's declaration, the language turned decidedly more emotional, with hopes that these final passages would drive readers to the Loyalist cause by appealing to their base political and religious instincts.[120] Readers were reminded that delegates who railed against the Quebec Act in 1774 were now "leagued with the eldest son of this bloody, impious, bigoted, and persecuting church, to ruin the nation from whose loins we sprung." There was more. "We think it not too severe to say," the author argued, "that we find them as intoxicated with ambition of Independent sovereignty, as that execrable Roman Daughter, who drove the wheels of her chariot over the mangled body of her murdered father, in her way to the capitol." Their fears of popery "have vanished," while they tried "to seduce the Canadian to their side." Even worse, they had neglected "their patriotic and religious ancestors . . . who chose rather to become exiles . . . than to submit to civil, but above all religious innovations." Now they were willing to destroy the constitution by "encouraging a religion which they held in abhorrence, as idolatrous and tyrannical." For these reasons, concluded the author, the "Natives and Citizens of America . . . do renounce and disclaim all allegiance, duty or submission to the Congress, or to any government under them."[121]

We are accustomed to thinking of the Battle of Yorktown as the decisive victory in the American fight for independence. Contemporary Americans certainly saw it as such, celebrating the defeat of Cornwallis's army with a degree of festivity unparalleled in the entirety of the war. The triumph stoked popular American attitudes of the virtuousness and magnanimity of their common cause, which they continued to frame in heavily racialized ways.[122] The British saw the writing on the wall, too. The war was nearing its seventh year, and the British had little to show for their effort. Since France's entry into the war, the nation had been stretched to its limits and suffered from repeated domestic turmoil, most famously in the 1780 Gordon Riots. Popular opposition to the American war grew in the aftermath of Yorktown. By March 1782, the marquess of Rockingham replaced Lord North at the head of the government and opened negotiations for an end to the conflict.

But there is another, largely forgotten narrative of post-Yorktown that describes neither American victory, nor British defeat. Rather this narrative tells the story of British independence, of loyal British subjects declaring their disavowal of the Patriot cause in favor of a renewed defense of Protestant Whig Loyalism. The Loyalist declaration demonstrated that a British common cause—committed to Protestantism, liberty, and monarchical government— had emerged from the war victorious, even in defeat. When read against the grain, in fact, the declaration's criticism of Congress for having incited crowd violence, destroyed trade, abandoned law and order, silenced opponents, and made friends with French Catholics, was actually a celebration of the British system of governance—a system that promoted order, constituted government, prosperity, freedom, and Protestantism. The American victory may have cost the empire its stake in much of North America, but despite their best efforts the Americans had not forced Britons to abandon their Britishness. The opposite was true. France's entry into the civil war had actually produced a more unwavering defense of loyalty and Loyalism among subjects throughout the North Atlantic.

It was of no surprise to readers on both sides of the ocean that this call for independence came from Rivington's print shop. Loyal refugees in New York City had the most to lose in the winter of 1781 and were most in need of making sense of the defeat. The declaration did not end hopes for reconciliation among many of the city's inhabitants, some of whom desperately wished to continue the war. But it did offer a clearer way of understanding the war, their enemy, and what it meant to be British. The same was true, though perhaps to a lesser degree, in places like Kingston and Halifax, where subjects had long struggled to make sense of the rebellion. The declaration, then, was both instructive—it explained to readers why they should reject Congress and what it meant to be British—and expressive, demonstrating the loyalty of a community at a crucial moment in the conflict.

Glaswegians did not read the declaration, unless they happened upon an issue of another city's newspaper in one of their many taverns or coffeehouses. But they did not need to see it. It was not necessary for them to declare independence from a foreign government thousands of miles away. Glaswegians certainly would have understood the declaration's contents, however. Congressional tyranny, mob violence, and the fear of popery were all common themes in the Glasgow press over the final years of the war. These themes had shaped popular attitudes toward the conflict and the enemy in Glasgow, just as they had among Glaswegians' fellow subjects in the colonies.

Ultimately, however, Glaswegians came to embrace a different understanding of Loyalism than their colonial counterparts in the aftermath of Yorktown. Glaswegians had spent the previous three years battling the spread of popery in their own country, occasioned not by some act of Congress, but by the designs of their own government. The No Popery cause had provoked a defense of a more radical vision of Protestant Whig Loyalism that shared more in common with the language of rebellious Americans in 1775 than it did with the more conservative loyalty expressed by British colonists in 1781.

It is impossible to overstate the importance of the Franco-American alliance on popular conceptions of Britishness in the latter years of the war. It is difficult, in fact, to even imagine how British subjects would have responded to American independence had France not joined the conflict. Britons' understanding of the war after 1778 depended entirely on the presence of their longstanding Catholic foes. Loyal subjects expressed a more determined defense of their nation, both because of who they were now fighting and because the war pushed into communities throughout the North Atlantic. The inhabitants of these four cities felt the war in profound ways after 1778, which forced them to think more seriously about their nation and national identity. In the end, they emerged from the nearly twenty-year conflict with a sharpened understanding of their Britishness. They were more committed to monarchy than ever before, but, crucially, they were also far more aware of the rights and liberties they enjoyed as British subjects. Unlike their American counterparts, loyal Britons across the North Atlantic remained convinced of the strength and resilience of their Protestant Empire and their place within it.

Conclusion

Reimagining Loyalism in a Postwar British Atlantic

In the late spring of 1782, thousands of Britons throughout the North Atlantic took part in the largest celebration for a battle victory during the entire American War for Independence. But there was something different about this battle. It was fought outside of the thirteen American colonies and against opponents who were not former British subjects. On April 12, just six months after Cornwallis's defeat at Yorktown, Admiral George Brydges Rodney defeated Comte de Grasse's French fleet at the Isles de Saintes, near the French Caribbean islands of Dominica and Guadeloupe. The victory was more of a rout. Rodney captured de Grasse and his flagship the *Ville de Paris* and four other French vessels, destroyed five more, took all of de Grasse's heavy artillery, and killed as many as six thousand French soldiers and sailors. The Battle of the Saintes, as it came to be known, thwarted an attempt by the French to capture Jamaica, the crown jewel of Britain's Atlantic empire.[1]

This was perhaps the greatest naval victory in British history until Horatio Nelson's success at Trafalgar more than twenty years later. Contemporary Britons certainly understood the significance of the moment. When Rodney returned to London in August, thousands paraded the famed admiral through the city's crowded streets amid cheers of "Rodney, Forever!"[2] Britons also gathered at local print shops to purchase popular prints of the victory over the French, which illustrated their nation's continued dominance of the Atlantic (figs. C.1 and C.2). Rodney, according to one historian, was "one of the few

FIGURE C.1.   *Taleo, or the Royal Sportsman, Running Down the Enemies of Great Britain* (1782). Rodney's victory convinced many Britons of the continued supremacy of their Atlantic empire, even after the loss of the thirteen American colonies. George III is shown here charging his European foes on horseback alongside a pack of dogs, each with collars bearing the names of famed British naval admirals. The Dutchman lays helpless on the ground amid two charging hounds, while the Spaniard fails to escape the jaws of another dog. Meanwhile, the dog named for Rodney locks its teeth into the leg of a Frenchman flailing his arms in panic as he leaps over a fence. *Courtesy of The Lewis Walpole Library, Yale University.*

British heroes of the Revolutionary War," which was made entirely possible by his improbable victory at the Saintes.[3]

News of this stunning success arrived in distant North Atlantic port cities ravaged by seven years of war and nearly two decades of political and social unrest. In fact, it is befitting of a revolution and war with such profound implications for inhabitants of the British Atlantic that the last major battle actually took place in that sea. Kingstonians certainly had cause to rejoice. Their city was spared the depredations of a French and Spanish invasion by the heroic actions of Rodney and his crew. "The demonstrations of Joy [shown] by the inhabitants of this Island [for Lord] George's glorious victory," reported one resident, "were [expressive] of the sense they entertain [of its] importance." The soldiers and island militia, who had been called into service when an invasion appeared imminent, fired a "general Feu de Joie," which rang from "all the forts in the harbor," while upward of three hundred of the town's merchants gathered for a celebratory dinner at a local tavern.[4] Kingstonians illuminated their town for two consecutive nights, and a band performed "God Save the King" and other patriotic songs from the balcony of the British

FIGURE C.2. *St. George & the Dragon* (1782). Some Britons, especially Loyalist refugees in New York, hoped Rodney's victory might lead to a renewed war against the rebellious colonists and their allies even as the newly appointed Rockingham administration began negotiating for peace. In this print, the gallant Rodney is seen slaying a dragon with wings covered in fleur-de-lis and spitting out frogs. Behind him, the new foreign secretary, Charles James Fox, offers Rodney a baron's coronet to stop fighting, fearing that the famed admiral's successes might derail the peace negotiations. *Courtesy of the John Carter Brown Library.*

Coffeehouse "amidst the joyful and repeated acclamations of a great number of inhabitants."[5]

Across the ocean, in Glasgow, "accounts of the gallant Admiral Rodney's complete victory over the French fleet in the West Indies, produced the greatest joy, which was visibly seen in ever countenance, from the highest to the lowest." In the evening, local officials ordered that "all the bells were set a-ringing, and the town [was] illuminated' to a degree not known "since the accession of his present Majesty." Chapman and Duncan's *Glasgow Mercury* also included a list of toasts delivered by the town magistrates and "principal inhabitants" expressive of the city's loyalty to the crown and empire. They raised their glasses to "the King, Queen, Royal Family, Sir G. Rodney, and all the Admirals, Captains, &c. who bore a share of the glorious and important victory obtained on the 12th of April, 1782." Similar reports of "bonfires, illuminations, [and] convivial meetings" from towns across the west of Scotland demonstrated the widespread loyalty of that region.[6]

New Yorkers also crowded the streets to celebrate the naval victory, even as they read rumors of the increasing likelihood of American independence. Rivington had news of Rodney's success proclaimed by handbill and published detailed accounts of "the glory of that triumphant, and ever to be recorded day, the twelfth of April eighty-two."[7] In nearby Brooklyn, a local tavern keeper hosted a dinner "fit for a conquering Sovereign" on a day in which "firm re-establishment . . . [was] given to Monarchy—Tyranny and its Republic are no more." The evening concluded with "amusements and decorations . . . to illustrate the Glories lately secured by his Majesty's arms in the West-Indies."[8] The following week, Loyalist refugees combined their elation for Rodney with celebrations of the king's birthday, which was given an added boost by the recent arrival of Prince William Henry, the king's third son and the future monarch. Soldiers fired a royal salute from Fort George, which was answered by the ships of war in the harbor, while leading military officials and other dignitaries congratulated the prince. The evening concluded with the firing of a "Feu de Joie . . . amongst many thousands of rejoicing inhabitants."[9]

News of Rodney's victory took a circuitous route to Halifax, arriving by way of a captured American vessel traveling from Antigua to Penobscot. The details were brief—the British had won a "decisive engagement" over their French foes—but Henry hoped that "by the first arrivals from New-York or the West-Indies, to give our Readers a more particular account of this interesting Event."[10] Unfortunately, no copies of his paper survive for the following three weeks, when celebrations likely occurred in that city. By early June, Lieutenant Governor Andrew Hamond wrote that it had produced a "perfect Tranquillity" in Halifax, while the council and assembly published addresses expressing their pleasure with "the present Appearance of public Affairs" on account of Rodney's success.[11] Haligonians also gathered at the Great Pontac Inn to sing "*The* WOODEN WALLS of ENGLAND," which celebrated the supremacy of the British navy over their European foes: "From Sea to Sea, from Shore to Shore, Bear then, ye Winds, the solemn Strain! This sacred Truth an Awe struck World appeals, *Britain's best Bulwark are her Wooden Walls.*"[12] Over the following weeks, the city's residents read of similar demonstrations of joy in the nation's capital, including James Fox's declaration that the defeat of de Grasse was "the most brilliant that this country had seen this century."[13]

Britons everywhere reveled in Rodney's success. They toasted, sang, and paraded, both in honor of the acclaimed general and with joy at the news of another crushing defeat of their longtime enemies.[14] Not since Wolfe's improbable victory at Quebec in 1759 had there been such an outpouring of joy in the streets of British towns and cities across the empire.[15] Yet, surprisingly, the Battle of the Saintes barely features in the historiography of the American Revolution, which largely centers on the march to independence after the American victory at Yorktown. The importance of Rodney's triumph has largely been reduced to its regional significance in having secured Jamaica from a devastating combined French and Spanish invasion.[16] Just one scholar has examined the battle beyond the shores of that island by looking at how mainland British subjects responded to news of the victory. Rodney was feted in towns in villages throughout the British Isles, the writer argues, because Rodney's defeat of the French represented a triumph of Britishness in a war that had questioned that very identity.[17]

Historians of Britain and the British Empire agree that the American Revolution led to a more determined but geographically narrower definition of Britishness. They argue that the revolution produced a "sharp move to the Right" in British political culture, a Thermidorean reaction that preceded the French by a decade. In the war's aftermath, officials in London embraced a far more conservative and authoritarian definition of Britishness that established clear distinctions between metropolitan and colonial subjects. Never again would Parliament presume that colonists enjoyed the same rights and liberties as their mainland counterparts. This attitude was shaped, in part, by the contentious political debates of the 1760s and 1770s, but also by the far more racially diverse population that now inhabited Britain's growing empire in the East. The celebrations in the British Isles surrounding Rodney's defeat of de Grasse, which were supposedly explicit in their support of this new conception of Britishness, are thought to illustrate this transformative moment.[18]

But this interpretation ignores the tens of thousands of subjects inhabiting the loyal British Atlantic. Their voices are lost in this narrow imperial perspective, where only metropolitan Britons (and mostly the English) were tasked with answering questions of loyalty and patriotism. For nearly two decades, Glaswegians, Kingstonians, Haligonians, and New Yorkers had also wrestled with questions prompted by the crisis and war. These subjects played just as an important role in shaping the British narrative of the conflict and in reimagining a popular, transatlantic understanding of what it meant to be British. France's participation in the latter years of the war was crucial to this process, but it did not necessarily lead these Britons to embrace a more conservative, authoritarian understanding of Loyalism. In Britain's postwar Atlantic empire, subjects in these four communities voiced a greater commitment to monarchical government, but they also expressed a more determined defense of the rights and liberties they enjoyed.

When viewed through the wider lens of the British Atlantic, this renewed embrace of Britishness also sits in tension with a diversity of local political cultures that were defined, in part, by their resident's revolutionary experiences.

Britons in these four communities often made sense of the debates surrounding this period, of questions of rights and liberties and what constituted tyranny, from distinct local perspectives. Of course, such differences did not originate in the 1760s and 1770s, nor were they previously incompatible with broader characterizations of British loyalty and Loyalism. But the events of this period forced these disparities into the open in ways previously unknown.

They revealed a shocking reality. There was little that actually bound together Britain's Atlantic empire. The actions of rebellious Americans certainly confirmed this point, but it was just as true of loyal Britons. Shared attitudes toward their nation and empire, their sense of loyalty and patriotism, collapsed in the face of rebellion predicated on a similar defense of Britishness. It was not so much that these loyal Britons lost their claim to an "empire of liberty," as several scholars contend, but that they simply could not agree on a shared understanding of British liberty.[19] Even the Franco-American alliance, which exposed the fraudulent nature of the American cause and helped to restore a triumphal narrative of Protestant Whig Loyalism, was unable to fully overcome how Britons across the North Atlantic came to understand the American Revolution.

On closer inspection, in fact, the celebrations surrounding Rodney's victory in these four communities reveal this tension between a shared defense of Britishness reinvigorated by the war against France and the more entrenched ideological divisions within the North Atlantic brought about by the events of the revolution and war. Loyal Britons expressed a greater, shared commitment to monarchy and empire but continued to defend a particular understanding of British liberty rooted in how they had experienced two decades of conflict.

The American Revolution muddied the waters of the North Atlantic. Over the previous twenty years, American Patriots thoroughly disrupted long-standing transatlantic narratives of Loyalism, calling into question the very beliefs and institutions central to eighteenth-century definitions of Britishness. Rebellious Americans rejected Parliamentary rule and legitimate government, which were previously thought to have secured the cherished rights and liberties of British subjects. They turned against mercantilism, a system of economy most Britons believed to have created widespread prosperity on both sides of the ocean. Rebel colonists also made their king into a Catholic and their former countrymen into friends of slaves and Indians, the very enemies who had proved so useful in uniting the empire's desperate population of subjects. Even more incomprehensible, these colonists defended their actions (at least until 1778) by laying claim to the very ideas and language that had previously bound together subjects across the North Atlantic. American Patriots not only robbed loyal Britons of a large swath of their empire but also stole away their sense of identity and belonging.

Rodney's triumph, and the Franco-American alliance more generally, helped to recover a shared Protestant British political culture ravaged by years of conflict. But neither were capable of completely overcoming the many divisions caused by the revolution. Popular understandings of Britishness were far more contingent on particular local political cultures shaped by the devastating events of the previous two decades. These divisions were especially apparent in the many celebrations surrounding de Grasse's defeat in the late spring of 1782. When Britons in each of these four communities took to the streets, they simultaneously affirmed the supremacy of their Protestant British empire and revealed the inescapable and entrenched differences among the nation's diverse Atlantic subjects.

White Kingstonians emerged from the revolution and war committed to a defense of monarchy, constituted government, and Protestantism, but, crucially, they had also come to believe that their liberty depended to a greater degree on the protection afforded by the British state. The crisis and war repeatedly reminded them of the precarious nature of freedom in a colony mostly inhabited by enslaved Africans and surrounded by French and Spanish colonies. At virtually every crucial moment over the previous twenty years, the island's residents were plagued by reports of rumored slave revolts or French and Spanish invasions. Kingstonians' failure to resist the Stamp Act was based, in part, on reports of an intended slave uprising on the island. They all but ignored the disputes over the Townshend duties, because they were too concerned with the outbreak of war with France over the Falkland Islands, which also led to new rumors of slave insurrections perhaps instigated by their Catholic foes. Kingstonians' trade suffered in the late 1760s and early 1770s as well, largely because of menacing Spanish *guarda costas* who opposed the opening of British free ports in the Caribbean. When the crisis began to turn toward rebellion early in 1775, Kingston representatives in the colonial assembly petitioned the king on behalf of the American colonists but admitted that the "peculiar situation" of their colony made resistance impossible.

Yet by the following year, fears of domestic revolts and foreign invasions were increasingly tied to the ideas and actions of American Patriots. From the start of the war, rebel privateers harassed the island's coastal communities, captured merchant ships traveling to and from Kingston, and actually conspired to incite slave revolts on the island. Most famously, the island's white inhabitants foiled a slave revolt in the fall of 1776 supposedly triggered by revolutionary rhetoric and colonial boycotts. After France and then Spain joined the war, stories of slave uprisings increasingly involved Britain's long-standing foes and their new American friends, while Jamaicans complained that the rebellion drew away soldiers needed to protect their island from such attacks. If some American colonists came to embrace a Patriot cause out of fear of British-instigated slave revolts and Indian attacks, it is just as likely that white Kingstonians were driven to loyalty by similar fears prompted by the actions of rebellious American colonists.[20] Loyalism, Kingstonians came to realize, was intimately bound to their right—their freedom—to own another person. Just as important, they believed it was the job of their government to protect this cherished right.

Their celebration of Rodney's victory demonstrated the island's dependency on the British state, which white Jamaicans understood as necessary given their "peculiar situation." In the days following news of the victory, Jamaican parishes drafted letters of thanks to the famed admiral, which were published in both local and British Atlantic newspapers. The letters acted as a kind of official statement for what the victory, and broader war, had come to mean to the colony's inhabitants. Across the island, Britons repeatedly described Rodney in paternalistic terms, for he had protected their city and colony from their many foes and, in doing so, secured to the inhabitants their cherished rights as British subjects. Kingstonians referred to him as the "guardian of Jamaica," for having defeated "the combined force of our enemies," and "restored us to the peaceable enjoyment of our civil rights."[21] The residents of St. Ann Parish on the north side of the island declared Rodney the "DELIVERER OF OUR COUNTRY" for having saved the island "from imminent danger."[22] The inhabitants of Hanover Parish described him as their "Protector" for securing "to us domestic happiness, personal safety, and quiet possession of our rights and properties."[23]

In 1783, the island assembly (in a rare display of planter-merchant unity) commissioned a statue of Rodney, which also spoke to the dependent nature of postwar Jamaican Loyalism. Unlike West's famous painting, *The Death of General Wolfe*, which portrayed the fallen general and unfurled flag as symbols of the future greatness of Britain's Protestant empire, Rodney appears in a more conservative, authoritarian, and classical form. Standing nearly eight feet tall, he is dressed in an antique naval costume and is in the stoic classical Apollo Belvedere pose, with his arm outstretched as though he has just slain his foe. It is an imposing statue, one that is meant both to recall the moment the famed naval commander defeated his French foe and to imagine Rodney (and the British state) as the great protector of the island colony. The reliefs across the base of the statue celebrate Britain's martial spirit but also the island's reliance on the state for its safety and prosperity. On one side Britannia stands with a raised shield and sword drawn, protecting an infant Jamaica who grabs at her leg while the British lion sits before them and a French standard retreats from the scene. The statue cost the assembly an enormous sum, more than £31,000, highlighting the loyalty of the island's white inhabitants and their immense wealth.[24]

Kingstonians saw Rodney as the great protector, as a Roman warrior defending the city and colony from their many internal and external enemies. They viewed his victory, and the Franco-American alliance more generally, as evidence of the continued superiority of a Protestant British imperial identity, and they remained convinced that Britain was an empire of liberty. But, importantly, white Kingstonians equated their notion of liberty with the right to enslave Africans and to resist menacing Catholic French and Spanish invaders. The city's white inhabitants had learned over the previous twenty years as well that their loyalty came at a cost to those who governed the colony. As loyal Protestant subjects, they expected, even demanded, that their government protect these very liberties, which were so crucial to their attachment to empire. Rodney's "glorious and ever-memorable VICTORY" proved so important to how the island's inhabitants self-identified as loyal subjects because it confirmed this very relationship.

Historians argue that there emerged a growing sense of civic pride, self-reliance, and independent thinking among white Jamaicans during the late 1780s and 1790s. This was the result, in part, of their cultural break from Britain's North American colonies, but also of the radical political ideas that circulated during the revolutionary era.[25] But it is just as true that central to this renewed expression of Britishness was their more determined defense of slavery, which they understood to be the greatest of all their cherished liberties and exactly what made them British. From their perspective, the revolution had affirmed and strengthened their belief in a broader imperial identity tied to their government's support of slavery.

In consequence, white Jamaicans felt betrayed by the growing movement in London to abolish the slave trade, itself the product of a revolutionary assault on British notions of liberty and also crucial to an emerging redefinition of Britishness on the mainland.[26] The island assembly and their lobbyists in London repeatedly sparred with Parliament over threats to the institution of slavery and the abolition of the slave trade, especially amid fears of the growing unrest in nearby Saint-Domingue and after the outbreak of the Second Maroon War in 1796.[27] In 1789, the assembly wrote to Parliament in response to recent debates on ending the slave trade, claiming, as they had in 1774, that their rights as British subjects were "as inviolable as those of their fellow-citizens within any part of the British dominions." They declared it an "unconstitutional assumption of power" for the government "to destroy . . . private properties," which, they feared, "must ultimately tend to alienate their affections from the parent state."[28] But the island's inhabitants also understood, just as they had at the outbreak of the American war, that their "peculiar situation" meant that opposing British rule was never an option. As such, in the first decades of the nineteenth century, white Jamaicans increasingly found themselves as outsiders to an empire and imperial identity increasingly tied to abolitionism.[29] Their understandings of loyalty and Loyalism—the reason they chose Britain over the Americans in the 1770s, and took to the streets to celebrate Rodney's victory in 1782—continued to rest on their belief in the right to own others and to have a government that protected this right.

The revolutionary experience of Haligonians revealed a community and colony deeply divided over questions of loyalty and patriotism. The city's inhabitants depended on the British state for the costs of governing the colony, for military protection, and for access to profitable British Atlantic trade routes. But their local political culture also reflected the close ties of many Haligonians with their more radical New England neighbors. The ruling elite sought desperately throughout the 1760s and 1770s to check this spirit of independence that was so common among the local populace. Officials repeatedly banned the publication of subversive writings, forced residents to take oaths of allegiance, and arrested known conspirators. The loyalty of many of the city's inhabitants during this period was, as one historian described it, "more by default than by declaration."[30]

Yet for nearly two decades, many Haligonians espoused radical conceptions of Britishness more in line with their rebellious neighbors to the south. They questioned government authority, demanded that they enjoy the same rights as mainland British subjects, and even considered joining the rebellion. During the Stamp Act Crisis, at least some residents tried to resist the implementation of the tax and threatened violence against the local stamp distributor, while they read in their local newspaper of other acts of violent resistance elsewhere in the British Atlantic. The same was true during the disputes of the late 1760s and early 1770s, when Haligonians read approvingly of radicals in the colonies opposing the Townshend duties and of the growing transatlantic support for the Wilkes and Liberty cause. After the loss of soldiers to Boston in 1768, many residents joined with several Indian tribes in the region to celebrate the Festival of St. Aspinquid, a multiethnic and religious event that could be understood as celebrating a new American identity in place of former ties to Britain.

When the crisis shifted to war, some Haligonians again made efforts to join with the rebellious American colonists. They disrupted British military efforts, allegedly destroyed boxes of tea, refused to join volunteer regiments, and sought to aid rebel colonists. Even the colony's more conservative assembly argued for a new plan of imperial-colonial relations that gave colonial assemblies a greater degree of control over taxation and limited the authority of royally appointed governors and their councils. The assembly also threatened to rebel if Crown officials did not remove from office the colony's unpopular governor, Francis Legge. Even after the first wave of Loyalist refugees began to arrive in the spring of 1776, the city and colony remained on the cusp of rebellion. The Franco-American alliance drew more Haligonians to the British cause, but even France's presence in the war was unable to entirely overcome many of the inhabitants' pro-American sympathies.

Haligonians emerged from the two-decade-long conflict without clear answers to questions of loyalty and patriotism, or what it meant to be British. Even Protestantism, and the fear of Catholic tyranny, appeared to recede in importance for many of the city's inhabitants. In June 1782, while Haligonians celebrated Rodney's victory, a small group of Irish Catholics in the city petitioned the governor for a repeal of the colony's penal laws, specifically those depriving Catholics of their right to practice their faith and to acquire land.[31] The petitioners were motivated by a growing settler population of disbanded Irish and Scottish Catholic soldiers and by the 1778 Irish and English Catholic Relief Acts, which they believed should be extended to those "professing the Roman Catholic Religion in all other His Majesty's Dominions."[32] The latter claim was especially interesting, given just how incredibly unpopular Catholic relief was on the British mainland, and is the only known instance of British Atlantic Catholics using that legislation to advance their own interests. The petitioners, although they did not so state, were also likely encouraged by the government's willingness to accommodate the colony's Catholic population since the late 1760s. Toleration, in fact, had proved to be a useful tool in securing the loyalty of previous hostile Indian and Acadian populations, much as it had done with French Canadians in Quebec.

The petition met with little opposition in the assembly, from the governor, or even from the public at large. Such a response was simply unimaginable just a decade earlier and at odds with a contemporary British Atlantic political culture so entirely dependent on anti-Catholic rhetoric. Two weeks after the petitioners submitted their request, the governor signed a bill repealing many of the 1758 penal laws, though it took another year before it received the king's assent.[33] By 1785, Nova Scotian Catholics had secured a priest and completed construction of St. Peter's Chapel in Halifax.[34] That Haligonians were apparently supportive of such legislation speaks to the ways in which the American Revolution led to the gradual emergence of an expanded definition of religious liberty in the remote North Atlantic colony.

But it is also useful to think of Catholic relief in the context of a broader postwar conception of Loyalism that expected from the empire's diverse subjects a degree of submission to imperial authority. Faced with a growing population of Catholic émigrés to the colony in the 1780s, officials in Halifax, and Nova Scotians more generally, possibly saw a repeal of the penal laws as the surest way to instill in those subjects a sense of loyalty and obedience to the British state.[35]

Catholic relief ultimately tried to encourage loyalty and a respect for authority at an especially critical moment in the city and colony's history. There was a significant amount of political upheaval in Nova Scotia in the 1780s and early 1790s, largely in consequence of the arrival of tens of thousands of Loyalist refugees.[36] Most eventually settled at Shelburne, south and west of Halifax, while a larger number traveled further north across the Bay of Fundy. In June 1784, that territory was partitioned from Nova Scotia to form the new colony of New Brunswick, governed almost exclusively by Loyalist refugees. Only a small percentage of the refugee population, black and white, free and enslaved, stayed in Halifax, where they began to arrive as early as the summer of 1782. The appearance of so many destitute people shocked colonial officials, who lacked the resources or internal infrastructure to settle the suffering exiles. The scarcity of usable land and good jobs also led to ongoing conflict between refugees and the original settlers, and between white and free black colonists.[37]

But these old and new inhabitants were less divided in their political interests, despite in many instances having supported opposite sides in the recent conflict. During the previous twenty years, both had suffered under oppressive governments, whether the political establishment in Halifax, Congress and its many committees and associations, or British military officials in occupied New York City. These experiences shaped inhabitants' attitudes toward government and their rights as British subjects.

With the opening of the Sixth Assembly in late 1785, refugees and old residents combined to push for reforms in colonial governance. Generally speaking, they sought to transfer power from the governor and council to the representative assembly, a move similar to the plan that had failed in 1775. They argued for control over elections, increased voting rights, and the expansion of representation (to account for the dramatic increase in population), in an effort to weaken the long-standing influence of Halifax representatives and their allies on the council. These residents targeted the colony's finances as well, reforming methods of customs collection and government spending, and by 1791 had acquired the right to initiate and amend money bills, which had previously been an important source of power for the ruling elite. They were not always successful in their efforts, but for a period of about six years, from 1785–91, they sought to transform the economy and government of Nova Scotia in ways previously unknown.

Governor Parr and his allies reacted by trying to sow seeds of divisions between refugees and old settlers, in part by turning to the language of rebellion that previously filled colonial newspapers. Parr characterized Loyalist representatives as transients and rabble-rousers, who had brought with them "a Republican Spirit" that threatened to undermine the colony's stability and prosperity.[38] When some Haligonians, old and new, led a campaign in the late 1780s to expand the number of judges in the colony and to ensure those tried for crimes were judged by a jury of their peers (an essential right of all Britons), Parr resorted to calling one of their leaders the "Wilkes of Nova Scotia."[39]

But the refugees, and their many friends in Halifax and across the colony, were hardly republicans, nor were they trying to dismantle the colony's government. They were simply exercising their rights as Protestant British subjects, which included their right to check government authority. They did not inherit these ideas from rebellious colonists, as Parr and subsequent historians suggest, but the events of the American Revolution did sharpen their understandings of what it meant to be British.[40] Popular demands for legitimate representative government were central to the British common cause formed in New York City in the winter of 1774–75. They were also just as useful in explaining why so many Haligonians lent their support to the American cause, at least until the alliance with France in 1778. That both groups reached the same conclusion by supporting opposite sides during the war hints at the ways in which the revolution had unsettled popular transatlantic definitions of British Loyalism. It also suggests that in the aftermath of the war, and in the absence of dangerous enemies, new and old Britons in Nova Scotia had come to demand a greater stake in the governing of their colony, in part because they shared a renewed commitment to their rights as British subjects.

This attempt at radical political change in the colony was short-lived, however. By the early 1790s, many of these refugees, and even some of the old inhabitants, departed the colony for places elsewhere in the empire or even to return to America. Their motives varied, with many complaining of poor land, abysmal weather, or limited economic opportunities. But others argued that, despite their best efforts at reform, they could no longer "live under the arbitrary, cruel & unjust Government as at present administer'd in Nova Scotia."[41] Their exodus thus spoke to the enduring resilience of the ruling elite in Halifax, who perhaps had found a greater degree of legitimacy with the emergence of a more authoritarian conception of loyalty radiating out from mainland Britain. But the departure of so many subjects in the early 1790s just as clearly expressed the strength and determination of Protestant Whig ideals, which had assumed new meaning and importance among the city's diverse population of subjects during and after the American Revolution.

Glaswegian attitudes toward their nation and empire were transformed by the ideas and events of the American Revolution. The conflict disrupted the city's profitable Atlantic tobacco trade, which had brought significant prosperity to many of the city's inhabitants and formed the basis of their loyal attachment to the empire. Yet Scots found opportunity in the many political crises of the period to refute long-standing national biases and to begin to push for a more inclusive British national identity. The events of the final years of the war also led Glaswegians to embrace a far more radical conception of their Britishness. Though loyal to the Crown, they emerged from two decades of conflict with a greater sense of their place in the empire and a greater commitment to defending their personal liberty and Protestant faith.

In the 1760s, Glaswegians expressed a more moderate brand of Loyalism, which celebrated order and government authority and defended mercantilist policies, which had brought significant wealth and fame to their city. They were vocal in their defense of the rights of mainland and colonial subjects, but they admonished colonial crowds for their violence, which Glaswegians associated with the Scotophobic Wilkite cause in England. By the end of the decade, they also began to push for a more inclusive understanding of Britishness that was capable of embracing both an English *and* Scottish past, which found meaning in the many public celebrations around the 1769 Douglas Cause.

The start of the war in North America, however, troubled Glaswegians, who, despite their loyal attachment to Great Britain, were fearful of supporting a war that would likely devastate their profitable colonial trade. In the first two years of the rebellion, they opted to remain neutral (or at least quiet) in hopes that the war would be short-lived and their city's economy would thus be saved. But like so many other Britons across the empire, their attitudes changed considerably in the spring of 1778, after learning of Burgoyne's humiliating defeat, war with France, and their government's plans for Catholic relief. Glaswegians began to express a militant, conservative brand of Loyalism that reimagined the war as a contest between Protestant liberty and Catholic tyranny. Rebellious colonists became peripheral figures in the conflict, proxies to a far greater enemy in Catholic France (and perhaps even their own government).

This renewed defense of Britishness ran headlong into government attempts to relieve Catholics in the British Isles. Beginning in the fall of 1778, Glaswegians wrote, spoke, and rioted against their government's attempts to favor Catholics while the nation was at war with France. At times, they questioned the very legitimacy of their government, hinted their king might be a disguised Catholic, and spoke of rebellion if officials carried through with their plans for relief. Even after Parliament withdrew the Scottish bill, and after the horrific riots in London in June 1780, many Glaswegians continued to oppose the spread of Catholicism in their country and were increasingly suspicious of the men and institutions that governed their society.

This remained true even two years later, long after the streets of London had been washed of the blood of Gordon's supporters. Just days after Glaswegians feted Rodney, they returned to the streets again to celebrate their king's birthday. Like New Yorkers, they combined their love of monarchy with Rodney's unforgettable victory. They toasted the king and queen before raising a glass to the famed admiral and "the Brave Tars who gained the late glorious victory over de Grasse." But significantly, amid these loud acclamations Glaswegians also drank to "Lord George Gordon, [and] the Praeses of the 85 Societies."[42] Their reasons for doing so are not entirely clear. Gordon and his friends in Glasgow possibly functioned as an affirmation of the city's commitment to a Protestant empire, itself a largely conservative statement shared by many Britons across the North Atlantic in the aftermath of the American war. But it is more likely their toast of Gordon acted as a check to these more conservative tendencies. Glaswegians had experienced a political awakening in the crisis over Catholic relief and came to view Gordon and his associates, not their king or imperial officials, as their nation's greatest defenders of Protestant liberty.

Of course, Glaswegians' opposition to Catholic relief was more than just an assertion of deeply held religious convictions. It was part of a broader agitation against the perceived corruption of British politics and political institutions, which had come under increased public scrutiny during the previous two decades. Beginning in 1782, Glaswegians embraced radical efforts to reform their political society that in many ways mirrored the efforts of Loyalist refugees and old inhabitants in Halifax. They campaigned for burgh reform, targeting the expansion of the franchise and changes to parliamentary election laws in an effort to weaken the various local oligarchies that dominated Scottish politics.[43] Glaswegians also sought the repeal of the 1712 Patronage Act, which had allowed for town councils to impose ministers on local churches. Many in Glasgow saw the dispute over patronage in classic Whig terms as a political contest between liberty and tyranny, and were quick to point out that the act was passed at a time when their country was under Jacobite control.[44]

Aware of the growing political transformation of Scots, leaders of the county reform movement in Yorkshire reached out for their support in the fall of 1782. Glasgow's city council did not back these measures but did take the opportunity to highlight the gross inequalities in parliamentary representation. They reported that the nearly one hundred thousand Scots who lived in the city and surrounding towns were represented "only by one Member, and that Member elected by four Delegates, of which this City only sends one, who is chosen by the corporation composed of no more than thirty individuals."[45] The English radical and reform leader Christopher Wyvill recognized the historical significance of the moment, even if Scots were reluctant to join his cause. That Englishmen and Scots espoused shared views on the corruption of government perhaps "evidenced a disposition to extinguish every remaining spark of those animosities which the writings of Mr. Wilkes, in opposition to Lord Bute, had been too successfully employed to excite."[46]

Glasgow was a trading town, however, and for many of the city's residents their sense of loyalty remained tied to the benefits of access to Atlantic trade routes. Remarkably, the American Revolution did little to change this belief. Despite their worst fears, Glasgow's tobacco merchants emerged largely unscathed from nearly twenty years of conflict, having profited from wartime shipping contracts and new markets in the Caribbean.[47] The latter was especially crucial to the postwar economic and urban development of the Scottish Lowlands. The importation of raw cotton from Jamaica fueled the country's early industrialization, while that island's enormous slave population provided a ready-made market for cheap linen cloth produced in Glasgow and the surrounding area.[48] The rapid growth of the economy transformed Glasgow into one of the great manufacturing centers of the British Empire in the early nineteenth century. This growth also strengthened patriotic attitudes toward the empire among the elite and middling Glaswegians who profited most from the expansion of industry.

Historians argue that Glaswegians, and Scots more generally, emerged from the American Revolution as loyal Protestant subjects. They were committed to monarchy and constituted government and active, if not leading, participants in the political and economic expansion of the British Empire. But among some circles in the city, another, more radical conception of Loyalism had also taken hold. These Glaswegians expressed a far more rigid defense of their Protestant liberties as a result, not of 1776, but of 1778. It was the war with France, and the crisis over Catholic relief, that spurred these Glaswegians to action. The threat of Catholicism in the latter years of the war awakened a spirit of Loyalism that demanded that their government remain the great bulwark of Protestant liberty. This was true of the campaigns for burgh and patronage reform in the mid-1780s and explains, in part, why the city and surrounding region were home to the most ardent supporters of the French

Revolution in the early 1790s.[49] The American Revolution, more than any other event of the eighteenth century, made Glaswegians British. It brought about a popular reimagining of Loyalism that remained deeply committed to monarchy but was also far more inclusive of Scots who expressed a greater determination to defend Protestant religious and political values within their nation and empire.

The American Revolution devastated loyal New Yorkers and the city in which they lived. The events of the previous two decades tore apart families, turned neighbors and friends against one another, and created divisions in the community that were ultimately resolved only by acts of violence and war. The revolution forcibly, violently, and necessarily shattered popular conceptions of Britishness that had tenuously bound together the city's residents for much of the eighteenth century. The very act of choosing sides, of declaring loyalty or rebellion, ultimately depended on embracing new conceptions of Loyalism that were capable of distinguishing friends from enemies.

The decade before the start of the war was especially crucial to a growing radical political culture in the city, which began to redefine popular understandings of Loyalism in reaction to events of both local and national importance. For many New Yorkers, tyranny appeared so widespread and unrelenting in its assault on colonial liberties that subjects needed to act. As the situation worsened, some began to embrace republican ideals and encouraged subjects to resist authority and ultimately to question the sovereignty of Parliament. But their fears were especially British, dependent on an established and oft-used language of Protestant loyalty that celebrated the right of subjects to check the dangerous tendencies of those in power. This was certainly true of the public's reaction to the 1774 Quebec Act. The king's willingness to tolerate Catholicism illustrated the growing corruption of the British government and led some New Yorkers to denounce their allegiance to the Crown. Such words and actions revealed the enduring significance of popular conceptions of Britishness but also showed how those ideas could be used to turn previously loyal Britons against their king.

While many New Yorkers began to openly reject monarchy in the winter and spring of 1775, others turned to a new, more moderate understanding of Loyalism. They celebrated an ordered British political society, which they contrasted with the licentiousness of colonial crowds and their seemingly indiscriminate attacks on people and their property. They elevated George III in the face of public declarations that he had abandoned their Protestant empire, believing instead that he was most capable of preserving their liberty and protecting their rights as British subjects. For these Britons, delegates to the First

Continental Congress, and their various committees and associations, were the ones acting the part of Catholic tyrannizers, not defenders of Protestant liberty. Yet, for all their criticism of the budding Patriot cause, loyal New Yorkers struggled to make their former friends into dangerous enemies worth fighting. Loyal New Yorkers believed instead that the Patriots were engaged in an unnatural rebellion, based not on principle but on self-interest, and that in their hearts rebellious colonists remained British subjects.

This belief changed in 1778 when Congress agreed to an alliance with France. Like Britons elsewhere in the North Atlantic, New Yorkers reimagined the war in far grander terms as another classic struggle between Protestant liberty and Catholic tyranny. This shift in thinking was more personal for Loyalist refugees, however, who had suffered for several years at the hands of violent Patriot crowds and soldiers. They came to understand the alliance as the natural outcome of a Patriot cause riddled from the start by popery. Over the remainder of the war, loyal New Yorkers embraced a far more vindictive and determined understanding of Britishness, which recast their American opponents as a dangerous threat to the liberty of Protestant Britons. They feared that defeat portended a dark future of Catholic despotism in North America and, worse yet, likely meant their forced exile from a land many had always called home.

This belief perhaps explains why New Yorkers crowded their streets twice on account of Rodney's defeat of de Grasse. Their celebrations, in fact, were at least as impressive as those in Jamaica, which had a far greater stake in the outcome of the battle. New Yorkers hoped that French defeat signified the approaching end of an unjust and illegitimate rebellion that had threatened to hand over Britain's North American colonies to its arch rivals. The American Revolution, it turns out, was as much a violent struggle between liberty and tyranny for loyal New Yorkers as it was for their American opponents.

The "loyal REFUGEES of the PROVINCE of New York" captured these feelings in a public address to Sir Guy Carleton, the newly appointed commander of British forces in North America, who had arrived in the city in May 1782. Writing in the days between the city's two celebrations of Rodney's triumph, these refugees expressed their admiration for Carleton and still believed their nation would "humble the pride of her natural enemies." But they described the war in especially personal terms as well, as one of unimaginable suffering at the hands of a brutal, oppressive enemy. They lamented the "ignominious deaths" suffered by many of the king's friends, who had been "imprisoned and banished from their estates and families . . . [and] treated with unparalleled cruelty and oppression." These refugees still prayed for a "happy

Reconciliation," in hopes of recovering much of what they had lost but were still prepared to "readily hazard our lives as we have sacrificed our fortunes" to defeat the unnatural rebellion.[50]

These were hardly the words of a defeated people. Loyal New Yorkers voiced a renewed commitment to the war in the summer of 1782, just as their nation's government was preparing for defeat. They continued to embrace a martial Loyalism shaped both by a broader vision of a Protestant empire and by a personal desire to revenge the suffering inflicted on them over the past decade or more. The address spoke to an understanding of British liberty crushed, in their eyes, by the tyranny of their American enemies. The loss of property, banishment, cruel treatment, and even death evidenced a society deprived of order, authority, and good government. The most basic rights of all Britons—the rights to life, liberty, and property—had been unfairly and brutally taken away. Such experiences not only convinced these loyal New Yorkers of the baseness of the American cause but also strengthened their attachment to the Crown and British government.

Loyal New Yorkers never abandoned this language of Loyalism. Even in the face of American independence, and even as they packed on to ships departing for ports elsewhere in the North Atlantic, these refugees remained convinced that monarchy offered the surest safeguard of liberty. They also continued to disparage their enemies, whom they regularly described as having succumbed to the "civil rage" of republican government.[51] In the final months of the war, New Yorkers regularly read of their opponents' immense debt and inflated currency and of Congress's exorbitant tax plans, which colonists were unwilling and unable to pay.[52] Congress, one writer gleefully argued, was "a bankrupt party, lessening hourly by converts to that mass of discontent."[53]

Loyalist writers continued to believe a debt-ridden, bankrupt America would ultimately be overtaken by France. One writer claimed that delegates to Congress had set about constructing a political culture of loyalty and devotion to their French allies precisely because Congress was so indebted to these supposed friends. The writer was astonished that the same people who had made so much noise "about Popery being tolerated in Canada" years ago were now willing to "sprinkle themselves with what they call holy water," as they allegedly had during the funeral for the Spanish ambassador in May 1780. More recently, delegates had even participated in lavish celebrations for the birth of the Dauphin, as "if a promised King of America had been born." The only hope for Americans, concluded the writer, was to seek a reunion with Great Britain and "leave the Congress to settle accounts with France."[54]

If this reunion did not happen, Loyalists were convinced that an independent America would suffer under the cruelty of French Catholic rule. One writer warned that with "France in the bosom of America, [and] in possession of her richest resources," nothing would stop the bourbon power and her allies from conquering the newly established nation. To the north, the writer argued, Canadians "under the standard of France" would seek "to revenge and enslave," while the Spaniards in the south, "united to France by a Family Compact," would take the opportunity to subdue Congress. Even out west, "Savages [were] converted into French and Spanish allies," while the French navy took possession of the profitable fisheries off the coast of Newfoundland, depriving Americans of one of their greatest sources of income.[55] So sure were Loyalist writers of future French rule in America that they even revived talk of the failed Carlisle peace proposal in hopes of persuading Congress to negotiate for reconciliation.[56]

These fears of a future of political tyranny in America, at the hands of either republican mobs or Catholic monarchs, were not mere hyperbole. They reflected the actual lived experiences of the tens of thousands of exiles who had sought refuge in New York City over the previous six years. The same was true in the months leading up to the British evacuation of the city. Loyal New Yorkers repeatedly suffered at the hands of returning Patriots in a bout of political violence that resembled the purging of British sympathizers from the city in the spring of 1775. The situation worsened after March 1783, when New Yorkers discovered that Article V of the peace treaty left it to each state to decide how to treat returning Loyalists and their property, a move that opened the door for retributive violence against those who had sided with Great Britain in the war.

Thereafter, stories circulated of Loyalists being whipped, beaten, and imprisoned for having supported Great Britain in the war. "This city swarms with those we lately called rebels," recorded one resident "and daily accounts are brought in of the most violent resolves entered into by different associations to murder all those who shall be found here upon the evacuation by the King's troops."[57] In October, Joshua Booth tried to reach his parents' home north of the city, but was captured by a group of forty Americans. They shaved his head and eyebrows, fixed a cow bell around his neck, and coated his head with "a very high cap of feathers . . . well plum'd with soft tar." They then stuck a paper on the front "with a man drawn with two faces, representing Arnold and the Devil's imps"[58] (fig. C.3).

James Rivington also suffered at the hands of emboldened Patriots, much as he had in the spring and fall of 1775. He was repeatedly taunted by Patriot writers for having served as the mouthpiece of the British cause during the war, and

FIGURE C.3. *The Savages Let Loose, or the Cruel Fate of the Loyalists* (1783). Loyalists felt betrayed by their government's decision to abandon them in the articles of peace, which left their lives and fortunes in the hands of revengeful Americans. In this print, the Americans are no longer cowering behind their European allies, but are now depicted as savage Indians, hanging, scalping, and hatcheting to death their former friends and countrymen. *Courtesy of the John Carter Brown Library.*

in November a group of Patriots stole his printing types.[59] A month later, Isaac Sears and company once again assaulted the famed printer, finally forcing him to quit his printing business. He stayed on in the city thereafter, but "to the joy of every whig in the United States, [his] political existence [was] terminated."[60]

But most loyal refugees did not stay. Beginning in the fall of 1782, tens of thousands departed the city, taking with them an experience of the revolution and war that had profoundly reshaped their understandings of loyalty and Loyalism. They had come to embrace a deeper devotion to monarchy and constituted government, but like Britons elsewhere in the North Atlantic, loyal refugees were more stubbornly committed to defending their rights and liberties as British subjects. The previous twenty years of conflict had sharpened their understandings of ideas like consent and representation, taxation and trade, and the nature and purpose of government more generally. But this change in thinking was not informed by the revolutionary ideals of American Patriots; it was defined against them. These Loyalists had escaped the tyranny of republican crowds and despotic Catholic French rule for a Protestant empire they believed to be still committed to popular notions of liberty and freedom. These refugees emerged from the American Revolution as committed monarchists but also devoted Whigs, identities they believed were entirely compatible with one another.

Scholars insist that American independence was a devastating blow to the British Empire. The loss of more than two million colonists and an enormous swath of land in North America threatened to upset the balance of power in Europe, where Britain had enjoyed the lion's share for the previous half century. American independence also led to the exile of tens of thousands of Britons who were forced to find new lives in an empire reeling from defeat and often incapable or ill-prepared for the challenges of resettlement. The loss, at least momentarily, unsettled Britain's dominant Atlantic economy by depriving merchants and traders of access to once lucrative colonial markets. Finally, the American victory was humiliating. Britons had forged an identity in the first half of the eighteenth century founded on the notion that they were an exceptional people. They inhabited a Protestant empire of liberty and prosperity and were seemingly invincible to the threats of their Catholic foes in Europe. The Americans unraveled such ideas and then combined with those foes to tear apart Britain's Atlantic empire.

But the view from the British Atlantic tells a very different story of the American Revolution. After the war, residents of these four communities described a renewed devotion to the British monarchy and constituted government. These loyal Britons resisted the revolutionary assault on Britishness by constructing a shared narrative of the crisis and war that framed both American republicanism and French Catholicism as far greater threats to personal liberty. Postwar conceptions of Britishness came to celebrate a balanced, representative British monarchy, which subjects believed to be most capable of creating political stability and economic prosperity in the empire. These attitudes were strongest in places where Britons suffered the most, such as with loyal refugees in New York City or even among white Kingstonians. But these attitudes attracted the support of Britons in Glasgow and Halifax, too, especially after 1778, when the war with France revived age-old definitions of Britishness.

The American Revolution strengthened attitudes toward monarchy, empire, and liberty among Britons in these four communities. In the aftermath of the conflict, they continued to share in an imperial political culture that celebrated their king and constituted government. But they embraced a more determined commitment to Whig ideas of liberty, as well. This language of Loyalism remained, in some sense, broadly conceived, but it increasingly took on a local dimension in consequence of how these Britons had experienced the events of this period. Kingstonians argued that their right to own slaves was a crucial component of their national identity, in part because the French, Spanish, and Americans had threatened to take away this right. Glaswegians emerged from the war convinced more than ever of the importance of Protestantism to their understandings of Britishness, both as a result of the war against France and their government's attempt to relieve Catholics in their country. They also championed radical Whig ideas of consent and representation, and pushed for a reform of political and religious institutions in the 1780s and 1790s. Haligonians and loyal refugees from New York City shared in this radical reimagining of their Britishness. They demanded greater rights and liberties in the aftermath of the war, in part because over the previous two decades they had been deprived of such rights by violent colonial crowds and committees, and oppressive civil and military governments.

The American Revolution ultimately failed to displace a popular Protestant Whig political culture that had taken hold in the British Atlantic during the first half of the eighteenth century. These loyal Britons rejected an American "contagion of liberty" for a more robust and determined understanding of what it meant to be British, which they continued to understand best within the context of their own particular local interests and political cultures.[61] The political conflicts of the 1780s and 1790s, over issues of representation, voting rights, Protestantism, and the slave trade, demonstrated this renewed commitment to Protestant Whig ideals. But these conflicts also revealed a British Atlantic still struggling to find commonality among an empire of diverse subjects. When imperial officials described a more narrowly defined and authoritarian image of Britishness in the aftermath of the war, perhaps then they were not acting on the reality that thousands of Protestant Britons had just rebelled. Rather, imperial officials were responding to the many more loyal Britons across the North Atlantic who remained stubbornly committed to an idea of Britishness often at odds with new forms of imperial rule and with the beliefs of their fellow Britons.

ACKNOWLEDGMENTS

This book covers the entirety of the American Revolution and War for Independence, and took nearly that length of time to write. As one might imagine, then, I have many debts to repay. I must begin with the late Drew Cayton, who is the reason I became an historian. Drew was a gifted scholar, engaging speaker (hands down the best lecturer I have ever heard), and quite possibly the nicest person I have ever met. He showed faith in me from the start and helped guide me toward graduate school. Even in the years after I left Miami, when we saw each other only occasionally at conferences, he was always eager to hear how things were going and showed interested in this project. It is my greatest regret that I was not able to finish this book before his sudden passing.

I wish to thank several faculty members who were especially supportive during my time at the University of Glasgow: Simon Ball, Susan Castillo, Ted Cowan, Lionel Glassey, Andrew Hook, Sam Maddra, Irene Maver, Marina Moskowitz, Phillips O'Brien, Thomas Munck, Nick Selby, and Don Spaeth. I was privileged to work with Colin Kidd, whose writing on eighteenth-century Scotland deeply informs my understanding of Glasgow during the revolution and war. Additionally, I am grateful to Doug Aiton, Jennifer Black, Mairi Langan, and Neil Murphy for their support and camaraderie during those years and ever since. Finally, I would like to thank Margo Hunter and the late Alison Peden for helping me to adjust to life in Scotland. It saddens me that I was not able to finish this book before Alison's sudden passing.

I was fortunate, as well, to have been a part of a small but close-knit Early Americanist community in Scotland and want to thank several faculty and graduate students, Vassiliki Karali, Ben Marsh, Colin Nicolson, Kirsten Phimister, Finn Pollard, Matthew Smith, Stewart Salmon, and David Watson. Frank Cogliano has been incredibly supportive of my work over these many years and has been a good friend. He and his wife, Mimi, are two of the kindest and most generous people I have known.

For the past nearly two decades, Simon Newman has been a wonderful adviser, mentor, and friend. Over these many years, he has given me space to pursue my own questions and to figure out what was interesting about my research, but he has also known when to help. In such moments, and with such ease, Simon could draw new and better connections in my work, reframe arguments, or make me see what was really of value in what I was trying to say. Those many conversations made this book possible. But so too did our friendship. Since the beginning, Simon has always—always—been there for me. He has been one of my greatest advocates and has continued to support me and this project even in the most difficult of times. I simply could not have written this book without him.

Much of the research for this book was made possible by the generous financial support of the Gilder Lehrman Institute, Friends of the Princeton Library, Henry E. Huntington Library, Library Company of Philadelphia, Smithsonian Institution, and the Robert H. Smith International Center for Jefferson Studies (ICJS). I also wish to thank the staff at those and the many other libraries my research has taken me, including the British Library, Glasgow's Mitchell Library, National Library of Scotland, New-York Historical Society, New York Public Library, Nova Scotia Archives, Society of Cincinnati Library, UK National Archives, University of Glasgow Special Collections, and University of Notre Dame Archives.

Many scholars have kindly taken the time to read drafts, sit for long conversations, respond to e-mail, or just show enthusiasm for my work. I wish to especially thank David Armitage, Trevor Burnard, Barbara Clark Smith, Linda Colley, Tom Humphrey, Maya Jasanoff, John Murrin, Amanda Moniz, Hannah Weiss Muller, Mary Beth Norton, Matthew Osborne, Andrew O'Shaughnessy, and David Waldstreicher. Some may have forgotten our conversations, but I have not and they mattered. The support and inspiration of these scholars helped to make this book possible, and for that I am deeply grateful.

As is often the case, several of the arguments in this book were first developed in papers delivered at various workshops and conferences. In 2013 and 2014, I came to realize the significance of the Quebec Act on British Loyalism (and the emerging Patriot cause) at a conference and then a workshop cosponsored by the Omohundro Institute of Early American History and Culture and Groupe d'histoire de l'Atlantique français, and organized by François Furstenberg and Ollivier Hubert. In 2015, Rob Parkinson invited me to workshop a very rough and poorly framed draft of chapter 3 at the Upstate Early American History Workshop at Binghamton University. Finally, in 2016, Andrew O'Shaughnessy invited me to participate in an ICJS conference, "Propaganda, Persuasion, the Press and the American Revolution, 1763–1783," where I first made the case for a Loyalist common cause in the months before the start of the American war. I owe thanks to the conference organizers and participants for their valuable feedback.

Portions of this book previously appeared in "The American Revolution, Glasgow, and the Making of the Second City of the Empire," in *Europe's Response to the American Revolution*, ed. Simon P. Newman (London: Palgrave, 2006), 1–25; "'In Favour of Popery': Patriotism, Protestantism, and the Gordon Riots in the Revolutionary British Atlantic," *Journal of British Studies* 52, no. 1 (January 2013), 79–102; and "A 'Fit Instrument': The Quebec Act and the Outbreak of Rebellion in Two British Atlantic Port Cities," in *Entangling the Quebec Act: Transnational Meanings, Contexts, and Legacies in North America and the British Empire*, ed. François Furstenberg and Ollivier Hubert (Montreal: McGill-Queen's University Press, 2020). I wish to thank Palgrave Macmillan, Cambridge University Press, and McGill-Queen's University Press, along with the many editors and anonymous readers who helped to improve early versions of my work.

Much of this book was written over the past seven years alongside the joys of parenting and the day-to-day challenges of working at a teaching university. The book simply could not have happened without the support of my friends and colleagues at Fresno State, especially Dan Cady, Honora Chapman, Lori Clune, Vernon Creviston, John Farrell, Romeo Guzmán, Ethan Kytle, Maria Lopes, Blain Roberts, and Bill Skuban. Deans Luz Gonzalez and Michelle DenBeste generously granted me multiple course releases that allowed for time to revise and rewrite the manuscript. Christian Bursett, Amy Noel Ellison, Stephen Mullen, and Michael Rettig graciously offered their time and scanning services to track down much-needed sources at distant archives. Finally, a special debt of gratitude goes to those who also found time in their own busy research and teaching lives to read the revised manuscript. Vernon Creviston commented on a very early (and very long) draft, while teaching a half-dozen or more classes. Andy Shankman, who wears more hats than one can count, offered his services at an especially difficult moment when (not for the first time) I doubted this "thing" would ever become a book. Finally, nearer to the finish line, Blain Roberts and Ethan Kytle generously responded to a last-minute request to read and comment on the entire manuscript.

And then there is Rob Parkinson, whom I first met in 2004 when we shared the top floor of the Library Company's Cassatt House. We instantly connected, in part, because of our shared research interests; Rob asks many of the same questions of the Patriot cause as I do of the Loyalists. His work is all over the pages of this book (he is practically the co-author of chapter 4) and has profoundly shaped how I think about the revolution and war. More than that, though, Rob has become one of my closest friends (despite his love of some really awful sports teams). There have been many times in the writing of this book that I just wanted to give it up, but Rob has always been there with encouraging words and offers to help. He is my most vocal supporter, has read and commented on most of the manuscript, and has always reminded me that what I am doing matters. I am not sure where I would be without our friendship.

I could not be happier that this project found a home at Cornell University Press. I wish to thank everyone at the Press, especially Clare Kirkpatrick Jones and Michael McGandy, for faithfully and patiently guiding this book to publication. A huge thanks goes to Mary Gendron as well for her meticulous editing of the manuscript, which she did without delay just as the coronavirus shut down the country. It was an absolute pleasure to work with Gerry Krieg, who drew the map that appears in the first chapter, and Beatrice Burton, who compiled an excellent index. Finally, I am especially grateful to Rachel Herrmann and the second anonymous reader for their close reading of the manuscript. This book is far better thanks to their insightful comments.

To my many friends—especially Lisa Bennett, Rob Bowie and Ashely Hoffman, Jackie Bryce, Anna Carr, Geoff and Linda Dervishian, Dave and Maryanne Esajian, Jeanne Johnson, Tom and Shannon Lei, Bruce Macleod, Bobby Pentorali, Neil Selvester, Dr. Greg and Karen Simpson, Ryan and Candice Smith, Andrew and Christa Wanger, and Andy and Shelly Watt—thank you for reminding me over the years that there is more to life than this book. A special thanks goes to three lifelong friends—Chris Bausano, Nate Bowie, and Darren Easton—who, despite living far from Fresno, remain my closest friends to this day.

Finally, I would be nowhere without the love and support of my family: my brothers, Todd and Matt, and their families, Jenn, Kara, Mallory, and Molly, as well as my in-laws, Alice and Eric Cheung, and Calvin and Jen. I am grateful for my parents, Maureena and Chuck, who have always encouraged me to pursue my passions and taught me at a young age to work hard and never give up. Those qualities made this book possible. I like to joke about the misery of fatherhood, but truth be told, I cannot imagine life without my two boys, Alastair and Oliver. I am proud of this book, but nothing brings me greater joy than these two kids. Except, of course, my two dogs, Bonnie and Lord Kelvin. They kept me company many a late night when much of the rewriting of this book took place.

No one has suffered more in the writing of this book than my spouse, Floridia Cheung. She has witnessed me express just about every kind of emotion imaginable, has endured hours upon hours of me talking about Loyalists, and has been dragged through many a city street to find a since forgotten site of some important event (she usually lost interest after the second wrong turn). She has also had three careers, returned to school for two of them, and has been an incredible mother to our two children, all the while showing me nothing but love and support. She is nothing short of amazing, and I could not have done this without her. I am also scared to death to tell her I plan to do it again.

Notes

Introduction

1. John Adams to Hezekiah Niles, February 13, 1818, in *The Works of John Adams, Second President of the United States*, ed. Charles Francis Adams (Boston: Little, Brown and Company, 1856), 10:282–83.

2. Adams, *The Works of John Adams*, 10:283–84.

3. Edmund S. and Helen M. Morgan, *The Stamp Act Crisis: Prologue to Revolution* (1953; reprint, with new preface by authors, New York: Collier Books, 1963); Edmund Morgan, *Birth of the Republic,1763–1789* (Chicago: University of Chicago Press, 1956); Bernard Bailyn, *The Ideological Origins of the American Revolution* (Cambridge, MA: Belknap Press of Harvard University Press, 1967); Gordon Wood, *The Creation of the American Republic, 1776–1787* (Chapel Hill: University of North Carolina Press, 1969); Pauline Maier, *From Resistance to Revolution: Colonial Radicals and the Development of American Opposition to Britain, 1765–1776* (New York: Alfred A. Knopf, 1972); J. G. A. Pocock, *The Machiavellian Moment: Florentine Political Thought and the Atlantic Republican Tradition* (Princeton, NJ: Princeton University Press, 1975); J. C. D. Clark, *The Language of Liberty, 1660–1832: Political Discourse and Social Dynamics in the Anglo-American World* (Cambridge: Cambridge University Press, 1994).

4. Contemporaries regularly referred to the rebellion as a civil war. To cite just one example, see New Yorker John Thurman's letter to a friend in London in September 1774, in which he says, "we dread the Consequences of Civil Warr & Fighting with our best friends," quoted in *The Iconography of Manhattan Island, 1498–1909*, ed. I. N. Phelps Stokes (1922; reprint, Union, NJ: The Lawbook Exchange, 1998), 4:866. Historians have also described the conflict as a civil war. For example, see Rebecca Brannon, *From Revolution to Reunion: The Reintegration of the South Carolina Loyalists* (Columbia: University of South Carolina Press, 2016), esp. chap. 1; John Shy, *A People Numerous and Armed: Reflections on the Military Struggle for American Independence* (New York: Oxford University Press, 1976), esp. chap. 8; Robert M. Calhoon, "A Special Kind of Civil War," in *Tory Insurgents: The Loyalist Perception and Other Essays*, ed. Robert M. Calhoon, Timothy M. Barnes, and Robert S. Davis (Columbia: University of South Carolina Press, 2010); Maya Jasanoff, *Liberty's Exiles: American Loyalists in the Revolutionary World* (New York: Alfred A. Knopf, 2011).

5. Jasanoff, *Liberty's Exiles*, 364–65n16. Of course, political allegiances were not static, often fluctuating with the events of the war and the proximity of armies. Problems of definition also make it difficult to accurately determine who was a Loyalist, with some believing that active military engagement was the only clear sign of

one's loyalty to the Crown. Paul H. Smith found that about nineteen thousand men fought in Loyalist regiments during the war and used that number to suggest that the total Loyalist population stood at roughly five hundred thousand, or about 20 percent of the total colonial population. "The American Loyalists: Notes on Their Organization and Numerical Strength," *William and Mary Quarterly* 25, no. 2 (April 1968): 259–77.

6. Andrew O'Shaughnessy, *An Empire Divided: The American Revolution and the British Caribbean* (Philadelphia: University of Pennsylvania Press, 2000), xi.

7. This argument is indebted to the work of Linda Colley in *Britons: Forging the Nation 1707–1837* (New Haven, CT: Yale University Press, 1992) and "Britishness and Otherness: An Argument," *Journal of British Studies* 31, no. 4 (October 1992): 309–29. Several historians have refined and challenged her argument. See Colin Kidd, *British Identities before Nationalism: Ethnicity and Nationhood in the Atlantic World, 1600–1800* (Cambridge: Cambridge University Press, 1999) and "North Britishness and the Nature of Eighteenth-Century British Patriotisms," *Historical Journal* 39, no. 2 (June 1996): 361–82; Kathleen Wilson, *The Sense of the People: Politics, Culture and Imperialism in England, 1715–1785* (Cambridge: Cambridge University Press, 1995); Steven Pincus, *1688: The First Modern Revolution* (New Haven, CT: Yale University Press, 2009); Gerald Newman, *The Rise of English Nationalism: A Cultural History, 1740–1830* (New York: St. Martin's Press, 1987); Carla Gardina Pestana, *Protestant Empire: Religion and the Making of the British Atlantic World* (Philadelphia: University of Pennsylvania Press, 2009); Owen Stanwood, *The Empire Reformed: English America in the Age of the Glorious Revolution* (Philadelphia: University of Pennsylvania Press, 2011); Brendan Mc-Conville, *The King's Three Faces: The Rise and Fall of Royal America, 1688–1776* (Chapel Hill: University of North Carolina Press, 2006); Eliga H. Gould, *The Persistence of Empire: British Political Culture in the Age of the American Revolution* (Chapel Hill: University of North Carolina Press, 2000); Francis D. Cogliano, *No King, No Popery: Anti-Catholicism in Revolutionary New England* (Westport, CT: Greenwood Press, 1995); Jack P. Greene, "Empire and Identity from the Glorious Revolution to the American Revolution," in *The Oxford History of the British Empire*, vol. 2, *The Eighteenth Century*, ed. P. J. Marshall (Oxford: Oxford University Press, 1998), 208–30; Colin Haydon, *Anti-Catholicism in Eighteenth-Century England, c. 1714–80: A Political and Social Study* (Manchester, UK: Manchester University Press, 1993); Tony Claydon and Ian McBride, eds., *Protestantism and National Identity: Britain and Ireland, c. 1650–c. 1850* (Cambridge: Cambridge University Press, 1998); S. J. Connolly, "Varieties of Britishness: Ireland, Scotland and Wales in the Hanoverian State," in *Uniting the Kingdom?: The Making of British History*, ed. Alexander Grant and Keith J. Stringer (New York: Routledge, 1995), 193–207; T. C. Smout, "Problems of Nationalism, Identity and Improvement in Later Eighteenth-Century Scotland," in *Improvement and Enlightenment: Proceedings of the Scottish Historical Studies Seminar, University of Strathclyde, 1987–88*, ed. T. M. Devine (Edinburgh: John Donald Publishers, 1989), 1–21. For the ways in which anti-Catholicism informed early modern English politics and society, see Peter Lake, "Anti-popery: The Structure of a Prejudice," in *Conflict in Early Stuart England: Studies in Religion and Politics, 1603–1642*, ed. Richard Cust and Ann Hughes (London: Longman, 1989), 73–82.

8. As John Murrin famously put it many years ago, "In a word, America was Britain's idea." "A Roof without Walls: The Dilemma of American National Identity," in *Beyond Confederation: Origins of the Constitution and American Identity*, ed. Richard Beeman, Stephen Botwin, and Edward C. Carter II (Chapel Hill: University of North

Carolina Press, 1987), 333–48, 339. See also John Murrin, "1776: The Countercyclical Revolution," in *Revolutionary Currents: Nation Building in the Transatlantic World*, ed. Michael A. Morrison and Melinda Zook (New York: Rowman & Littlefield, 2004), 65-90; Greene, "Empire and Identity," 227–29; Jasanoff, *Liberty's Exiles*, 9; Dror Wahrman, "The English Problem of Identity in the American Revolution," *American Historical Review* 106, no. 4 (October 2001): 1236–62.

9. P. J. Marshall, "The First British Empire," in *The Oxford History of the British Empire*, vol. V, *Historiography*, ed. Robin W. Winks (Oxford: Oxford University Press, 1999), 43–55. The traditional view was that the American Revolution marked the end of this empire as Britain turned to the east, to India and Southeast Asia. Recently, Marshall has challenged that assertion, as does this study. *The Making and Unmaking of Empires: Britain, India, and America c. 1750–1783* (New York: Oxford University Press, 2007) and *Remaking the British Atlantic: The United States and the British Empire after American Independence* (New York: Oxford University Press, 2012).

10. Colley, *Britons*, 144–45, and "Britishness and Otherness," 309–29; Gould, *Persistence of Empire*, chap. 6, and "American Independence and Britain's Counter-revolution," *Past & Present*, 154 (February 1997): 108–12; Stephen Conway, *The British Isles and the War for American Independence* (Oxford: Oxford University Press, 2000), chap. 9, and "'A Joy Unknown for Years Past': The American War, Britishness, and the Celebration of Rodney's Victory at the Saints," *History* 86, no. 282 (April 2001): 194; Jasanoff, *Liberty's Exiles*, chap. 4; Marshall, *Making and Unmaking*, chap. 11, and *Remaking the British Atlantic*, chap. 6.

11. My argument is indebted to the work of J. G. A. Pocock, who famously called for a decentering of British history that was less English centric and more representative of the reach and diversity of the nation's Atlantic empire. "British History: A Plea for a New Subject," *The Journal of Modern History* 47, no. 4 (December 1975): 601–21, and "The New British History in Atlantic Perspective: An Antipodean Commentary," The American Historical Review 104, no. 2 (April 1999): 490–500. For an excellent discussion of the field of "New British History," see the essays in, "AHR Forum: The New British History in Atlantic Perspective," *The American Historical Review* 104, no. 2 (April 1999): 426–500.

12. Edward Brathwaite, *The Development of Creole Society in Jamaica, 1770–1820* (New York: Oxford University Press, 1971), parts I and II; Richard B. Sheridan, *Sugar and Slavery: An Economic History of the British West Indies, 1623–1775* (Baltimore: Johns Hopkins University Press, 1974); Trevor Burnard, *Jamaica in the Age of Revolution* (Philadelphia: University of Pennsylvania Press, 2020) and *Mastery, Tyranny, and Desire: Thomas Thistlewood and His Slaves in the Anglo-Jamaican World* (Chapel Hill: University of North Carolina Press, 2004); O'Shaughnessy, *Empire Divided*, part I; Christer Petley, *White Fury: A Jamaican Slaveholder and the Age of Revolution* (Oxford: Oxford University Press, 2018), part I; T. R. Clayton, "Sophistry, Security and Socio-political Structures in the American Revolution; or, Why Jamaica Did Not Rebel," *Historical Journal* 29, no. 2 (June 1986): 319–44.

13. Elizabeth Mancke, *The Fault Lines of Empire: Political Differentiation in Massachusetts and Nova Scotia, Ca. 1760–1830* (New York: Routledge, 2005), esp. chaps. 4 and 5; J. B. Brebner, *The Neutral Yankees of Nova Scotia: A Marginal Colony during the Revolutionary Years* (1937; reprint: New York: Russell & Russell, 1970); Gordon Stewart and George Rawlyk, *A People Highly Favoured of God: The Nova Scotia Yankees and the American*

Revolution (Hamden, CT: Archon Books, 1972); George Rawlyk, *Nova Scotia's Massachusetts: A Study of Massachusetts–Nova Scotia Relations, 1630–1784* (Montreal: McGill-Queen's University Press, 1973) and Rawlyk, ed., *Revolution Rejected, 1775–1776* (Scarborough, ON: Prentice-Hall, 1968); Wilfred Brenton Kerr, *The Maritime Provinces of British North America and the American Revolution* (Sackville, NB: Busy East Press, 1942), chaps. 4 and 5, and "The Merchants of Nova Scotia and the American Revolution," *Canadian Historical Review* 13, no. 1 (March 1932): 20–36.

14. Joyce D. Goodfriend, *Before the Melting Pot: Society and Culture in Colonial New York City, 1664–1730* (Princeton: Princeton University Press, 1992); Jill Lepore, *New York Burning: Liberty, Slavery, and Conspiracy in Eighteenth-Century Manhattan* (New York: Vintage, 2005); Carl Bridenbaugh, *Cities in Revolt: Urban Life in America, 1743–1776* (New York: Alfred A. Knopf, 1955); Gary Nash, *Urban Crucible: Social Change, Political Consciousness, and the Origins of the American Revolution* (Cambridge, MA: Harvard University Press, 1979); Benjamin L. Carp, *Rebels Rising: Cities and the American Revolution* (Oxford: Oxford University Press, 2007), chap. 2.

15. T. M. Devine, *The Tobacco Lords: A Study of the Tobacco Merchants of Glasgow and Their Trading Activities c. 1740–90* (Edinburgh: John Donald Publishers, 1975); Jacob M. Price, "The Rise of Glasgow in the Chesapeake Tobacco Trade, 1707–1775," *William and Mary Quarterly* 11, no. 2 (April 1954): 179–99; Gordon Jackson, "Glasgow in Transition, c. 1660 to c. 1740," in *Glasgow*, vol. 1, *Beginnings to 1830*, ed. T. M. Devine and Gordon Jackson (Manchester, UK: Manchester University Press, 1995), 63–105; M. L. Robertson, "Scottish Commerce and the American War of Independence," *Economic History Review* 9, no. 1 (August 1956): 123–31; Dalphy I. Fagerstrom, "Scottish Opinion and the American Revolution," *William and Mary Quarterly* 11, no. 2 (April 1954): 252–275; D. B. Swinfen, "The American Revolution in the Scottish Press," in *Scotland, Europe and the American Revolution*, ed. Owen Dudley Edwards and George Shepperson (New York: St. Martin's Press, 1977), 66–74; Robert Kent Donovan, "The Popular Party of the Church of Scotland and the American Revolution," in *Scotland and America in the Age of Enlightenment*, ed. Richard B. Sher and Jeffrey R. Smitten (Edinburgh: Edinburgh University Press, 1990); Bruce P. Lenman, "Aristocratic 'Country' Whiggery in Scotland and the American Revolution," in *Scotland and America*, ed. Sher and Smitten, 180–92.

16. See chapter 4 and McConville, *King's Three Faces*, 288–90; Cogliano, *No King*, esp. chap. 3; Vernon Creviston, "'No King Unless it be a Constitutional King': Rethinking the Place of the Quebec Act in the Coming of the American Revolution," *Historian* 73, no. 3 (Fall 2011): 463–79.

17. Robert Parkinson, *The Common Cause: Creating Race and Nation in the American Revolution* (Chapel Hill: University of North Carolina Press, 2016); Cogliano, *No King*. Other historians have argued for the importance of the Coercive Acts in shaping the common cause. David Ammerman, *In the Common Cause: American Response to the Coercive Acts of 1774* (Charlottesville: University Press of Virginia, 1974); T. H. Breen, *American Insurgents, American Patriots: The Revolution of the People* (New York: Hill & Wang, 2010) and *The Marketplace of Revolution: How Consumer Politics Shaped American Independence* (New York: Oxford University Press, 2004), esp. chap. 8.

18. Historians, while certainly aware of the importance of the Franco-American alliance for British understandings of the war, have not thought about it in the con-

text of the wider British Atlantic. Conway, *British Isles*, chap. 5, and his two articles on the subject: "'A Joy Unknown,'" 180–99, and "From Fellow-Nationals to Foreigners: British Perceptions of the Americans, circa 1739–1783," *William and Mary Quarterly* 59, no. 1 (January 2002): 65–100; Colley, *Britons*, 132–45; Troy O. Bickham, *Making Headlines: The American Revolution as Seen through the British Press* (DeKalb: Northern Illinois University Press, 2009), chap. 5; Ruma Chopra, *Unnatural Rebellion: Loyalists in New York City during the Revolution* (Charlottesville: University of Virginia Press, 2011), 92–94, 192–93.

19. This is true of virtually every one of the most indispensable works on Loyalism. William Nelson, *The American Tory* (New York: Oxford University Press, 1961); Robert McClure Calhoon, *The Loyalist in Revolutionary America, 1760–1781* (New York: Harcourt Brace Jovanovich, 1965); Wallace Brown, *The King's Friends: The Composition and Motives of the American Loyalist Claimants* (Providence, RI: Brown University Press, 1966); Bernard Bailyn, *The Ordeal of Thomas Hutchinson* (Cambridge, MA: Harvard University Press, 1974); Janice Potter, *The Liberty We Seek: Loyalist Ideology in Colonial New York and Massachusetts* (Cambridge, MA: Harvard University Press, 1983); Brannon, *From Revolution*. Ruma Chopra, *Unnatural Rebellion* and *Choosing Sides: Loyalists in Revolutionary America* (New York: Roman & Littlefield, 2013); Kacy Dowd Tillman, *Stripped and Script: Loyalist Women Writers of the American Revolution* (Amherst: University of Massachusetts Press, 2019); Rebecca Brannon and Joseph Moore, *The Consequences of Loyalism: Essays in Honor of Robert M. Calhoon* (Columbia: University of South Carolina Press, 2019). There are a couple of exceptions to this narrow approach, such as Maya Jasanoff's wonderful global history of the post-war Loyalist experience. *Liberty's Exiles*. Additionally, Jerry Bannister and Liam Riordan's excellent introductory essay seeks to position Loyalism in a broader North Atlantic context. Introduction to *The Loyal Atlantic: Remaking the British Atlantic in the Revolutionary Era*, ed. Bannister and Riordan (Toronto: University of Toronto Press, 2012).

20. Historians who describe enslaved Africans who sided with the British as Loyalists tend to do so by embracing a more general definition of a Loyalist as someone who simply opposed the rebellion or fought for broader universal rights. For example, see James W. St. G. Walker, *The Black Loyalists: The Search for a Promised Land in Nova Scotia and Sierra Leone, 1783–1870* (New York: Longman, 1976); Jasanoff, *Liberty's Exiles*, 9; Michael E. Goth, "Black Loyalists and African American Allegiance in the Mid-Hudson Valley," in *The Other Loyalists: Ordinary People, Royalism, and the Revolution in the Middle Colonies, 1763–1787*, ed. Joseph S. Tiedemann, Eugene R. Fingerhut, and Robert W. Venables (Albany: SUNY Press, 2009), 81–104. Cassandra Pybus's work on runaway slaves during the American Revolution is often described by others as a history of Black Loyalists, though she never actually uses that term. *Epic Journeys of Freedom: Runaway Slaves of the American Revolution and Their Global Quest for Freedom* (Boston, MA: Beacon Press, 2006). For a useful critique of the idea of a Black Loyalist, see Barry Cahill, "The Black Loyalist Myth in Atlantic Canada," *Acadiensis* 29, no. 1 (Autumn 1999): 76–87. Historians also tend to equate Indian support for the British with loyalty or allegiance to the Crown, while acknowledging that Indian motives were substantially different from those of white British subjects. For example, see Colin Calloway, *The American Revolution in Indian Country: Crisis and Diversity in Native American Communities* (Cambridge: Cambridge University Press, 1995), esp. 29–42; Jim Piecuch,

Three Peoples, One King: Loyalists, Indians, and Slaves in the Revolutionary South, 1775–1782 (Columbia: University of South Carolina Press, 2013). The Mohawk sachem Joseph Brant is most often characterized as a Loyalist, though he too acted in the interest of protecting Iroquois land and political autonomy. Alan Taylor, *The Divided Ground: Indians, Settlers, and the Northern Borderland of the American Revolution* (New York: Vintage, 2006); Jasanoff, *Liberty's Exiles*, 189–98.

21. Jasanoff, *Liberty's Exiles*, esp. part I.

22. David Armitage, "Three Concepts of Atlantic History," in *The British Atlantic World, 1500–1800*, ed. David Armitage and Michael J. Braddick (New York: Palgrave, 2002) 11–27. See also Trevor Burnard, "The British Atlantic," in *Atlantic History: A Critical Appraisal*, ed. Jack P. Green and Philip D. Morgan (Oxford: Oxford University Press, 2009), 111–36.

1. A Body Politic

1. Isaiah Thomas, *The History of Printing in America, with a Biography of Printers and an Account of Newspapers* (1810; reprint, Barre, MA: Imprint Society, 1970), 1:332–37.

2. *New-Hampshire Gazette*, October 14, 1756.

3. While scholars recognize this fact, surprisingly few studies actually examine the complex ways in which news and information traveled, or how an emerging British Atlantic print culture shaped popular understandings of Britishness. Ian K. Steele is the only historian to have given careful consideration to the growth of an English Atlantic printing industry and the various communication networks that supported it. Frustratingly, however, his study ends in 1740, just before the rapid expansion of this industry and these networks, and at the moment when Britons were just beginning to forge a national identity. *The English Atlantic* (New York: Oxford University Press, 1986). There is very good scholarship on the regional importance of the printing industry in shaping political cultures and identities. For Great Britain, see John Brewer, *Party Ideology and Popular Politics at the Accession of George III* (Cambridge: Cambridge University Press, 1976); Troy O. Bickham, *Making Headlines: The American Revolution as Seen through the British Press* (DeKalb: Northern Illinois University Press, 2009); Hannah Barker, *Newspapers, Politics and English Society, 1695–1855* (New York: Longman, 2000); Jeremy Black, *The English Press in the Eighteenth Century* (Philadelphia: University of Pennsylvania Press, 1987). For America and the American colonies, see Simon Newman, *Parades and the Politics of the Street: Festive Culture in the Early American Republic* (Philadelphia: University of Pennsylvania Press, 1999); David Waldstreicher, *In the Midst of Perpetual Fetes: The Making of American Nationalism, 1776–1820* (Chapel Hill: University of North Carolina Press, 1997); Robert Parkinson, *The Common Cause: Creating Race and Nation in the American Revolution* (Chapel Hill: University of North Carolina Press, 2016); Joseph M. Adelman, *Revolutionary Networks: The Business and Politics of Printing the News, 1763–1789* (Baltimore: Johns Hopkins University Press, 2019); Charles E. Clark, "The Newspapers of Provincial America," in *Three Hundred Years of the American Newspaper*, ed. John B. Hench (Worcester, MA: American Antiquarian Society, 1991), 367–89. For British Canada, see Michael Eamon, *Imprinting Britain: Newspapers, Sociability, and the Shaping of British North America* (Montreal: McGill-Queen's University Press, 2015).

4. Newman, *Parades and the Politics*, 187.

5. Benedict Anderson, *Imagined Communities: Reflections on the Origins and Spread of Nationalism* (London: Verso, 1983), 44–45, 61, 62. Many historians have applied this idea to their own work. Some of the best are Linda Colley, *Britons: Forging the Nation 1707–1837* (New Haven, CT: Yale University Press, 1992); Waldstreicher, *In the Midst*; Newman, *Parades and the Politics*; Parkinson, *Common Cause*.

6. During the so-called slave conspiracy of 1741, it was widely believed that a suspected Catholic and Spanish sympathizer encouraged slaves to burn the city. Jill Lepore, *New York Burning: Liberty, Slavery, and Conspiracy in Eighteenth-Century Manhattan* (New York: Vintage, 2005), 170–97. The same is true of the 1712 slave conspiracy, which many contemporaries believed was caused by Spanish Catholic slaves in the city. Jason K. Duncan, *Citizens or Papists?: The Politics of Anti-Catholicism in New York, 1685–1821* (New York: Fordham University Press, 2005), 19–20.

7. Trevor Burnard and Kenneth Morgan, "The Dynamics of the Slave Market and Slave Purchasing Patterns in Jamaica, 1655–1788," *William and Mary Quarterly* 58, no. 1 (January 2001): 205–7 and "European Migration to Jamaica, 1655–1780," *William and Mary Quarterly* 53, no. 4 (October 1996): 772, table 1. A writer in a 1782 Jamaican almanac reported that there were 5,000 whites, 1,200 free people of color, and 8,000 slaves living in Kingston. *Douglass & Aikman's Almanack and Register for the Island of Jamaica: Calculated for the Year of Our Lord 1782* (Kingston: Douglass & Aikman, 1781), 67, National Library of Jamaica, accessed July 15, 2015, https://nljdigital.nlj.gov.jm/files /original/bd477cd209ff67acb704964172c9ce0b.pdf. Throughout the seventeenth and eighteenth centuries, slaves attempted to revolt nearly every five years in Jamaica, more than anywhere else in the empire. Orlando Patterson, *The Sociology of Slavery: An Analysis of the Origins, Development and Structure of Negro Slave Society in Jamaica* (London: MacGibbon & Kee, 1967), 273–74.

8. Simon Newman, "Theorizing Class in Glasgow and the Atlantic World," in *Class Matters: Early North America and the Atlantic World*, ed. Simon Middleton and Billy G. Smith (Philadelphia: University of Pennsylvania Press, 2008), 16–34.

9. Twenty newspapers were published in London at the time, more than the number printed in Glasgow, New York City, Halifax, and Kingston combined. William Speck, "Politics and the Press," in *The Press in English Society from the Seventeenth to Nineteenth Centuries*, ed. Michael Harris and Alan Lee (Rutherford, NJ: Farleigh Dickinson University Press, 1986), 48.

10. Hannah Barker, *Newspapers, Politics and Public Opinion in Late Eighteenth-Century England* (Oxford: Oxford University Press, 1998), 96–97.

11. Brewer, *Party Ideology*, 139–60.

12. For England, see G. A. Cranfield, *The Development of the Provincial Newspaper, 1700–1760* (Oxford: Oxford University Press, 1962), 1–27; Brewer, *Party Ideology*, 142–43. For Scotland, see Mary Elizabeth Craig, *The Scottish Periodical Press, 1750–1789* (Edinburgh: Oliver and Boyd, 1931). For British North America, see William David Sloan and Julie Hedgepeth Williams, *The Early American Press, 1690–1783* (Westport, CT: Greenwood Press, 1994), 104–5; Charles E. Clark, *The Pubic Prints: The Newspaper in Anglo-American Culture, 1665–1740* (New York: Oxford University Press, 1994), 59–73. For the British Caribbean, and Jamaica in particular, see John A. Lent, *Third World Mass Media and Their Search for Modernity: The Case of Commonwealth Caribbean, 1717–1976* (Lewisburg, PA: Bucknell University Press, 1977), 323–43, app. A.

13. E. A. Wrigley, *Poverty, Progress, and Population* (Cambridge: Cambridge University Press, 2004), 257–259; Jan de Vries, *European Urbanization, 1500–1800* (Cambridge: Cambridge University Press, 1984); Barker, *Newspapers, Politics and English Society*, 29–45.

14. New York City: Gary Nash, *Urban Crucible: Social Change, Political Consciousness, and the Origins of the American Revolution* (Cambridge, MA: Harvard University Press, 1979), 4, 54, 313, 409, fig. 1; Evarts B. Green and Virginia D. Harrington, *American Population before the Federal Census of 1790* (1932; reprint, New York: Columbia University Press, 1981), 94–102. Glasgow: T. C. Smout, *A History of the Scottish People, 1560–1830* (New York: Charles Scribner's Sons, 1969), 157, 261, table 2; Jeremy Black, *Eighteenth-Century Britain, 1688–1783* (New York: Palgrave Macmillan, 2001), 122.

15. Kingston: Trevor Burnard, "'The Grand Mart of the Island': The Economic Function of Kingston, Jamaica in the Mid-eighteenth Century," in *Jamaica in Slavery and Freedom: History, Heritage and Culture*, ed. Kathleen E. A. Monteith and Glen Richards (Kingston, Jamaica: University of the West Indies Press, 2002), 227. Halifax: Charles Morris, "A Description of the Several Towns in This Province the Lands Comprehended within and Bordering on Said Towns," in *Report Concerning Canadian Archives for the Year 1904* (Ottawa: S. E. Dawson, 1905), 290.

16. Jill Lepore, *The Name of War: King Philip's War and the Origins of American Identity* (New York: Vintage, 1999), x.

17. Konstantin Dierks, *In My Power: Letter Writing and Communications in Early America* (Philadelphia: University of Pennsylvania Press, 2011), chap. 1; Lindsay O'Neill, *The Open Letter: Networking in the Early Modern British World* (Philadelphia: University of Pennsylvania Press, 2015), esp. 2–9.

18. The two earliest known Scottish newspapers were both printed in Edinburgh: *Edinburgh Gazette* (1699) and the *Edinburgh Courant* (1705). Stephen W. Brown, "Newspapers and Magazines," in *Edinburgh History of the Book in Scotland*, vol. 2, *Enlightenment and Expansion, 1707–1800*, ed. Stephen W. Brown and Warren McDougall (Edinburgh: Edinburgh University Press, 2011), 354–55.

19. A. R. B. Haldane, *Three Centuries of Scottish Posts: An Historical Survey to 1836* (Edinburgh: Edinburgh University Press, 1971), 39; William Lewins, *Her Majesty's Mails: An Historical and Descriptive Account of the British Post-Office* (London: Sampson, Low, Son, and Marston, 1864), 88–89.

20. Steele, *English Atlantic*, chap. 9; Dierks, *In My Power*, chap. 1; L. E. Britnor, *The History of the Sailing Packets to the West Indies, Paper No. 5* (London: British West Indies Study Circle, 1973), 1–15; Thomas Foster, *The Postal History of Jamaica, 1662–1880* (London: Robson Lowe, 1968), 9–12.

21. For news of the first packet service, see *Whitehall Evening Post or London Intelligencer*, October 25, 1755.

22. Drawing on Lloyd's List and newspaper reports, John S. Olenkiewicz has charted every packet ship that crossed the Atlantic between 1756 and 1840. For the Falmouth to New York City voyages between 1756 and 1783, see *British Packet Sailings, Falmouth to North America: 1755–1840*, 1–42, accessed August 1, 2015, http://www.rfrajola.com/Mercury/British%20Packet%20NA%201755-17840%20with%20Mailboats.pdf.

23. *New York Mercury*, January 26, 1756. By the early 1760s, postal riders traveled to and from New York and Philadelphia three times a week, a trip that usually took fif-

teen hours. Michael G. Kammen, *Colonial New York: A History* (New York: Oxford University Press, 1975), 338. For more on the inconsistences that plagued the postal system in the middle of the eighteenth century, see *Journal Kept by Hugh Finlay, Surveyor of the Post Roads on the Continent of North America . . . Begun the 13th Septr. 1773 and Ended 26th June 1774* (Brooklyn, NY: Frank H. Horton, 1867). Finlay provides a weekly chart for the mail service in New York City on p. 48.

24. William Smith, *The History of the Post Office in British North America, 1639–1870* (Cambridge: Cambridge University Press, 1920), 176.

25. Olenkiewicz, *British Packet Sailings*.

26. For example, see the ship *Harriot* in Olenkiewicz, *British Packet Sailings*.

27. For example, see the account of the *General Wall* in *Caledonian Mercury*, March 31, 1760.

28. Howard Robinson, *Carrying British Mails Overseas* (New York: G. Allen & Unwin, 1964), 39–50; Britnor, *History of the Sailing Packets*, 17–32.

29. On average, between 1781 and 1788, it took forty-two days for a packet boat to travel from Falmouth to Kingston. B. W. Higman, *Plantation Jamaica, 1750–1850: Capital and Control in a Colonial Economy* (Kingston, Jamaica: University of the West Indies Press, 2005), 130.

30. Higman, *Plantation Jamaica*, 113–33. For the use of slaves to deliver mail, see Roderick Cave, *Printing and the Book Trade in the West Indies* (London: Pindar Press, 1987), 32.

31. Steele, *English Atlantic*, 275.

32. *Pennsylvania Gazette*, February 19, 1756.

33. Steele, *English Atlantic*, 92.

34. Walter S. Dunn, *The New Imperial Economy: The British Army and the American Frontier, 1764–1768* (Westport, CT: Praeger, 2001), 32–34.

35. Virginia Harrington, *The New York Merchant on the Eve of the Revolution* (1935; reprint, Gloucester, MA: Peter Smith, 1964), 190, 193–95; Steele, *English Atlantic*, 32, 63, 66–70, 296, table 4.5.

36. Steele, *English Atlantic*, 69–70, 298, table 4.7.

37. T. M. Devine, *The Tobacco Lords: A Study of the Tobacco Merchants of Glasgow and Their Trading Activities c. 1740–90* (Edinburgh: John Donald Publishers, 1975), 55–71.

38. Richard F. Dell, "The Operational Record of the Clyde Tobacco Fleet, 1747–1775," *Scottish Economic & Social History* 2, no. 1 (1982): 5, table 1, 15.

39. Devine, *Tobacco Lords*, chap. 7.

40. Warren McDougall, "Scottish Books for America in the Mid-18th Century," in *Spreading the Word: The Distribution Networks of Print 1550–1850*, ed. Robin Myers and Michael Harris (Winchester, UK: St. Paul's Bibliographies, 1990), 21–46.

41. Jack P. Greene found that in 1752, nearly 50 percent of all ships trading in Jamaica came from Britain's North American colonies. *Settler Jamaica in the 1750s: A Social Portrait* (Charlottesville: University of Virginia Press, 2016), 17–18, table 1.5. The Kingston printer William Daniell purchased his paper from Ben Franklin in Philadelphia, who often included copies of his gazette in his correspondence. For example, see "Daniell to Franklin, 29 June 1754," in *The Papers of Benjamin Franklin*, vol. 5, *July 1, 1753, through March 31, 1755*, ed. Leonard W. Labaree (New Haven, CT: Yale University Press, 1962), 364.

42. Alejandra Dubcovsky draws similar conclusions about "the tension between imperial ambitions and local arrangements," which found meaning in the complicated, uneven nature of communication networks in the early American South. *Informed Power: Communication in the Early American South* (Cambridge, MA: Harvard University Press, 2016), 6. Imperial officials, like Thomas Pownall, worried aloud in the 1760s that these smaller networks might weaken the influence of the metropole. William B. Warner, "Communicating Liberty: The News of the British Empire as a Matrix for the American Revolution," *ELH* 72, no. 2 (Summer 2005): 347–51.

43. Julie Hedgepeth Williams, *The Significance of the Printed Word in Early America: Colonists' Thoughts on the Role of the* Press (Westport, CT: Greenwood Press, 1999), 135–62.

44. For example, see *Glasgow Mercury*, January 8, 1778. I would like to thank Stephen Mullen for help with locating this particular issue of the *Mercury*. See also *Nova-Scotia Gazette: and the Weekly Advertiser*, January 3, 1769; *Rivington's New-York Gazetteer; Or, The Connecticut, Hudson's River, New-Jersey, and Quebec Weekly Advertiser*, April 22, 1773. Rivington's paper went through several titles during its run. Hereafter, it will be referred to as *Rivington's Gazette*.

45. Tony Claydon, "Daily News and the Construction of Time in Late Stuart England, 1695–1714," *Journal of British Studies* 52, no. 1 (January 2013): 55–78.

46. I have not been able to locate the original publication of the letter in the Dublin newspaper. *Pennsylvania Gazette*, March 27, 1766; *New York Gazette*, March 31, 1766; *Newport Mercury*, April 7, 1766; *Boston Post-Boy*, April 7, 1766; *London Evening Post*, May 6, 1766; *Caledonian Mercury*, May 10, 1766; *Jackson's Oxford Journal*, May 10, 1766; *Dublin Courier*, May 12, 1766; *Leeds Intelligencer*, May 13, 1766.

47. My understanding of the public sphere is informed by Jürgen Habermas, *The Structural Transformation of the Public Sphere: An Inquiry into a Category of Bourgeois Society*, trans. Thomas Burger with the assistance of Frederick Lawrence (Cambridge, MA: MIT Press, 1989). I disagree, however, with Habermas's claim that ordinary Britons operated within a separate public sphere (an "us versus them" scenario) that increasingly forced state officials toward accepting a more democratic, equal society. These lines were not so clearly drawn during the revolutionary era, especially in the context of print and politics. Some of the best works in this field that draw on Habermasian theory are Waldstreicher, *In the Midst of Perpetual Fetes*; Newman, *Parades and the Politics*; David S. Shields, *Civil Tongues and Polite Letters in British America* (Chapel Hill: University of North Carolina Press, 1997); Michael Warner, *The Letters of the Republic: Publication and the Public Sphere in Eighteenth-Century America* (Cambridge, MA: Harvard University Press, 1990).

48. Halifax's population was similar to that of other middle-tier towns in the thirteen American colonies, like Portsmouth, New Hampshire, or Williamsburg, Virginia, both of which also produced at least one newspaper during this period. For population tables, see Thomas L. Purvis, ed., *Colonial America to 1763* (New York: Facts on File, 1999), 128–67. For a brief period in 1769 and 1770, two newspapers were published in the city. For a history of printing in Nova Scotia, see Isaiah Thomas, *The History of Printing in America, with a Biography of Printers and an Account of Newspapers* (Worcester, MA: From the Press of Isaiah Thomas, June 1810), 2:179–81; Dean Jobb, "'The First That Ever Was Publish'd in the Province': John Bushell's *Halifax Gazette*, 1752–1761," *Journal*

of the *Royal Nova Scotia Historical Society*, 11 (2008): 1–22; J. J. Stewart, "Early Journalism in Nova Scotia," in *Collections of the Nova Scotia Historical Society, For the Year 1887–88*, vol. 6 (Halifax, NS: Nova Scotia Printing Company, 1888), 91–122.

49. "Memoir of Isaiah Thomas, By His Grandson, Benjamin Franklin Thomas," in Thomas, *History of Printing*, 1:xxvii, xxxi–xxxii.

50. Beginning in 1780, John Howe, a Loyalist exile from Boston, published the *Halifax Journal*, which competed with Henry for readers over the remainder of the war. No copies survive today, however, and we know nothing of its circulation or readership. Stewart, "Early Journalism," 117–20.

51. In 1718, Robert Baldwin began publishing the *Weekly Jamaica Courant*, the second oldest newspaper in all of Britain's Atlantic colonies. At the time, Governor Sir Nicholas Laws argued, "I am of opinion if a press were set up in Jamaica it would be of great use, and benefit for publick intelligence, advertisements, and many other things." Douglas C. McMurtrie, *The First Printing in Jamaica* (Evanston, IL: n.p., 1942), 3.

52. Sara Yeh, "Colonial Identity and Revolutionary Loyalty: The Case of the West Indies," in *British North America in the Seventeenth and Eighteenth Centuries*, ed. Stephen Foster (Oxford: Oxford University Press, 2013), 195–226.

53. In 1755, the planter elite in nearby Spanish Town began their own newspaper, the *Weekly St. Jago Intelligencer*. In 1773, a fourth newspaper, the *Cornwall Chronicle or Country Gazette*, began at Montego Bay, the largest port on the northwest corner of the island. Cave, *Printing and the Book Trade*, 20, 108–9; Frank Cundall, *The Press and Printers of Jamaica Prior to 1820* (Worcester, MA: American Antiquarian Society, 1916), 298–99.

54. Aikman was a bookseller in Annapolis, Maryland, who fled to Kingston in October 1775. Douglass was the manager of the famed American Company of Comedians, who were forced to flee the colonies in 1775 when Patriot committees shut down theaters. Aikman's younger brother, Alexander Aikman, fled from Charleston to Jamaica in 1779 and took over the printing of the *Intelligencer*. *Jamaica Mercury and Kingston Weekly Advertiser*, May 1, 1779.

55. In 1715, Donald Govan founded the city's first newspaper, the *Glasgow Courant*. David Murray, *Robert & Andrew Foulis and the Glasgow Press, with Some Account of the Glasgow Academy of Fine Arts* (Glasgow: J. Maclehose and Sons, 1913), 14; Craig, *Scottish Periodical Press*, 9.

56. *Chronicles of Saint Mungo: or, Antiquities and Traditions of Glasgow* (Glasgow: John Smith & Son, 1843), 143–48.

57. From as early as 1654, the town council employed an agent to obtain the latest newsletters in Edinburgh. Dale Cragsley, "The Glasgow Periodical Press in the Eighteenth Century," *Scottish Notes and Queries* 13, no. 3 (1935): 166.

58. William Couper, *The Edinburgh Periodical Press: Being a Bibliographical Account of the Newspapers, Journals, and Magazines Issued in Edinburgh from the Earliest Times to 1800* (Stirling, UK: Eneas Mackay, 1908), 2:71–83.

59. Clark, *Public Prints*, 178–88. For more on Zenger and the origins of a free press, see James Alexander, *A Brief Narrative of the Case and Trial of John Peter Zenger*, ed. Stanley N. Katz (Cambridge, MA: Harvard University Press, 1963); Leonard Levy, *Legacy of Suppression: Freedom of Speech and Press in Early America* (Cambridge, MA: Harvard University Press, 1960).

60. Isaiah Thomas questioned Gaine's political beliefs, arguing that his creed "was to join the strongest party." Thomas, *History of Printing*, 2:103. From 1768, Gaine's newspaper was called the *New-York Gazette; and the Weekly Mercury*. Hildeburn, *Sketches of Printers and Printing in Colonial New York* (Detroit, MI: Gale Research, 1969), 35–54.

61. Hildeburn, *Sketches of Printers*, 89–96; Thomas, *History of Printing*, 2:116–20. For more on the emergence of these networks and the role printers played in creating and sustaining them, see Adelman, *Revolutionary Networks*, chaps. 3 and 4. There were several other short-lived newspapers: the *New-York Chronicle* (1769–70), the *Constitutional Gazette* (1775–76), and the *New York Packet* (1776).

62. Leroy Hewlett, "James Rivington, Loyalist Printer, Publisher, and Bookseller of the American Revolution, 1774–1802: A Biographical, Bibliographical Study" (Ph.D. diss., University of Michigan, 1958), 15–17; Hildeburn, *Sketches of Printers*, 105–41. Rivington may have briefly lived in Halifax. See the advertisement for a "James Rivington, Book Seller Stationer from London" in *Halifax Gazette*, May 14, 1761.

63. The four newspapers were the *New-York Gazette and Weekly Mercury* (Monday); *Rivington's Gazette* (Wednesdays and Saturdays); *Royal American Gazette* (Thursdays); *New-York Mercury; or General Advertiser* (Fridays). Thomas, *History of Printing*, 2:110, 120–24; Hildeburn, *Sketches of Printers*, 98–104, 168–70.

64. Barker, *Newspapers, Politics, and English Society*, 43. Scottish Clerks of the Road had franking privileges since the late seventeenth century, and the right was extended to government officials in 1764. Haldane, *Three Centuries*, 167–68. For an especially good example of the franking privilege, see the subscription book for William Brown, printer of the *Quebec Gazette*. Subscription Book, 1768–1769, MG 24, B 1, Neilson Collection, vol. 46, file 3, Reel C-15611, Library and Archives of Canada (hereafter cited as LAC). The practice of taking news from other newspapers is called "exchanging." Parkinson, *Common Cause*, 15; Ben Paul Lafferty, "Joseph Dennie and *The Farmer's Weekly Museum*: Readership and Pseudonymous Celebrity in Early National Journalism," *American Nineteenth Century History* 15, no. 1 (2014): 67–87.

65. In 1769, Halifax's Anthony Henry resumed printing his gazette and thus re-entered Brown's subscription list. Subscription Book, LAC.

66. Haldane, *Three Centuries*, 42–45.

67. *Glasgow Mercury*, November 10, 1780. The city's printers also depended on these networks to acquire news from around Scotland that they could publish in their newspapers. Couper, *Edinburgh Periodical Press*, 1:109.

68. His letter was printed as a pamphlet and sold in Glasgow in 1774 as *News from America: From Alexander Thomson . . . to a Gentleman near Glasgow* (Glasgow, 1774), 1. Rare Books, John Witherspoon Library, vol. 49, Princeton University.

69. *New-York Mercury*, March 22, 1762.

70. *Rivington's Gazette*, October 13, 1774.

71. Thomas also claimed that Henry married a local pastry cook "of African extraction" whose income he used to purchase his printing press. Thomas, *History of Printing*, 2:177–81.

72. *New-York Mercury*, December 23, 1765. Conversely, when Thomas took to the *Halifax Gazette* to rail against the dreaded tax, he was aided in part by the arrival of a ship from Philadelphia, which "brought some of the newspapers published in that city." Thomas, *History of Printing*, 1:159.

73. *Jamaica Mercury, and Kingston Weekly Advertiser*, November 27, 1779.

74. *Jamaica Mercury, and Kingston Weekly Advertiser*, May 1, 1779.

75. Parkinson, *Common Cause*, 26–77, esp. 44–60 and 704, app. B. For Bradford's 1774 subscription book, see "List of Customers for Pennsylvania Journal Taken January 1774," Bradford Family Papers, Collection 1676, 2d Ser., box 9, folder 1, Historical Society of Pennsylvania. I would like to thank Robert Parkinson for sharing this with me.

76. We have no way of knowing who took up Dunlap's offer or whether those agents served more areas beyond their own locale (they likely did), but the list gives us some idea of where Dunlap believed his paper might travel. *Pennsylvania Packet; and the General Advertiser*, October 28, 1771. Similar listings of agents can be found in the *New-York Mercury*, November 27, 1752; *New York Journal; or, the General Advertiser*, May 25, 1769; *American Journal; and General Advertiser*, April 1, 1779.

77. *Nova-Scotia Gazette: and the Weekly Chronicle*, September 29, 1772. See also *American Journal; and General Advertiser*, April 1, 1779; *Connecticut Courant*, October 29, 1764.

78. Cranfield, *Provincial Newspaper*, chap. 1; C. Y. Ferdinand, *Benjamin Collins and the Provincial Newspaper Trade in the Eighteenth Century* (New York: Oxford University Press, 1997), chap. 3.

79. Cranfield, *Provincial Newspaper*, 200.

80. Victoria E. M. Gardner, *The Business of News in England, 1760–1820* (London: Palgrave Macmillan, 2016), 148.

81. Parkinson, *Common Cause*, 61. Jamaican networks were likely much smaller, given the location of that island. For example, see the *Savanna-la-Mar Gazette*, July 15, 1788.

82. *New-Hampshire Gazette*, October 14, 1756.

83. *New-York Gazette*, February 22, 1762.

84. I have not located the version published in Edinburgh, though the essay did appear in New York City under the heading "*From the* Edinburgh Evening Post." *New-York Gazette; and the Weekly Mercury*, August 4, 1783. *Quidnunc* was a popular term used to refer to someone who obsessed over the latest news. Uriel Heyd, *Reading Newspapers: Press and Public in Eighteenth-Century Britain and America* (Oxford: Voltaire Foundation, 2012), 94–98, 195–230.

85. For example, see Bickham, *Making Headlines*, 36–39.

86. A yearly subscription to the *Glasgow Mercury* in 1780 sold for 12s. 8d., if the buyer obtained the weekly paper from the printing office; 13s. 2d., if the buyer had it sent to his or her home in town; and 15s. 2.d., if sent by post outside of the city. *Glasgow Mercury*, June 29, 1780. Residents of New Jersey could purchase an annual subscription to *Rivington's Gazette* in 1774 for "one dollar and a half," or roughly twelve shillings. *Rivington's Gazette*, September 2, 1774. In 1773, Anthony Henry's *Nova Scotia Gazette: and the Weekly Chronicle*, went for a flat-rate 10s., with the only option being for consumers to pick up their papers at Henry's printing office on Sackville Street. *Nova Scotia Gazette: and the Weekly Chronicle*, January 12, 1773.

87. Black, *English Press*, 106–8.

88. This is much lower than Joseph Addison's 1711 claim of twenty readers for every issue of his *Spectator*. Hannah Barker, "England, 1760–1815," in *Press, Politics and the Public Sphere in Europe and America, 1760–1820*, ed. Hannah Barker and Simon Burrows (Cambridge: Cambridge University Press, 2002), 104–5.

89. It is difficult to establish clear links between literacy rates and readership, since the normal indicators of a literate person—the ability to sign his or her name—does not necessarily mean the person could also read. R. A. Houston, *Scottish Literacy and the Scottish Identity: Illiteracy and Society in Scotland and Northern England, 1600–1800* (Cambridge: Cambridge University Press, 1985), esp. 46–49; T. C. Smout, "Born Again at Cambulsang: New Evidence on Popular Religion and Literacy in Eighteenth-Century Scotland," *Past & Present* 97, no. 1 (November 1982): 114–27.

90. Barry Reay, *Popular Cultures in England, 1550–1750* (New York: Longman, 1998), 48. See also Nicholas Hudson, "Constructing Oral Tradition: The Origins of the Concept in Enlightenment Intellectual Culture," in *The Spoken Word: Oral Culture in Britain, 1500–1850*, ed. Adam Fox and Daniel Woolf (Manchester, UK: Manchester University Press, 2002), 240–77.

91. Clark, *Public Prints*, 217–20; Claydon, "Daily News," 55–78.

92. *New-York Journal; or, The General Advertiser*, July 11, 1776.

93. Roger S. Schofield, "The Measurement of Literacy in Pre-industrial England," in *Literacy in Traditional Societies*, ed. James Goody (Cambridge: Cambridge University Press, 1968), 312–13; Brewer, *Party Ideology*, 155–58.

94. Newman, "Theorizing Class in Glasgow," 16–34. The rise in Gaelic-speaking Highlanders during this period led the editors of the *Scots Magazine* to begin to print lists of common Scottish phrases, which they dubbed *Scotticisms*, alongside their English translations, so that "our countrymen [can avoid them] in speaking and writing." *Scots Magazine*, 22 (November 1760), 686–87.

95. John M'Ure, *Glasghu Facies: A View of the City of Glasgow* (Glasgow: John Tweed, 1872), 2:462. See also Robert Alison, *The Anecdotage of Glasgow Comprising Anecdotes and Anecdotal Incidents of the City of Glasgow and Glasgow Personages* (Glasgow: Thomas D. Morison, 1892), 204.

96. John Strang, *Glasgow and Its Clubs* (Glasgow: Richard Griffin and Co., 1857), 175–78.

97. Claude Galarneau and Gilles Gallichan make a similar case for John Bushell's shop in Halifax. "Working in Trades," in *History of the Book in Canada*, vol. 1, *Beginnings to 1840*, ed. Patricia Lockhart Fleming, Gilles Gallichan, and Yvan Lamonde (Toronto: University of Toronto Press, 2004), 85–86.

98. Ewald Schaukirk, "Occupation of New York City by the British," *Pennsylvania Magazine of History and Biography* 10, no. 4 (January 1885): 440–41.

99. Quoted in Patricia Lockhart Fleming, "Public Print," in *History of the Book in Canada*, vol. 1, *Beginnings to 1840*, ed. Patricia Lockhart Fleming, Gilles Gallichan, and Yvan Lamonde (Toronto: University of Toronto Press, 2004), 113.

100. Brian Cowan, *The Social Life of Coffee: The Emergence of the British Coffeehouse* (New Haven, CT: Yale University Press, 2005), 172–75; Peter Thompson, *Rum Punch & Revolution: Taverngoing & Public Life in Eighteenth-Century Philadelphia* (Philadelphia: University of Pennsylvania Press, 1999), esp. chaps. 3 and 4.

101. *New-York Gazette Revived in the Weekly Post-Boy*, August 20, 1750. See also the advertisement for the Whitehall Coffee House in the *New-York Gazette*, June 21, 1762.

102. L. H. Butterfield, ed., *Diary and Autobiography of John Adams* (Cambridge, MA: Harvard University Press, 1961), 2:103.

103. *Rivington's Gazette*, January 15, 1780.

104. Haldane, *Three Centuries*, 38.

105. *Glasgow, Past and Present: Illustrated in Dean of Guild Reports and in the Reminiscences and Communications of Senex [R. Reid], Aliquis, &c.*, ed. James Pagan (Glasgow: James MacNab, 1851), 113–14.

106. For mention of publications being sent to Durie, see *Glasgow Mercury*, April 11, 1780. For evidence of his ownership of the Swann Inn, see Robert Brown, *The History of Paisley: From the Roman Period Down to 1884* (Paisley, UK: J&J Cook, 1886), 2:159. Other Glaswegians formed reading clubs and gathered regularly at local taverns to read the latest gazettes. Strang, *Glasgow and Its Clubs*, 100–101.

107. J. B. Brebner, *The Neutral Yankees of Nova Scotia: A Marginal Colony During the Revolutionary Years* (1937; reprint: New York: Russell & Russell, 1970), 199–201; T. B. Akins, *History of Halifax City*, 2nd ed. (1895; reprint, Belleville, ON: Mica Pub., 1973), 78–84; Marjorie Major, "The Great Pontack Inn," *Nova Scotia Historical Society* 3, no. 3 (September 1973): 171–90; George Mullane, "Old Inns and Coffee Houses of Halifax," *Collections of the Nova Scotia Historical Society* (1933), 22:1–23.

108. *Jamaica Mercury, and Kingston Weekly Advertiser*, March 4, 1780. See also *Jamaica Mercury, and Kingston Weekly Advertiser*, July 24, 1779.

109. Alfred Spencer, ed., *Memoirs of William Hickey* (New York, Alfred A. Knopf, 1921), 2:45.

110. Quoted in Richard B. Sheridan, "The Jamaican Slave Insurrection Scare of 1776 and the American Revolution," *Journal of Negro History* 61, no. 3 (July 1976): 300. Heather Andrea Williams argues that African American slaves in the antebellum South were particularly adept at listening, a skill made necessary by the refusal of whites to teach their slaves how to read and write. *Self-Taught: African American Education in Slavery and Freedom* (Chapel Hill: University of North Carolina Press, 2005), 7–10.

111. *New-Hampshire Gazette*, October 14, 1756.

112. Colley, *Britons*; Carla Gardina Pestana, *Protestant Empire: Religion and the Making of the British Atlantic World* (Philadelphia: University of Pennsylvania Press, 2009); Owen Stanwood, *The Empire Reformed: English America in the Age of the Glorious Revolution* (Philadelphia: University of Pennsylvania Press, 2011); Brendan McConville, *The King's Three Faces: The Rise and Fall of Royal America, 1688–1776* (Chapel Hill: University of North Carolina Press, 2006); Eliga H. Gould, *The Persistence of Empire: British Political Culture in the Age of the American Revolution* (Chapel Hill: University of North Carolina Press, 2000); Francis D. Cogliano, *No King, No Popery: Anti-Catholicism in Revolutionary New England* (Westport: Greenwood Press, 1995). For more on the importance of *red letter days*, see David Cressy, *Bonfires and Bells: National Memory and the Protestant Calendar in Elizabethan and Stuart England* (Berkeley: University of California Press, 1989).

113. David Armitage put it more succinctly, describing the British Empire from the 1740s as "Protestant, commercial, maritime and free." *The Ideological Origins of the British Empire* (Cambridge: Cambridge University Press, 2000), 173.

114. See the impressive work of Fred Anderson, *Crucible of War: The Seven Years' War and the Fate of Empire in British North America, 1754–1766* (New York: Alfred A. Knopf, 2000) and *A People's Army: Massachusetts Soldiers and Society in the Seven Years' War* (Chapel Hill: University of North Carolina Press, 1984).

115. David Copeland, "'Join, or Die': America's Press during the French and Indian War," *Journalism History* 24, no. 3 (1998): 112–21. This was true of mainland Britain as well. Kathleen Wilson, *The Sense of the People: Politics, Culture and Imperialism in England, 1715–1785* (Cambridge: Cambridge University Press, 1995), chap. 3; Bob Harris, *Politics and the Nation: Britain in the Mid-Eighteenth Century* (Oxford: Oxford University Press, 2002), chap. 3.

116. "Corruption of News-writers, No. 30. Saturday, November 11 [1758]," *Idler* (London: n.p., 1761), 1:169.

117. *Glasgow Courant*, July 14, 1755.

118. *New-York Gazette: or, the Weekly Post-Boy*, January 17, 1757.

119. *New York Gazette: or, the Weekly Post-Boy*, September 23, 1754; *Glasgow Journal*, January 13, 1755; *Halifax Gazette*, February 15, 1755.

120. David Copeland found a sharp increase in the reporting of Indian violence during the 1750s. *Colonial American Newspapers: Character and Content* (Newark: University of Delaware Press, 1997), 42–68. See also Peter Silver, *Our Savage Neighbors: How Indian War Transformed Early America* (New York: W. W. Norton, 2008), esp. chap. 4; Stanwood, *Empire Reformed*, chap. 2.

121. For example, see *New-York Mercury*, March 25, 1754.

122. For example, see *Caledonian Mercury*, July 6 and August 12, 1756; *Scots Magazine*, 19 (February 1757), 75–76; *Scots Magazine*, 19 (November 1757), 599. Troy Bickham found that during the war British writers described Indians as both feared enemies and possible allies. *Savages Within the Empire: Representations of American Indians in Eighteenth-Century Britain* (Oxford: Oxford University Press, 2005), 84–92.

123. *Whitehall Evening Post, or London Intelligencer*, January 10, 1760. Trevor Burnard and John Garrigus, *The Plantation Machine: Atlantic Capitalism in French Saint-Domingue and British Jamaica* (Philadelphia: University of Pennsylvania Press, 2016), chap. 4.

124. Slaves also felt the effects of the war more than the white inhabitants. Planters cut their rations and worked them longer hours to produce supplies for the British army and navy. Michael Craton, *Testing the Chains: Resistance to Slavery in the British West Indies* (Ithaca, NY: Cornell University Press, 1982), 126–27.

125. Edward Long, *The History of Jamaica: Or, General Survey of the Ancient and Modern State of That Island* (1774; reprint, Montreal: McGill-Queen's University Press, 2002), 2:456. Some of the slaves involved in the uprising came from French Guadeloupe, where they had seen "something of military operations," which they planned to use against white Jamaicans. Burnard and Garrigus, *Plantation Machine*, 128.

126. Long, *History of Jamaica*, 2:447.

127. The best contemporary accounts of the rebellion are Long, *History of Jamaica*, 2:447–75; Bryan Edwards, *The History Civil and Commercial of the British West Indies* (London: J. Stockdale, 1793), 2:75–79. See also Vincent Brown, *Tacky's Revolt: The Story of an Atlantic Slave War* (Cambridge, MA: Belknap Press of Harvard University Press, 2020), esp. chap. 4, and *The Reaper's Garden: Death and Power in the World of Atlantic Slavery* (Cambridge, MA: Harvard University Press, 2008), 144–52; Trevor Burnard, *Jamaica in the Age of Revolution* (Philadelphia: University of Pennsylvania Press, 2020), chap. 4; Craton, *Testing the Chains*, chap. 11; Maria A. Bollettino, "Slavery, War, and Britain's Atlantic Empire: Black Soldiers, Sailors, and Rebels in the Seven Years' War" (Ph.D. diss., University of Texas, 2009), chap. 5.

128. Trevor Burnard argues that Tacky's Revolt was major turning point in securing the loyalty of the island's white inhabitants to the British state. *Jamaica in the Age of Revolution*, chap. 4.

129. Wolfe died from gunshot wounds to his chest and abdomen on September 13, 1759. In the hours after his demise, the British defeated the French, capturing the capital of French Canada in what was the most important battle of the war and one of Britain's greatest victories of the eighteenth century. Anderson, *Crucible of War*, 344–68.

130. Simon Schama, *Dead Certainties (Unwarranted Speculations)* (New York: Alfred A. Knopf, 1991), 21–28.

131. Some of these works appear in the exhibition catalogue for the 2012 exhibit *Benjamin West: General Wolfe and the Art of Empire*, held at the University of Michigan Museum of Art. Carole McNamara, with an essay by Clayton A. Lewis, *Benjamin West: General Wolfe and the Art of Empire* (Ann Arbor: University of Michigan Museum of Art, 2012). The famed engraver William Woollett was thought to have sold ten thousand reproductions of the print. Alan McNairn, *Behold the Hero: General Wolfe and the Arts in the Eighteenth Century* (Liverpool, UK: Liverpool University Press, 1997), 147–51. New Yorker Oliver DeLancey erected a monument to Wolfe on his estate on the northwestern edge of the city. Its whereabouts today are not known. Joan Coutu, *Persuasion and Propaganda: Monuments and the Eighteenth-Century British Empire* (Montreal: McGill-Queen's University Press, 2006), 211–12.

132. Nicholas Rogers, "Brave Wolfe: The Making of a Hero," in *A New Imperial History: Culture, Identity, and Modernity in Britain and the Empire, 1660–1840*, ed. Kathleen Wilson (Cambridge: Cambridge University Press, 2004), 239–59.

133. "Popery," and other words like "papists" and "popish," were derogatory terms used by Protestants to describe Catholics and Catholicism. In his seminal work on the topic, Peter Lake defines popery as an "anti-religion, a perfectly symmetrical negative image of true Christianity." "Anti-popery: The Structure of a Prejudice," in *Conflict in Early Stuart England: Studies in Religion and Politics, 1603–1642*, ed. Richard Cust and Ann Hughes (London: Longman, 1989), 73–74.

134. For a detailed account of the individuals surrounding Wolfe, see McNairn, *Behold the Hero*, 136–41. The identity of the provincial ranger is not known, though some have speculated it was either Sir William Howe or Sir William Johnson. Colonel C. P. Stacey, "Benjamin West and 'The Death of Wolfe,'" *National Gallery of Canada Bulletin, No. 7*, 4, no. 1 (1966): 1–5.

135. McNairn, *Behold the Hero*, 167–76. The inclusion of an Indian was clearly for symbolic purposes. As far as we know, none fought with the British at the Battle of Quebec, and a vast majority sided with the French during the war. Britons often argued that the incivility of Indians was partly the consequence of the influence of the Catholic faith. Sophie White, *Wild Frenchmen and Frenchified Indians: Material Culture and Race in Colonial Louisiana* (Philadelphia: University of Pennsylvania Press, 2012).

2. Liberty Triumphant

1. *New-York Gazette*, June 9, 1766.

2. The session is famously known in French history as *séance de la flagellation*, or "session of the scourging." The king's speech is quoted in R. R. Palmer, *The Age of the*

Democratic Revolution: A Political History of Europe and America, 1760–1800 (Princeton, NJ: Princeton University Press, 1959), 1: 95–96.

3. *New York Gazette*, June 9, 1766.

4. Edmund S. and Helen M. Morgan, *The Stamp Act Crisis: Prologue to Revolution* (1953; reprint, with new preface by authors, New York: Collier Books, 1963).

5. Justin du Rivage comes to a similar conclusion, arguing that "the controversy over the Stamp Act drew the British Empire together, even as it threatened to tear it apart." *Revolution Against Empire: Taxes, Politics, and the Origins of American Independence* (New Haven, CT: Yale University Press, 2017), chap. 4.

6. For New York City: F. L. Engelman, "Cadwallader Colden and the New York Stamp Act Riots," *William and Mary Quarterly* 10, no. 4 (October 1953): 560–78; Pauline Maier, *From Resistance to Revolution: Colonial Radicals and the Development of American Opposition to Britain, 1765–1776* (New York: Alfred A. Knopf, 1972), 51–76. For Halifax: Wilfred B. Kerr, "The Stamp Act in Nova Scotia," *New England Quarterly* 6, no. 3 (September 1933): 552–66. For Kingston: Andrew O'Shaughnessy, "The Stamp Act Crisis in the British Caribbean," *William and Mary Quarterly* 51, no. 2 (April 1994): 203–26; Donna J. Spindel, "The Stamp Act Crisis in the British West Indies," *Journal of American Studies* 11, no. 2 (August 1977): 209.

7. Morgan and Morgan, *Stamp Act Crisis*, 36.

8. Morgan and Morgan, *Stamp Act Crisis*, 37.

9. James A. Henretta, *Salutary Neglect: Colonial Administration Under the Duke of Newcastle* (Princeton, NJ: Princeton University Press, 1972).

10. John Brewer, *Party Ideology and Popular Politics at the Accession of George III* (Cambridge: Cambridge University Press, 1976), 163–200, and "The Misfortunes of Lord Bute: A Case-Study in Eighteenth-Century Political Argument and Public Opinion," *Historical Journal* 16, no. 1 (March 1973): 3–43; Linda Colley, *Britons: Forging the Nation 1707–1837* (New Haven, CT: Yale University Press, 1992), 113–17; Kathleen Wilson, *The Sense of the People: Politics, Culture and Imperialism in England, 1715–1785* (Cambridge: Cambridge University Press, 1995), 206–36.

11. P. D. G. Thomas, *British Politics and the Stamp Act Crisis: The First Phase of the American Revolution, 1763–1767* (Oxford: Clarendon Press, 1975), chap. 3; John L. Bullion, *A Great and Necessary Measure: George Grenville and the Genesis of the Stamp Act, 1763–1765* (Columbia, MO: University of Missouri Press, 1982), chap. 1; Eliga H. Gould, *The Persistence of Empire: British Political Culture in the Age of the American Revolution* (Chapel Hill: University of North Carolina Press, 2000), 110–22.

12. The 1764 Sugar Act, which lowered the duty on foreign molasses and expanded the authority of vice-admiralty courts, benefited Caribbean sugar planters at the cost of North American merchants and traders. Andrew O'Shaughnessy, *An Empire Divided: The American Revolution and the British Caribbean* (Philadelphia: University of Pennsylvania Press, 2000), 65–67.

13. Such a tax was certainly not new to mainland Britons, who had been paying one since 1712. Similar kinds of taxes also appeared briefly in both New York and Jamaica, but those bills originated in their own representative assemblies, not from an outside legislative body. Lynne Oats, Pauline Sadler, and Carlene Wynter, "Taxing Jamaica: The Stamp Act of 1760 and Tacky's Rebellion," *EJournal of Tax Research* 12, no. 1 (2014): 162–84; Mack Thompson, "Massachusetts and New York Stamp Acts," *William and Mary Quarterly* 26, no. 2 (April 1969): 253–58.

14. Thomas, *British Politics*, 69–100; Morgan and Morgan, *Stamp Act Crisis*, chap. 5; du Rivage, *Revolution Against Empire*, 111–14.

15. Morgan and Morgan, *Stamp Act Crisis*, esp. chaps. 6 and 7; Bernard Bailyn, *The Ideological Origins of the American Revolution* (Cambridge, MA: Belknap Press of Harvard University Press, 1967), 99–102.

16. *Caledonian Mercury*, November 25, 1765.

17. *Scots Magazine*, 27 (December 1765), 633. du Rivage argues that colonial attitudes toward liberty and property were part of a radical Whig embrace of republican values, which he termed "republican imperialism." I agree, though I would suggest that these ideas were not so radical by the 1760s and enjoyed the broad support of moderate Britons on both sides of the ocean. *Revolution Against Empire*, 117–19.

18. *New-York Mercury*, September 30, 1765; *Halifax Gazette*, October 24, 1765; *Caledonian Mercury*, November 11, 1765.

19. *Liberty, Property, and No Stamps* (New York, 1765), Evans 10041.

20. *New-York Mercury*, October 21, 1765. See also William H. W. Sabine, ed., *Historical Memoirs from 16 March 1763 to 9 July 1776 of William Smith* (New York: Colburn & Tegg, 1956), 1:29–32; Andrew David Edwards, "Grenville's Silver Hammer: The Problem of Money in the Stamp Act Crisis," *Journal of American History* 104, no. 2 (September 2017): 337–62.

21. *Halifax Gazette*, November 14, 1765.

22. Frances Armytage, *The Free Port System in the British West Indies: A Study in Commercial Policy, 1766–1822* (London: Longmans, Green & Co., 1953), 13–27; Allan Christelow, "Contraband Trade Between Jamaica and the Spanish Main, and the Free Port Act of 1766," *Hispanic American Historical Review* 22, no. 2 (May 1942): 309–43; Richard B. Sheridan, *Sugar and Slavery: An Economic History of the British West Indies, 1623–1775* (Baltimore: Johns Hopkins University Press, 1974), 459–60; Adrian J. Pearce, *British Trade with Spanish America, 1763–1808* (Liverpool, UK: Liverpool University Press, 2007), 55–57.

23. "To the Hon[ble] the Commons of great Britain in Parliament assembled," February 15, 1765, Fuller Letter Book, 1762–1773, Nicholas M. Williams Ethnological Collection, Boston College Library. I would like to thank Amy Noel Ellison for providing me with copies of Fuller's letter book.

24. *Caledonian Mercury*, September 23, 1765. See also *Caledonian Mercury*, August 26, 1765.

25. *Scots Magazine*, 27 (October 1765), 553.

26. *Caledonian Mercury*, December 9, 1765.

27. *Caledonian Mercury*, November 11, 1765; *Scots Magazine*, 27 (December 1765), 663; *New-York Mercury*, October 28, 1765; *Halifax Gazette*, November 7, 1765.

28. *New-York Mercury*, November 7, 1765; *Halifax Gazette*, December 19, 1765; *Scots Magazine*, 27 (December 1765), 663.

29. *Halifax Gazette*, November 14, 1765.

30. T. H. Breen, *The Marketplace of Revolution: How Consumer Politics Shaped American Independence* (New York: Oxford University Press, 2004), 218–34.

31. *Caledonian Mercury*, October 5, 1765.

32. *New-York Gazette, and Weekly Post-Boy*, June 6, 1765. His essay also appeared in the *Boston Evening-Post*, June 24, 1765; *Georgia Gazette*, September 19, 1765.

33. *Scots Magazine*, 27 (December 1765), 635. In the January 1766 issue, the magazine's editors dismissed two pro-tax pamphlets, describing "some strictures on the

late occurrences in North America" as "weak and trivial," and "the justice and necessity of taxing the American colonies, demonstrated" as "more ignorant than the preceding, [and] ten times more furious." *Scots Magazine*, 28 (January 1766), 39.

34. Quoted in O'Shaughnessy, *Empire Divided*, 86.

35. Colin Kidd, *Subverting Scotland's Past: Scottish Whig Historians and the Creation of an Anglo-British Identity, 1689–c. 1830* (Cambridge: Cambridge University Press, 2003), 144–65.

36. *Scots Magazine*, 27 (August 1765), 409.

37. I have not been able to locate the original essay in the *New-York Gazette*, but it was exchanged in the *Boston Evening-Post*, July 22, 1765.

38. Bender was a city in the Ottoman Empire. *Halifax Gazette*, December 5, 1765. The poem is addressed "New York, To the Printer," though I have not been able to locate the original.

39. Gordon Wood, *The Creation of the American Republic, 1776–1789* (Chapel Hill: University of North Carolina Press, 1972), 319–28; Barbara Clark Smith, *The Freedoms We Lost: Consent and Resistance in Revolutionary America* (New York: New Press, 2010), esp. chap. 2; Maier, *Resistance to Revolution*, chaps. 1 and 2; George Rudé, "The London 'Mob' of the Eighteenth Century," *Historical Journal* 2, no. 1 (1959): 1–18.

40. Hugh Gaine advertised for sale copies of Trenchard and Gordon's *Cato Letters* in a December issue of his gazette. *New-York Mercury*, December 23, 1765. On the resurgence of this republican discourse in the 1760s, see Brewer, *Party Ideology*, esp. chaps. 1, 8–10.

41. Joseph Addison, "Cato: A Tragedy" (1712; reprint, Glasgow, 1765), *Eighteenth Century Collections Online, Gale*, accessed August 3, 2018, http://find.gale.com/ecco/info mark.do?&source=gale&prodId=ECCO&userGroupName=csufresno&tabID=T001 &docId=CB126737685&type=multipage&contentSet=ECCOArticles&version=1.0 &docLevel=FASCIMILE.

42. *Caledonian Mercury*, October 30, 1765.

43. John Locke, *Two Treatises of Government* (1689; reprint, London, 1824), 263.

44. E. P. Thompson, "The Moral Economy of the English Crowd in the Eighteenth Century," *Past & Present* 50 (February 1971): 76–136; Barbara Clark Smith, "Food Rioters and the American Revolution," *William and Mary Quarterly* 51, no. 1 (January 1994): 3–38.

45. Maier recognizes that there were "just and unjust uprisings," but allows radical Whig writers and actors to determine whether or not the Stamp Act riots were just. Maier, *Resistance to Revolution*, chap. 2, esp. 61–66.

46. Morgan and Morgan, *Stamp Act Crisis*, 241–44; Donald-Thiery Ruddel, *Quebec City, 1765–1832: The Evolution of a Colonial Town* (Ottawa, ON: University of Ottawa Press, 1987), 150.

47. *New-York Mercury*, October 28, 1765.

48. "Maryland Gazette," *Halifax Gazette*, November 14, 1765; New York and Philadelphia papers, *Halifax Gazette*, December 5, 1765. See also Joseph M. Adelman, *Revolutionary Networks: The Business and Politics of Printing the News, 1763–1789* (Baltimore: Johns Hopkins University Press, 2019), 59–63.

49. *Halifax Gazette*, November 21, 1765, and January 2, 1766.

50. *New-London Gazette*, November 15, 1765. See also *New-York Gazette, and Weekly Post-Boy*, October 31, 1765.

51. Morgan and Morgan were unable to discover the author of this resolution, though they believe it failed by only a narrow margin. *Stamp Act Crisis*, 120–33. The resolutions appeared in both New York and Glasgow newspapers and were likely printed in Halifax and Kingston, though no copies survive from that period: *New-York Gazette, and Weekly Post-Boy*, July 11, 1765; *Caledonian Mercury*, October 23, 1765.

52. Quoted in Morgan and Morgan, *Stamp Act Crisis*, 131.

53. *New-York Gazette, and Weekly Post-Boy*, June 6, 1765.

54. *Halifax Gazette*, December 5, 1765.

55. Joseph S. Tiedemann, *Reluctant Revolutionaries: New York City and the Coming of the American Revolution, 1763–1776* (Ithaca, NY: Cornell University Press, 1997), 69–71.

56. Simon Middleton traces the origins of this growing republican political culture to the words and actions of the city's artisan community during the political and economic crises of the 1730s. *From Privileges to Rights: Work and Politics in Colonial New York City* (Philadelphia: University of Pennsylvania Press, 2006), chap. 6. See also Roger J. Champagne, "Liberty Boys and Mechanics of New York City, 1764–1774," *Labor History* 8, no. 2 (Spring 1967): 115–35; Herbert M. Morais, "The Sons of Liberty in New York," in *The Era of the American Revolution: Studies Inscribed to Evarts Boutell Green*, ed. Richard B. Morris (New York: Harper & Row, 1939), 269–89; Tiedemann, *Reluctant Revolutionaries*, 47–48, 71–73.

57. *New-York Gazette*, June 6 and 13, 1765.

58. Several New England newspapers published a list of the distributors' names and locations: *Boston Evening-Post*, August 5, 1765; *Boston Post-Boy & Advertiser*, August 5, 1765; *Newport Mercury*, August 12, 1765; *Connecticut Courant*, August 12, 1765.

59. Dirk Hoerder, *Crowd Action in Revolutionary Massachusetts, 1760–1780* (New York: Academic Press, 1977), chap. 2; Alfred Young, "Ebenezer Mackintosh: Boston's Captain General of the Liberty Tree," in *Revolutionary Founders: Rebels, Radicals, and Reformers in the Making of the Nation*, ed. Alfred F. Young, Gary B. Nash, and Ray Raphael (New York: Vintage, 2011), 15–33; Gary Nash, *Urban Crucible: Social Change, Political Consciousness, and the Origins of the American Revolution* (Cambridge, MA: Harvard University Press, 1979), 292–300; Morgan and Morgan, *Stamp Act Crisis*, 161–70.

60. *Glasgow Journal*, October 17, 1765; *Caledonian Mercury*, October 12 and 14, and November 2, 1765.

61. *Caledonian Mercury*, November 23, 1765. In reality, several communities burned Mercer in effigy before he even arrived in the colony. When he landed in Williamsburg, he was attacked by a crowd who forced him to resign from office. Charles R. Hildeburn, "Notes on the Stamp Act in New York and Virginia," *Pennsylvania Magazine of History and Biography* 2, no. 3 (1878): 299–301.

62. *New-York Mercury*, August 26, 1765.

63. News of his appointment appeared in the *New-York Mercury*, July 1, 1765. For his resignation, see McEvers to Cadwallader Colden, August 1765, *Letters and Papers of Cadwallader Colden*, vol. 7, *1765–1775*, in *Collections of the New-York Historical Society*, (New York: New York Historical Society, 1923), 56:56–57.

64. *New-York Gazette*, October 17, 1765.

65. Gage to Colden, August 31, 1765, in *The Iconography of Manhattan Island, 1498–1909*, ed. I. N. Phelps Stokes (1922; reprint, Union, NJ: The Lawbook Exchange, Ltd., 1998), 4:749–50.

66. *New-York Mercury*, September 2 and 16, 1765; *Halifax Gazette*, October 3 and 24, November 7 and 14, and December 5 and 19, 1765; *Caledonian Mercury*, October 21 and 23, and November 2, 1765; *Scots Magazine*, 27 (October 1765), 548–50.

67. *New-York Mercury*, September 16, 1765.

68. In August, he wrote to a friend in London convinced of the need for a local "military force to keep the rabble in order." Archibald Hinshelwood to Joshua Mauger, August 19, 1765, *The Gilder Lehrman Institute of American History*, accessed August 31, 2017, https://www.gilderlehrman.org/collections/6a466274-0656-4f28-92f3-641772644195.

69. News of the event was carried in several North American newspapers. For example, see *New-York Mercury*, November 7, 1765. For the poem, see *New-York Mercury*, November 25, 1765.

70. Gordon Stewart and George Rawlyk, *A People Highly Favoured of God: The Nova Scotia Yankees and the American Revolution* (Hamden, CT: Archon Books, 1972), 3–23.

71. For example, see *New-York Mercury*, November 7, 1765.

72. *New-York Mercury*, November 18, 1765.

73. L. H. Butterfield, ed., *Diary and Autobiography of John Adams* (Cambridge, MA: Harvard University Press, 1961), 1:285; *The Montresor Journals*, ed. G. D. Scull, in *Collections of the New-York Historical Society*, vol. 14 (New York: New York Historical Society, 1882), 346.

74. *Scots Magazine*, 28 (February 1766), 67.

75. The report appeared in several New England newspapers and across the ocean in Scotland. For example, see *Boston Evening Post*, January 13, 1766; *Caledonian Mercury*, March 12, 1766.

76. Carl Anthony Lane, "The Roots of Jamaican Loyalism, 1760–1766," (Ph.D. diss., City University of New York, 1978), 364–66.

77. Howell to the Secretary of State, May 31, 1766, Public Records Office (hereafter cited as PRO) CO 137/62, 208, The National Archives (hereafter cited as TNA).

78. Quoted in Spindel, "Stamp Act Crisis," 209.

79. Howell to the Secretary of State, May 31, 1766, PRO CO 137/62, 208, TNA.

80. *A Providence Gazette, Extraordinary*, March 12, 1766.

81. *Halifax Gazette: or the Weekly Advertiser*, January 16, 1766.

82. *New-York Mercury*, October 28, 1765.

83. A copy of the broadside appears in Colden to Henry S. Conway, October 26, 1765, PRO CO/5/1098, TNA.

84. It is not clear whether the funeral procession actually happened. Tiedemann believes the crowd might have been motivated by the account of a similar demonstration reported in Holt's newspaper nearly two months earlier. Tiedemann, *Reluctant Revolutionaries*, 75. It is more likely the protesters were acting on a recent report from Philadelphia of residents mourning the loss of liberty. *New-York Mercury*, October 14, 1765. See also Jason Shaffer, *Performing Patriotism: National Identity in the Colonial and Revolutionary American Theatre* (Philadelphia: University of Pennsylvania Press, 2007), 50–52.

85. Scull, ed., *Montresor Journals*, 336.

86. For an account of the riot, see *New-York Mercury*, November 4, 1765; *New-York Gazette, or, The Weekly Post-Boy*, November 7, 1765; *No Stamped Paper to Be Had (Philadelphia), 7 November 1765* (New York, 1765), Evans 10106. It also appeared in the *Glasgow Journal*, December 19, 1765. The Porteous note was exchanged in several

British and American newspapers. For example, see *Public Ledger* [London], December 13, 1765.

87. Porteous's trial and death were covered extensively in colonial newspapers. For example, see *New-York Weekly Journal*, November 8, 1736; *New-York Weekly Journal*, December 13, 1736.

88. Paul A. Gilje, *The Road to Mobocracy: Popular Disorder in New York City, 1763–1834* (Chapel Hill: University of North Carolina Press, 1987), 47; Peter C. Messer, "Stamps and Popes: Rethinking the Role of Violence in the Coming of the American Revolution," in *Between Sovereignty and Anarchy: The Politics of Violence in the American Revolutionary Era*, ed. Patrick Griffin, Robert G. Ingram, Peter S. Onuf, and Brian Schoen (Charlottesville: University of Virginia Press, 2015), 114–38. Pope's Day had long been used to advance political causes. David Cressy, "The Fifth of November Remembered," in *Myths of the English*, ed. Roy Porter (Cambridge: Polity Press, 1992), 68–90.

89. Scull, ed., *Montresor Journals*, 337–39.

90. Stokes, ed., *Iconography of Manhattan Island*, 4:754.

91. O'Shaughnessy, "Stamp Act Crisis," 205. For consignment and expenditure numbers, see Lynne Oats and Pauline Sadler, "Accounting for the Stamp Act Crisis," *Accounting Historians Journal* 35, no. 2 (December 2008): 123, fig. 4; 135, fig. 7.

92. Marcus Rediker and Peter Linebaugh, *The Many-Headed Hydra: The Hidden History of the Revolutionary Atlantic* (Boston: Beacon Press, 2000).

93. *New-York Gazette*, December 2, 1765. See also *Massachusetts Gazette*, December 6, 1765; *Pennsylvania Gazette*, December 12, 1765.

94. *Halifax Gazette*, November 21, 1765. The statement offended city officials, who threatened Thomas with charges of sedition. Isaiah Thomas, *The History of Printing in America, with a Biography of Printers and an Account of Newspapers* (1810; reprint, Barre, MA: Imprint Society, 1970), 1:158. See also *Boston Evening Post*, November 25, 1765. Kerr, "Stamp Act in Nova Scotia," 560; M. Louise English Anderson, "Crowd Activity in Nova Scotia During the American Revolution" (master's thesis, Queen's University, Kingston, ON, 1987), 102.

95. *Connecticut Courant*, March 24, 1766.

96. North America, Nova Scotia: John Brettell, Stamp Office, Enclosing Copy of a Threatening Letter Sent to Mr. Hinshelwood, Distributor for Nova Scotia, January 31, 1766, PRO T 1/449/368-71, TNA.

97. For example, see *Boston Evening Post*, December 30, 1765. A similar report appeared in Scotland in February. *Scots Magazine*, 28 (February 1766), 102.

98. *Massachusetts Gazette*, January 30, 1766.

99. For example, see *Halifax Gazette*, November 7, December 5, and December 19, 1765.

100. *Halifax Gazette: or the Weekly Advertiser*, February 13, 1766.

101. *Boston Evening-Post*, January 27, 1766; *Boston Post-Boy & Advertiser*, January 27, 1766; *Massachusetts Gazette*, January 30, 1766; *New-York Gazette*, February 10, 1766; *Pennsylvania Gazette*, February 13, 1766; *Newport Mercury*, February 10, 1766; *Connecticut Courant*, February 10, 1766. Similar reports appeared in the *Virginia Gazette* [Purdie & Dixon], March 7, 1766; *Scots Magazine*, 28 (April 1766), 217.

102. *Halifax Gazette: or the Weekly Advertiser*, February 20, 1766.

103. For example, see *Pennsylvania Journal*, March 6, 1766.

104. *Boston Evening-Post*, March 24, 1766.

105. *Caledonian Mercury*, March 8, 1766. Fearing a slave revolt, white Jamaicans called up the militia in the spring of 1766. *Glasgow Journal*, May 15, 1766. Trevor Burnard, *Jamaica in the Age of Revolution* (Philadelphia: University of Pennsylvania Press, 2020), 122-23.

106. Butterfield, ed., *Diary of John Adams*, 1:285. See also *Pennsylvania Gazette*, February 6, 1766.

107. Jack P. Greene, "The Jamaica Privilege Controversy, 1764–66: An Episode in the Process of Constitutional Definition in the Early Modern British Empire," *Journal of Imperial and Commonwealth History* 22, no. 1 (1994): 16–53; O'Shaughnessy, *Empire Divided*, 111–15.

108. For reasons not known, Nova Scotia was also excluded from this meeting. C. A. Weslager, *The Stamp Act Congress: With an Exact Copy of the Complete Journal* (Newark: University of Delaware Press, 1976), 61.

109. Morgan and Morgan, *Stamp Act Crisis*, 257–60; Maier, *Resistance to Revolution*, chap. 4.

110. *New-York Gazette, and Weekly Post-Boy*, January 2, 1766.

111. *New-York Mercury*, January 13 and February 24, 1766.

112. Thomas Reid to Dr. Andrew Skene, Glasgow, December 30, 1765, in *The Works of Thomas Reid, D.D., Now Fully Collected, with Selections from his Unpublished Letters*, ed. Sir William Hamilton, Bart. (Edinburgh: Maclachlan and Stewart, 1846), 43.

113. Archibald Henderson to Edmund Burke, February 9, 1766, in *The Works and Correspondence of the Right Honourable Edmund Burke* (London: Rivington, 1852), 1:50–51.

114. Petition of Merchants of Glasgow, March 7, 1766, HL/PO/JO/10/3/256/50, Parliamentary Archives. Similar petitions were produced in many of Britain's leading trading towns. *Scots Magazine*, 28 (October 1766), 527–31. See also Thomas, *British Politics*, 216–19; du Rivage, *Revolution Against Empire*, 139–41; Morgan and Morgan, *Stamp Act Crisis*, 331–32.

115. Thomas, *British Politics*, chaps. 11 and 12; Robert J. Chaffin, "The Declaratory Act of 1766: A Reappraisal," *Historian* 37, no. 1 (November 1974): 5–25.

116. *New-York Gazette*, June 9, 1766.

117. *Caledonian Mercury*, March 8, 1766.

118. *Caledonian Mercury*, March 15, 1766.

119. *Virginia Gazette* [Purdie & Dixon], May 2, 1766; *New-York Gazette*, May 19, 1766.

120. *Georgia Gazette*, May 21, 1766.

121. Harold A. Innis, ed., *The Diary of Simeon Perkins, 1766–1780* (Toronto: Champlain Society, 1948), 1:3; Elizabeth Mancke, *The Fault Lines of Empire: Political Differentiation in Massachusetts and Nova Scotia, Ca. 1760–1830* (New York: Routledge, 2005), 72.

122. Benjamin Thomas Hill, ed., *The Diary of Isaiah Thomas, 1805–1828* (Worcester, MA: Published by the Society, 1909), 1:vi.

123. Kerr, "Stamp Act in Nova Scotia," 565.

124. J. B. Brebner, *The Neutral Yankees of Nova Scotia: A Marginal Colony During the Revolutionary Years* (1937; reprint: New York: Russell & Russell, 1970), 163.

125. Kerr, "Stamp Act in Nova Scotia," 565–66.

126. Reports of the celebration appeared in newspapers from Georgia to Massachusetts. For example, see *Pennsylvania Journal; And the Weekly Advertiser*, July 3, 1766.

127. *Newport Mercury*, July 14, 1766.

128. *Joy to America. At 3 this day . . . New-York, 20 May 1766* (New York, 1766), Evans 10347.

129. *New-York Gazette, or, The Weekly Post-Boy*, May 22, 1766.

130. Scull, ed., *Montresor Journals*, 368. Paul Gilje notes that the words *Pitt* and *Liberty* were printed in larger letters than *George 3d*, emphasizing their importance in relation to the king. *Road to Mobocracy*, 53.

131. *New-York Mercury*, May 26, 1766; *New-York Gazette*, May 26 and June 2, 1766.

132. *New-York Gazette*, June 9, 1766; Stokes, ed., *Iconography of Manhattan Island*, 4:765.

133. *New-York Gazette*, June 9, 1766.

3. In Search of Common Happiness

1. *Connecticut Gazette; and the Universal Intelligencer*, January 7, 1774.

2. Poplicola, or "Friend of the People," was the agnomen for Publius Valerius Publicola, one of the four Roman aristocrats who founded the first Roman Republic in the sixth century B.C.E. Vardill admitted to writing under this name after the war in his memorial to the Loyalist Claims Commission. Hugh Edward Egerton, ed., *The Royal Commission on the Losses and Services of American Loyalists, 1783 to 1785* (Oxford: Oxford University Press, 1915), 254–56. Rev. Myles Cooper may have been involved with the writing of this letter; the two men were known to have worked together on previous essays. Timothy M. Barnes, "Loyalist Newspapers of the American Revolution, 1763–1783: A Bibliography," *Proceedings of the American Antiquarian Society* 83, no. 2 (October 1973): 228.

3. The letter first appeared as a broadside, published by James Rivington on November 12, and subsequently reprinted in his gazette the following week. Vardill, *To The Worthy Inhabitants of the City of New-York* (New York, 1773), Evans 12956; *Rivington's Gazette*, November 18, 1773. The letter appeared in just one other North American newspaper: *Norwich Packet*, December 2, 1773. John Holt claimed he did not have space to print Vardill's essay. *New-York Journal; or, The General Advertiser*, November 18, 1773.

4. For more on the place of virtue in revolutionary-era American political culture, see Gordon S. Wood, *The Creation of the American Republic, 1776–1787* (Chapel Hill: University of North Carolina Press, 1969), 65–70; Ann Fairfax Withington, *Toward a More Perfect Union: Virtue and the Formation of American Republics* (New York: Oxford University Press, 1991), esp. the introduction. The classic text on the emergence of a common cause is David Ammerman, *In the Common Cause: American Response to the Coercive Acts of 1774* (Charlottesville: University Press of Virginia, 1974). The subject has received renewed interest in recent years. For example, see T. H. Breen, *American Insurgents, American Patriots: The Revolution of the People* (New York: Hill & Wang, 2010) and *The Marketplace of Revolution: How Consumer Politics Shaped American Independence* (New York: Oxford University Press, 2004); Robert Parkinson, *The Common Cause: Creating Race and Nation in the American Revolution* (Chapel Hill: University of North Carolina Press, 2016).

5. John W. Tyler, *Smugglers and Patriots: Boston Merchants and the Advent of the American Revolution* (Boston: Northeastern University Press, 1986), esp. chap. 5; Thomas M.

Truxes, *Defying Empire: Trading with the Enemy in Colonial New York* (New Haven, CT: Yale University Press, 2008), 188–209.

6. *Rivington's Gazette*, November 18, 1773. Vardill's essay is briefly discussed in Benjamin Woods Labaree, *The Boston Tea Party* (New York: Oxford University Press, 1964), 94–95.

7. Frances Armytage, *The Free Port System in the British West Indies: A Study in Commercial Policy, 1766–1822* (London: Longmans, Green & Co., 1953), 28–51; P. D. G. Thomas, *British Politics and the Stamp Act Crisis: The First Phase of the American Revolution, 1763–1767* (Oxford: Clarendon Press, 1975), 265–75; Andrew O'Shaughnessy, *An Empire Divided: The American Revolution and the British Caribbean* (Philadelphia: University of Pennsylvania Press, 2000), 66–69.

8. Edward Long, *The History of Jamaica: Or, General Survey of the Ancient and Modern State of That Island* (1774; reprint, Montreal: McGill-Queen's University Press, 2002), 2:198. The illicit trade with Spain is covered in Armytage, *Free Port System*, 13–27; Allan Christelow, "Contraband Trade Between Jamaica and the Spanish Main, and the Free Port Act of 1766," *Hispanic American Historical Review* 22, no. 2 (May 1942): 309–43; Nuala Zahedieh, "The Merchants of Port Royal, Jamaica, and the Spanish Contraband Trade," *William and Mary Quarterly* 43, no. 4 (October 1986): 570–93.

9. *Gentlemen's Magazine, and Historical Chronicle* (July 1766), 301–3. Similar complaints were lodged against the governor in March 1766 by the island's grand jury. *New-York Gazette*, July 14, 1766.

10. *Glasgow Journal*, May 15, 1766.

11. Armytage, *Free Port System*, 29–30.

12. The Dutch, Danes, and French had experimented with free ports earlier in the century, and the English had temporarily opened several of their colonial ports during the previous century. Christelow, "Contraband Trade," 334–35.

13. During his brief stint as president of the Board of Trade in 1763, Townshend pushed for a reduction in the duty on foreign sugar from 6 pennies to 2 pennies per gallon, a rate aggressively opposed by both Jamaican planters and merchants. Thomas, *British Politics*, 39–40. Townshend also opposed the repeal of the stamp tax, arguing for the need to assert "the supremacy of this country over the colonies." Thomas, *British Politics*, 88; Cornelius P. Forster, *The Uncontrolled Chancellor: Charles Townshend and His American Policy* (Providence: Rhode Island Bicentennial Foundation, 1978), 93.

14. R. C. Simmons and P. D. G. Thomas, eds., *Proceedings and Debates of the British Parliaments Respecting North America, 1754–1783* (Millwood, NY: Kraus International, 1983), 2:377; Patrick Griffin, *The Townshend Moment: The Making of Empire and Revolution in the Eighteenth Century* (New Haven, CT: Yale University Press, 2017), 133–34. Rockingham reported to the king that Townshend "took a forward part and did admirably well" during the debate over free ports. Forster, *Uncontrolled Chancellor*, 94.

15. Steven Pincus offers a very good summary of the long history of mercantilist consensus scholarship, which he argues does not reflect the far more complex and contentious nature of political economic thinking in early modern Britain. "Rethinking Mercantilism: Political Economy, the British Empire, and the Atlantic World in the Seventeenth and Eighteenth Centuries," *William and Mary Quarterly* 69, no. 1 (January 2012): 3–34.

16. *New York Gazette*, September 1, 1766.

17. Armytage, *Free Port System*, 28–51. Gregory E. O'Malley misdates the act to 1767, but does show the importance of British slave trading interests in shaping the legislation. *Final Passages: The Intercolonial Slave Trade of British America, 1619–1807* (Chapel Hill: University of North Carolina Press, 2014), 301–16.

18. Perry Gauci, *William Beckford: First Prime Minister of the London Empire* (New Haven, CT: Yale University Press, 2013), 123–24; Armytage, *Free Port System*, 40–41.

19. Long, *History of Jamaica*, 2:195. Tensions over the illicit French sugar trade had been brewing for several years. In 1762, the planter-controlled assembly attempted to pass legislation making it punishable by death for Kingston merchants to take part in such trade. The Board of Trade disallowed the law, which they found "repugnant," especially since it was actually legal to import some foreign goods so long as duties were paid. Trevor Burnard, "Harvest Years?: Reconfigurations of Empire in Jamaica, 1756–1807," *Journal of Imperial and Commonwealth History* 40, no. 4 (November 2012): 536–37.

20. Trevor Burnard, "'The Grand Mart of the Island': The Economic Function of Kingston, Jamaica in the Mid-eighteenth Century," in *Jamaica in Slavery and Freedom: History, Heritage and Culture*, ed. Kathleen E. A. Monteith and Glen Richards (Kingston: University of the West Indies Press, 2002), 225–41; O'Malley, *Final Passages*, esp. chap. 6.

21. "An Act for dividing the Island of Jamaica into three Counties . . . Said Counties." *Acts of Assembly, Passed in the Island of Jamaica, from the Year 1681 to the Year 1769 Inclusive* (Kingston, Jamaica: Printed by Alexander Aikman, 1787), 2:7. The author of a 1756 pamphlet, published in both Dublin and London, framed Price Sr. as the greatest threat to the freedom of the island's inhabitants. "A Letter from a Citizen of Port-Royal in Jamaica to a Citizen of New-York; Relating to Some Extraordinary Measures, Lately Set on Foot in That Island" (London: Printed for J. Johnson, 1766), *Eighteenth Century Collections Online, Gale*, accessed November 11, 2014, http://find.gale.com /ecco/infomark.do?&source=gale&prodId=ECCO&userGroupName=csu fresno&tabID=T001&docId=CW3304897469&type=multipage&contentSet=ECCO Articles&version=1.0&docLevel=FASCIMILE. See also Michael Craton and James Walvin, *A Jamaican Plantation: The History of Worthy Park 1670–1970* (Toronto: University of Toronto Press, 1970), 71–94.

22. Jack P. Greene, "'Of Liberty and of the Colonies': A Case Study of Constitutional Conflict in the Mid-eighteenth Century British American Empire," in *Liberty and American Experience in the Eighteenth Century*, ed. David Womersley (Indianapolis, IN: Liberty Fund, 2006), 48–92; James Robertson, *Gone Is the Ancient Glory: Spanish Town, Jamaica, 1534–2000* (Kingston, Jamaica: Ian Randle, 2005), 89–93; George Metcalf, *Royal Government and Political Conflict in Jamaica, 1729–1783* (London: Longman, 1965), 122–38.

23. Memorial of the Merchants and Factors of Kingston to the Board of Trade, January 1754, Public Records Office (PRO) CO 137/27/176-87, The National Archives (TNA). I would like to thank Christian Bursett for providing me with a copy of this petition.

24. For example, see *Pennsylvania Gazette*, March 26, 1754. Many port cities on the mainland petitioned Parliament in 1757 to keep the capital in Kingston. *New York Gazette, or the Weekly Post-Boy*, August 1, 1757.

25. Simon Taylor to Chaloner Arcedekne, Kingston, November 29, 1766, in *Travel, Trade and Power in the Atlantic, 1765–1884*, Camden Miscellany, vol. 35, ed. Betty Wood and Martin Lynn (Cambridge: Cambridge University Press, 2002), 32–35.

26. *Newport Mercury*, April 6, 1767; *New-York Gazette, or the Weekly Post-Boy*, April 9, 1767. The two newspapers do not agree on the actual date of the riot. The report printed in the *Newport Mercury* says the riot took place on November 29; Parker places it on November 22.

27. For more on the nature of eighteenth-century crowd culture in the British Atlantic, see Dirk Hoerder, *Crowd Action in Revolutionary Massachusetts, 1760–1780* (New York: Academic Press, 1977); Pauline Maier, "Popular Uprisings and Civil Authority in Eighteenth-Century America," *William and Mary Quarterly* 27, no. 1 (January 1970): 3–35; Nicholas Rogers, *Crowds, Culture, and Politics in Georgian Britain* (Oxford: Clarendon Press, 1998).

28. For example, see *New-York Gazette*, July 14 and October 6, 1766.

29. For example, see *New-York Gazette*, July 14, 1766.

30. John Gilbert McCurdy, *Quarters: The Accommodation of the British Army and the Coming of the American Revolution* (Ithaca, NY: Cornell University Press, 2019); Bernard Bailyn, *The Ideological Origins of the American Revolution* (Cambridge, MA: Belknap Press of Harvard University Press, 1967), 55–93, esp. 61–66; John Philip Reid, *In Defiance of Law: The Standing Army Controversy, the Two Constitutions, and the Coming of the American Revolution* (Chapel Hill: University of North Carolina Press,1981), esp. chap. 9.

31. *New-York Journal; or, the General Advertiser*, March 16, 1769. Holt reprinted a 1697 London pamphlet arguing that liberty could never exist in a nation that kept a standing army during peacetime. *New-York Journal, or General Advertiser*, December 11 and 24, 1766, and January 1, 8, 22, and 29, 1767.

32. *To the Sons of Liberty in this City* (New York, February 3, 1770), Evans 11891. See also J. David Harden, "Liberty Caps and Liberty Trees," *Past & Present* 146, no. 1 (1995): 66–102; Arthur Schlesinger, "Liberty Trees: A Genealogy," *New England Quarterly* 25, no. 4 (December 1952): 435–58. Liberty poles and trees had their origins in sixteenth- and seventeenth-century English maypole celebrations. David Cressy, *Bonfires and Bells: National Memory and the Protestant Calendar in Elizabethan and Stuart England* (Berkeley: University of California Press, 1989), 21–23.

33. *New-York Gazette, or the Weekly Post-Boy*, August 14, 1766.

34. *The Montresor Journals*, ed. G. D. Scull, in *Collections of the New-York Historical Society* (New York: New York Historical Society, 1882), 14:382–84.

35. I. N. Phelps Stokes, ed., *The Iconography of Manhattan Island, 1498–1909* (1922; reprint, Union, NJ: The Lawbook Exchange, 1998), 4:769.

36. John C. Travis, ed., "The Memoirs of Stephen Allen, 1767–1852, Typescript," 6, New-York Historical Society (hereafter cited as NYHS).

37. Quoted in Adrian J. Pearce, *British Trade with Spanish America, 1763–1808* (Liverpool, UK: Liverpool University Press, 2007), 55.

38. Christelow, "Contraband Trade," 339–40.

39. *Caledonian Mercury*, June 1, 1767; *Scots Magazine*, 29 (May 1767), 277; *New-York Gazette, or the Weekly Post-Boy*, August 20, 1767.

40. *New-York Journal; or, the General Advertiser*, October 12, 1769.

41. Quoted in Pearce, *British Trade*, 52.

42. Long, *History of Jamaica*, 2:199.

43. *Gazetteer and New Daily Advertiser* [London], January 26, 1768.

44. Very little has been written on the Douglas Cause. Karl Sabbagh, *The Trials of Lady Jane Douglas: The Scandal That Divided 18th Century Britain* (Newbold on Stour, UK: Skyscraper Publications, 2014); Percy Fitzgerald, *Lady Jean: The Romance of the Great Douglas Cause* (London: T. Fisher Unwin, 1904); A. Francis Steuart, ed., *The Douglas Cause*, Notable Scottish Trials *Series* (Glasgow and Edinburgh: W. Hodge & Co., 1909).

45. In his massive two-volume hagiography of the family, David Hume of Godscroft declared, "For what Family can boast of such a series of great Commanders, so many zealous Asserters of Liberty and Independency of their native Country, and so eminently distinguished by their great Actions through all Europe." *The History of the House and Race of Douglas and Angus*, 4th ed. (Edinburgh, 1748), 2:v.

46. In July 1748, Lady Jane Douglas supposedly gave birth to twin sons, Archibald (Archy) and Sholto, in France. Sholto and Lady Jane both died unexpectedly in 1753. Steuart, ed., *Douglas Cause*, 14–16.

47. Quoted in Sabbagh, *Trials of Lady Jane*, 235.

48. *New-York Journal; or, the General Advertiser*, July 30, 1767.

49. Boswell's father, Lord Auchinleck, was one of the fifteen judges presiding over the case. Boswell's only published novel, *Dorando: A Spanish Tale* (1767), was loosely based on the Douglas Cause. Peter Martin, *A Life of James Boswell* (New Haven, CT: Yale University Press, 2002), 230–34.

50. John Brewer, *Party Ideology and Popular Politics at the Accession of George III* (Cambridge: Cambridge University Press, 1976), 163–200. Scottish migration to England in the latter half of the eighteenth century played into popular anti-Scottish attitudes. Paul Langford, "South Britons' Reception of North Britons, 1707–1820," in *Anglo-Scottish Relations from 1603 to 1900*, ed. T. C. Smout (Oxford: Oxford University Press, 2005), 143–69. Wilkite Scotophobia was also a response to the obvious (and, for some, unsettling) fact that many Scots were actively engaged in the commercial and military expansion of the empire, and celebrated their newfound Britishness. One Scot proclaimed, "Let then our southern brethren rail at us for the lead we take in war and commerce, in the arts and in the sciences; their jealousy is the strongest and most sincere acknowledgement of our superiority." The essay first appeared as a broadside, entitled "A North Briton Extraordinary," in Edinburgh early in 1765. No copy is known to have survived. It was reprinted in the *Gentleman's Magazine*, 35 (March 1765), 130–33.

51. *Caledonian Mercury*, September 5 and 21, 1768. The anonymous writer was likely the popular Scottish philosopher David Hume, who was a vocal critic of the Wilkite cause. Donald W. Livingston, "Hume, English Barbarism and American Independence," in *Scotland and America in the Age of Enlightenment*, ed. Richard B. Sher and Jeffrey R. Smitten (Princeton, NJ: Princeton University Press, 1990), 133–47.

52. *A Mirror for the Multitude; Or, Wilkes and His Abettors No Patriot* (Glasgow, 1770), 38, 48, *Eighteenth Century Collections Online, Gale*, accessed December 15, 2014, http:// find.gale.com / ecco / infomark.do?&source=gale&prodId=ECCO&userGroupName =csufresno&tabID=T001&docId=CW3304725761&type=multipage&contentSet =ECCOArticles&version=1.0&docLevel=FASCIMILE.

53. *Scots Magazine*, 32 (February 1770), 82–83. It was customary in Scotland at this time to burn Wilkes in effigy on Pope's Day. John Strang, *Glasgow and Its Clubs*

(Glasgow: Richard Griffin and Co., 1857), 179. This was especially true after Wilkes's victory in the 1768 Middlesex election. *Caledonian Mercury*, April 6, 1768.

54. *Scots Magazine*, 29 (July 1767), 387–88.

55. Dickinson's *Letters* appeared in several New York City newspapers between December 1767 and March 1768 and were printed as a pamphlet by John Holt in May 1768. John Dickinson, *Letters from a Farmer in Pennsylvania to the Inhabitants of the British Colonies* (New York, 1768), Evans 10878. As far as I am aware, his letters were not published in Halifax, Kingston, or Glasgow, though it is likely that copies were brought to these communities.

56. Carl F. Kaestle, "The Public Reaction to John Dickinson's Farmer's Letters," *Proceedings of the American Antiquarian Society* 78, no. 2 (October 1968): 325–26n4. Readership is always difficult to determine, but given the popularity of newspapers and pamphlets it is likely that a vast majority of adult white colonists read his letters or listened as someone else read them. Kaestle suggests readership was somewhere between eighty thousand and two hundred thousand colonists. "Public Reaction," 352–53, app. B.

57. Jack P. Greene, *The Constitutional Origins of the American Revolution* (Cambridge: Cambridge University Press, 2011), 115; Pauline Maier, *From Resistance to Revolution: Colonial Radicals and the Development of American Opposition to Britain, 1765–1776* (New York: Alfred A. Knopf, 1972), 114–15; Bailyn, *Ideological Origins*, 145; Milton E. Flower, *John Dickinson: Conservative Revolutionary* (Charlottesville: University Press of Virginia, 1983), 62; Jane E. Calvert, *Quaker Constitutionalism and the Political Thought of John Dickinson* (New York: Cambridge University Press, 2009), 220–21.

58. Nicole Eustace, *Passion Is the Gale: Emotion, Power, and the Coming of the American Revolution* (Chapel Hill: University of North Carolina Press, 2008), 418–22.

59. Dickinson, *Letters*, 49.

60. Dickinson, *Letters*, 18–19.

61. Public toasts were instrumental in shaping local political cultures and their appearance in newspapers allowed this culture to extend to communities elsewhere in the empire. Simon Newman, *Parades and the Politics of the Street: Festive Culture in the Early American Republic* (Philadelphia: University of Pennsylvania Press, 1999), 29–31.

62. *The Following Patriotic Toasts* (New York, 1770), Evans 49255. "Alderman Wilks," of course, referred to John Wilkes. Sidney and Hampden were revered by radicals for having opposed the arbitrary rule of former English kings. Pasquale Paoli was a Corsican Patriot who rose to fame in Britain in 1768–69 for leading Corsican resistance to French invaders. The French prevailed in the conflict, and Paoli was forced into exile in Britain in May 1769. Peter Adam Thrasher, *Pasquale Paoli: An Enlightened Hero, 1725–1807* (Hamden, CT: Archon Books, 1970). Finally, "Mrs. M'Auley" referred to Catharine Macaulay, a popular writer and historian whose eight-volume history of England drew rave reviews from radicals on both sides of the Atlantic. Bridget Hill, *The Republican Virago: The Life and Times of Catherine Macaulay, Historian* (New York: Oxford University Press, 2002).

63. For more on the bishop controversy, see Carl Bridenbaugh, *Mitre and Sceptre: Transatlantic Faiths, Ideas, Personalities, and Politics, 1689–1775* (New York: Oxford University Press, 1962), chap. 10; James B. Bell, *A War of Religion: Dissenters, Anglicans, and the American Revolution* (New York: Palgrave Macmillan, 2008), 107–20. For more on the city's factional politics, see Patricia U. Bonomi, *A Factious People: Politics and Society in*

Colonial New York (New York: Columbia University Press, 1971), 229–78; Roger Champagne, "Family Politics versus Constitutional Principles: The New York Assembly Elections of 1768 and 1769," *William and Mary Quarterly* 20, no. 1 (January 1963): 57–79; Joseph S. Tiedemann, *Reluctant Revolutionaries: New York City and the Coming of the American Revolution, 1763–1776* (Ithaca, NY: Cornell University Press, 1997), 105–71.

64. The boycott had an immediate and profound effect on the city's economy. Imports declined from £482,930 in 1767 to just £74,918 the following year. Arthur M. Schlesinger, *The Colonial Merchants and the American Revolution, 1763–1776* (New York: Atheneum, 1968), 187–90.

65. *Scots Magazine*, 30 (September 1768), 481–82.

66. The editor of the *Whisperer*, William Moore, admitted to despising "Tories, Jacobites and Scotchmen," though he was just as critical of the Hanoverian monarchy, which he believed to be succumbing to the same popish tendencies as its predecessors. Paul Kléber Monod, *Jacobitism and the English People, 1688–1788* (Cambridge: Cambridge University Press, 1993), 41.

67. *Scots Magazine*, 32 (July 1770), 395.

68. For example, see *Nova-Scotia Gazette*, December 1, 1768; *Nova Scotia Chronicle, And Weekly Advertiser*, February 14, 1769, and January 30, 1770.

69. *Nova-Scotia Gazette*, June 2 to August 4, 1768.

70. P. D. G. Thomas, *The Townshend Duties Crisis: The Second Phase of the American Revolution, 1767–1773* (New York: Oxford University Press, 1987), 78.

71. Francklin to Shelburne, March 29, 1768, quoted in Emily P. Weaver, "Nova Scotia and New England during the Revolution," *American Historical Review* 10, no. 1 (October 1904): 60.

72. Hillsborough to governor of Nova Scotia, April 21, 1768, quoted in Weaver, "Nova Scotia," 60.

73. Reports of colonists toasting the "patriotic 92" appeared in the *Nova Scotia Gazette* later in the year. For example, see *Nova-Scotia Gazette*, December 1, 1768.

74. *Nova-Scotia Gazette*, June 16, 1768. Haligonians also read of Scots in Edinburgh burning Wilkes in effigy. *Nova-Scotia Gazette*, June 30, 1768.

75. "It is, in some measure, the unavoidable consequence of Liberty," admitted one writer, "which will every now and then run into Licentiousness.—But still, take us for all, in all, we are the happiest Nation this World ever contained." *Nova-Scotia Gazette*, July 14, 1768.

76. *Nova-Scotia Gazette*, June 30, 1768.

77. Francklin to Hillsborough, July 10, 1768, in *Report on Canadian Archives, 1894*, ed. Douglas Brymner (Ottawa, ON: S.E. Dawson, 1895), 287.

78. Campbell to Hillsborough, September 12, 1768, in Brymner, ed., *Canadian Archives*, 290.

79. J. B. Brebner, *The Neutral Yankees of Nova Scotia: A Marginal Colony during the Revolutionary Years* (1937; reprint: New York: Russell & Russell, 1970), 93, 128–29.

80. There were approximately two thousand Acadians in Nova Scotia in the mid-1770s. John Mack Faragher, *A Great and Noble Scheme: The Tragic Story of the Expulsion of the French Acadians from their American Homeland* (New York: W.W. Norton, 2005), 438–39.

81. According to the 1767 census, Catholics made up roughly 25 percent of the population, and most were of Irish decent. Catholics constituted more than half the

population in nearby Cape Breton and St. John's Island, though they were likely Mi'kmaq, French, and Acadian, not Irish. "A General Return of the several Townships in the Province of Nova Scotia the first day of January 1767," RG 1, 443: 1, Public Archives of Nova Scotia (hereafter cited as PANS).

82. John G. Reid, *"Pax Britannica* or *Pax Indigena?* Planter Nova Scotia (1760–1782) and Competing Strategies of Pacification," *Canadian Historical Review* 85, no. 4 (December 2004): 669–82. Reid also explores the complexities of this relationship during the Revolutionary War in, "Imperial-Aboriginal Friendship in Eighteenth-Century Mi'kma'ki/Wulstukwik," in *The Loyal Atlantic: Remaking the British Atlantic in the Revolutionary Era,* ed. Jerry Bannister and Liam Riordan (Toronto: University of Toronto Press, 2012), 75–102. See also L. F. S. Upton, *Micmacs and Colonists: Indian-White Relations in the Maritimes, 1713–1867* (Vancouver: University of British Columbia Press, 1979), 61–78; Geoffrey Plank, *An Unsettled Conquest: The British Campaign against the Peoples of Nova Scotia* (Philadelphia: University of Pennsylvania Press, 2001), esp. 122–39; Daniel N. Paul, *We Were Not the Savages: A Micmac Perspective on the Collision between European and Native American Civilizations,* 3rd ed. (Halifax, NS: Nimbus, 1994), 130–76; Peter M. Doll, *Revolution, Religion, and National Identity: Imperial Anglicanism in British North America, 1745–1795* (Madison, NJ: Farleigh Dickinson University Press, 2000), 35–65.

83. Campbell to Hillsborough, September 12, 1768, quoted in M. Louise English Anderson, "Crowd Activity in Nova Scotia During the American Revolution" (master's thesis, Queen's University, Kingston, ON, 1987), 59.

84. Campbell to Hillsborough, October 25, 1768, in Brymner, ed., *Canadian Archives,* 292.

85. *New-York Gazette, or the Weekly Post-Boy,* December 19, 1768.

86. *New-York Gazette; and the Weekly Mercury,* October 31, 1768; *New-York Gazette, or the Weekly Post-Boy,* October 31, 1768; *New-York Journal; or, the General Advertiser,* November 3, 1768. Francklin claimed there was no truth to this rumor. Francklin to Lords of Trade, November 29, 1768, in Brymner, ed., *Canadian Archives,* 293.

87. Reid, "Pax Britannica," 686–87.

88. Since 1758, Nova Scotian law forbade the practice of Catholicism and required Catholic priests and missionaries to leave the province or face "perpetual Imprisonment." *N.S. Laws, 1758–1765* (n.p.: [1766?]), 49.

89. Claude Galarneau, "Charles François Bailly de Messein," *Dictionary of Canadian Biography,* vol. 4 (Toronto: University of Toronto/Université Laval, 1979), accessed November 12, 2017, http://www.biographi.ca/en/bio/bailly_de_messein _charles_francois_4E.html.

90. Francklin to Hillsborough, July 20, 1768, in Brymner, ed., *Canadian Archives,* 288.

91. Quoted in Upton, *Micmacs and Colonists,* 67. In 1769 and 1770, Mi'kmaq converts attended service at St. Paul's Church in Halifax, where they were said to have "prayed for the prosperity of the Province and the blessing of Almighty God on King George, the Royal family and the Governor of the Province." T. B. Akins, *History of Halifax City,* 2nd ed. (1895; reprint, Belleville, ON: Mica Pub., 1973), 71.

92. Campbell to Hillsborough, August 7, 1769, in Brymner, ed., *Canadian Archives,* 298. Campbell even proposed creating a Mi'kmaq settlement near Halifax, which could be used to turn hostile Indians into "peaceable subjects." Campbell to Hillsborough, December 22, 1770, in Brymner, ed., *Canadian Archives,* 303.

93. *New-York Journal; or, the General Advertiser,* November 23, 1769.

94. *New-York Journal; or, the General Advertiser*, January 4, 1770.

95. Supreme Court Records, RG 39, PANS. Bailly claimed that "opposition came from the Presbyterians and people of New England." "An Historical Centennial," *Catholic Historical Review* 7, no. 1 (April 1921): 62.

96. *New-York Journal; or, the General Advertiser*, December 28, 1769.

97. *Pennsylvania Chronicle, and Universal Advertiser*, May 1, 1769.

98. *Caledonian Mercury*, March 15, 1769.

99. *Caledonian Mercury*, March 6, 1769.

100. For example, see *New-York Gazette, or the Weekly Post-Boy*, July 24, 1769.

101. Though he does not discuss the Douglas Cause, Colin Kidd argues that such displays of "Scotocentric patriotism" demonstrated the failure of mid-eighteenth-century politicians and writers "to construct an influential and genuinely pan-British national identity." "North Britishness and the Nature of Eighteenth-Century British Patriotisms," *Historical Journal* 39, no. 2 (June 1996): 377–82.

102. *Caledonian Mercury*, April 22, 1769; *Lloyd's Evening Post* [London], 1 May 1769. Scots continued to remember the importance of the Douglas Cause well into the nineteenth century. Reuben Percy, *Relics of Literature* (London: Thomas Boys, 1823), 27–30; Ralston Inglis, *The Dramatic Writers of Scotland* (Glasgow: G.D. Mackellar, 1868), 143.

103. For the relationship between patriotism and commercial interests, see Breen, *Marketplace of Revolution*, 235–93. New Yorkers destroyed their theater in early 1768. *New-York Journal; or, the General Advertiser*, April 9, 1768. On the relationship between the theater and revolutionary politics, see Withington, *More Perfect Union*, 20–47. Edward Countryman describes these actions as traditional eighteenth-century English moral economy protests. *A People in Revolution: The American Revolution and Political Society in New York, 1760–1790* (Baltimore: Johns Hopkins University Press, 1981), 55–63.

104. *Caledonian Mercury*, September 25, 1769.

105. Cooley's case was carried in many colonial American newspapers. It appeared first in the *New-York Journal; or, the General Advertiser*, July 20, 1769, and then as a pamphlet, *To the Public . . . New-York, 21st July, 1769* (New York, 1769), Evans 11224. Sam Adams referred to Cooley's case in his popular, mostly fake newspaper, *Journal of Occurrences*. *New-York Journal; or, the General Advertiser*, November 30, 1769.

106. For other cases, see *New-York, September 18, 1769. Advertisement* (New York, 1769), Evans 11381; *Advertisement, of great importance to the public* (New York, 1769), Evans 11137; *New-York Journal; or, the General Advertiser*, October 5, 1769. Benjamin H. Irvin, "Tar, Feathers, and the Enemies of American Liberties, 1768–1776," *New England Quarterly* 76, no. 2 (June 2003): 230. Tiedemann downplays the violent methods used to enforce the boycott. *Reluctant Revolutionaries*, 154–58.

107. *New-York Journal; or, the General Advertiser*, November 2, 1769. William Bingley, printer of Wilkes's *North Briton* newspaper, was imprisoned for refusing to speak with officials about accusations he made against Lord Mansfield in issues 50 and 51. Robert R. Bataille, *The Writing Life of Hugh Kelly: Politics, Journalism, and Theater in Late-Eighteenth-Century London* (Carbondale: Southern Illinois University Press, 2000), 67–68. William Lucas, a popular Irish politician, was known as the "Wilkes of Ireland" for his opposition to the presence of a standing army.

108. *Caledonian Mercury*, September 25, 1769. In December, Holt reprinted a copy of Cooley's account, which likely amused many of his readers. *New-York Journal; or, the General Advertiser*, December 14, 1769.

109. *A Son of Liberty* [Alexander McDougall], *To the Betrayed Inhabitants of the City and Colony of New York, December 16, 1769* (New York, 1769), Evans 11319. Bonomi, *Factious People,* 267–78; William L. MacDougall, *American Revolutionary: A Biography of General Alexander McDougall* (Westport, CT: Greenwood Press, 1977), 27–38; Tiedemann, *Reluctant Revolutionaries,* 143–49.

110. Colden declared the broadside "a false, seditious, and infamous Libel" and offered a £100 reward to anyone who could name the author. *By the Honourable Cadwallader Colden . . . A Proclamation* (New York, 1769), Evans 11362.

111. *New-York Gazette, or the Weekly Post-Boy,* January 15, 1770.

112. *New-York Gazette, or the Weekly Post-Boy,* January 22, 1770.

113. The soldiers had posted a handbill around the city critical of New Yorkers and the liberty pole. *Whereas an Uncommon and Riotous Disturbance* (New York, 1770), Evans 11936. See also Lee R. Boyer, "Lobster Backs, Liberty Boys, and Laborers in the Streets: New York's Golden Hill and Nassau Street Riots," *New-York Historical Society Quarterly* 57, no. 4 (October 1973): 281–308; McCurdy, *Quarters,* 193-96.

114. *New-York Gazette, or the Weekly Post-Boy,* February 5, 1770; *Supplement to the Boston-Gazette, And Country Journal,* February 19, 1770; *Supplement to the Boston Evening-Post,* February 19. 1770; *Essex Gazette,* February 27, 1770; *New-York Journal; or, the General Advertiser,* March 1, 1770; *Georgia Gazette,* March 28, 1770. Boyer relied on private letters to argue that reports of the Battle of Golden Hill often conflicted. For most colonists who did not witness the event, however, "an Impartial Citizen's" account was likely responsible for their understanding of what had happened. Boyer, "Lobster Backs," 281–308.

115. A broadside published in New York City carrying news of the Boston massacre was appropriately titled *An Account of a late Military Massacre at Boston, or the Consequences of Quartering Troops in a Populace Town* (New York, 1770), Evans 11543.

116. *Pennsylvania Journal, And Weekly Advertiser,* February 22, 1770.

117. For example, see *New-York Gazette, or the Weekly Post-Boy,* April 2, 1770. To refresh New Yorkers' memories, local printers also republished Wilkes' controversial *North Briton No. 45.* Andrew Hook, *Scotland and America: A Study of Cultural Relations, 1750–1835* (Glasgow: Blackie, 1975), 62. McDougall was toasted alongside Wilkes and Dickinson during the Stamp Act repeal anniversary weeks later. *The Following Patriotic Toasts* (New York, 1770), Evans 49255. For more on the influence of Wilkes on the American cause, see Pauline Maier, "John Wilkes and the American Disillusionment with Britain," *William and Mary Quarterly* 20, no. 3 (July 1963): 373–95, esp. 385–86.

118. *New-York Journal; or, the General Advertiser,* February 8, 1770.

119. There were rumors in the fall of 1770—after the repeal of most of the duties—that "a non-importation party has lately started up" in Jamaica, but there is no evidence that it ever happened. *Public Advertiser* [London], September 14, 1770; O'Shaughnessy, *Empire Divided,* 106–7.

120. In reality, the British had no legal grounds to defend their settlement at Port Egmont. Imperial officials argued for the "right by discovery" and claimed they could establish settlements in the South Atlantic based on the 1748 Treaty of Utrecht. The point was disputed by Spain and France, and even the British were aware that France had settled a small outpost on the islands two years before them. Julius Goebel Jr., *The Struggle for the Falkland Islands: A Study in Legal and Diplomatic History* (1927; reprint,

Port Washington, NY: Kennikat Press, 1971), 221–70. Brendan Simms, *Three Victories and a Defeat: The Rise and Fall of the First British Empire, 1714–1783* (New York: Basic, 2008), 561–64.

121. *Scots Magazine*, 32 (December 1770), 647–56.

122. Nicholas Tracy, "The Falkland Islands Crisis of 1770: Use of Naval Force," *English Historical Review* 90, no. 354 (January 1975): 68–69.

123. *Pennsylvania Chronicle*, November 26, 1770.

124. For example, see *New-York Journal; or, the General Advertiser*, February 22, 1770.

125. *St. James's Chronicle or British Evening Post* [London], May 16, 1769.

126. *Nova Scotia Chronicle, And Weekly Advertiser*, June 19, 1770.

127. *New-York Journal; or, the General Advertiser*, November 22, 1770. The Spaniards also targeted the island's profitable lumber trade along the coast of Honduras. *New-York Journal; or, the General Advertiser*, November 29, 1770.

128. *Caledonian Mercury*, February 25, 1771.

129. *New-York Gazette, or the Weekly Post-Boy*, December 31, 1770.

130. *Middlesex Journal or Chronicle of Liberty* [London], September 20, 1770.

131. *Public Advertiser* [London], June 15, 1770.

132. *Northampton Mercury*, February 26, 1770.

133. *Nova-Scotia Gazette*, May 11, 1769.

134. Brebner described "the origins and ultimate fate" of the festival as "shrouded in mystery." *Neutral Yankees*, 201. See also Thomas H. Raddall, "The Feast of St. Aspinquid," *Nova Scotia Historical Quarterly* 1, no. 1 (March 1971), 1–9. Some believe the saint was actually the popular Pennacook sachem and prophet Passaconaway, while others think he was invented by white Europeans (though possibly based on Passaconaway) to advance their own religious and political agendas. Mi'kmaq tradition, on the other hand, suggests that he was actually Apenquid, a seventeenth-century Catholic sachem who lived along the northern New England coast in present-day Maine. Don (Byrd) Awalt, "The Mi'kmaq and Point Pleasant Park" (unpublished essay), 2–3.

135. *Nova-Scotia Gazette*, May 12, 1768.

136. Henry included the names and tribes of the twelve sachems, though I have not been able to identify all of them. Many appear to have not been contemporaries of Aspinquid, and some were known to have allied with both the English and French in previous wars. I have included Henry's list, along with the more common spelling of the sachem's names in brackets. "Sacham Hindrick [Hendrick Theyanoguin], Chief of the Mohawks, Sacham Unkeas [Uncas], Chief of the Mohegans, Sacham Woompakkoooanaugh, Chief of the Narragansetts, Sacham Massasoiett [Massasoit or Ousamequin], Chief of the Wampenoogs, Sacham Waban, Chief of the Naticks, Sacham Peagan, Chief of the Asscooomisscoos, Sacham Pomhammoon, Chief of the Nipmags [possibly the Nipmuc], Sacham Wookooocoonaught, Chief of the Poonkkapoogs [Ponkapoag], Sacham Boombarreen [possibly Bomazeen or Bomoseen], Chief of the Norndgwoaks [Norridgewock], Sacham Wewoookkadondona, Chief of the Pennobscotts, Sacham Eegerermmitt [Egeremet], Sacham of the Passamanquada [Passamaquoddy], Sacham Pier Thomas [Pierre Tomah], Woompakkamunnyquassen, Chief of the St. John's [Maliseet or Malicite]." *Nova-Scotia Chronicle And Weekly Advertiser*, June 5, 1770.

137. *Nova-Scotia Gazette: and the Weekly Chronicle*, June 1, 1773.

138. *Nova-Scotia Gazette*, May 11, 1769. The 1767 census counted 1,351 Americans, who represented 45 percent of the city's population. "A General Return," 1.

139. *Nova-Scotia Gazette: and the Weekly Chronicle*, May 25, 1773.

140. Gordon Stewart and George Rawlyk, *A People Highly Favoured of God: The Nova Scotia Yankees and the American Revolution* (Hamden, CT: Archon Books, 1972), 24–44.

141. Akins, *Halifax City*, 218n.

142. For example, see *New-York Gazette; and the Weekly Mercury*, July 23, 1770; *New-York Gazette; and the Weekly Mercury*, August 27, 1770.

143. *Rivington's Gazette*, December 2, 1773. See also Janice Potter, *The Liberty We Seek: Loyalist Ideology in Colonial New York and Massachusetts* (Cambridge, MA: Harvard University Press, 1983), 15–38.

144. That Vardill was attacked so often and by so many suggests the persuasiveness of his arguments against opponents of the Tea Act. For example, see "Brutus," *Rivington's Gazette*, December 16, 1773; "An Old Prophet," *Rivington's Gazette*, December 9, 1773; *A Tradesman, To the Free-Holders and Free-Men, of the City, and Province of New-York* (New York, 1773), Evans 13040; *The Student of the Law, Fellow Citizens, Friends of Liberty and Equal Commerce* (New York, 1773), Evans 12765; *The Mechanic, To the Worthy Inhabitants of New-York* (New York, 1773), Evans 13042.

145. *Rivington's Gazette*, December 28, 1773. His essay appeared as a broadside as well. *To the Worthy Inhabitants of the City of New York* (New York, 1773), Evans 12955. Vardill's criticisms were echoed by a group of merchants in Plymouth, Massachusetts. *Rivington's Gazette*, January 20, 1774.

4. King-Killing Republicans

1. These ceremonies drew upon the more elaborate royal entry ceremonies common in Western Europe since the fourteenth century, especially in France. Neil Murphy, *Ceremonial Entries, Municipal Liberties and the Negotiation of Power in Valois France, 1328–1589* (Leiden, NL: Brill, 2016); Peter Borsay, "'All the town's a stage': Urban Ritual and Ceremony 1660–1800," in *The Transformation of English Provincial Towns 1600–1800*, ed. Peter Clark (London: Hutchinson, 1984), 228–58.

2. Fred Anderson, *Crucible of War: The Seven Years' War and the Fate of Empire in British North America, 1754–1766* (New York: Alfred A. Knopf, 2000), 344–68.

3. Carleton did advise members of Parliament who were responsible for drafting the legislation. P. D. G. Thomas, *Tea Party to Independence: The Third Phase of the American Revolution, 1773–1776* (Oxford: Clarendon Press, 1991), 88–117.

4. *New-York Journal; or, The General Advertiser*, October 6, 1774; *Rivington's Gazette*, October 6, 1774; *Nova-Scotia Gazette: and the Weekly Chronicle*, November 8, 1774; *Glasgow Journal*, November 17, 1774. This account appeared in many other North American and mainland British newspapers.

5. The Quebec Act included four main provisions: it extended the province's territory into the Ohio Country; it reinstated French law in civil cases; it created a new colonial government that would be run by a royally appointed governor and council; and, finally, it tolerated Catholicism in the colony, though Catholics would be required to take an oath of allegiance to the Crown. For imperial bureaucrats, Catholic

toleration proved politically expedient and possibly revealed an increasingly enlightened attitude among some of the British elite toward their traditional Gallic adversaries. Peter M. Doll, *Revolution, Religion, and National Identity: Imperial Anglicanism in British North America, 1745–1795* (Madison, NJ: Farleigh Dickinson University Press, 2000), 146–53; Hilda Neatby, *The Quebec Act: Protest and Policy* (Scarborough, ON: Prentice-Hall of Canada, 1972); Reginald Coupland, *The Quebec Act: A Study in Statesmanship* (Oxford: Clarendon Press, 1925); Philip Lawson, *The Imperial Challenge: Quebec and Britain in the Age of the American Revolution* (Montreal: McGill-Queen's University Press, 1989).

6. Peter Force, ed., *American Archives: A Documentary History of the English Colonies in North America*, 4th ser. (Washington, DC: M. St. Claire Clarke & Peter Force, 1846), 6:14.

7. Robert Parkinson addresses the role of both groups in shaping a nascent American identity. *The Common Cause: Creating Race and Nation in the American Revolution* (Chapel Hill: University of North Carolina Press, 2016). See also Peter Silver, *Our Savage Neighbors: How Indian War Transformed Early America* (New York: W. W. Norton, 2008), esp. chap. 2; Jill Lepore, *The Name of War: King Philip's War and the Origins of American Identity* (New York: Vintage, 1999), chap. 7; James D. Rice, *Tales from a Revolution: Bacon's Rebellion and the Transformation of Early America* (New York: Oxford University Press, 2012), esp. 171–85; Edmund Morgan, *American Slavery, American Freedom: The Ordeal of Colonial Virginia* (New York, 1975), chap. 18.

8. Benjamin Irvin, *Clothed in Robes of Sovereignty: The Continental Congress and the People Out of Doors* (Oxford: Oxford University Press, 2014); Richard R. Beeman, *Our Lives, Our Fortunes and Our Sacred Honor: The Forging of American Independence, 1774–1776* (New York: Basic, 2013), 163–74.

9. *To the Public. An Application having been Made . . . [September 28, 1774]* (New York, 1774), Evans 13667. See also Joseph S. Tiedemann, *Reluctant Revolutionaries: New York City and the Coming of the American Revolution, 1763–1776* (Ithaca, NY: Cornell University Press, 1997), 199–201; T. H. Breen, *American Insurgents, American Patriots: The Revolution of the People* (New York: Hill & Wang, 2010), chap. 5.

10. One writer admitted that it was the absence of "that great priviledge, Town-Meetings" in Nova Scotia, which prevented them from taking a firmer stance. *Boston-Gazette, And Country Journal*, August 15, 1774. See also Elizabeth Mancke, *The Fault Lines of Empire: Political Differentiation in Massachusetts and Nova Scotia, Ca. 1760–1830* (New York: Routledge, 2005).

11. *Nova-Scotia Gazette: and the Weekly Chronicle*, September 20, 1774. Legge wrote to Dartmouth in October that "the inhabitants have behaved with decorum; the East India Company's tea has been disposed of and dispersed through the country." Legge to the Earl of Dartmouth, September 10 and October 18, 1774, quoted in J. B. Brebner, *The Neutral Yankees of Nova Scotia: A Marginal Colony During the Revolutionary Years* (1937; reprint: New York: Russell & Russell, 1970), 168.

12. For example, see *New-York Journal; or, The General Advertiser*, September 15, 1774.

13. *New-York Journal; Or, the General Advertiser*, September 15, 1774.

14. Patriot writers drew from the writings of Opposition Whigs in London. Vernon Creviston, "'No King Unless it be a Constitutional King': Rethinking the Place of

the Quebec Act in the Coming of the American Revolution," *Historian* 73, no. 3 (Fall 2011): 463–79.

15. Several delegates debated its inclusion before deciding to frame their opposition to the bill as a threat to their personal safety. David Ammerman, *In the Common Cause: American Response to the Coercive Acts of 1774* (Charlottesville: University Press of Virginia, 1974), 70–71.

16. Notes of Debates in the Continental Congress, October 17, 1774, *Diary and Autobiography of John Adams*, ed. L. H. Butterfield (Cambridge, MA: Harvard University Press, 1961), 2:154–55. Others, like Richard Henry Lee, Thomas McKean, and Joseph Reed, expressed concerns similar to Adams's. Edmund C. Burnett, ed., *Letters of Members of the Continental Congress* (Washington: Carnegie Institution, 1921), 1:77–79; Bernard Donoughue, *British Politics and the American Revolution: The Path to War, 1773–1775* (New York: Macmillan, 1964), 106.

17. Peter Force, ed., *American Archives: A Documentary History of the English Colonies in North America*, 4th ser. (Washington, DC: M. St. Claire Clarke & Peter Force, 1837), 1:927. See also Congress's *Declaration and Resolves* in Force, ed., *American Archives*, 1:912.

18. *Rivington's Gazette*, September 22, 1774.

19. Force, ed., *American Archives*, 1:917. The address was reprinted in *Rivington's Gazette*, November 3, 1774; *Nova-Scotia Gazette: and the Weekly Chronicle*, January 10, 1775; *Scots Magazine*, 36 (Appendix 1774), 691–95.

20. Force, ed., *American Archives*, 1:913. Nearly every British Atlantic newspaper printed the Continental Association, including three of the communities in this study. It is likely that it also appeared in a Jamaican newspaper, though no copies exist for this period. *New-York Gazette; and the Weekly Mercury*, October 31, 1774; *Nova-Scotia Gazette: and the Weekly Chronicle*, November 22, 1774; *Scots Magazine*, 36 (December 1774), 657–60. The boycott on the importation of goods from Britain, Ireland, and the Caribbean began December 1, 1774. The ban on exportation to Britain was to start on September 10, 1775.

21. *Lord North's Soliloquy* (New York, 1774), Evans 42633. It first appeared in the *London Evening Post*, September 20, 1774.

22. For example, see *New-York Gazette; and the Weekly Mercury*, October 31, 1774.

23. *New-York Journal; or, The General Advertiser*, November 3, 1774. For reasons not known, Holt printed the same letter three weeks later: *New-York Journal; or, The General Advertiser*, November 24, 1774. Similar reports surfaced during the summer and fall months. For example, see *New-York Journal; or, The General Advertiser*, July 7, 1774; *Nova-Scotia Gazette: and the Weekly Chronicle*, October 11, 1774.

24. Brendan McConville, *The King's Three Faces: The Rise and Fall of Royal America, 1688–1776* (Chapel Hill: University of North Carolina Press, 2006), 288–90; Creviston, "No King," 463–79; Francis D. Cogliano, *No King, No Popery: Anti-Catholicism in Revolutionary New England* (Westport: Greenwood Press, 1995), esp. chap. 3.

25. *Nova-Scotia Gazette: and the Weekly Chronicle*, September 20, 1774. See also *New-York Journal; or, The General Advertiser*, February 9, 1775.

26. *New-York Journal; or, The General Advertiser*, October 20, 1774.

27. *New York Journal*, November 10, 1774. The writer also believed that Gage's army had recently attacked Boston, even though these rumors had long since been discounted.

28. Tiedemann, *Reluctant Revolutionaries*, 204.

29. At least six thousand New Yorkers, and likely more, refused to sign the Association even after reports of fighting at Lexington and Concord. Half of the colony's fourteen counties either ignored or suppressed the implementation of the Association in the spring of 1775. Alexander Flick, *Loyalism in New York During the American Revolution* (New York: Macmillan, 1901), 47. See also Edward Countryman, "Consolidating Power in Revolutionary America: The Case of New York, 1775–1783," *Journal of Interdisciplinary History* 6, no. 4 (Spring 1976): 651–54; Carl Becker, *The History of Political Parties in the Province of New York, 1760–1776* (Madison: University of Wisconsin Press, 1968), 173. In February, the colony's assembly voted two to one to not recognize the proceedings of Congress or endorse the Continental Association, while only the city and three county committees—Ulster, Albany, and Suffolk—actually came out in support of Congress. Carl Becker, "Election of Delegates from New York to the Second Continental Congress," *American Historical Review* 9, no. 1 (October 1903): 73. For examples of communities where Patriots failed to gain a stronghold, see Sung Bok Kim, "The Limits of Politicization in the American Revolution: The Experience of Westchester County, New York," *Journal of American History* 80, no. 3 (December 1993): 868–89; Joseph S. Tiedemann, "Patriots by Default: Queens County, New York, and the British Army, 1776–1783," *William and Mary Quarterly* 43, no. 1 (January 1986): 35–63, and "A Revolution Foiled: Queens County, New York, 1775–1776," *Journal of American History* 75, no. 2 (September 1988): 417–44; Ruth M. Keesey, "Loyalism in Bergen County, New Jersey," *William and Mary Quarterly* 18, no. 4 (October 1961): 558–76. Philip Ranlet disputes claims of widespread Loyalism in the region. *The New York Loyalists* (Knoxville: University of Tennessee Press, 1986), 52–67.

30. For a useful summary of the debate over how many colonists were Loyalists, see Maya Jasanoff, *Liberty's Exiles: American Loyalists in the Revolutionary World* (New York: Alfred A. Knopf, 2011), 364–65n16.

31. The list of those with such interests is extensive: wealthy merchants, local officials, Anglican ministers and their parishioners, recent immigrants, ethnic and religious minorities, tenants along the Hudson River Valley, and devotees of the more conservative De Lanceyite faction. Wallace Brown, *The Good Americans: The Loyalists in the American Revolution* (New York: Morrow & Co., 1969), 44–81, and *The King's Friends: The Composition and Motives of the American Loyalists Claimants* (Providence, RI: Brown University Press, 1966); Robert McClure Calhoon, *The Loyalist in Revolutionary America, 1760–1781* (New York: Harcourt Brace Jovanovich, 1965), 370–81; William Nelson, *The American Tory* (New York: Oxford University Press, 1961), 85–115; Patricia U. Bonomi, *A Factious People: Politics and Society in Colonial New York* (New York: Columbia University Press, 1971), chaps. 7 and 8; Ranlet, *New York Loyalists*, 52–71; Joseph S. Tiedemann, Eugene R. Fingerhut, and Robert W. Venables, eds., *The Other Loyalists: Ordinary People, Royalism, and the Revolution in the Middle Colonies, 1763–1787* (Albany: SUNY Press, 2009); Esmond Wright, "The New York Loyalists: A Cross-Section of Colonial Society," in *The Loyalist Americans: A Focus on Greater New York*, ed. Robert A. East and Jacob Judd (Tarrytown, NY: Sleepy Hollow Restorations, 1975), 74–94; Thomas J. Humphrey, *Land and Liberty: Hudson Valley Riots in the Age of Revolution* (DeKalb: Northern Illinois University Press, 2004). Maya Jasanoff does argue for a shared Loyalist cause, what she calls the "Spirit of 1783," but it emerged only after

the end of the revolution. At the outbreak of the war, she claims instead that "choices about loyalty depended more on employers, occupations, profits, land, faith, family, and friendships than on any implicit identification as an American or a Briton." *Liberty's Exiles*, 24. Ruma Chopra argues that Loyalists had a "deep ideological commitment and sentimental attachment to empire," but argues in the following paragraph that "more than ideological commitments, the proximity of the British army and the threat of local coercion dramatically affected people's choices." *Choosing Sides: Loyalists in Revolutionary America* (New York: Rowman and Littlefield, 2013), 3. Mary Beth Norton similarly identifies Loyalists' arguments against their opponents but does not tie those arguments to broader understandings of what it meant to be British. *The British Americans: The Loyalist Exiles in England, 1774–1789* (Boston: Little, Brown, 1972), 16–24, 130–54. In her analysis of Southern Loyalism, Rebecca Brannon claims that Loyalists were not committed to a particular political ideology, but rather "understood loyalty viscerally." Rebecca Brannon, *From Revolution to Reunion: The Reintegration of the South Carolina Loyalists* (Columbia: University of South Carolina Press, 2016), 15. Donald F. Johnson admits that there existed "a rich literature of loyalism," by the early 1770s, but he contends that colonists living in British occupied cities during the war held "flexible loyalties," and only turned to this language of Loyalism to advance their own political, economic, or social interests. "Ambiguous Allegiances: Urban Loyalties During the American Revolution," *Journal of American History* 104, no. 3 (December 2017): 610-31. Christopher Minty attributes political allegiances to the influence of local institutions, like the various committees of safety or the British military, and not to a set of competing ideas. "Mobilization and Voluntarism: The Political Origins of Loyalism in New York, c. 1768–1778" (Ph.D. diss., University of Stirling, 2014), and "'Of One Hart and One Mind': Local Institutions and Allegiance during the American Revolution," *Early American Studies* 15, no. 1 (Winter 2017): 99–132. Christopher Sparshott argues that popular loyalism did not emerge from a set of shared political ideals, but was rather "fluid, contingent, and ultimately unpredictable." "The Popular Politics of Loyalism During the American Revolution, 1774–1790" (Ph.D. diss., Northwestern University, 2007), 24. Finally, Edward Larkin claims Loyalists were motivated by "a variety of reasons that often had little to do with the politics and the grand ideals of the American Revolution." "Loyalism," in *The Oxford Handbook of The American Revolution*, ed. Edward G. Gray and Jane Kamensky (Oxford: Oxford University Press, 2013), 291, and "What Is a Loyalist? The American Revolution as Civil War," *Common-Place* 8, no. 1 (October 2007), http://commonplace.online/article/what-is-a-loyalist/. For an exception to this thinking, see Janice Potter, *The Liberty We Seek: Loyalist Ideology in Colonial New York and Massachusetts* (Cambridge, MA: Harvard University Press, 1983), esp. 39–61; Timothy M. Barnes and Robert C. Calhoon, "Loyalist Discourse and the Moderation of the American Revolution," in *Tory Insurgents: The Loyalist Perception and Other Essays*, ed. Robert M. Calhoon, Timothy M. Barnes, and Robert S. Davis (Columbia: University of South Carolina Press, 2010), 160–203; Mary Beth Norton, "The Loyalist Critique of the Revolution," in *The Development of a Revolutionary Mentality: Library of Congress Symposia on the American Revolution* (Washington, DC: n.p., 1972), 127–50.

On the other hand, historians have been much more willing to acknowledge an underlying shared ideology that came to define the Patriot cause. To name just a few examples: Bernard Bailyn, *The Ideological Origins of the American Revolution* (Cambridge, MA: Belknap Press of Harvard University Press, 1967); Gordon S. Wood, *The Radicalism of the American Revolution* (New York: Vintage, 1991); Pauline Maier, *From Resistance to Revolution: Colonial Radicals and the Development of American Opposition to Britain, 1765–1776* (New York: Alfred A. Knopf, 1972), esp. chaps. 8 and 9; Breen, *American Insurgents* and *The Marketplace of Revolution: How Consumer Politics Shaped American Independence* (New York: Oxford University Press, 2004); Ammerman, *In the Common Cause*; Parkinson, *Common Cause.*

32. This is certainly true of Bernard Bailyn's portrayal of Thomas Hutchinson. *The Ordeal of Thomas Hutchinson* (Cambridge, MA: Harvard University Press, 1974). See also Nelson, *American Tory,* 19; Janice Potter and Robert M. Calhoon, "The Character and Coherence of the Loyalist Press," in *The Press and the American Revolution,* ed. Bernard Bailyn and John B. Hench (Worcester, MA: American Antiquarian Society, 1980), 272. In the first number of *The American Crisis,* Thomas Paine had this to say about Loyalists: "And what is a Tory? Good GOD! what is he? I should not be afraid to go with a hundred Whigs against a thousand Tories, were they to attempt to get into arms. Every Tory is a coward, for a servile, slavish, self-interested fear is the foundation of Toryism; and a man under such influence, though he may be cruel, never can be brave." "The American Crisis, Number 1, Dec. 19, 1776," *Paine: Collected Writings,* ed. Eric Foner (New York: Library of America, 1995), 94.

33. Rivington initially refuted Patriot claims that he was a tool of the ministry and changed the subheading of his newspaper to "Printed at his Open and Uninfluenced Press, fronting Hanover-Square." *Rivington's Gazette,* May 12, 1774. In the winter of 1774–75, there were only three other significant Loyalist newspapers in the colonies, Margaret Draper's *Massachusetts Gazette and Boston News Letter,* Nathaniel Mills and John Hick's *Massachusetts Gazette, and the Boston Post-Boy Advertiser,* and James Humphreys's *Pennsylvania Ledger: or the Virginia, Maryland, Pennsylvania, & New Jersey Weekly Advertiser.* None of them matched the reach or influence of *Rivington's Gazette.* Timothy M. Barnes, "Loyalist Newspapers of the American Revolution, 1763–1783: A Bibliography," *Proceedings of the American Antiquarian Society* 83, no. 2 (October 1973): 219–23, 232–33.

34. Ebenezer Hazard to Silas Deane, March 1, 1775, quoted in Leroy Hewlett, "James Rivington, Loyalist Printer, Publisher, and Bookseller of the American Revolution, 1774–1802: A Biographical, Bibliographical Study" (Ph.D. diss., University of Michigan, 1958), 74. Patriot printers depended on similar networks of writers. Parkinson, *Common Cause,* chap. 1.

35. This statement appears in Seabury's written testimony submitted to the Loyalist Claims Commission. Quoted in Philip Davidson, *Propaganda and the American Revolution, 1763–1783* (Chapel Hill: University of North Carolina Press, 1941), 250.

36. Davidson, *Propaganda,* 249–311. In March 1775, booksellers in both Edinburgh and Glasgow advertised for sale a collection of "PAMPHLETS imported from NORTH AMERICA" that included all four of Seabury's pamphlets along with Thomas Chandler's "What Think Ye of Congress Now?" *Caledonian Mercury,* March 22, 1775. Anthony Henry published Chandler's "The American Querist" and "A Friendly Address to All Reasonable Americans" during the fall and winter of 1774–75. "The American Querist": *Nova-Scotia Gazette: and the Weekly Chronicle,* November 1 and 8,

1774; "What Think Ye of Congress Now": *Nova-Scotia Gazette: and the Weekly Chronicle*, December 20, 1774, to February 14, 1775. No copies of Jamaican newspapers exist for this period, though it is likely these pamphlets also appeared there.

37. *A Letter from Thomas Lord Lyttelton, to William Pitt, Earl of Chatham, on the Quebec Bill* (New York, 1774), 19, Evans 13386.

38. Thomas Chandler, *A Friendly Address to All Reasonable Americans, on the Subject of our Political Confusions . . . are Fairly Stated* (New York, 1774), 20, 53–55, Evans 13224.

39. *A Letter from Thomas Lord Lyttelton*, 13.

40. Samuel Seabury, *The Congress Canvassed: or, An Examination into the Conduct of the Delegates, at their Grand Convention . . . To the Merchants of New-York* (New York, 1774), 14–16, Evans 13601.

41. Mary V. V. [pseud.], *A Dialogue, Between a Southern Delegate and His Spouse, on His Return from the Grand Continental Congress. A Fragment, Inscribed to the Married Ladies of America* (New York, 1774), 13, Evans 13245. See also *The Poor Man's Advice to His Poor Neighbors* (New York, 1774), 17, Evans 13551.

42. *Rivington's Gazette*, March 9, 1775.

43. John Lind, *An Englishman's Answer, to the Address from the Delegates to the People of Great-Britain . . . in the late Continental Congress* (New York, 1775), 21–23, Evans 14159.

44. Philip Gould, *Writing the Rebellion: Loyalists and the Literature of Politics in British America* (Oxford: Oxford University Press, 2013), 144–67. Peter Walker argues that both antipopery and antipuritanism assumed similar meaning during protests over the 1774 Quebec Act and the 1778 Catholic relief bills. Peter W. Walker, "Tolerating Protestants: Antipopery, Antipuritanism, and Religious Toleration in Britain, 1776–1829," in *Against Popery: Anti-Catholicism and the British-American World*, ed. Evan Haefeli (Charlottesville: University of Virginia Press, forthcoming).

45. Seabury, *Congress Canvassed*, 10.

46. *The Triumph of the Whigs: or, T'other Congress Convened* (New York, 1775), 7, Evans 14523. See also *Rivington's Gazette*, January 26, 1775.

47. *To the Worthy Inhabitants of the City of New-York, 16th September 1774* (New York, 1774), Evans 13100. See also *Rivington's Gazette*, October 13, 1774, and January 12, 1775; *New-York Gazette; and the Weekly Mercury*, April 24, 1775; "Narrative or Journal of Capt. John Ferdinand Dalziel Smyth, of the Queen's Rangers," *Pennsylvania Magazine of History and Biography* 39, no. 2 (1915): 144–45.

48. Seabury, *Congress Canvassed*, 20.

49. Samuel Seabury, *An Alarm to the Legislature of the Province of New-York* (New York, 1775), 7, Evans 14453, 7.

50. Samuel Seabury, *Free Thoughts, on the Proceedings of the Continental Congress, Held at Philadelphia Sept. 5, 1774* (New York, 1774), 23–24.

51. Seabury, *Congress Canvassed*, 15, 17. See also Samuel Seabury, *An Alarm to the Legislature of the Province of New-York* (New York, 1775), 7, Evans 14453.

52. Barnes and Calhoon refer to this thinking as Loyalist moderation. "Loyalist Discourse," 175–84.

53. Donald Desserud, "An Outpost's Response: The Language and Politics of Moderation in Eighteenth-Century Nova Scotia," *American Review of Canadian Studies* 29, no. 3 (Fall 1999): 379–405.

54. For example, see *Nova-Scotia Gazette: and the Weekly Chronicle*, October 11 and November 22, 1774, and January 10 and February 28, 1775.

55. Legge worried about the support of Acadians as tensions in the thirteen colonies escalated. Legge to Dartmouth, August 20, 1774, in *Report on Canadian Archives, 1894*, ed. Douglas Brymner (Ottawa, ON: S.E. Dawson, 1895), 320.

56. Local merchants depended on New England traders and their ships to export goods to places elsewhere in the empire. In 1764, of the £64,790 in goods exported from Nova Scotia, £17,000 went through Boston. Viola F. Barnes, "Francis Legge, Governor of Loyalist Nova Scotia, 1773–1776," *New England Quarterly* 4, no. 3 (July 1931): 425.

57. Barnes, "Francis Legge," 425–29; W. S. MacNutt, *The Atlantic Provinces: The Emergence of Colonial Society, 1712–1857* (Toronto: McClelland and Stewart, 1965), 77–81; George A. Rawlyk, ed., *Revolution Rejected, 1775–1776* (Scarborough, ON: Prentice-Hall, 1968), 30–33; Brebner, *Neutral Yankees*, 303–5. Lewis R. Fischer, "Revolution without Independence: The Canadian Colonies, 1749–1775," in *The Economy of Early America: The Revolutionary Period, 1763–1790*, ed. Ronald Hoffman, John J. McCusker, Russell R. Menard, and Peter J. Albert (Charlottesville: University Press of Virginia, 1988), 94–123.

58. Brebner, *Neutral Yankees*, 150–55.

59. Quoted in Desserud, "An Outpost's Response," 385.

60. *Nova-Scotia Gazette: and the Weekly Chronicle*, May 9, 1775.

61. *New-York Gazette; and the Weekly Mercury*, June 12, 1775.

62. *Nova-Scotia Gazette: and the Weekly Chronicle*, June 27, 1775; Executive Council Minutes, June 23, 1775, RG 1, 170: 166–67, Public Archives of Nova Scotia (hereafter cited as PANS).

63. Robert Kent Donovan, "The Popular Party of the Church of Scotland and the American Revolution," in *Scotland and America in the Age of Enlightenment*, ed. Richard B. Sher and Jeffrey R. Smitten (Edinburgh: Edinburgh University Press, 1990), 81–99.

64. For example, see *Nova-Scotia Gazette: and the Weekly Chronicle*, September 20, 1774.

65. For example, see *Scots Magazine*, 36 (June 1774), 298–307, 307–9; *Scots Magazine*, 37 (January 1775), 18–21; (May 1775), 240–45.

66. *Scots Magazine*, 36 (October 1774), 536. See also James MacPherson's defense of the bill in his widely read response to Congress's *Declaration of the Causes and Necessity of Taking Up Arms*. *Scots Magazine*, 38 (March 1776), 122.

67. By 1775, 43 percent of Scottish imports were from North America, with tobacco accounting for nearly 38 percent. M. L. Robertson, "Scottish Commerce and the American War of Independence," *Economic History Review* 9, no. 1 (August 1956): 123.

68. Seabury, *Free Thoughts*, 4–15, and *The Poor Man's Advice*, 9–11.

69. *Caledonian Mercury*, January 4, 1775. See also *Edinburgh Advertiser*, April 14, 1775.

70. Woody Holton, *Forced Founders: Indians, Debtors, Slaves, and the Making of the American Revolution in Virginia* (Chapel Hill: University of North Carolina Press, 1999), chaps. 3 and 4; Michael A. McDonnell, *The Politics of War: Race, Class, and Conflict in Revolutionary Virginia* (Chapel Hill: University of North Carolina Press, 2007), 34–35. The extent of Virginian indebtedness was staggering. Richard Sheridan found that in

1772, 37 tobacco firms held "31,000 debts to 112 stores in Virginia." "The British Credit Crisis of 1772 and the American Colonies," *Journal of Economic History* 20, no. 2 (June 1960): 161–86.

71. Samuel Seabury, *A View of the Controversy between Great-Britain and Her Colonies* (New York, 1774), 60, Evans 13603.

72. *Caledonian Mercury*, October 31, 1774. See also *Caledonian Mercury*, December 26, 1774.

73. *Caledonian Mercury*, November 22, 1774. See also T. M. Devine, *The Tobacco Lords: A Study of the Tobacco Merchants of Glasgow and Their Trading Activities c. 1740–90* (Edinburgh: John Donald Publishers, 1975), 104.

74. The letter was titled "extract of a letter from a gentleman in Westmoreland county (Virginia) to his friend in *Glasgow*, dated June 30." *Glasgow Journal*, August 18, 1774.

75. *Virginia Gazette* [Pickney], February 9, 1775; Force, ed., *American Archives*, 1: 970–72.

76. *Scots Magazine*, 37 (February 1775), 75–78.

77. Stephen Conway, *The British Isles and the War for American Independence* (Oxford: Oxford University Press, 2000), 272; Dalphy I. Fagerstrom, "Scottish Opinion and the American Revolution," *William and Mary Quarterly* 11, no. 2 (April 1954): 264.

78. *The Journals of the House of Commons* (London, 1803), 35:74–75. Patriot printers reported on the petition in positive terms, suggesting it revealed a broad transatlantic support for their cause. For example, see *Essex Gazette*, March 21, 1775.

79. Seabury, *Free Thoughts*, 6–10. Delegates to the First Continental Congress shared these concerns and recognized that economic boycotts could jeopardize political unity at a critical moment in the imperial conflict. When drafting the Continental Association, New York representative Isaac Low wondered aloud whether colonists could "live without rum, sugar, and molasses?" I. N. Phelps Stokes, ed., *The Iconography of Manhattan Island, 1498–1909* (1922; reprint, Union, NJ: The Lawbook Exchange, 1998), 4:865–66. On the other hand, some colonists argued in favor of boycotting the Caribbean colonies as the most effective way to convince Parliament to repeal the Coercive Acts. *Boston Evening-Post*, September 5, 1774.

80. *Rivington's Gazette*, January 12, 1775.

81. *Craftsman or Say's Weekly Journal* [London], August 13, 1774.

82. *Edinburgh Advertiser*, July 21, 1775.

83. Betty Wood and Martin Lynn, eds., *Travel, Trade and Power in the Atlantic, 1765–1884*, Camden Miscellany, vol. 35 (Cambridge: Cambridge University Press, 2002), 148–49.

84. Quoted in Andrew O'Shaughnessy, *An Empire Divided: The American Revolution and the British Caribbean* (Philadelphia: University of Pennsylvania Press, 2000), 146–47.

85. *Scots Magazine*, 37 (February 1775), 105.

86. For example, see *London Evening Post*, September 20, 1774.

87. For example, see *Rivington's Gazette*, December 8, 1774. Other rumors spread that the Spanish were building fortifications at Havana in preparation for war. For example, see *New-York Journal; or, The General Advertiser*, January 5, 1775.

88. *Pennsylvania Ledger*, April 22, 1775.

89. *Rivington's Gazette*, June 15, 1775.

90. The Kingston faction waited to draft the petition until after the planters departed for the Christmas holiday. O'Shaughnessy, *Empire Divided*, 144–45.

91. Humble Petition and Memorial of the Assembly of Jamaica, Force, ed., *American Archives*, 1:1072–74. See also Jack P. Greene, *Peripheries and Center: Constitutional Development in the Extended Politics of the British Empire and the United States, 1607-1788* (Athens: University of Georgia Press, 1986), 139; Sara Yeh, "Colonial Identity and Revolutionary Loyalty: The Case of the West Indies," in *British North America in the Seventeenth and Eighteenth Centuries*, ed. Stephen Foster (Oxford: Oxford University Press, 2013), 208-9; Trevor Burnard, *Jamaica in the Age of Revolution* (Philadelphia: University of Pennsylvania Press, 2020), 200-2. Andrew O'Shaughnessy dismisses the petition as the work of an assembly mostly concerned about losing the North American trade, which would likely have led to an increase in slave rebellions on the island. *Empire Divided*, 143–46.

92. Quoted in O'Shaughnessy, *Empire Divided*, 139. While several London newspapers printed reports that the assembly had produced a petition, I cannot find a single newspaper that published the actual document.

93. *Morning Chronicle and London Advertiser*, January 11, 1775.

94. *Pennsylvania Evening Post*, February 23, 1775; *Norwich Packet and the Connecticut, Massachusetts, New-Hampshire, and Rhode-Island Weekly Advertiser*, February 23, 1775; *New-York Journal; or, The General Advertiser*, February 23, 1775; *Connecticut Gazette; And the Universal Intelligencer*, February 24, 1775; *Providence Gazette; And Country Journal*, February 25, 1775; *Pennsylvania Ledger or the Virginia, Maryland, Pennsylvania, & New-Jersey Weekly Advertiser*, February 25, 1775; *Boston Evening-Post*, February 27, 1775; *Dunlap's Pennsylvania Packet or, the General Advertiser*, February 27, 1775; *New-York Gazette; and the Weekly Mercury*, February 27, 1775; *Newport Mercury*, February 27, 1775; *Essex Gazette*, February 28, 1775; *Der Wöchentliche Pennsylvanische Staatsbote*, February 28, 1775; *Connecticut Journal, And the New-Haven Post-Boy*, March 1, 1775; *Massachusetts Spy or, Thomas's Boston Journal*, March 2, 1775; *New-Hampshire Gazette, And Historical Chronicle*, March 3, 1775; *Boston Evening-Post*, March 6, 1775; *Connecticut Courant, And Hartford Weekly Intelligencer*, March 6, 1775; *Virginia Gazette* [Dixon and Hunter], March 11, 1775; *Nova-Scotia Gazette: and the Weekly Chronicle*, March 14, 1775.

95. *Massachusetts Gazette; And the Boston Post-Boy and Advertiser*, February 13, 1775. See also *New-York Gazette, and Weekly Mercury*, February 13, 1775. Roderick Cave, "Early Printing and the Book Trade in the West Indies," *Library Quarterly* 48, no. 2 (April 1978): 172.

96. Another letter attributed the assembly's petition to the widespread popularity of Dickinson's *Farmer's Letters*. *Pennsylvania Ledger or the Virginia, Maryland, Pennsylvania, & New-Jersey Weekly Advertiser*, February 11, 1775.

97. Virginia address: *Pennsylvania Evening Post*, April 29, 1775. Connecticut address: *Connecticut Courant, And Hartford Weekly Intelligencer*, April 3, 1775. There is no evidence that Jamaicans created Committees of Correspondence. In November, however, the same assemblymen who petitioned the king a year earlier defeated a motion to prevent the assembly from receiving "letters from any of the assemblies or congresses in North America during the present disturbances." *Journal of the Assembly of Jamaica*, vol. 6 (Kingston: Alexander Aikman, 1800), 576.

98. O'Shaughnessy, *Empire Divided*, 137–46.

99. *Rivington's Gazette*, October 13, 1774.

100. Hewlett, *James Rivington*, 60–105; Schlesinger, *Prelude to Independence: The Newspaper War on Britain, 1764–1776* (New York: Alfred A. Knopf, 1957), 224–27; Breen, *American Insurgents*, 232–37; Holger Hoock, *Scars of Independence: America's Violent Birth* (New York: Crown, 2017), 36–40; Joseph M. Adelman, *Revolutionary Networks: The Business and Politics of Printing the News, 1763–1789* (Baltimore: Johns Hopkins University Press, 2019), 126–29.

101. Silas Deane to Mrs. Elizabeth Deane, September 8, 1774, in *Collections of the New York Historical Society for the Year 1886* (New York: Printed for the Society, 1887), 16.

102. "Jacobite Priest," Force, ed., *American Archives*, 1:1051–52. "Elizabethtown," *Boston Evening-Post*, January 16, 1775. A writer in Philadelphia claimed that Rivington had been "gratified with a Pension of some pounds sterling, and has received, from the Pope, absolution for all the lies he has told, and is to tell in the New-York Gazetteer." *Pennsylvania Journal; and the Weekly Advertiser*, March 8, 1775.

103. Force, ed., *American Archives*, 1:1106. At the same time, a New Yorker declared Rivington to be one of the "few remaining enemies of American Freedom" in the colonies. *New-York Journal; or, the General Advertiser*, February 9, 1775.

104. The following communities agreed to a boycott of Rivington's press. In Connecticut: Hartford, *Connecticut Courant*, January 30, 1775; Fairfield, Force, ed., *American Archives*, 1:1075–76; Litchfield, *Connecticut Courant*, February 27, 1775. In New Jersey: Elizabethtown, Force, ed., *American Archives*, 1:1051–52; Morristown, Force, ed., *American Archives*, 1:1106; Woodbridge, *New-York Journal; or, The General Advertiser*, January 19, 1775; Force, ed., *American Archives*, 1:1103; Hanover, Force, ed., *American Archives*, 1:1240–41; Freehold, Peter Force, ed., *American Archives: A Documentary History of the English Colonies in North America*, 4th ser. (Washington, DC: M. St. Claire Clarke & Peter Force, 1839), 2:35–36; Newark, Force, ed., *American Archives*, 1:1029–30. In New York: Suffolk County (Long Island), *Virginia Gazette* [Pinkney], March 23, 1775; New Windsor, Force, ed., *American Archives*, 2:132–33. In Rhode Island: Newport, *Newport Mercury*, March 6, 1775; Force, ed., *American Archives*, 2:12–13; Providence, Force, ed., *American Archives*, 2:15. In Massachusetts: Worcester, *Norwich Packet*, February 23, 1775. There were also reports from as far away as Baltimore, Maryland, and Charleston, South Carolina, of colonists canceling their subscriptions to Rivington's newspaper. Baltimore: *To the PUBLIC. NEW-YORK, November 16th, 1774* (New York, 1774), Evans 13667; *New-York Journal; or, the General Advertiser*, November 17, 1774. South Carolina: *New-York Journal; or, the General Advertiser*, December 8, 1774; *Nova-Scotia Gazette: And the Weekly Chronicle*, February 21, 1775.

105. *Rivington's Gazette*, November 17, 1774; Force, ed., *American Archives*, 2:132–33; *New-York Journal; or, The General Advertiser*, December 8, 1774. For the Freehold incident: Force, ed., *American Archives*, 2:35–36.

106. Force, ed., *American Archives*, 2:15.

107. Baltimore: Hewlett, *James Rivington*, 63. Philadelphia: Force, ed., *American Archives*, 1:1233.

108. Force, ed., *American Archives*, 2:50.

109. James Madison to William Bradford, [early March] 1775, in *The Papers of James Madison*, vol. 1, *16 March 1751–16 December 1779*, ed. William T. Hutchinson and William M. E. Rachal (Chicago: University of Chicago Press, 1962), 141–42.

110. Thomas Chandler, *What Think Ye of the Congress Now?* (New York, 1775), 1–2, Evans 13866. According to a letter from Annapolis, Maryland, Chandler's pamphlet was persuading residents to support the Loyalist cause. *Rivington's Gazette*, February 9, 1775.

111. *Rivington's Gazette*, 6 April 1775; Force, ed., *American Archives*, 2:36–37.

112. Thomas Jones, *History of New York during the Revolutionary War* (New York: Printed for the New York Historical Society, 1879), 1:64–5. See also "Anti-Tyrannicus" essay in *Rivington's Gazette*, March 23, 1775.

113. Breen, *American Insurgents*, esp. chaps. 7 and 8; Irvin, *Robes of Sovereignty*, 75–96; Ammerman, *Common Cause*, esp. 103–24.

114. This reassertion of monarchy was, in many ways, a response to the erosion of royal authority during this critical period in the conflict. McConville, *King's Three Faces*, 281–311.

115. *Rivington's Gazette*, March 9, 1775.

116. Force, ed., *American Archives*, 2:252–53.

117. *Rivington's Gazette*, January 12, 1775. See also Creviston, "No King," 476–77; Ruma Chopra, *Unnatural Rebellion: Loyalists in New York City during the Revolution* (Charlottesville: University of Virginia Press, 2011), 32; Benjamin L. Carp, *Rebels Rising: Cities and the American Revolution* (Oxford: Oxford University Press, 2007), 62–63.

118. Becker offers a brief discussion of several of these declarations in *Political Parties*, 170–73. Edward Countryman mentions them only to suggest the relative size of the Loyalist population in the region surrounding New York City. *A People in Revolution: The American Revolution and Political Society in New York, 1760–1790* (Baltimore: Johns Hopkins University Press, 1981), 148–51.

119. For example, see the New York Assembly's petition to the king in March 1775. While they renounced Congress and restated their loyalty to the Crown, they also defended colonists' opposition to the Stamp Act, Townshend duties, Quebec Act, and Coercive Acts, and questioned the right of Parliament to raise revenue in the colonies. "The Humble Petition of the Assembly, 25 March 1775," in Force, ed., *American Archives*, I:1313–16.

120. Maya Jasanoff referred to this as "the mounting pressure of revolutionary events," though she focuses mostly on events after Lexington and Concord. *Liberty's Exiles*, 24.

121. Pauline Maier, *American Scripture: Making the Declaration of Independence* (New York: Vintage, 1997), 69–96.

122. Ulster County, *Rivington's Gazette*, January 26, 1775; Dutchess County, *Rivington's Gazette*, February 9, 1775; Reading, *Rivington's Gazette*, February 23, 1775; Westchester, *New-York Gazette; and the Weekly Mercury*, April 17, 1775. Rivington included the names of signers: *Rivington's Gazette*, April 20, 1775. Similar declarations of loyalty to the king appeared in Jamaica (on Long Island), *Rivington's Gazette*, February 2, 1775; New Milford, *Rivington's Gazette*, March 16, 1775; Danbury, *Rivington's Gazette*, February 23, 1775; Hampstead, *Rivington's Gazette*, April 6, 1775; Cortlandt Manor, *Rivington's Gazette*, February 16, 1775; White Plains, *Rivington's Gazette*, January 12, 1775; *New-York Gazette; and the Weekly Mercury*, January 16, 1775; John's-Town, *Rivington's Gazette*, April 6, 1775; King's District in Albany County, *New-York Gazette; and the Weekly Mercury*, February 6, 1775; Ridgefield, *New-York Gazette; and the Weekly*

Mercury, February 20, 1775; Anson County, North Carolina, *Rivington's Gazette*, April 6, 1775; Rowan and Surry Counties, North Carolina, *Rivington's Gazette*, April 6, 1775; *New-York Gazette; and the Weekly Mercury*, April 10, 1775.

123. Newtown, *Rivington's Gazette*, January 19, 1775; Dutchess County, *Rivington's Gazette*, February 9, 1775; Hampstead, *Rivington's Gazette*, April 6, 1775; Cortlandt Manor, *Rivington's Gazette*, February 16, 1775.

124. Reading, *Rivington's Gazette*, February 23, 1775; Hampstead, *Rivington's Gazette*, April 6, 1775; Ulster County, *Rivington's Gazette*, March 2, 1775.

125. *Rivington's Gazette*, March 2, 1775. John's-Town residents made a similar argument: *Rivington's Gazette*, April 6, 1775.

126. Dutchess, *Rivington's Gazette*, February 9, 1775; Reading, *Rivington's Gazette*, February 23, 1775; Ridgefield, *New-York Gazette; And the Weekly Mercury*, February 20, 1775. Residents of the seven precincts of Dutchess County made a similar declaration in April, just as news of fighting at Lexington arrived in New York City. *New-York Gazette; And the Weekly Mercury*, April 24, 1775.

127. *Rivington's Gazette*, March 2, 1775. The episode is briefly mentioned in Eugene R. Fingerhut, *Survivor: Cadwallader Colden II in Revolutionary America* (Washington, DC: University Press of America, 1983), 42–43.

128. For example, see *Craftsman or Say's Weekly Journal* [London], March 4 and 15 and April 22, 1775.

129. For example, see *Bath Chronicle*, March 9, 1775. For Scottish newspapers, see *Caledonian Mercury*, April 17 and 24, May 10, and June 19, 1775.

130. Thomas Jones described the gathering that day as another example of Patriots using violent methods to oppose legitimate, representative government in their community: "The republican party in order to swell their numbers, marched round all the docks and wharves, with trumpets blowing, fifes playing, drums beating, and colours flying; by this means collecting all the boys, sailors, negroes, New England and Jersey boatmen, that could be mustered." *History of New York*, 1:37–38.

131. *New-York Journal; or, The General Advertiser*, March 9, 1775. These "Friends of Freedom" were the ones who tried to force William Cunningham to "damn his popish King George."

132. *New-York Journal; or, The General Advertiser*, April 13, 1775.

133. William Bell Clark, ed., *Naval Documents of the American Revolution* (Washington, DC: Naval History Division, 1964) 1:406–8, 415–17. Ranlet claims that New England merchants, who were illicitly supplying the British army and navy in Boston, created many of these rumors to direct the public's attention away from their activities. *New York Loyalists*, 56.

134. "Voluntary Corps," "Colonel Marinus Willett's Narrative," in *New York City during the American Revolution: Being a Collection of Original Papers (Now First Published) from the Manuscripts in the Possession of the Mercantile Library Association of New York City*, ed. Abraham Tomlinson and Henry B. Dawson (New York: Privately Printed for the Association, 1861), 54–55; "Insulted," Catherine S. Crary, *The Price of Loyalty: Tory Writings from the Revolutionary Era* (New York: McGraw-Hill, 1973), 45. See also Stokes, ed., *Iconography of Manhattan Island*, 4:881–82; Jones, *History of New York*, 1:39–40; William H. W. Sabine, ed., *Historical Memoirs from 16 March 1763 to 9 July 1776 of William Smith* (New York: Colburn & Tegg, 1956), 1:221–23; Chopra, *Unnatural Rebellion*, 35–38.

135. *To the Public . . . April 27, 1775* (New York, 1775), Evans 14435; *Rivington's Gazette*, May 4, 1775.

136. One Patriot writer reported that "JAMES RIVINGTON, printer, and Parson COOPER, a writer on the side of TYRANNY, with some other *ministerial tools*, have decamped, and taken passage for the land of SLAVERY." *Newport Mercury*, May 8, 1775. Newspapers in London recorded their arrival. *General Evening Post* [London], 29 June 1775. Cooper eventually settled in Edinburgh, where he died in 1785. Jones, *History of New York*, 1:59–61.

137. Colden to the Earl of Dartmouth, May 3, 1775, Jones, *History of New York*, 1:497.

138. Jones, *History of New York*, 1:42–43.

5. The Madness of these Deluded People

1. *New-York Gazette; and the Weekly Mercury*, November 4, 1776. The address was also reprinted in Abraham Tomlinson and Henry B. Dawson, eds., *New York City during the American Revolution: Being a Collection of Original Papers (Now First Published) from the Manuscripts in the Possession of the Mercantile Library Association of New York City* (New York: Privately Printed for the Association, 1861), 117–38. According to Christopher Minty, Charles Inglis wrote this declaration. "Mobilization and Voluntarism: The Political Origins of Loyalism in New York, c. 1768–1778" (Ph.D. diss., University of Stirling, 2014), 69–73. See also Ruma Chopra, *Unnatural Rebellion: Loyalists in New York City during the Revolution* (Charlottesville: University of Virginia Press, 2011), 64–68.

2. For reasons that are not known, this address was never published. Loyalist Declaration of Dependence, November 28, 1776, MSS.Y1776, New-York Historical Society (hereafter cited as NYHS). See also R. W. G. Vail, "The Loyalist Declaration of Dependence of November 28, 1776," *New-York Historical Society Quarterly* 31, no. 2 (April 1947): 68–71.

3. During the Canada campaign, Washington actively discouraged anti-Catholic attitudes among his soldiers and banished celebrations of Pope's Day. F. J. Zwierlein, "End of No-Popery in Continental Congress," *Thought* 11, no. 3 (December 1936): 357–77.

4. Robert Parkinson, *The Common Cause: Creating Race and Nation in the American Revolution* (Chapel Hill: University of North Carolina Press, 2016).

5. Janice Potter and Robert M. Calhoon, "The Character and Coherence of the Loyalist Press," in *The Press and the American Revolution*, ed. Bernard Bailyn and John B. Hench (Worcester, MA: American Antiquarian Society, 1980), 234–72; Chopra, *Unnatural Rebellion*, 3.

6. Thomas Paine, "The American Crisis, Number 1, Dec. 19, 1776," in *Paine: Collected Writings*, ed. Eric Foner (New York: Library of America, 1995), 91.

7. Worthington C. Ford et al., eds., *Journals of the Continental Congress, 1774–1789*, vol. 2, *May 10–September 20, 1775* (Washington, DC: Government Printing Office, 1905), 79, 80, 204–6.

8. *Kingston Journal*, August 3, 1776; *General Evening Post* [London], October 22, 1776.

9. Richard B. Sheridan, "The Crisis of Slave Subsistence in the British West Indies during and after the American Revolution," *William and Mary Quarterly* 33, no. 4 (October 1976): 621–22.

10. *Journal of the Assembly of Jamaica* (Kingston: Alexander Aikman, 1800), 6:635.

11. Quoted in Andrew O'Shaughnessy, *An Empire Divided: The American Revolution and the British Caribbean* (Philadelphia: University of Pennsylvania Press, 2000), 152.

12. Quoted in O'Shaughnessy, *Empire Divided*, 153.

13. *Caledonian Mercury*, August 7, 1776. There were also concerns that Patriot sympathizers living in Kingston were sending weapons and ammunition to Washington's army. *Caledonian Mercury*, August 17, 1776.

14. T. M. Devine, *The Tobacco Lords: A Study of the Tobacco Merchants of Glasgow and Their Trading Activities c. 1740–90* (Edinburgh: John Donald Publishers, 1975), chap. 7, esp. 108–9, 119–20.

15. *Caledonian Mercury*, March 13, 1776.

16. *Caledonian Mercury*, October 11, 1775. Stephen Conway, *The British Isles and the War for American Independence* (Oxford: Oxford University Press, 2000), 272; Devine, *Tobacco Lords*, 124.

17. *Virginia Gazette* [Purdie], June 9, 1775; Peter Force, ed., *American Archives: A Documentary History of the English Colonies in North America*, 4th ser. (Washington, DC: M. St. Claire Clarke & Peter Force, 1839), 2:115.

18. *Caledonian Mercury*, January 13, 1776; Harry Lumsden, ed., *The Records of the Trades House of Glasgow, 1713–1777* (Glasgow: n.p., 1934), 571–72.

19. *Scots Magazine*, 36 (February 1776), 108; *Caledonian Mercury*, February 10, 1776. See also Devine, *Tobacco Lords*, 124–50, esp. 132.

20. Peter Force, ed., *American Archives: A Documentary History of the English Colonies in North America*, 4th ser. (Washington, DC: M. St. Claire Clarke & Peter Force, 1846), 6:61–4; *Scots Magazine*, 36 (January 1776), 9–12. Desserud asserts, correctly I believe, that this petition represents a very good, though largely ignored, example of British American constitutional thinking, which emphasized a mixed and balanced government. Desserud, "An Outpost's Response," 379–405. See also J. Bartlet Brebner, "Nova Scotia's Remedy for the American Revolution," *Canadian Historical Review*, 15, no. 2 (June 1934): 171–81.

21. Quoted in Desserud, "An Outpost's Response," 391.

22. Executive Council Minutes, July 5, 1775, RG 1, 170: 169–70, Public Archives of Nova Scotia (hereafter cited as PANS).

23. Executive Council Minutes, August 1775, RG 1, 170: 176–78, PANS.

24. Executive Council Minutes, August 29, 1775, RG 1, 170: 182–84, PANS; Executive Council Minutes, November 4, 1775, RG 1, 170: 185, PANS.

25. William Harrison deposition, December 19, 1776, RG I, 342, 60, PANS.

26. Quoted in David Jaffee, *People of the Wachusett: Greater New England in History and Memory, 1630–1860* (Ithaca, NY: Cornell University Press, 1999), 185.

27. Barry Cahill, "The Sedition Trial of Timothy Houghton: Repression in a Marginal New England Planter Township during the Revolutionary Years," *Acadiensis* 24, no. 1 (October 1994): 35–58. Early historians downplayed the significance of the case. J. B. Brebner, *The Neutral Yankees of Nova Scotia: A Marginal Colony During the Revolutionary Years* (1937; reprint: New York: Russell & Russell, 1970), 341–42; Wilfred Brenton Kerr, *The Maritime Provinces of British North America and the American Revolution* (Sackville, NB: Busy East Press, 1942), 83.

28. The report appeared in several London newspapers. For example, see *Gazetteer and New Daily Advertiser* [London], October 31, 1775.

29. *Nova-Scotia Gazette: and the Weekly Chronicle*, September 26, 1775. By comparison, several American printers (including Anthony Henry) had published William Henry Drayton's charge to South Carolina's grand jury, which questioned the supremacy of the monarch, denied Parliament's sovereignty in the colonies, and urged the jury to protect society from "Roman Catholic doctrines . . . which tend to establish a most cruel tyranny in Church and state." *Nova-Scotia Gazette: and the Weekly Chronicle*, March 28, 1775.

30. *Nova-Scotia Gazette: and the Weekly Chronicle*, September 26, 1775.

31. There were rumors that Legge's real intentions were to send these men to Boston to enlist in Gage's army, while others complained that they could not afford the additional taxes. Residents of both Yarmouth and Cumberland County argued against fighting, because as former New Englanders they refused to go to war "against their friends and relations." Their petitions reveal the extent to which the revolution was a civil war, but they also demonstrated just how ineffective was the British common cause. Residents of these two counties were willing to risk losing their colony to the Americans than to take up arms against their former countrymen. Cumberland County petition, George A. Rawlyk, ed., *Revolution Rejected, 1775–1776* (Scarborough, ON: Prentice-Hall, 1968), 28. Yarmouth petition, Brebner, *Neutral Yankees*, 291. See also Donald Desserud, "Nova Scotia and the American Revolution: A Study of Neutrality and Moderation in the Eighteenth Century," in *Making Adjustments: Change and Continuity in Planter Nova Scotia, 1759–1800*, ed. Margaret Conrad (Fredericton, NB: Acadiensis Press 1991), 89–112. Elizabeth Mancke argues that the petitions focused on particular local political issues and did not call into question the inhabitant's broader loyalty to the empire. Elizabeth Mancke, *The Fault Lines of Empire: Political Differentiation in Massachusetts and Nova Scotia, Ca. 1760–1830* (New York: Routledge, 2005), 78–80.

32. "Copy of letter from Arbuthnot to Mr. Stephen, Halifax yard Dec. 26, 1775, that was then given to the Lords of Admiralty," PRO CO 5/123/205-6, TNA.

33. Captain Alexander McDonald to Gage, January 27, 1776, "Letter-Book of Captain Alexander McDonald, of the Royal Highland Emigrants, 1775–1779," in *Collections of the New-York Historical Society for the Year 1882* (New York: Printed for the Society, 1883), 240–41. Legge was able to muster fewer than one hundred men, most of whom were recent Irish immigrants. Paul H. Smith, *Loyalists and Redcoats: A Study in British Revolutionary Policy* (New York: W.W. Norton, 1972), 69; Barry Cahill, "Record Keeping in a Provincial Regiment: The Strange Case of the Loyal Nova Scotia Volunteers, 1775–1783," *Archivaria* 26 (Summer 1988): 81–90; Mancke, *Fault Lines*, chap. 5.

34. The Petition of the Principal Gentlemen and inhabitants of your Majestys faithfull & Loyal Province of Nova Scotia, January 2, 1776, PRO CO 217/27/218-23, TNA. I would like to thank Michael Rettig for providing me with copies of this petition.

35. Lieutenant Governor Thomas Oliver to Germaine, Halifax, April 21, 1776, PRO CO 5/175/80-1, TNA.

36. The best account of Eddy's Rebellion is Ernest Clarke, *The Siege of Fort Cumberland, 1776: An Episode in the American Revolution* (Montreal: McGill Queen's University Press, 1995).

37. Viola F. Barnes, "Francis Legge, Governor of Loyalist Nova Scotia, 1773–1776," *New England Quarterly* 4, no. 3 (July 1931): 444–47.

38. Peter Force, ed., *American Archives: A Documentary History of the English Colonies in North America*, 5th ser. (Washington, DC: M. St. Claire Clarke & Peter Force, 1851), 2:189–90.

39. Executive Council Minutes, July 13, 1776, RG 1, 170: 210–12, PANS.

40. Alexander Flick, *Loyalism in New York During the American Revolution* (New York: Macmillan, 1901), 58–77.

41. *Rivington's Gazette*, April 20, 1775.

42. Sears and his men acted against the wishes of the Provincial Assembly and Continental Congress, both of which worried that violence against the press would look bad publicly. Sears, however, had grown to despise Rivington, who had repeatedly attacked the character of the famed New York radical. Sears and others also sought revenge after learning that Virginia's governor, Lord Dunmore, had confiscated the press of John Hunter Holt, printer of the *Virginia Gazette* and nephew to the New York printer, John Holt. Parkinson, *Common Cause*, 146–49, 176–79.

43. Extract of a letter from Mr. Foxcroft to Anthony Todd, New York, December 6, 1775, PRO CO 5/135/78, TNA.

44. One resident described the streets as "plague-stricken," while another warned, "we are Now a City of Waar." "Plague-stricken," Ewald Schaukirk, "Occupation of New York City by the British," *Pennsylvania Magazine of History and Biography* 10, no. 4 (January 1887): 420. "City at Waar," quoted in Tomlinson and Dawson, eds., *New York City*, 85–86.

45. Memorial of George Birks, PRO AO 12/24/376-81, TNA; Memorial of John Lewis, PRO AO 12/18/230, TNA; Memorial of James Deas, PRO AO 12/24/383-6, TNA. Deas and Lewis signed the October 1776 loyalty declaration addressed to the Howe brothers. Tomlinson and Dawson, eds., *New York City*, 124, 129.

46. Samuel Seabury, *Free Thoughts, on the Proceedings of the Continental Congress, Held at Philadelphia Sept. 5, 1774* (New York, 1774), 23–24.

47. Peter Elting to Capt. Richard Varick, June 13, 1776, quoted in Tomlinson and Dawson, eds., *New York City*, 97.

48. Thomas Paine, "Common Sense: Addressed to the Inhabitants of America, February 14, 1776," in Foner, ed., *Paine: Collected Writings*, 15.

49. The event worried Loudon, who feared that America "may fall a sacrifice to a more fatal despotism than that with which we are threatened." Peter Force, ed., *American Archives: A Documentary History of the English Colonies in North America*, 4th ser. (Washington, DC: M. St. Claire Clarke & Peter Force, 1844), 5:439–40. Inglis's pamphlet appeared two months later in Philadelphia under a new title, *The True Interest of America Impartially Stated in Certain Strictures on a Pamphlet Intitled Common Sense* (Philadelphia, 1776).

50. *New-York Journal; or, the General Advertiser*, July 11, 1776. Winthrop D. Jordan, "Familial Politics: Thomas Paine and the Killing of the King, 1776," *Journal of American History* 60, no. 2 (September 1973): 294–308; Arthur S. Marks, "The Statue of King George III in New York and the Iconology of Regicide," *American Art Journal* 13, no. 3 (Summer 1981): 61–82. Jefferson's explanation of the Quebec Act reflected the public's fear that it was to serve as "an example and fit instrument" to subject North American colonists to tyranny and arbitrary rule. He intentionally placed the grievance directly preceding the ones that blamed the king for actually doing this (the 1774

Massachusetts Government Act and the 1767 New York Restraining Act, respectively) to convince readers that such fears were real. Pauline Maier, *American Scripture: Making the Declaration of Independence* (New York: Vintage, 1997), 116–19.

51. *New-York Journal; or, the General Advertiser*, July 11, 1776. The number is taken from an account current found in the papers of Oliver Wolcott, future governor of Connecticut. *Proceedings of the New York Historical Society for the Year 1843* (New York: Printed for the Society, 1844), 172–74.

52. Edward H. Tatum, Jr., ed., *The American Journal of Ambrose Serle, Secretary to Lord Howe, 1776–1778* (San Marino, CA: Huntington Library, 1940), 30.

53. *Scots Magazine*, 38 (August 1776), 436.

54. John Lind, *An Answer to the Declaration of the American Congress* (London, 1776), 12. Lind's introduction, which includes this passage, was published in the *Scots Magazine*, 38 (October 1776), 652–55.

55. Thomas Hutchinson, *Strictures Upon the Declaration of the Congress at Philadelphia; In a Letter to a Noble Lord, &c.* (London, 1776), 8.

56. Benjamin L. Carp, "The Night the Yankees Burned Broadway: The New York City Fire of 1776," *Early American Studies* 4, no. 2 (Fall 2006): 471–511. For more on the plundering committed by British and Hessian soldiers, see Chopra, *Unnatural Rebellion*, 62–64.

57. Tatum Jr., ed., *Ambrose Serle*, 110.

58. I. N. Phelps Stokes, ed., *The Iconography of Manhattan Island, 1498–1909* (1926; reprint, Union, NJ: The Lawbook Exchange, 1998), 5:1015.

59. Carl Leopold Baurmeister, *Revolution in America: Confidential Letters and Journals, 1776–1784, of Adjutant General Major Baurmeister of the Hessian Forces*, trans. and annot. Bernhard A. Uhlendorf (New Brunswick, NJ: Rutgers University Press, 1957), 50. During the British invasion, one officer reported that Loyalists "Voluntirely formed themselves in a Town Guard & secured possession of the Forts & Batteries which in the course of the day had been evac[u]ated by the Rebels." Revolutionary War Journal of Lachlan Campbell, September 14, 1776, MSS, Society of the Cincinnati.

60. *New-York Gazette; and the Weekly Mercury*, October 28, 1776.

61. Loyalists living in and around New York City made up two-thirds of all Loyalists who served in provincial regiments during the war. Smith, *Loyalists and Redcoats*, 48–49. Philip Ranlet argues that the British mostly relied on recent Scottish and Irish immigrants to fill these regiments. *The New York Loyalists* (Knoxville: University of Tennessee Press, 1986), chap. 7.

62. *New-York Gazette; and the Weekly Mercury*, November 11 and 25 and December 9, 1776. See also Minty, "Mobilization and Voluntarism," chap. 1.

63. Linda Colley, "The Apotheosis of George III: Loyalty, Royalty and the British Nation, 1760–1820," *Past & Present* 102, no. 1 (February 1984): 94–129, and *Britons: Forging the Nation 1707–1837* (New Haven, CT: Yale University Press, 1992), chap. 5; Marilyn Morris, *The British Monarchy and the French Revolution* (New Haven, CT: Yale University Press, 1998), chap. 8; Andrew Jackson O'Shaughnessy, *The Men Who Lost America: British Leadership, the American Revolution, and the Fate of the Empire* (New Haven, CT: Yale University Press, 2013), 43–46.

64. "Pleasing terror," Tatum, Jr., ed., *Ambrose Serle*, 130; "so noble an Appearance," *New-York Gazette; and the Weekly Mercury*, October 28, 1776; "a monument of insult,"

William Tryon to Lord George Germain, November 26, 1776, Stokes, ed., *Iconography of Manhattan Island*, 5:1032; "stick of wood," *New York Gazette; and Weekly Mercury*, January 18, 1770.

65. *Royal American Gazette*, January 23, 1777.

66. Paul Leicester Ford, ed., *The Journals of Hugh Gaine, Printer*, vol. II, *Journals and Letters* (New York: Dodd, Mead & Co., 1902), 35.

67. *New-York Gazette; and the Weekly Mercury*, June 9, 1777. See also Friedrich von Muenchhausen, *At General Howe's Side, 1776–1778: The Diary of General William Howe's Aide de Camp, Captain Friedrich von Muenchhausen*, trans. Ernst Kipping, annot. Samuel Smith (Monmouth Beach, NJ: Philip Freneau Press, 1974), 13.

68. *Royal American Gazette*, September 25, 1777.

69. *New-York Gazette; and the Weekly Mercury*, September 29, 1777.

6. The British Lion Is Rouzed

1. Joyce Lee Malcolm, *The Tragedy of Benedict Arnold: An American Life* (New York: Pegasus, 2018); Stephen Brumwell, *Turncoat: Benedict Arnold and the Crisis of American Liberty* (New Haven, CT: Yale University Press, 2018); Willard Sterne Randall, *Benedict Arnold: Patriot and Traitor* (New York: Morrow, 1990); James Kirby Martin, *Benedict Arnold, Revolutionary Hero: An American Warrior Reconsidered* (New York: New York University Press, 1997).

2. Linda Colley, *Captives: Britain, Empire, and the World, 1600–1850* (London: Pimlico, 2003), 203–8; Judith L. Van Buskirk, *Generous Enemies: Patriots and Loyalists in Revolutionary New York* (Philadelphia: University of Pennsylvania Press, 2002), 91–105; Sarah Knott, *Sensibility and the American Revolution* (Chapel Hill: University of North Carolina Press, 2009), 153–84.

3. Most famously, in Philadelphia a crowd of patriotic citizens twice burned in effigy their former and not well-liked military governor. Benjamin H. Irvin, "The Streets of Philadelphia: Crowds, Congress, and the Political Culture of Revolution, 1774–1783," *Pennsylvania Magazine of History and Biography* 129, no. 1 (January 2005): 32–44. Patriot writers also necessarily sought to turn the once acclaimed general into a dangerous and foreign enemy by placing him alongside Britain's other nefarious allies, Indians and runaway slaves. Robert Parkinson, *The Common Cause: Creating Race and Nation in the American Revolution* (Chapel Hill: University of North Carolina Press, 2016), 477–78.

4. Patriot printers produced their own version of the address in which Arnold admitted to defecting on the grounds that his "ruling passion is, and ever has been, vanity and a love of money." For example, see *Pennsylvania Packet or the General Advertiser*, October 17, 1780. See also Charles Royster, "'The Nature of Treason': Revolutionary Virtue and American Reactions to Benedict Arnold," *William and Mary Quarterly* 36, no. 2 (April 1979): 164–93.

5. The first address appeared in all four communities: *Rivington's Gazette*, October 10, 1780; *Royal Gazette* [Kingston], November 23, 1780; *Caledonian Mercury*, November 20, 1780; *Scots Magazine*, 42 (November 1780), 595–96. Anthony Henry was unable to publish the address in his Nova Scotia gazette for want of space. *Nova Scotia Gazette: and the Weekly Chronicle*, January 2, 1781. By 1780, however, many Haligonians subscribed to

Rivington's newspaper and would have been able to read it there. *Nova-Scotia Gazette: and the Weekly Chronicle*, February 13, 1781. Patriot printers carried the address with a short introductory paragraph arguing that nothing Arnold wrote was true. For example, see *Pennsylvania Packet or the General Advertiser*, October 17, 1780.

6. American colonists were offered direct representation in Parliament, complete control over taxation, a withdrawal of British troops in peacetime, the permanent establishment of Congress, and a guarantee that colonial and customs officials would be drawn from residents of their respective colonies. Those who had participated in the rebellion were also promised full pardon, amnesty, and indemnity. Andrew Jackson O'Shaughnessy, *The Men Who Lost America: British Leadership, the American Revolution, and the Fate of the Empire* (New Haven, CT: Yale University Press, 2013), 61–65. On Patriot efforts to discount the commissioners, see Leonard J. Sadosky, *Revolutionary Negotiations: Indians, Empires, and Diplomats in the Founding of America* (Charlottesville: University of Virginia Press, 2009), 106–15; Parkinson, *Common Cause*, 384–97.

7. Benedict Arnold, *To the inhabitants of America . . . October 7, 1780* (New York, 1780), Evans 16701.

8. That this proclamation also appeared in all four communities suggests that it was more than just a recruitment advertisement. *Rivington's Gazette*, October 23 to December 6, 1780; *Royal Gazette* [Jamaica], November 25, 1780; *Edinburgh Advertiser*, December 1, 1780; *Scots Magazine*, 42 (December 1780), 596–98; *Nova Scotia Gazette: and the Weekly Chronicle*, January 9, 1781. Several other English, Scottish, and Irish newspapers carried the proclamation, as well. For example, see *London Packet; Or, New Lloyd's Evening Post*, December 1, 1780; *Dublin Evening Post*, December 5, 1780; *Aberdeen Journal; And North-British Magazine*, December 11, 1780.

9. O'Shaughnessy, *Men Who Lost America*, 154–64, 166–67; Troy O. Bickham, *Making Headlines: The American Revolution as Seen through the British Press* (DeKalb: Northern Illinois University Press, 2009), 105–17.

10. *Rivington's Gazette*, March 21, 1778.

11. Kathleen Wilson argues that the general public in England resisted efforts to enlist, but that does not seem to be the case in Glasgow. *The Sense of the People: Politics, Culture and Imperialism in England, 1715–1785* (Cambridge: Cambridge University Press, 1995), 253.

12. *Caledonian Mercury*, March 11, 1778. See also Edward Curtis, *The Organization of the British Army in the American Revolution* (1926; reprint: New York: AMS Press, 1969), 75–77; Steven Conway, "The Politics of British Military and Naval Mobilization, 1775–83," *English Historical Review* 112, no. 449 (November 1997): 1179–1201.

13. Eliga H. Gould, *The Persistence of Empire: British Political Culture in the Age of the American Revolution* (Chapel Hill: University of North Carolina Press, 2000), 156–64; Gillian Russell, *The Theatres of War: Performance, Politics, and Society, 1793–1815* (New York: Oxford University Press, 1995), 33–46. For contemporary accounts of the king reviewing the encampments, see *Morning Chronicle, and London Advertiser*, October 21 and November 4, 1778.

14. *Glasgow Mercury*, January 8, 1778; *Scots Magazine*, 40 (January 1778), 48. The address was exchanged in several London newspapers. For example, see *London Gazette*, January 17, 1778.

15. On news of a French war, see *Glasgow Mercury*, January 8, 1778. Other communities in Scotland took part in enlistment drives early in 1778. For example, see *Glasgow Mercury*, January 8 and February 19, 1778; *Caledonian Mercury*, February 7 and 21 and March 21, 1778.

16. *Glasgow Mercury*, January 8, 1778; *Scots Magazine*, 40 (January 1778), 48; *Rivington's Gazette*, March 21, 1778.

17. *Caledonian Mercury*, January 17, 1778. See also *Glasgow Mercury*, January 8 and March 19, 1778. One writer remarked that Glaswegians "have ever been distinguished for their loyalty and patriotism; but upon no occasion have they exerted themselves more than in the present case." *London Chronicle*, January 15, 1778.

18. *Newcastle Chronicle Or, Weekly Advertiser*, January 31, 1778. Similar processions occurred in Perth and Strathaven when the Dukes of Atholl and Hamilton, respectively, arrived to fill their regiments. *Glasgow Mercury*, January 15 and February 12, 1778.

19. For example, see James Denholm, *The History of the City of Glasgow and Suburbs* (Glasgow: Printed by and for R. Chapman, 1798), 38–39; James Cleland, *Annals of Glasgow: Comprising an Account of the Public Buildings, Charities, and the Rise and Progress of the City* (Glasgow: Printed by James Hedderwick, 1816), 1:35; Robert Reid, *Old Glasgow and Its Environs: Historical and Topographical* (Glasgow: David Robertson, 1864), 166–70.

20. *Rivington's Gazette*, March 21, 1778.

21. *Rivington's Gazette*, April 4, 1778.

22. In part, this narrative had to do with the unwillingness of British officials to employ Loyalists in active military service. Henry Clinton believed they could not be trusted—further evidence of the difficulties of defining loyalties in the midst of a civil war—and feared their lack of training and discipline threatened the safety of British regulars. Paul H. Smith, *Loyalists and Redcoats: A Study in British Revolutionary Policy* (New York: W.W. Norton, 1972), chap. 3; Philip Ranlet, *The New York Loyalists* (Knoxville: University of Tennessee Press, 1986), 106–19; Ruma Chopra, *Unnatural Rebellion: Loyalists in New York City during the Revolution* (Charlottesville: University of Virginia Press, 2011), 103–7, 114–22.

23. *Rivington's Gazette*, April 11, 1778. Timothy M. Barnes and Robert C. Calhoon characterize these sentiments as belonging only to a small minority of extremists, though the success of the recruitment drives suggests their views enjoyed broad support among loyal refugees in the city. "Loyalist Discourse and the Moderation of the American Revolution," in *Tory Insurgents: The Loyalist Perception and Other Essays*, ed. Robert M. Calhoon, Timothy M. Barnes, and Robert S. Davis (Columbia: University of South Carolina Press, 2010), 173–75.

24. *Rivington's Gazette*, May 2, 16, and 20, 1778.

25. Advertisements for the Caledonian Volunteers and Lord Rawdon's Volunteers of Ireland appeared in *Rivington's Gazette*, May 2, 1778.

26. Thomas Jones, *History of New York During the Revolutionary War* (New York: Printed for the New York Historical Society, 1879), 1:264–5.

27. *Rivington's Gazette*, February 21, 1778; *New-York Gazette; and The Weekly Mercury*, February 23, 1778. By the end of 1778, as many as 7,400 men served in various provincial regiments, almost double the number from a year before. The number increased to nearly 9,000 in December 1779 and more than 10,000 by the end of 1780. Smith, *Loyalists and Redcoats*, 77.

28. In the summer of 1776, Congress sent William Bingham to St. Pierre, the main port at Martinique, to oversee the privateering operation and to encourage French officials to support the war. Robert C. Alberts, *The Golden Voyage: The Life and Times of William Bingham, 1752–1804* (Boston: Houghton Mifflin, 1969); Margaret L. Brown, "William Bingham, Agent of the Continental Congress in Martinique," *Pennsylvania Magazine of History and Biography* 61, no. 1 (January 1937): 54–87; Selwyn H. H. Carrington, *The British West Indies during the American Revolution* (Providence, RI: Foris Publications, 1988), chap. 6.

29. *London Evening Post*, February 7, 1778.

30. *Kentish Gazette*, January 10, 1778.

31. Dalling to Governor Comte D'Argout, January 31, 1778, *Naval Documents of the American Revolution*, ed. Michael J. Crawford (Washington, DC: Naval Historical Center, 2005), 11:252–53. See also Dalling to Germain, April 25, 1778, *Naval Documents of the American Revolution*, ed. Michael J. Crawford (Washington, DC: Naval History and Heritage Command, 2013), 12:194–95; *Jamaica Gazette*, February 21, 1778; *Daily Advertiser* [London], April 25, 1778.

32. *Hampshire Chronicle*, January 19, 1778.

33. For example, see *Reading Mercury*, March 23, 1778.

34. To the King's Most Excellent Majesty in Council, November 21, 1777, *Journals of the Assembly of Jamaica* (Kingston: Alexander Aikman, 1802), 7:18. The assembly also increased extraordinary taxes at a rate greater than at any point in the past twenty years, with the revenue mostly used to improve military barracks and fortifications. Andrew O'Shaughnessy, *An Empire Divided: The American Revolution and the British Caribbean* (Philadelphia: University of Pennsylvania Press, 2000), 197.

35. *Derby Mercury*, January 2, 1778.

36. *Cumberland Pacquet, and Ware's Whitehaven Advertiser*, March 10, 1778.

37. Eliphalet Fitch, a Boston native who moved to Kingston in 1761, carried on an extensive smuggling operation with the Spanish throughout much of the war, supplying them with ships, goods, and intelligence. J. H. Parry, "Eliphalet Fitch: A Yankee Trader in Jamaica during the War of Independence," *History: The Journal of the Historical Association* 40, no. 138/139 (February 1955): 85–98.

38. A copy of the essay appeared in *Rivington's Gazette*, June 27, 1778, under the heading "*The Jamaica Gazette*, 14 March 1778." Unfortunately, there are no extant copies of the original issue of the *Jamaica Gazette*.

39. *Royal Pennsylvania Gazette*, May 5, 1778.

40. Parker to Secretary of the Admiralty Philip Stephens, April 19, 1778, in Crawford, ed., *Naval Documents*, 12:143.

41. Between 1775 and 1783, American privateers captured at least 225 ships traveling to and from Nova Scotia. Julian Gwyn, *Frigates and Foremasts: The North American Squadron in Nova Scotia Waters, 1745–1815* (Vancouver: University of British Columbia Press, 2003), 56. The privateer war mattered a great deal to Haligonian merchants, as evidenced by their reaction in the spring of 1777 to British naval commander Sir George Collier's capture of the *Rainbow*. After entering the harbour, "the Merchantmen . . . Ornamented their Vessels with Colors, firing their Guns, and huzzaing, as the Rainbow passed along, giving every Token of the highest Joy and Satisfaction." "A Detail of some particular Services performed in America during the Years 1776–1777–1778.

& 1779 (Compiled from Journals & original Papers)," Andre De Coppet Collection, C0036, no. 15, Princeton University.

42. Arbuthnot to Germain, December 23, 1777, in *Report on Canadian Archives, 1894*, ed. Douglas Brymner (Ottawa, ON: S.E. Dawson, 1895), 374.

43. Massey to Germain, December 10, 1777, in Brymner, ed., *Canadian Archives*, 373–74.

44. The Memorial and Petition of the Subscribers, late Inhabitants of the Province of Nova Scotia, March 3, 1778, Papers of the Continental Congress, 1774–1789, Memorials Addressed to Congress, item 41, vol. 7, 21–23, National Archives and Records Administration (hereafter cited as NARA). Congress's Committee for Foreign Affairs wrote in May 1778 that "Nova Scotia has long ago expressed its wishes to be adopted by Us, and now afresh Solicits." Committee of Foreign Affairs to William Lee, May 14, 1778, *Letters of Delegates to Congress*, vol. 9, *February 1–May 31, 1778*, ed. Paul H. Smith et al. (Washington, DC: Library of Congress, 1982), 665. Congress read the address on May 6 and appointed a committee to review its contents. On May 21, the committee reported that they supported an invasion, but wanted to wait until France joined the war, which "shall render an attempt upon Nova Scotia more likely to succeed." *Journals of the Continental Congress, 1774–1789*, vol. 11, *May 2–September 1, 1778*, ed. Worthington C. Ford et al. (Washington, DC: Government Printing Office, 1908), 498, 518.

45. *Independent Chronicle and the Universal Advertiser*, June 18, 1778. It is likely that Congress's report was the source for this story.

46. "Letter-Book of Captain Alexander McDonald, of the Royal Highland Emigrants, 1775–1779," in *Collections of the New-York Historical Society for the Year 1882* (New York: Printed for the Society, 1883), 395.

47. *Nova Scotia Gazette: and the Weekly Chronicle*, January 2, 1781.

48. Arbuthnot to Germain, May 27, 1778, in Brymner, ed., *Canadian Archives*, 376–77.

49. Arbuthnot to Germain, April 8, 1778, in Brymner, ed., *Canadian Archives*, 376.

50. Éloi Degrâce, "Bourg, Joseph-Mathurin," *Dictionary of Canadian Biography*, vol. 4 (Toronto: University of Toronto/Université Laval, 1979), accessed April 5, 2017, http://www.biographi.ca/en/bio/bourg_joseph_mathurin_4E.html.

51. J. B. Brebner, *The Neutral Yankees of Nova Scotia: A Marginal Colony During the Revolutionary Years* (1937; reprint: New York: Russell & Russell, 1970), 323–27; George Rawlyk, *Nova Scotia's Massachusetts: A Study of Massachusetts–Nova Scotia Relations, 1630–1784* (Montreal: McGill-Queen's University Press, 1973), 241–46. In 1775, Allan joined Jonathan Eddy in his failed rebellion and in early 1776 petitioned the Massachusetts assembly and Congress to invade the colony. In 1777, Congress appointed Allan superintendent of Indian affairs for the Eastern Department. Alice R. Stewart, "Allan, John," *Dictionary of Canadian Biography*, vol. 5 (Toronto: University of Toronto/Université Laval, 1983), accessed April 6, 2017, http://www.biographi.ca/en/bio/allan_john_5E.html.

52. Francklin to Germain, June 6, 1778, in Brymner, ed., *Canadian Archives*, 378. The petitioners to the Massachusetts assembly also claimed that "the Residence of the Mischeat and Mickamack tribes of Indians . . . on several occasions have manifested a friendly Disposition to the [Patriot] Cause." Memorial and Petition of the Subscribers, 22.

53. *Nova-Scotia Gazette: and the Weekly Chronicle*, October 6, 1778.

54. Hughes to Germain, October 12, 1778, in Brymner, ed., *Canadian Archives*, 380.

55. Brebner, *Neutral Yankees*, 313.

56. Quoted in Dror Wahrman, "The English Problem of Identity in the American Revolution," *American Historical Review* 106, no. 4 (October 2001): 7.

57. Several historians have looked at how the alliance shaped popular understandings of Britishness within certain regions of the empire. Gould, *Persistence of Empire*, chap. 5; O'Shaughnessy, *Empire Divided*, chap. 9; Bickham, *Making Headlines*, chaps. 5 and 6; Stephen Conway, "'A Joy Unknown for Years Past:' The American War, Britishness, and the Celebration of Rodney's Victory at the Saints," *History* 86, no. 282 (April 2001): 180–99, and "From Fellow-Nationals to Foreigners: British Perceptions of the Americans, circa 1739–1783," *William and Mary Quarterly* 59, no. 1 (January 2002): 65–100.

58. *Rivington's Gazette*, June 6, 1778.

59. *Rivington's Gazette*, June 13, 1778.

60. *Nova Scotia Gazette: and the Weekly Chronicle*, January 12, 1779.

61. *Glasgow Mercury*, November 12, 1778.

62. *Rivington's Gazette*, January 2, 1779.

63. *Nova Scotia Gazette: and the Weekly Chronicle*, September 5, 1780.

64. Don Francisco Saavedra de Sangronis, *Journal of Don Francisco Saavedra de Sangronis during the Commission which he had in his Charge from 25 June until the 20th of the same month of 1783*, ed. Francisco Morales Padrón, trans. Aileen Moore Topping (Gainesville: University of Florida Press, 1989), 50–51.

65. *Rivington's Gazette*, July 29, 1778; *Caledonian Mercury*, October 28, 1778.

66. *Rivington's Gazette*, August 22, 1778; *Caledonian Mercury*, November 4, 1778; *Glasgow Mercury*, November 5, 1778; *Scots Magazine*, 40 (November 1778), 598–99.

67. *Rivington's Gazette*, May 20, 1780; *Nova-Scotia Gazette: and the Weekly Chronicle*, June 6, 1780; *Caledonian Mercury*, June 26, 1780; *Glasgow Mercury*, June 29, 1780; *Scots Magazine*, 42 (June 1780), 300; *Royal Gazette* [Kingston], July 1, 1780.

68. For example, see "The able Doctor, or America Swallowing the Bitter Draught, [May 1, 1774]" in *The American Revolution in Drawings and Prints, A Checklist of 1765–1790 Graphics in the Library of Congress*, ed. Donald H. Cresswell (Washington, DC: Library of Congress, 1975), 270.

69. Diplomatic historians have argued for the importance of the alliance in shifting the government's attention away from the colonial rebellion and toward a war with France. H. M. Scott, *British Foreign Policy in the Age of the American Revolution* (Oxford: Clarendon Press, 1990), 277; Jeremy Black, *War for America: The Fight for Independence* (New York: St. Martin's Press, 1991), 146; Piers Mackesy, *The War for America, 1775–1783* (Cambridge, MA: Harvard University Press, 1964), 147–61. Eliga Gould argues that the alliance was most important to Britain, because France's use of a colonial revolt to justify war against their old enemies ultimately threatened the sovereignty of every European state. "American Independence and Britain's Counter-Revolution," *Past & Present*, 154 (February 1997): 119–21.

70. *Scots Magazine*, 40 (August 1778), 439. See also Atticus's essay in the *Caledonian Mercury*, September 21, 1778; *Scots Magazine*, 40 (September 1778), 457–58; *Jamaica Mercury, and Kingston Weekly Advertiser*, September 11, 1779.

71. *Royal Gazette* [Kingston], May 15, 1779.

72. *Rivington's Gazette*, June 13, 1778. See also *New-York Gazette; and The Weekly Mercury*, September 21, 1778.

73. Saut[d] June 6, 1778, Diary of Alex[r] Houston at New York and Shelburne, N.S., 1778–1788, MG 1, vol. 483c, Nova Scotia Archives and Records Management (hereafter cited as NSARM). "Let me seriously ask you, where is your liberty now?" asked another Loyalist writer. "You were told that [the rebellion] was to avoid the establishing of *Popery*. . . . Is not Popery now as much established by law in your state as any other religion? So that your Governor and all your rulers may be *Papists*, and you may have a Mass-House in every corner of your country." *Rivington's Gazette*, January 6, 1779.

74. *Rivington's Gazette*, August 22, 1778; *Caledonian Mercury*, November 9, 1778; *Scots Magazine*, 40 (November 1778), 598–99.

75. *Glasgow Mercury*, November 12, 1778. The following April, a letter taken from Gaine's New York newspaper reported again that "the people daily grow more and more disaffected to the Congress's alliance with a Popish King." *Glasgow Mercury*, April 1, 1779.

76. *Rivington's Gazette*, October 28, 1778.

77. *Rivington's Gazette*, June 20, 1778. See also Edgar's essay in *Rivington's Gazette*, October 10, 1778.

78. *Rivington's Gazette*, September 23, 1778.

79. *Rivington's Gazette*, November 25, 1778.

7. In Defence of the Protestant Religion

1. *London Evening-Post*, May 30, 1780.

2. *London Evening-Post*, June 3, 1780.

3. The best contemporary account of the riots is *London Evening-Post*, June 6 to 10, 1780. Many historians have written about the riots. See J. Paul de Castro, *The Gordon Riots* (London: Milford, 1926); Christopher Hibbert, *King Mob: The Story of Lord George Gordon and the Riots of 1780* (1958; reprint, Stroud, UK: Sutton, 2004); George Rudé, "The Gordon Riots: A Study of the Rioters and Their Victims," *Transactions of the Royal Historical Society* 5th ser., vol. 6 (January 1956): 93–114; Nicholas Rogers, "Crowd and People in the Gordon Riots," in *The Transformation of Political Culture: England and Germany in the Late Eighteenth Century*, ed. Eckhart Hellmuth (Oxford: Oxford University Press, 1990), 39–55; Eugene Charlton Black, *The Association: British Extraparliamentary Organization, 1769–1793* (Cambridge, MA: Harvard University Press, 1963), 131–73; Ian Haywood and John Seed, eds., *The Gordon Riots: Politics, Culture and Insurrection in Late 18th Century Britain* (Cambridge,: Cambridge University Press, 2015); Colin Haydon, "The Gordon Riots in the English Provinces," *Historical Research* 63, 152 (October 1990): 354–59, "'Popery at St. James's': The Conspiracy Theses of William Payne, Thomas Hollis, and Lord George Gordon," in *Conspiracies and Conspiracy Theory in Early Modern Europe: From the Waldensians to the French Revolution*, ed. Barry Coward and Julian Swann (Aldershot, UK: Ashgate, 2004), 173–95, and *Anti-Catholicism in Eighteenth-Century England, c. 1714–80: A Political and Social Study* (New York: Manchester University Press, 1993), 204–44.

4. Cards were distributed among the populace to be carried as a badge of support for the cause. One proclaimed that "Georg 3[d] is a Roman Catholick. No popery Down with

it. Dethrone him or else he will Masacree you all. If your king's Not Dethron'd he will be your Utter ruin for he is a true Roman Catholick . . . he should lose his Head." Letter from Jn° Mansel, Lᵗ Colˡ, 3rd Dragoon, Artilery Ground to [unknown], June 12, 1780, Public Records Office (hereafter cited as PRO) WO 34/103/367–68, The National Archives (hereafter cited as TNA). See also letter from Richard Worsley, Hyde Park Camp to [unknown], June 11, 1780, PRO WO 34/103/325–26, TNA.

5. It was later reported that 1,294 prisoners escaped during the riots. PRO PC 1/3097: June 15, 1780, TNA.

6. Rudé, "Gordon Riots," 99, 105. These are conservative numbers based on official government records. Hibbert suggests the total number of those killed was closer to 850. *King Mob*, 144n1.

7. Accurate battle death statistics for the American War for Independence are especially difficult to come by, though it appears that deaths typically numbered less than five hundred in any given battle. Henry H. Peckham, ed., *The Toll of Independence: Engagements and Battle Casualties of the American Revolution* (Chicago: University of Chicago Press, 1974). One exception is the 1782 Battle of the Saints, where contemporary reports estimate that as many as six thousand French sailors and soldiers perished in the fighting. Andrew Jackson O'Shaughnessy, *The Men Who Lost America: British Leadership, the American Revolution, and the Fate of the Empire* (New Haven, CT: Yale University Press, 2013), 315.

8. See especially de Castro, *Gordon Riots*; Hibbert, *King Mob*; Black, *Association*, 131–73, Haywood and Seed, eds., *The Gordon Riots*. For an exception, see my article, "'In Favour of Popery': Patriotism, Protestantism, and the Gordon Riots in the Revolutionary British Atlantic," *Journal of British Studies* 52, no. 1 (January 2013): 79–102.

9. Robert Kent Donovan, "Voices of Distrust: The Expression of Anti-Catholic Feeling in Scotland, 1778–1781," *Innes Review* 30 (June 1979): 62–63. The Irish bill was more modest. It allowed Catholics to lease land, but only for up to 999 years, denying them the opportunity to acquire political rights through land ownership. The bill did, however, abolish the gavel system, which sought to break up the Catholic landed aristocracy by requiring landowners to either divide their land among all sons upon their death or give it to the eldest son if he converted to Protestantism. Robert E. Burns, "The Catholic Relief Act in Ireland, 1778," *Church History* 32, no. 2 (June 1963): 181–206.

10. This was true of places like Quebec, Grenada, and to a lesser degree Nova Scotia. Peter M. Doll, *Revolution, Religion, and National Identity: Imperial Anglicanism in British North America, 1745–1795* (Madison, NJ: Farleigh Dickinson University Press, 2000), 146–53; Hannah Weiss Muller, "Bonds of Belonging: Subjecthood and the British Empire," *Journal of British Studies* 53, no. 1 (January 2014): 29–58; Karen Stanbridge, "Quebec and the Irish Catholic Relief Act of 1778: An Institutional Approach," *Journal of Historical Sociology* 16, no. 3 (September 2003): 375–404. For Nova Scotia, see chap. 3 and conclusion.

11. By the 1770s, there were roughly eighty thousand Catholics living in England (1.3 percent of the population) and thirty thousand in Scotland (2.5 percent), whereas Irish Catholics amounted to between 70 and 80 percent of all Irelanders. Robert Kent Donovan, "The Military Origins of the Roman Catholic Relief Programme of 1778," *Historical Journal* 28, no. 1 (March 1985): 82–83. For more on the nature of Highland

loyalty, see Matthew P. Dziennik, *The Fatal Land: War, Empire, and the Highland Soldier in British America* (New Haven, CT: Yale University Press, 2015), 184–97.

12. Letter from Oughton to Lord Suffolk, Edinburgh, April 27, 1778, PRO SP 54/47/131, TNA. See also letter from Oughton to Lord Suffolk, Edinburgh, May 19, 1778, PRO SP 54/47/135, TNA.

13. Letter from Oughton to George III, Edinburgh, September 7, 1778, PRO SP 54/47/187, TNA. See also letter from W. Hamilton to Lord Viscount Weymouth, Edinburgh, October 29, 1779, PRO SP 54/47/346-47, TNA.

14. Robert Kent Donovan, *No Popery and Radicalism: Opposition to Roman Catholic Relief in Scotland, 1778–1782* (New York: Garland Publishing, 1987).

15. *Scotland's Opposition to the Popish Bill: A Collection of All the Declarations and Resolutions . . . for Preventing the Growth of Popery* (Edinburgh: Printed by David Paterson, 1780), 4; *Caledonian Mercury*, October 17 and 26, 1778; *Scots Magazine*, 40 (October 1778), 565–66.

16. *Glasgow Mercury*, October 22, 1778; *Scots Magazine*, 40 (December 1778), 685.

17. Stuart Salmon, "The Loyalist Regiments of the American Revolutionary War, 1775–1783" (Ph.D. diss., University of Stirling, 2009), 96–97. According to Philip Ranlet, by 1780 Irish soldiers made up nearly 38 percent of the Queen's Rangers, though we know nothing of their religious affiliation. *The New York Loyalists* (Knoxville: University of Tennessee Press, 1986), 113. During St. Patrick's Day celebrations in March 1779, "four hundred *strapping Fellows*" of Rawdon's Volunteers marched through the city. *New-York Gazette; and The Weekly Mercury*, March 22, 1779. For Halifax, see Terrence Murphy, "The Emergence of Maritime Catholicism, 1781–1830," *Acadiensis* 13, no. 2 (Spring 1984): 29–32. In Jamaica, Edward Long predicted that as much as a third of the white population in 1774 was Scottish. *The History of Jamaica: Or, General Survey of the Ancient and Modern State of that Island* (1774; reprint, Montreal: McGill-Queen's University Press, 2002), 2:287; David Dobson, *Scottish Emigration to Colonial America, 1607–1785* (Athens: University of Georgia Press, 1994), 122–34. William Dalrymple's Loyal Irish Corps was stationed in Kingston in the latter years of the war, though it is unclear whether his soldiers were Catholic. *Scots Magazine*, 41 (December 1779), 670.

18. O. F. Christie, ed., *The Diary of the Revd. William Jones, 1777–1821* (London: Brentano, 1929), 39, 42. See also *Morning Chronicle, and London Advertiser*, October 8, 1778; *Saunders's News-Letter*, October 13 and November 14, 1778

19. *Reading Mercury*, January 11, 1779.

20. Executive Council Minutes, August 27, 1778, RG 1, 170: 264–68, Public Archives of Nova Scotia (hereafter cited as PANS).

21. *New-York Gazette; and the Weekly Mercury*, August 3, 1778; "Journal of Lieutenant John Charles Philip Von Krafft, of the Regiment Von Bose, 1776–1784," in *Collections of the New-York Historical Society for the Year 1882* (New York: Printed for the Society, 1883), 58.

22. *The Journal of a Voyage from Charlestown, S.C., to London, Undertaken during the American Revolution. By a Daughter of an Eminent American Loyalist [Louisa Susannah Wells] in the Year 1778. And Written from Memory Only in 1779* (New York: Printed for the New York Historical Society, 1906), 23; "Proceedings of a Board of General Officers of the British Army at New York, 1781," in *Collections of the New-York Historical Society for the Year 1916* (New York: Printed for the Society, 1916), 99–101.

23. Calhoon attributes the increased militancy of Loyalist refugees after 1778, not to France's entry in the war, but to the Loyalists' belief that the rebellion was collapsing, and a quick, retributive bout of violence would end the war more quickly. Robert M. Calhoon, "Civil, Revolutionary, or Partisan: The Loyalists and the Nature of the War for Independence," in *Tory Insurgents: The Loyalist Perception and Other Essays*, ed. Robert M. Calhoon, Timothy M. Barnes, and Robert S. Davis (Columbia: University of South Carolina Press, 2010), esp. 212–16.

24. Robert Parkinson, *The Common Cause: Creating Race and Nation in the American Revolution* (Chapel Hill: University of North Carolina Press, 2016), 384–99.

25. *Manifesto and Proclamation. To the Members of the Congress . . . This Third Day of October, 1778* (New York, 1778), Evans 15832. The Loyalist judge William Smith had a hand in writing the manifesto. William H. W. Sabine, ed., *Historical Memoirs from 26 August 1778 to 12 November 1783 of William Smith* (New York: New York Times & Arno Press, 1971), 2:28–31. Rivington printed thirteen separate copies, one for each assembly, which Clinton personally signed. Sabine, ed., *Historical Memoirs*, 2:31. Rivington also took the unprecedented step of providing a free copy of the manifesto to those who purchased the October 7 issue of his gazette. He then printed the manifesto in nine consecutive issues of his paper, and once in German. *Rivington's Gazette*, October 7 to November 4, 1778. The German addition appears in the October 14 issue. Hugh Gaine also carried the manifesto in his paper for four consecutive weeks. *New-York Gazette; and The Weekly Mercury*, October 12 to November 2, 1778. Many Patriot newspapers published the manifesto. For example, see *Pennsylvania Packet or the General Advertiser*, October 15, 1778. The manifesto appeared in Glasgow. *Scots Magazine*, 40 (November 1778), 607–10. There are no extant copies of the *Nova-Scotia Gazette* or any of the Jamaican newspapers for the last months of 1778, though it is very likely that the manifesto made its way to both cities.

26. Sam Adams authored the manifesto. Harry Alonzo Cushing, ed. *The Writings of Samuel Adams* (New York: G.P. Putnam's Sons, 1908), 4:84–86.

27. In September, Massachusetts passed an act banishing more than three hundred Loyalists from the state, and the following spring, the assembly agreed to confiscate the property of known Loyalists. Refugees in New York City responded with a declaration of war against "the rebels and their adherents" that was read in both Halifax and Glasgow. *Rivington's Gazette*, February 13, 1779; *Scots Magazine*, 41 (March 1779), 147; *Nova-Scotia Gazette: and the Weekly Chronicle*, May 18, 1779. The New York Assembly passed a similar confiscation bill in October 1779, though county committees had been confiscating Loyalist property since the start of the war. Alexander Flick, *Loyalism in New York during the American Revolution* (New York: Macmillan, 1901), chap. 7; Matthew P. Dziennik, "New York's Refugees and Political Authority in Revolutionary America," *William and Mary Quarterly* 77, 1 (January 2020), 65–96.

28. *Rivington's Gazette*, October 10, 1778. See also *Rivington's Gazette*, December 16, 1778.

29. *Rivington's Gazette*, December 8, 1778. See also *Royal American Gazette*, January 28, 1779.

30. Kacy Dowd Tillman, *Stripped and Script: Loyalist Women Writers of the American Revolution* (Amherst: University of Massachusetts Press, 2019); Janice Potter-MacKinnon, *While the Women Only Wept: Loyalist Refugee Women* (Montreal: McGill-Queen's University Press, 1993); Judith L. Van Buskirk, *Generous Enemies: Patriots*

and Loyalists in Revolutionary New York (Philadelphia: University of Pennsylvania Press, 2002), chap. 2, esp. 63–65; Mary Beth Norton, "Eighteenth-Century American Women in Peace and War: The Case of the Loyalists," *William and Mary Quarterly 33*, no. 3 (July 1976): 386–409; Konstantin Dierks, *In My Power: Letter Writing and Communications in Early America* (Philadelphia: University of Pennsylvania Press, 2011), 218–20. Popular pro-British prints often ridiculed the presence of women in colonial protests for having abandoned their traditional roles as mothers and wives. For example, see "The Alternative of Williams-burg" and "Society of Patriotic Ladies, at Edenton in North Carolina," in *The American Revolution in Drawings and Prints: A Checklist of 1765–1790 Graphics in the Library of Congress*, ed. Donald H. Cresswell (Washington, DC: Library of Congress, 1975), 280–81.

31. *Rivington's Gazette*, January 6, 1779.

32. *Rivington's Gazette*, January 16, 1779. In February, Tryon reported to Germain that "Ladies in this City" had fitted out another privateer, *The Royal Charlotte*. Tryon to Germain, February 5, 1779, in *Documents Relative to the Colonial History of the State of New-York*, ed. E. B. O'Callaghan (Albany, NY: Weed, Parsons and Company, 1857), 8:757.

33. By the end of the year, more than seven thousand Loyalists served in provincial regiments, though Isaac Ogden believed the British could have gotten ten thousand had they focused their efforts on recruiting. Ruma Chopra, *Unnatural Rebellion: Loyalists in New York City during the Revolution* (Charlottesville: University of Virginia Press, 2011), 108–17.

34. Sabine, ed., *Historical Memoirs*, 2:58–59. In his letter to Germain, he removed mention of the Canadians. Tryon to Germain, December 24, 1778, in *Documents Relative*, 8:755–56.

35. Donovan, *No Popery*, 58; Hisashi Kuboyama, "The Politics of the People in Glasgow and the West of Scotland, 1707–c. 1785" (Ph.D. diss., University of Edinburgh, 2012), 150–57.

36. *Transactions of the Eighty-Five Societies, in and about Glasgow: United . . . to Oppose a Repeal of the Penal Statues against Papists in Scotland* (Glasgow: Printed by William Smith, 1779), 227–28.

37. Supplement to the Glasgow Journal, No. 1957, PRO SP 54/47/210-211, TNA; *Scotland's Opposition*, 31–2. See also *Scotland's Opposition*, 90, 193.

38. *Scotland's Opposition*, 59.

39. *Glasgow Mercury*, February 4, 1779; *Scotland's Opposition*, 63. See also "A True Whig," in Supplement to the Glasgow Journal, No. 1957; William Thom, *Achan's Trespass, in the Accursed Thing, Considered: A Sermon Preached in the Church of Govan on the Public Fast, February 26, 1778* (Glasgow: James Duncan, 1778), 42; *Eighteenth Century Collections Online*, Gale, accessed April 14, 2017, <http://find.gale.com/ecco/infomark.do ?&source=gale&prodId=ECCO&userGroupName=csufresno&tabID=T001&docId =CW118654922&type=multipage&contentSet=ECCOArticles&version=1 .0&docLevel=FASCIMILE>

40. *Scotland's Opposition*, 296, 154.

41. *Scotland's Opposition*, 193–94.

42. *Scotland's Opposition*, 56.

43. *Scotland's Opposition*, 46.

44. *Scotland's Opposition*, 63.

45. *Scotland's Opposition*, 154.

46. *Scots Magazine*, 41 (February 1779), 107.

47. *Scotland's Opposition*, 124; *Glasgow Mercury*, January 28, 1779.

48. *Scotland's Opposition*, 245.

49. *Scotland's Opposition*, 270–71; *Glasgow Mercury*, February 25, 1779.

50. *Glasgow Mercury*, January 28, 1779. Editors of the *Scots Magazine* declared the Carluke petition "the boldest that we have seen." *Scots Magazine*, 41 (February 1779), 109–10. A similar declaration appeared in *London Evening-Post*, February 9, 1779.

51. *Glasgow Mercury*, February 11, 1779; J. Oughton to Lord Suffolk, Edinburgh, February 12, 1779, PRO SP 54/47/228, TNA. An even more violent riot occurred at the same time in Edinburgh. *Glasgow Mercury*, February 11, 1779. Weeks before the riot in Glasgow, Oughton had warned the king of the likelihood of violence: "The people in all Parts have been alarmed with an Idea that Popery is about to be re-established among them. The Pulpits, Presbiteries, Synods, Burgess meetings, and associations all speak the same language, expressive of their Fears, and declaration of their Resolutions to oppose by all legal and constitutional means—Terms too often employed to cloak the worst of Purposes. The most moderate Clergy of the estab-lished Church are obliged, for their own sake, to join in the Cry; the enthusiastick Preachers, Nonjurors, and Republicans of all Denominations labour assiduously to spread the alarm." J. Oughton to the king, dated Carline Park [Edinburgh], January 21. 1779, PRO SP 54/47/206, TNA.

52. *Jamaica Mercury, and Kingston Weekly Advertiser*, May 8, 1779.

53. *Nova-Scotia Gazette: and the Weekly Chronicle*, June 1, 1779

54. For example, see *Nova-Scotia Gazette: and the Weekly Chronicle*, January 12, Feb-ruary 16 and 23, March 23, and May 18, 1779.

55. *Nova-Scotia Gazette: and the Weekly Chronicle*, March 30, 1779.

56. *Nova-Scotia Gazette: and the Weekly Chronicle*, April 6, 1779. The winner of the election was John George Pyke, a prominent merchant, militia officer, and supporter of the Crown. *Nova-Scotia Gazette: and the Weekly Chronicle*, May 25, 1779. Andrew Robb, "Pyke, John George," in *Dictionary of Canadian Biography*, vol. 6 (Toronto: Uni-versity of Toronto/Université Laval, 1987), accessed June 23, 2017, http://www.biographi.ca/en/bio/pyke_john_george_6E.html.

57. Lord Justice Clerk Thomas Miller to Lord Viscount Weymouth, Edinburgh, February 27, 1779, PRO SP 54/47/230, TNA.

58. *Scots Magazine*, 41 (March 1779), 131–33.

59. The report appeared in several London newspapers, which said it came from the "Glasgow Papers," though I have not been able to confirm this. For example, see *Public Advertiser*, March 17, 1779. For a report of the riot, see *Glasgow Mercury*, March 18, 1779.

60. *Scots Magazine*, 41 (March 1779), 134, 140.

61. Oughton to Weymouth, Caroline Park, October 9, 1779, PRO SP 54/47/342, TNA. Gordon drew support from the weaver community for his opposition to the repeal of the cambric laws. *Glasgow Mercury*, September 9, 1779; "A Short Account of the Kindly Reception the Right Honourable Lord George Gordon Met within the City of Glasgow, and Other Places in the West," in *Transactions of the Eighty-Five Private Societies*, 26–27.

62. Eliga H. Gould, *The Persistence of Empire: British Political Culture in the Age of the American Revolution* (Chapel Hill: University of North Carolina Press, 2000), 164–78, esp. 172–75.

63. *Caledonian Mercury*, December 1, 1779; *Glasgow Mercury*, December 9, 1779.

64. Andrew O'Shaughnessy, *An Empire Divided: The American Revolution and the British Caribbean* (Philadelphia: University of Pennsylvania Press, 2000), 188–89, and *Men Who Lost America*, 178–85.

65. T. M. Devine has written extensively on the increase in importance of the Caribbean trade in Glasgow. "A Glasgow Tobacco Merchant during the American War for Independence: Alexander Speirs of Elderslie, 1775 to 1781," *William and Mary Quarterly* 33, no. 3 (July 1976): 501–13; "An Eighteenth-Century Business Elite: Glasgow-West India Merchants, c. 1785–1815," *Scottish Historical Review* 57, no. 1 (April 1978): 40–67; "Did Slavery Make Scotia Great?," *Britain and the World* 4, no. 1 (March 2011): 40–64. See also Stephen Mullen, "The Glasgow West India Interest: Integration, Collaboration and Exploitation in the British Atlantic World, 1776–1846" (Ph.D. diss., University of Glasgow, 2015), chap. 2.

66. Petition of the Merchants of Glasgow to the King, January 21, 1779, PRO CO 5/116/50, TNA.

67. For more on the free trade crisis, see Maurice R. O'Connell, *Irish Politics and Social Conflict in the Age of the American Revolution* (Philadelphia: University of Pennsylvania Press, 1965), 129–67; Martyn J. Powell, *Britain and Ireland in the Eighteenth-Century Crisis of Empire* (New York: Palgrave Macmillan, 2003), 158–77; Vincent Morley, *Irish Opinion and the American Revolution* (Cambridge: Cambridge University Press, 2002), 223–30.

68. *Edinburgh Advertiser*, December 31, 1779; *Scots Magazine*, 41 (Appendix 1779), 728.

69. *Jamaica Mercury, And Kingston Weekly Advertiser*, November 20 and December 4 and 25, 1779.

70. Dalling to Germain, August 6–23, 1779, PRO CO 137/49/1-5, TNA; *Jamaica Mercury, And Kingston Weekly Advertiser*, September 4, 1779. By November, the owners of Lloyd's Coffeehouse in London were so sure of Jamaica falling to the French and Spanish that they began to offer insurance policies on the island's estates. *Caledonian Mercury*, November 3, 1779.

71. O'Shaughnessy, *Empire Divided*, 193.

72. *Jamaica Mercury, And Kingston Weekly Advertiser*, September 4, 1779. D'Estaing captured St. Vincent in June and Grenada in early July. Robert Neil McLarty, "Jamaica Prepares for Invasion, 1779," *Caribbean Quarterly* 4, no. 1 (January 1955): 62–63.

73. *Jamaica Mercury, And Kingston Weekly Advertiser*, October 2, 1779.

74. Samuel Jones to the Earl of Shelburne, Kingston, September 10, 1779, quoted in McLarty, "Jamaica Prepares," 65–66.

75. *Jamaica Mercury, And Kingston Weekly Advertiser*, May 15 and August 28, 1779.

76. Stephen Fuller argued from London that "the arming of Domestic Negroes is a policy . . . promising relief for the present, but pregnant with future evils." Quoted in O'Shaughnessy, *Empire Divided*, 181.

77. *Jamaica Mercury, And Kingston Weekly Advertiser*, August 21, 1779.

78. *Jamaica Mercury, And Kingston Weekly Advertiser*, August 28, 1779.

79. "Spirit of loyalty," *Jamaica Mercury, And Kingston Weekly Advertiser*, September 4, 1779; "take up arms," *Jamaica Mercury, And Kingston Weekly Advertiser*, August 14, 1779.

80. *Caledonian Mercury*, February 5, 1780. Gordon also presented a petition to Parliament from the eighty-five societies "praying for a repeal of the acts passed last session in favor of Papists." *Scots Magazine*, 42 (March 1780), 120.

81. *London Evening-Post*, May 11, 1780.

82. For reports of the riots in these four communities, see *Glasgow Mercury*, June 15, 22, and 29, 1780; *Rivington's Gazette*, August 23 and 26, 1780; *Royal Gazette* [Kingston], August 12, 19, and 26, 1780; *Nova-Scotia Gazette: and the Weekly Chronicle*, September 26 and November 14 and 28, 1780.

83. See especially Thomas Holcroft, *A Plain and Succinct Narrative of the Late Riots and Disturbances in the Cities of London and Westminster, and Borough of Southwark* (London, 1780). Hibbert's first chapter is titled "The Mad Scotchman." *King Mob*, ch. 1. Castro began his book by quoting Edward Gibbon, who said the riots were marked "by a dark and diabolical fanaticism." *Gordon Riots*, 1. Eugene Black titled his chapter on the riots "The Children of Darkness." *Association*, chap. 4.

84. *Rivington's Gazette*, September 6, 1780; *Scots Magazine*, 42 (July 1780), 344.

85. *Rivington's Gazette*, August 26, 1780. For the Methodist response, see *Rivington's Gazette*, September 3, 1780. For the relationship between antipopery and antipuritanism during the riots, see Peter W. Walker, "Tolerating Protestants: Antipopery, Antipuritanism, and Religious Toleration in Britain, 1776–1829," in *Against Popery: Anti-Catholicism and the British-American World*, ed. Evan Haefeli (Charlottesville: University of Virginia Press, forthcoming).

86. *Rivington's Gazette*, September 6, 1780; *Royal American Gazette*, September 19, 1780.

87. "Diabolical tumults," *Royal Gazette* [Kingston], August 12, 1780; "French money," *Glasgow Mercury*, June 15, 1780.

88. *Glasgow Mercury*, June 22, 1780.

89. *Scots Magazine*, 42 (July 1780), 344.

90. *Rivington's Gazette*, September 6, 1780. See also *New-York Gazette; and The Weekly Mercury*, September 4, 1780.

91. *Rivington's Gazette*, September 6, 1780.

92. *Nova Scotia Gazette: and the Weekly Chronicle*, September 26, 1780.

93. Officials in London, worried that the violence might spread to Scotland, ordered soldiers to search the homes and arrest several of the leaders of the movement. Donovan, *No Popery*, 43–45.

94. Provost, etc. of Glasgow declaring their loyalty after rioting in the capital, August 16, 1780, PRO HO 55/31/11, TNA.

95. *Glasgow Mercury*, June 22, 1780.

96. *Jamaica Mercury, And Kingston Weekly Advertiser*, March 25, 1780. See also *Rivington's Gazette*, June 3, 1780.

97. Johann Conrad Döhla, *A Hessian Diary of the American Revolution*, trans. and ed. Bruce E. Burgoyne (Norman: University of Oklahoma Press, 1990), 123, and Johann Ernst Prechtel, *A Hessian Officer's Diary of the American Revolution*, trans. and ed. Bruce E. Burgoyne (Bowie, MD: Heritage Books, 1994), 57. Henry praised the local militia for exerting "themselves like Men of Spirit and true Loyalty. . . . we shall be redy to Rebel the attacks of our perfidious Enemies the French and all their abbettors." *Nova-Scotia Gazette: and the Weekly Chronicle*, May 30, 1780.

98. "Spanish Main," *Nova-Scotia Gazette: and the Weekly Chronicle*, August 1, 1780; "Dread of France," *Nova-Scotia Gazette: and the Weekly Chronicle*, August 22, 1780.

99. *Rivington's Gazette*, September 23, 1780; Diary entry, September 22, Typed Mimeograph Copy of the Diary of Thomas Buchanan, Merchant, NYC, for the Year 1780, New-York Historical Society (hereafter cited as NYHS); Ewald Schaukirk, "Occupation of New York City by the British," *Pennsylvania Magazine of History and Biography* 10, no. 4 (January 1885): 433; Burgoyne, ed., *Hessian Diary*, 138.

100. Charles Royster, *A Revolutionary People at War: The Continental Army and American Character, 1775–1783* (Chapel Hill: University of North Carolina Press, 1979), chap. 7.

101. *Caledonian Mercury*, November 25, 1780.

102. *Caledonian Mercury*, December 2, 1780.

103. *Glasgow Journal*, February 1, 1781; *Scots Magazine*, 43 (February 1781), 106–7.

104. Quoted in Donovan, *No Popery*, 46–47.

105. *Glasgow Journal*, February 15, 1781. The provost's letter appears in David Baird Smith, "Glasgow in 1781," *Scottish Historical Review* 16, no. 63 (April 1919): 226–27.

106. *Caledonian Mercury*, February 17, 1781.

107. O'Shaughnessy, *Men Who Lost America*, 178–85; Robert J. Bennett, "Collective Action when Needed: The Kingston Chamber of Commerce in Jamaica, 1778–85," *Journal of Imperial and Commonwealth History* 43, no. 2 (2015): 170–71; Don Francisco Saavedra de Sangronis, *Journal of Don Francisco Saavedra de Sangronis during the Commission Which He Had in His Charge from 25 June until the 20th of the Same Month of 1783*, ed. Francisco Morales Padrón, trans. Aileen Moore Topping (Gainesville: University of Florida Press, 1989), 41.

108. *Royal Gazette* [Kingston], October 14, 1780. Matthew Mulcahy, *Hurricanes and Society in the British Greater Caribbean, 1624–1783* (Baltimore: Johns Hopkins University Press, 2010), chap. 7.

109. O'Shaughnessy, *Men Who Lost America*, 297–313.

110. O'Shaughnessy, *Men Who Lost America*, 260–82.

111. Schaukirk, "Occupation of New York City," 439. Similar accounts likely appeared in Halifax, though no copies of the *Nova-Scotia Gazette* exist today.

112. Miles Cooper to Peter Stuyvesant, December 4, 1781, Stuyvesant-Rutherfurd Papers, Box 10, Folder 1u, NYHS.

113. Sabine, ed., *Historical Memoirs*, 2:462.

114. *Cornwall-Chronicle, and Jamaica General Advertiser*, December 15, 1781.

115. *Royal Gazette* [Kingston], January 19 and February 7, 9, and 16, 1782.

116. *Glasgow Mercury*, December 6, 1781.

117. *Nova-Scotia Gazette: and the Weekly Chronicle*, January 22, 1782; *Gazette of Saint Jago de la Vega*, January 31, 1782. In March 1782, Rivington published the declaration alongside Jefferson's declaration as an addendum to a pamphlet containing Silas Deane's private letters. *Paris Papers; Or Mr. Silas Deane's Late Intercepted Letters, To His Brothers, and Other Intimate Friends, in America* (New York, 1782), Evans 17509. Rivington might have also sold the declaration separately. *A Declaration of Independence Published by Congress at Philadelphia in 1776, with a Counter-Declaration Published at New-York in 1781* (New York, 1782).

118. To the best of my knowledge, the declaration appeared in just two newspapers: *Hampshire Chronicle*, March 11, 1782, and *Public Advertiser* [London], July 12, 1782.

119. Philip Gould argues that the shared language of the two declarations "compresses that imagined distance and portrays inevitable intimacy instead." This is true to some degree, though to be clear, the purpose of the Loyalist declaration was to convince colonists to separate from Congress, which it did by attacking the very basis of the Patriot cause. *Writing the Rebellion: Loyalists and the Literature of Politics in British America* (Oxford: Oxford University Press, 2013), 78–80.

120. Parkinson, *Common Cause*, 249–59.

121. *Rivington's Gazette*, November 17, 1781.

122. Royster, *Revolutionary People*, 327–30. On race, see Parkinson, *Common Cause*, 522–26.

Conclusion

1. Alfred Thayer Mahan, *Types of Naval Officers: Drawn from the History of the British Navy* (London: Sampson Low, Marston & Company, 1902), 225–53; David Hannay, *Life of Rodney* (London: Macmillan, 1891), 174–222; Andrew O'Shaughnessy, *An Empire Divided: The American Revolution and the British Caribbean* (Philadelphia: University of Pennsylvania Press, 2000), 227–37, and *The Men Who Lost America: British Leadership, the American Revolution, and the Fate of the Empire* (New Haven, CT: Yale University Press, 2013), 313–19.

2. O'Shaughnessy, *Men Who Lost America*, 315.

3. O'Shaughnessy, *Men Who Lost America*, 319.

4. One resident reported that "2500 regulars, with 16,000 militia, resolved to defend the place to the utmost in case it should be attacked." *London Chronicle*, May 16, 1782. See also Christer Petley, *White Fury: A Jamaican Slaveholder and the Age of Revolution* (Oxford: Oxford University Press, 2018), 114–15.

5. *Gazette of St. Jago de la Vega*, May 2, 1782; *Rivington's Gazette*, May 29, 1782; *New-York Gazette; and The Weekly Mercury*, June 3, 1782.

6. *Glasgow Mercury*, May 30, 1782; *Glasgow Journal*, May 30, 1782.

7. This is the event referred to in chapter 1 that angered the minister, Ewald Schaukirk. "Glory of that triumphant," *Rivington's Gazette*, June 8, 1782.

8. *Rivington's Gazette*, May 29, 1782. See also *Rivington's Gazette*, June 8, 1782.

9. *Rivington's Gazette*, June 5, 1782. See also Carl Leopold Baurmeister, *Revolution in America: Confidential Letters and Journals, 1776–1784, of Adjutant General Major Baurmeister of the Hessian Forces*, trans. and annot. Bernhard A. Uhlendorf (New Brunswick, NJ: Rutgers University Press, 1957), 509; Ewald Schaukirk, "Occupation of New York City by the British," *Pennsylvania Magazine of History and Biography* 10, no. 4 (January 1885): 442.

10. *Nova-Scotia Gazette: and the Weekly Chronicle*, May 28, 1782.

11. Sir And: Snape Hammond, Halifax 12 June, Recd the 1st July by Higginbottom, add. 21809, f.244, British Library. Council and assembly addresses: *Nova-Scotia Gazette: and the Weekly Chronicle*, June 18, 1782.

12. *Nova-Scotia Gazette: and the Weekly Chronicle*, September 3, 1782.

13. *Nova-Scotia Gazette: and the Weekly Chronicle*, August 27, 1782. See also *Scots Magazine*, 44 (September 1782), 461.

14. Patriot leaders worried that the defeat could stall peace negotiations and might even convince the British public to push for a renewed war in North America. Adams to

Jenings, July 5, 1782, *Papers of John Adams*, vol. 13, *May-October 1782*, ed. Gregg L. Lint et al. (Cambridge, MA: Belknap Press of Harvard University Press, 2008), 157. Patriot writers also ridiculed Britons who celebrated a victory as they were about to lose the war. For example, see *Pennsylvania Evening Post, and Public Advertiser*, June 25, 1782.

15. The Battle of the Saintes was the only event of the revolutionary era that future British subjects actively commemorated. For New York City, see *Rivington's New-York Pocket Almanack, for . . . 1783* (New York, 1783), Evans 17706. For Nova Scotia, see *Royal American Gazette* [Shelburne], April 18, 1785. For Jamaica, see "Almanack and register for the island of Jamaica: calculated for the year of our Lord 1783 . . . or leap-year," *National Library of Jamaica Digital Collection*, accessed June 21, 2017, http://nljdigital.nlj.gov.jm/items/show/3294. *State Gazette of South Carolina*, June 23, 1788, *National Library of Jamaica Digital Collection*, accessed June 21, 2017, http://nljdigital.nlj.gov.jm/items/show/3503.

16. For the importance of Rodney's victory in the British Caribbean, see O'Shaughnessy, *Empire Divided*, 227–37, and *Men Who Lost America*, 313–19. Military historians note both the strategic and tactical importance of the victory. W. M. James, *The British Navy in Adversity: A Study of the War of American Independence* (1926; reprint, New York: Russell & Russell, 1970), 337–53, 448–50; Piers Mackesy, *The War for America, 1775–1783* (Cambridge, MA: Harvard University Press, 1964), 457–59; Sam Willis, *Fighting at Sea in the Eighteenth Century: The Art of Sailing Warfare* (Rochester, NY: Boydell & Brewer, 2008), 130–31; Stephen Conway, *The War for American Independence, 1775–1783* (New York: St. Martin's Press, 1995), 140–41.

17. Stephen Conway, "'A Joy Unknown for Years Past': The American War, Britishness, and the Celebration of Rodney's Victory at the Saints," *History* 86, no. 282 (April 2001): 180–99.

18. Linda Colley, *Britons: Forging the Nation 1707–1837* (New Haven, CT: Yale University Press, 1992) 144–45; Eliga H. Gould, *The Persistence of Empire: British Political Culture in the Age of the American Revolution* (Chapel Hill: University of North Carolina Press, 2000), chap. 6, and "American Independence and Britain's Counter-Revolution," *Past & Present*, 154 (February 1997): 108–12; Stephen Conway, *The British Isles and the War for American Independence* (Oxford: Oxford University Press, 2000), chap. 9, and "A Joy Unknown," 194; Maya Jasanoff, *Liberty's Exiles: American Loyalists in the Revolutionary World* (New York: Alfred A. Knopf, 2011), chap. 4; P. J. Marshall, *The Making and Unmaking of Empires: Britain, India, and America c.1750–1783* (New York: Oxford University Press, 2007), chap. 11, and *Remaking the British Atlantic: The United States and the British Empire after American Independence* (New York: Oxford University Press, 2012), chap. 6.

19. Conway, *The British Isles*, 332–34; Christopher Leslie Brown, *Moral Capital: Foundations of British Abolitionism* (Chapel Hill: University of North Carolina Press, 2006).

20. Robert Parkinson, *The Common Cause: Creating Race and Nation in the American Revolution* (Chapel Hill: University of North Carolina Press, 2016).

21. The Magistrates, and other Inhabitants of the Town of Kingston, Public Records Office (hereafter cited as PRO) 30/20/21/5, The National Archives (hereafter cited as TNA).

22. *Gazette of St. Jago de la Vega*, June 20, 1782.

23. *Morning Post* [London], August 17, 1782.

24. Kingstonians vied to have the statue erected along the harbor at the south end of King Street to greet visitors as they arrived in the city, but the planter-controlled assembly chose instead to place it in Spanish Town. Joan Coutu, *Persuasion and Propaganda: Monuments and the Eighteenth-Century British Empire* (Montreal: McGill-Queen's University Press, 2006), 240–50; Frank Cundall, *Historic Jamaica* (London: Institute of Jamaica, 1915), 119–23.

25. Edward Brathwaite, *The Development of Creole Society in Jamaica, 1770–1820* (New York: Oxford University Press, 1971), 67–101; Eric Williams, *Capitalism and Slavery* (New York: Capricorn Books, 1966), 199–200; O'Shaughnessy, *Empire Divided*, 245–48; Coutu, *Persuasion and Propaganda*, chap. 8.

26. David Brion Davis, *The Problem of Slavery in the Age of Revolution, 1770–1823* (Ithaca, NY: Cornell University Press, 1975), chaps. 8–9; Brown, *Moral Capital*; Edward L. Cox, "The British Caribbean in the Age of Revolution," in *Empire and Nation: The American Revolution in the Atlantic World*, ed. Eliga H. Gould and Peter S. Onuf (Baltimore: Johns Hopkins University Press, 2005), 275–94.

27. David Beck Ryden, *West Indian Slavery and British Abolition, 1783–1807* (New York: Cambridge University Press, 2009), chap. 3.

28. To the honourable the House of Commons of Great-Britain, December 10, 1789, *Journals of the Assembly of Jamaica* (Kingston: Alexander Aikman, 1804), 8:536.

29. Petley, *White Fury*, chaps. 5 and 6; Sara Yeh, "Colonial Identity and Revolutionary Loyalty: The Case of the West Indies," in *British North America in the Seventeenth and Eighteenth Centuries*, ed. Stephen Foster (Oxford: Oxford University Press, 2013), 220–22; Trevor Burnard, *Jamaica in the Age of Revolution* (Philadelphia: University of Pennsylvania Press, 2020), esp. epilogue, and "Harvest Years? Reconfigurations of Empire in Jamaica, 1756–1807," *Journal of Imperial and Commonwealth History* 40, no. 4 (November 2012): 545–55; Burnard correctly argues that in the aftermath of the revolution, white Jamaicans were likely envious of South Carolinian slave owners, whose wealth and status improved significantly under a new pro-slavery American government. Trevor Burnard, "Freedom, Migration, and the American Revolution," in Gould and Onuf, eds., *Empire and Nation*, 295–314.

30. Jasanoff, *Liberty's Exiles*, 159.

31. The four petitioners were John Cody, John Mullowny, William Meany, and James Kavanagh. Letter of July 8, 1782, Archdiocese of Westminster Collection (hereafter cited as DWE), University of Notre Dame Archives (hereafter cited as UNDA). Terrence Murphy, "The Emergence of Maritime Catholicism, 1781–1830," *Acadiensis* 13, no, 2 (Spring, 1984): 29–49; Terrence Punch, "The Irish Catholics, Halifax's First Minority Group," *Nova Scotia Historical Quarterly* 10, no. 1 (March 1980): 23–40; Luca Codignola, "Roman Catholic Conservatism in a New North Atlantic World, 1760–1829," *William and Mary Quarterly* 64, no. 4 (October 2007): 717–56; John Garner, "The Enfranchisement of Roman Catholics in the Maritimes," *Canadian Historical Review* 34, no. 3 (September 1953): 203–18; Mark G. McGowan, "Canadian Catholics, Loyalty, and the British Empire, 1763–1901," in *Loyalism and the Formation of the British World, 1775–1914*, ed. Frank O'Gorman and Allan Blackstock (Woodbridge, UK: Boydell Press, 2014), 201–21.

32. "Extract of Proceedings respecting the Roman Catholics of the Province of Nova-Scotia, 18 June 1782," DWE, UNDA.

33. *Nova-Scotia Gazette: and the Weekly Chronicle*, July 9, 1782.

34. Terrence Murphy, "Trusteeism in Atlantic Canada: The Struggle for Leadership among the Irish Catholics of Halifax, St John's, and Saint John, 1780–1850," in *Creed and Culture: The Place of English-Speaking Catholics in Canadian Society, 1750–1930*, ed. Terrence Murphy and Gerald Stortz (Montreal: McGill-Queen's University Press, 1993), 129.

35. Officials were also reassured by the Catholic Church in British North America openly opposing American republican ideals. Codignola, "Roman Catholic Conservatism," esp. 753–54.

36. By 1784, as many as thirty thousand white refugees, three thousand free blacks, and another twelve hundred slaves had emigrated to the region. Jasanoff, *Liberty's Exile*, 160. For more on the free black population, see Jasanoff, *Liberty's Exiles*, chap. 5, esp. 172–75. For more on the enslaved population, see Harvey Armani Whitfield, *North to Bondage: Loyalist Slavery in the Maritimes* (Vancouver: University of British Columbia Press, 2016), chap. 2.

37. Jasanoff, *Liberty's Exiles*, 157–98.

38. Parr to Evan Nepean, March 8, 1788, PRO CO 217/690, TNA.

39. Neil MacKinnon, *This Unfriendly Soil: The Loyalist Experience in Nova Scotia, 1783–1791* (Kingston, ON: McGill-Queen's University Press, 1986), 127–36. The Wilkes quote appears on page 129.

40. Jasanoff, for example, argues that Loyalist refugee rhetoric during the 1785 election riot in Shelburne sounded as though it came from the mouths of American Patriots. However, Loyalists expressed similar views of Congress at the start of the war. *Liberty's Exile*, 180–89.

41. Quoted in MacKinnon, *Unfriendly Soil*, 165.

42. *Glasgow Journal*, June 6, 1782.

43. Fewer Scots enjoyed the right to vote than Britons anywhere else in the British Isles. John Cannon, *Parliamentary Reform, 1640–1832* (New York: Cambridge University Press, 1973), 108. For more on the burgh reform movement, see Henry W. Meikle, *Scotland and the French Revolution* (1912; reprint, New York: A.M. Kelly, 1969), 16–24; Bob Harris, *The Scottish People and the French Revolution* (London: Pickering & Chatto, 2008), 14–25.

44. For example, see *Caledonian Mercury*, July 24, 1782. Harris, *Scottish People*, 32–38; Meikle, *French Revolution*, 14–40.

45. Christopher Wyvill, *Political Papers* (York: Printed by W. Blanchard, 1794), 2:82–85.

46. Christopher Wyvill, *Political Papers* (York: Printed by W. Blanchard, 1802) 4:197–98.

47. The merchants were also able to revive their Atlantic tobacco trade. Exports to the newly independent Americans reached their prewar levels by as early as the middle of the 1780s. T. M. Devine, *The Tobacco Lords: A Study of the Tobacco Merchants of Glasgow and Their Trading Activities c. 1740–90* (Edinburgh: John Donald Publishers, 1975), 161–67.

48. T. M. Devine, "An Eighteen-Century Business Elite: Glasgow-West India Merchants, c. 1750–1815," *Scottish Historical Review* 57, no. 1 (April 1978): 40–67, "Did Slavery Make Scotia Great?," *Britain and the World* 4, no. 1 (March 2011): 40–64, esp. 61, and *Scotland's Empire, 1600–1815* (New York: Penguin, 2003), 221–49; Stephen Mullen, "The Glasgow West India Interest: Integration, Collaboration and Exploitation in

the British Atlantic World, 1776–1846" (Ph.D. diss., University of Glasgow, 2015), chap. 2, and "A Glasgow-West India Merchant House and the Imperial Dividend, 1779–1867," *Journal of Scottish Studies* 33, no. 2 (October 2013): 196–233. For more on the growth of the textile industry, see Anthony Cooke, "An Elite Revisited: Glasgow West India Merchants, 1783–1877," *Journal of Scottish Historical Studies* 32, no. 2 (November 2012): 127–65, esp. 144–46.

49. Harris, *Scottish People*, chap. 3.

50. *Rivington's Gazette*, June 1, 1782.

51. *Rivington's Gazette*, July 6, 1782.

52. For example, see "'The Freeholder" essays, which are believed to have been written by Charles Inglis. *Rivington's Gazette*, June 15, 22, and 29, July 13, 20, and 27, and August 3, 1782. Ross N. Hebb, *Samuel Seabury and Charles Inglis: Two Bishops, Two Churches* (Madison, NJ: Farleigh Dickinson University Press, 2010), 39.

53. *Rivington's Gazette*, September 25, 1782.

54. *Rivington's Gazette*, December 11, 1782. American Patriots admitted that celebrations of the birth of the Dauphin were intended to convince the French of their commitment to the alliance. Madison to Edmund Randolph, May 14, 1782, in *The Papers of James Madison, Congressional Series*, vol. 4, *1 January 1782–31 July 1782*, ed. William T. Hutchinson et al. (Chicago: University of Chicago Press, 1965), 242. See also Benjamin Irvin, *Clothed in Robes of Sovereignty: The Continental Congress and the People Out of Doors* (Oxford: Oxford University Press, 2014), 265–68.

55. *Rivington's Gazette*, July 20, 1782.

56. *Rivington's Gazette*, July 13, and August 7, 1782.

57. *Glasgow Journal*, June 19, 1783. See also Robert Ernst, "A Tory-Eye View of the Evacuation of New York," *New York History* 64, no. 4 (October 1983): 382–85.

58. Ruma Chopra, *Unnatural Rebellion: Loyalists in New York City during the Revolution* (Charlottesville: University of Virginia Press, 2011), 212. For a contemporary account of the attack on Booth, see *Newport Mercury*, November 15, 1783.

59. For example, see John Holt's scathing attack on Rivington and other Loyalists. *Independent New-York Gazette*, December 13, 1783.

60. *Pennsylvania Packet, and General Advertiser*, January 15, 1784. See also Philip Freneau's poem, "Rivington's Reflections," which appeared in the *Independent Ledger and the American Advertiser*, December 23, 1782, and January 13, 1783.

61. The phrase was first used by Bernard Bailyn in *The Ideological Origins of the American Revolution* (Cambridge, MA: Belknap Press of Harvard University Press, 1967), chap. 6.

INDEX

Italicized page numbers refer to illustrations.

CPSIA information can be obtained
at www.ICGtesting.com
Printed in the USA
LVHW030341230221
679657LV00021BB/279/J

9 781501 754012